The New
CAMBRIDGE
English Course

TEACHER
1

MICHAEL SWAN
CATHERINE WALTER

CAMBRIDGE
UNIVERSITY PRESS

Published by the Press Syndicate of the University of Cambridge
The Pitt Building, Trumpington Street, Cambridge CB2 1RP
40 West 20th Street, New York, NY1011–4211, USA
10 Stamford Road, Oakleigh, Melbourne 3166, Australia

© Michael Swan and Catherine Walter 1990

First Published 1990
Fifth printing 1994

Designed by Banks and Miles, London
Cover design by Michael Peters & Partners Limited, London
Typeset by Wyvern Typesetting, Bristol
Origination by Eric Linsell / Progress Colour Limited
Printed in Italy by G. Canale & C. S.p.A. - Borgaro T.se - TURIN

ISBN 0 521 37665 3 Teacher's Book 1

ISBN 0 521 37637 8 Student's Book 1

Student's Book 1 split edition:
ISBN 0 521 37641 6 Student's Book 1A
ISBN 0 521 37642 4 Student's Book 1B

ISBN 0 521 37649 1 Practice Book 1

Practice Book 1 split edition:
ISBN 0 521 37653 X Practice Book 1A
ISBN 0 521 37654 8 Practice Book 1B

ISBN 0 521 37661 0 Practice Book 1 with Key

ISBN 0 521 37669 6 Test Book 1

ISBN 0 521 37502 9 Class Cassette Set 1

ISBN 0 521 37506 1 Student's Cassette Set 1

Student's Cassettes 1 split edition:
ISBN 0 521 38222 X Student's Cassette 1A
ISBN 0 521 38223 8 Student's Cassette 1B

ISBN 0 521 42728 2 Video 1 (VHS PAL)
ISBN 0 521 42729 0 Video 1 (VHS SECAM)
ISBN 0 521 42730 4 Video 1 (VHS NTSC)
ISBN 0 521 42731 2 Video 1 Teacher's Guide with photocopiable tasks
ISBN 0 521 44704 6 Video Teacher's Guide
ISBN 0 521 44703 8 Video Student Activity Book

Authors' acknowledgements

We are grateful to all the people who have helped us
with this book. Our thanks to:
- The many people whose ideas have influenced our
  work, including all the colleagues and students from
  whom we have learnt.
- Those institutions and teachers who were kind
  enough to comment on their use of *The Cambridge
  English Course*, and whose suggestions have done so
  much to shape this new version.
- The Cambridge University Press representatives and
  agents, for their valuable work in transmitting
  feedback from users of the original course.
- The people who agreed to talk within range of our
  microphones: Alwyn Anchors, Dai Colven, Steve
  Dixon, Lorna Higgs, Marilyn Norvell, Ruth Swan,
  Mark Walter Swan, Sue Ward, Adrian Webber and
  Celia Wilson.
- Steve Hall of Bell Voice Recordings, for doing a
  wonderful job on the songs.
- Peter Taylor of Taylor Riley Productions Ltd; Peter
  and Diana Thompson and Andy Tayler of Studio
  AVP; and all the actors and actresses; they made
  recording sessions seem easy and created an excellent
  end product.
- Susan Sheppard, Sally Palmer-Smith, Marjorie Pereira,
  and Denise Quinton of Banks and Miles, for their
  creativity, skill and hard work in the design of the
  printed components of the course.
- Val Mercer and Lindsey Cunningham of Michael
  Peters & Partners Limited for their excellent cover
  design.
- Eric Linsell and his colleagues at Progress Colour
  Limited, and all the staff at Wyvern Typesetting, for
  their care and attention to detail.
- Gill Clack, Cathy Hall, Avril Price-Budgen, David
  Seabourne and Clare Walshe for their careful and
  professional help with production.
- Mark Walter Swan, Helen Walter Swan and Inge
  Bullock, for keeping us in touch with what really
  matters.
- Adrian du Plessis, Colin Hayes and Peter Donovan of
  Cambridge University Press, whose confidence and
  support have made the author-publisher relationship
  so unproblematic.
- Desmond Nicholson of Cambridge University Press,
  whose encouragement and suggestions helped to get
  The New Cambridge English Course underway.
- And finally Desmond O'Sullivan of ELT Publishing
  Services: his skills in dealing with people and with
  print, his devotion, patience, stamina and unfailing
  good humour have made this course possible.

Contents

Map of Book 1

	Grammar	**Phonology**
	Students will learn these grammar points	Students will work on these aspects of pronunciation
1 to 4	Present tense of *be*; *have got*; *a* and *an*; noun plurals; subject personal pronouns; possessives; possessive *'s* and *s'*; predicative use of adjectives; questions (question word and yes/no); *be* with ages; prepositions of place; *this*; *any* in questions.	Word and sentence stress; rhythm; linking; intonation; consonant clusters; /θ/ and /ð/; /ə/; pronunciation of *'s*; weak form of *from*.
5 to 8	Simple Present tense; *there is/are*; imperatives; *was* and *were* (introduction); countable and uncountable; *some/any*, *much/many* and other quantifiers; *the*; omission of article in generalisations; object personal pronouns; attributive use of adjectives; frequency adverbs; adverbs of degree; prepositions of time, place and distance; omission of article in *at home* etc.; *-ing* for activities; *be* with prices.	Word and sentence stress; rhythm; linking; intonation, including polite intonation; weak forms; /ɪ/; /θ/ in ordinals; pronunciations of *the*.
9 to 12	*Have got*; Present Progressive tense (introduction); more Simple Present tense; Simple Past tense; past tense of *be*; *I'd like* + noun phrase / infinitive; *when*-clauses; demonstratives; *be* and *have*; *both* and *all*; *a . . . one*; prepositions of place; *say* and *tell*; *ago*; *What (a) . . . !*	Linking; sentence stress; weak forms; hearing unstressed syllables; rhythm and stress in questions; rising intonation for questions; high pitch for emphasis; stress in negative sentences; stress for contrast; spelling/pronunciation difficulties; /h/; voiced *s* in verb endings; Simple Past endings; strong form of *have*.
13 to 16	*Can*; Present Progressive tense (present and future meanings); *be* with ages and measures; difficult question structures; comparative and superlative adjectives; structures used for comparison; *a bit / much* before comparative adjectives; *good at* + noun/gerund; *look like* + noun phrase; *look* + adjective; *What is . . . like?*; prepositions in descriptions; prepositions of time.	Stress and rhythm recognition and production; decoding rapid speech; hearing unstressed syllables; pronunciations of the letter *a*; pronunciations of the letter *e*; pronunciations of the letter *i*; /ə/ and stress; weak and strong forms of *can* and *can't*; weak forms of *as*, *than* and *from*; /θ/ in ordinals.
17 to 20	Present Perfect tense; more Simple Past tense; verbs with two objects; *Could you*, *Why don't we*, *Let's* and *Shall we* + infinitive without *to*; question words as subjects; elementary reported speech; reply questions; *So . . . I*; *say* and *tell*; *for* and *since*; *How long . . . ?*; *no = not any*; *some* and *something* in offers and requests; article and prepositional usage; sequencing and linking words; *both . . . and*; *neither . . . nor*; *Do you mind if . . . ?*	Decoding rapid speech; linking with initial vowels; contrastive stress; pronunciations of the letter *u*; /iː/ and /ɪ/; polite intonation for requests; rising intonation in reply questions; weak forms of *was* and *were*.
21 to 24	*Going to*; *will*-future; infinitive of purpose; imperatives; conditional structures; structures with *get*; adverbs vs. adjectives; adverbs of manner; paragraph-structuring adverbials; position of *always* and *never* in imperatives.	Spellings of /ɜː/; 'long' pronunciation of vowel letters before (consonant +) *e*; pronunciations of the letter *o*; /w/; /iː/ and /ɪ/; 'dark' *l* in Future tense contractions; recognition and pronunciation of *going to*; pronunciation of *won't*.

Functions

Students will learn to

Greet; introduce; begin conversations with strangers; participate in longer conversations; say goodbye; ask for and give information; identify themselves and others; describe people; ask for repetition; enquire about health; apologise; express regret; distinguish levels of formality; spell and count.

Ask for and give information, directions, personal data, and opinions; describe places; indicate position; express likes and dislikes; tell the time; complain; participate in longer conversations; express politeness.

Ask for and give information; describe people and things, and ask for descriptions; talk about resemblances; greet; make arrangements to meet; ask for information about English; make and reply to offers and requests; narrate; shop; make travel enquiries and hotel bookings; change money.

Compare; ask for and give information and opinions; describe and compare people; speculate; make and reply to requests; invite and reply; describe and speculate about activities; plan; count (ordinals); telephone.

Request and reply; borrow; suggest; agree, disagree and negotiate; invite and reply; narrate; report what people have said; ask for, give and refuse permission; show interest; compare; ask for and give information and opinions; distinguish levels of formality; ask for information about English; start conversations; make arrangements to meet; order food *etc.* in a restaurant.

Talk about plans; make predictions; guess; make suggestions; express sympathy; give instructions; give advice; warn; announce intentions; raise and counter objections; narrate.

Topics and notions

Students will learn to talk about

People's names; age; marital status; national origin; addresses; jobs; health; families; physical appearance; relationships; numbers and letters; approximation; place.

Addresses; phone numbers; furniture; houses and flats; work; leisure occupations and interests; food and drink; prices; likes and dislikes; preferences; things in common and differences; days of the week; ordinal numbers; existence; time; place; relative position; generalisation; countability; quantification; degree; frequency; routines.

People's appearances; families; colours; parts of the body; relationships; physical and emotional states; clothes; places; prices; sizes; people's pasts; history; poverty; happiness; racism; childhood; growing up; resemblance.

Abilities; physical characteristics and qualities; weights and measures; numbers (cardinal and ordinal); ages; personalities; professions; names of months; future plans; the weather; holidays; places; travel; time; similarities and differences; temporary present and future actions and states.

Holidays; going out; food and drink; daily routines; historical personalities; people's careers; interests and habits; likes and dislikes; contrast; sequence; past time; frequency; duration up to the present; similarity.

Houses; seasons; holidays; places; plans; health and illness; sports; machines; horoscopes; danger; purpose; intention; manner; the future.

Skills

The Student's Book and Practice Book between them provide regular practice of the basic 'four skills'. Special skills taught or practised at Level 1 include decoding rapid colloquial speech, reading and listening for specific information, writing longer sentences, writing paragraphs, writing formal letters, writing friendly letters and notes, and filling in forms.

Vocabulary

Students will learn 900 or more common words and expressions during Level 1 of the course.

Introduction

The nature and purpose of the course

The New Cambridge English Course is designed for people who are learning English for general practical or cultural purposes. The course generally presupposes a European-type educational background, but with some adaptation it can be used successfully with learners from other cultural environments. The course teaches British English, but illustrates other varieties as well.

The material at each level includes a Student's Book, a Teacher's Book and a set of Class Cassettes (for classwork); a Practice Book, with or without Key (for homework); two optional Student's Cassettes; and an optional Test Book for teachers. Split editions of the Student's Book, Practice Book and Student's Cassettes are also available.

A set of two video cassettes and an accompanying Teacher's Guide are also available for use with Level 1. The Teacher's Guide contains photocopiable tasks for students to use with the video. For teachers who do not wish to photocopy, a Teacher's Guide without tasks and separate Student's Activity Books are available.

Level 1 is for complete beginners and false beginners. It teaches language forms and their uses, and practises receptive and productive skills. All aspects of language are covered – this is a multi-syllabus course, not just a grammar course or a skills course. It will take students up to a point where they can begin to use English to achieve a certain number of simple practical aims.

The approach is different from that of some other beginners' courses. Features which may be new to your students include:
– multi-syllabus course organisation
– wide variety of presentation methodology
– mixture of factual and fictional topics
– opportunities for student choice
– emphasis on systematic vocabulary learning
– regular pronunciation and spelling work
– some use of authentic listening material
– deliberate inclusion of some 'too difficult' material (see *Basic principles*)
– active and varied 'communicative' practice.
These points are dealt with in more detail in the following sections.

The organisation of the course

Level 1 of *The New Cambridge English Course* consists of six blocks of four units, each unit divided into four lessons. A lesson provides enough work for 45 minutes upwards (depending on the learners' speed, motivation and previous knowledge), so each unit will take three hours or more of class time. The first three units of a block are topic- or function-based. Work on grammar, vocabulary, pronunciation, etc. leads up to exchange of real information, dramatisation, or writing exercises related to the theme of the unit. Every fourth unit is a 'Consolidation' unit: it displays, revises and tests the language learned in the previous three units.

Basic principles

The pedagogic design of *The New Cambridge English Course* reflects the following beliefs.

Respecting the learner

People generally learn languages best when their experience, knowledge of the world, interests and feelings are involved, and a course must allow students to 'be themselves' as fully as possible. But not everybody learns in the same way, and not everything can be taught in the same way. A course must provide fiction as well as fact; role play as well as real communication activities; personal as well as impersonal discussion topics; learner-centred as well as teacher-centred activities. Beginners' course material should not be childish and patronising, and it is worth remembering that the best classroom humour generally comes from the students, not from the textbook.

The language: multi-syllabus course design

A complete English language beginners' course will incorporate at least eight main syllabuses:
– **Vocabulary:** students must acquire a 'core' vocabulary of the most common and useful words in the language, as well as learning more words of their own choice.
– **Grammar:** basic structures must be learnt and revised.
– **Pronunciation** work is important for many students. Learners need to speak comprehensibly, and to understand people with different accents speaking in natural conditions (not just actors speaking standard English in recording studios).
– **Notions:** students must know how to refer to common concepts such as *sequence*, *contrast*, or *purpose*.
– **Functions:** learners must be able to do things such as *complaining*, *describing*, *suggesting*, or *asking for permission* in English.
– **Situations:** a course must teach the stereotyped expressions associated with situations like *shopping*, *making travel enquiries*, *booking hotel rooms*, *telephoning*, etc.
– **Topics:** students need to learn the language used to talk about subjects of general interest. The coursebook should include some controversial and emotionally engaging material, rather than sticking to bland middle-of-the-road 'safe' topics.
– **Skills:** learners need systematic practice in both receptive and productive skills. Reading and listening work will include some authentic interviews and texts, as well as specially written material.

How important is grammar?

Obviously grammar is important, especially at the early stages of learning a language, but it can be overvalued at the expense of other areas such as skills development and vocabulary growth. (Vocabulary mistakes tend to outnumber grammar mistakes by more than three to one.) Students often feel that a lesson with no new grammar in 'doesn't teach anything'; they must learn not to judge their progress simply by the number of new structures taught.

For students who do not speak Western European languages, the English articles present special problems. Some extra explanations and model exercises on the use of the articles, designed for such students, will be found in an appendix on pages 135–137.

'Learning' and 'acquisition'

Most people seem to learn a foreign language more effectively if it is 'tidied up' for them. This helps them to focus on high-priority language and to see the grammatical regularities.

However, learners also need to encounter a certain amount of 'untidy' natural language (even if this seems a bit too difficult for them). Without some unstructured input, people's unconscious mechanisms for acquiring languages may not operate effectively.

A course should cater for both these ways of approaching a language (sometimes called 'learning' and 'acquisition' respectively). The occasional use of unsimplified authentic materials may require a change in learner expectations: many students and teachers are used only to texts in which every new word and structure has to be explained and learnt.

Methodology

- **Communicative practice:** where possible, language practice should resemble real-life communication, with genuine exchange of information and opinions. Pair and group work can greatly increase the quantity and quality of practice.
- **Input and output; creativity:** students generally learn what they use and forget what they don't use. At least some lessons should lead up to genuine conversations, role play or writing activities in which students use creatively what they have learnt. If they can use their new language to entertain, inform or amuse each other, so much the better.
- **Error** is a natural part of learning, and over-correction can destroy confidence. Some learners will need a high level of accuracy, but very few will ever be perfect. Students' achievement should not be measured negatively (by how far away they are from perfection), but positively (by how successfully they can use the language for their own purposes).
- **Regularity and variety** need to be carefully balanced. If all the lessons are constructed in the same way, a course is easy to use but monotonous. Variety makes lessons more interesting, but too much variety can make material more difficult for teachers to prepare and students to get used to.
- **Study and memorisation** are necessary, for most learners, for really thorough learning.

- **Learning and acquisition** should both be catered for. This will mean that students will sometimes focus intensively on language items, and sometimes do tasks involving 'untidy' texts where only a part of the material need be understood. Likewise, there will sometimes be 'preview' appearances (for instance in exercise rubrics) of language items that will be studied intensively somewhat later.
- **The mother tongue,** if it can be used, can help to make explanations faster and more precise. The same is true of bilingual dictionaries, and students should practise their use.

Knowing where you are

Students can easily get lost in the complicated landscape of language study. A course must supply some kind of 'map' of their language-learning, so that they can understand the purpose of each kind of activity, and can see how the various lessons add up to a coherent whole. Regular revision should be provided, helping students to place the language items they are learning into the context of what they already know.

Using the course

(Many teachers will of course know very well how to adapt the course to their students' needs. These suggestions are meant mainly for less experienced teachers who are unfamiliar with this approach.)

Preparation

You may need to prepare the first lessons carefully in advance, until everybody is used to the approach. Later, less work should be needed – the teachers' notes will guide you through each lesson.

Choice

You may not feel it necessary to do absolutely all the lessons in the book. (But if you drop a lesson, check that you don't 'lose' language material which is important for your students.)

If you are teaching in Britain or another English-speaking country, you may wish to bring forward some language areas that are important for your students' 'survival needs'. Examples are lessons 10B, 10D and 14D.

Leave out exercises that cover points of language which your class don't need.

Don't do an exercise if you or your students really dislike it. (But don't leave out a strange-looking activity without giving it a try!)

Don't force a lesson on your students if it bores everybody; find another way to teach the material. But don't automatically drop a topic because it makes people angry – rage can get people talking!

Timing

Motivated students should average three hours or more per unit. (Some units will of course go more quickly or more slowly than others.) So the book should take a minimum of 72 hours to complete (plus any time spent on tests, homework correction, etc.). If you don't have that much time, you will need to look through the book in advance and decide what to leave out.

Authentic recordings

The course contains some 'real-life' recordings of conversations, interviews and other material. These teach vocabulary, stimulate discussion, and train learners to understand natural speech (in a variety of accents). Students may not understand every word of what they hear. THIS DOES NOT MATTER! They need to experience some language which is beyond their present capacities – this happens in natural language learning all the time. (You can help by sometimes talking naturally in English about your interests, events in your life, etc.).

Discourage students from asking for complete transcriptions and explanations of long recordings – this is not usually an efficient use of time.

Vocabulary learning

Words and expressions to learn are listed at the end of each lesson. You may need to suggest techniques of learning this vocabulary. Some possible approaches are:
- Copy new words with their translations in special notebooks. Cover the words and try to recall them from the translations.
- Note English-language explanations or examples of the use of new words. Write more examples.
- Keep 'vocabulary diaries', listing new words under subject/grammatical headings (e.g. 'verbs of movement'; 'professions'). Revise occasionally by trying to write from memory as many words as possible from each list.

Different people learn best in different ways – but for most students, some systematic vocabulary study is necessary.

You may want to point out to students that there is an alphabetical index of vocabulary at the back of their books (pages 124–130). This includes phonetic transcriptions; you may wish to introduce your students gradually to their use.

Consolidation units

You may need to show students how to use the 'A' lessons of the Consolidation units (Units 4, 8, 12, 16, 20 and 24). They should spend time, with you or on their own, looking at the material and studying the structures and vocabulary. Encourage them to look back at the lessons to see exactly how the new items are used.

The 'B' and 'C' lessons of the Consolidation units revise the major items taught in the previous three units, and in each Consolidation unit there is an opportunity for extended speaking practice. Doing these exercises will help learning and build confidence. The 'D' lesson of each Consolidation unit is a test of the language from the previous three units. It is meant to give students and teacher an idea of how well the material has been assimilated. Only use those parts of the test that cover material important to your students. If you wish to administer unseen tests as well, the Test Book provides a parallel test at the level of each Consolidation unit.

Practice Book

The Practice Book is an essential part of the course. It provides a choice of consolidation and revision exercises, together with regular work on reading and writing skills; it also includes activities using the Student's Cassettes. Together with the Consolidation units, the Practice Book ensures that students integrate current learning with areas previously covered and get sufficient opportunities for skills development. A 'with Key' version of the Practice Book contains answers to all the exercises, where appropriate, for learners wishing to do further homework on a self-study basis.

The Practice Book also includes a 'Mini-grammar': a concise summary of all the grammar points covered up to the end of Level 1 of the course.

Student's Cassettes

The Student's Cassette set consists of a selection of material from Class Cassette set 1, including all the recordings for the optional listening exercises in the Practice Book, a dramatised reading of the Practice Book serial story and songs from the Student's Book. Motivated learners who have the time can thus make active use of the Student's Cassettes at home.

Supplementing the course

The course is relatively complete, and it should not need much supplementation. But of course, the more extra reading, listening and speaking students can do – in or out of class – the better. A circulating class library of supplementary readers can be useful. *Something to Read 1* by Christine Lindop and Dominic Fisher (Cambridge University Press, 1988) has been written especially for students working with this course.

Learner expectations and learner resistance

Students have their own ideas about language learning. Up to a point, these must be respected – individuals have different learning strategies, and will not respond to methods which they distrust. However, learners sometimes resist important and useful activities which do not fit in with their preconceptions, and this can hinder progress. So you may have to spend time, early in the course, training students in new attitudes to language learning. Problems are especially likely to arise over questions of grammar and correction (students may want too much), over the use of authentic materials, and over exercises involving group work.

Comments

The New Cambridge English Course, as a completely revised edition of a very successful course series, has had the benefit of the best sort of piloting programme – thousands of teachers have used the original edition over several years, and their feedback has helped us to shape the present version. But improvements are always possible, and we would be delighted to hear from users. Letters can be sent to us c/o Cambridge University Press (ELT), The Edinburgh Building, Shaftesbury Road, Cambridge CB2 2RU, Great Britain.

Michael Swan   Catherine Walter   August 1989

Unit 1 Hello

1A What's your name?

Greeting and introducing; questions and answers; *it*; *is*; *my* and *your*; *not*.

1 Listen to the conversations. Then put the sentences into the pictures.

What's your name?
Hello. My name's Mary Lake.
No, it isn't.
Catherine.
Hello. Yes, room three one
    two, Mrs Lake.
What's *your* name?
Is your name Mark Perkins?
John.
Thank you.
It's Harry Brown.

2 Pronunciation. Say these words and expressions after the recording.

what   what's   your   my   name
it   it's   isn't
Yes, it is.   No, it isn't.

3 Say your name.

'Hello. My *name's* ....'

4 Ask other students' names.

'*What's your name?*'

5 Ask and answer.

'*Is your name Anne?*'   '*Yes, it is.*'
'*Is your name Alex?*'   '*No, it isn't. It's Peter.*'

> **Learn:** Hello; my; your; it; is; what; not (n't);
> Thank you; yes; no; name; one; two; three.

This symbol means that all or part of the recording for this exercise is on one of the Student's Cassettes.

6

Unit 1: Lesson A

Students learn to ask people's names and to give their own. They learn numbers up to three.
Structures: third person of *be*: affirmatives, negatives, questions with *what*, *yes/no* questions, short answers, contractions; first and second person possessives.
Phonology: consonant clusters /ts/ and /znt/; linking in *Yes, it is* and *No, it isn't*.

Language notes and possible problems

1. *Name* In English, *name* can be used to mean 'first name', 'surname', or 'full name'. Some students may assume it means only one of these.
2. *'s* The contracted *'s* is difficult to handle at first: look out for **What's your name's?*[1] and **My name Maria*.
3. Vocabulary Make sure students know they are to learn and remember the words in the vocabulary box. Note that the words and expressions listed are those which students are expected to learn and remember now. Other items (i.e. *room*, *Mrs*) are previewed here, but need not be learnt until later.
4. Practice Book The Practice Book is an important part of the course, and students should consolidate their learning by doing some Practice Book exercises after every lesson. Initially, you will probably want to go over homework exercise instructions in class to make sure that the students understand what to do.

Optional extra materials

Name-cards for each student (see Optional activity).

1 Listening and matching[2]

- This can be done before or after the personal exchanges in Exercises 3–5.
- Tell students to look at the illustrations.
- Play the three conversations through once or twice.
- Ask students to look at the sentences in the box.
- Ask what sentence goes into the first speech-balloon.
- Write the answer on the board:
  1. Hello. My name's Mary Lake.
- Do the same with the second speech-balloon.
- Then let students continue by themselves, writing the numbers and sentences on a piece of paper.
- Go over the answers and play the recording again.

Alternative Exercise 1 for 'false beginners'

- If your students already know some English, ask them to try the exercise *before* hearing the conversations.

Tapescript for Exercise 1

1. Hello. My name's Mary Lake.
2. Hello. Yes, room three one two, Mrs Lake.
3. Thank you.

4. What's your name?
5. Catherine.
6. What's *your* name?
7. John.

8. Is your name Mark Perkins?
9. No, it isn't.
10. It's Harry Brown.

2 Pronunciation

- This is an opportunity to work on problem sounds. Don't be too perfectionist at this stage.
- The main points to work on are the consonant clusters in *what's*, *it's*, and *isn't*, and the linking in *Yes, it is* and *No, it isn't*.
- In a small class, get everybody to try each word or expression. In a larger class, do chorus work, and then pick out one or two individuals.

3 Saying your name

- This can be done with books closed. Say: '*My name is . . .*' (giving your name). '*My name's . . .*'
- Write both forms on the board.
- Point out that we mostly use the contraction in speaking and the uncontracted form in writing.
- Ask students '*What's your name?*' and get them to answer '*My name's . . .*'

4 Asking people's names

- Write on the board: *What is your name? What's your name?*
- Practise *What's your name?*
- Tell students to walk round the room asking everybody's names. (If this is difficult, students can just find out the names of their near neighbours.)

5 Yes/no questions: short answers

- Ask a student '*Is your name . . . ?*' Teach '*Yes, it is.*'
- Ask another student '*Is your name . . . ?*' (wrong name) and teach '*No, it isn't.*'
- Elicit or explain that *isn't = is not*.
- Show the examples in the book. Practise the pronunciation once again, paying attention to /ts/ and /znt/ and to the linking.
- Practise with a walk-round exercise (or ask students to check up on the names of their neighbours). Work on first names and surnames.

Optional activity

- Prepare cards or slips of paper with various names of famous people (e.g. *William Shakespeare, Greta Garbo*).
- Shuffle the cards and give them out to students.
- Practise *What's your name?*, *My name's . . .*, *Is your name . . . ?*, and so on, using the new names.
- Alternatively, give students English first names.

Vocabulary to learn

- Point out that you expect students to learn the words and phrases that appear at the bottom of each page in the *Learn* section.

Practice Book exercises: choose two or more

1. Revision of lesson structures and vocabulary.
2. Writing full forms of contractions.
3. Writing the names of numbers 1 to 3.
4. Pronunciation (consonant clusters and linking).
5. Translation of sentences from the lesson.
6. Student's Cassette exercise (Student's Book Exercise 1). Writing (dictation from cassette). When students do this exercise at home they should close their books and play the recording, as many times as they need to in order to write the conversation down, using the pause buttons on their cassette players. Students then practise saying the sentences.

---

[1] A star marks an unacceptable utterance.
[2] Explicit exercise instructions are given in the Student's Book from the beginning, for two reasons: to accustom the student to the language used in the instructions, and to make it easier for the teacher to see what is going on. Obviously complete beginners will not understand the instructions, and will need to be told (by demonstration, gesture, or mother-tongue explanation) what to do.
[3] This recording symbol means the recording is essential to the exercise. The symbol in Exercise 2 means that the teacher has the choice of using the recording or reading out the words and phrases for pronunciation practice.
   If you fast forward in 'Play' mode, you will hear a signal at the end of each exercise on the recording which will help you find your place.

Unit 1: Lesson B

Students learn to talk about other people's names, and to spell. They learn the numbers *four* to *six*.
Structures: possessives (*his, her*).
Phonology: pronunciation of the letters of the alphabet.

Language notes and possible problems

1. *His* and *her* Speakers of Romance languages, and some others, will need to work hard on the difference between *his* and *her*. (French, for example, uses the same word for both; the word varies in form according to the gender of the *thing possessed*, not the possessor.)

2. *First name, surname* Some students may already have learnt expressions such as *Christian name, given name, family name*. We use *first name* and *surname* here, but you can of course teach other terms if you wish. Note that Chinese family names come before other names, so *first name* may give Chinese a false impression of the meaning of *first. Name* is a 'false friend' for some learners; for instance, German *Name* means 'surname'.

Optional extra materials

Pictures of well-known people (cut from magazines, for example), and separate cards with their names on. Flashcards with letters of the alphabet.

1 Matching names and pictures: *his* and *her*

• Give students a chance to look over the pictures of the people and the documents. Then go through the people in order and ask for the names. Make sure students get *his* and *her* right.
• Point out the pronunciation of *four, five* and *six*.
• Do further practice by asking for the names of 'number six', 'number three', and so on. Students answer in complete sentences.

The people in the pictures are:
1. Denise Quinton   4. Lewis Dorrington
2. Gavin Jowitt   5. James Wharton
3. Jean Sheppard   6. Gillian Sharpe

• Further practice is possible with pictures of famous people cut out of magazines.

2 *First name* and *surname*

• Get the students to copy and complete the table, and check that they have done so correctly.

3 Writing

• Ask students to write several sentences about the pictures, like those in the examples.
• Point out that contracted forms are more common in speech, and full forms in writing.
• Get volunteers to read some of their sentences, and the other students to say which number picture they are talking about. This can be done in pairs or small groups after a class demonstration.

4 Personalisation

• Practise the examples.
• Ask a few questions about students' names, using the third person as in the examples. Call on selected students to answer.
• Get volunteers to ask questions. You or other students answer.
• Continue the work in small groups.
• Finally, get students to test *your* knowledge by asking 'What's his/her name?'

5 The alphabet: names of the letters

• Run through the alphabet with the students (you may like to use the recording).
• Say (or play) each group of letters several times and get students to practise them.
• Look out for confusions between *G* and *J*, *A* and *R*, *V* and *W*, *A* and *E*, *E* and *I* (depending on nationality). If you plan to teach the students to read phonetic symbols, this is a good place to introduce a few.
• Use flashcards (or write letters on the board) for further practice. This can be continued in groups.
• Note that students will need to know the alphabetical order of letters by heart in order to work properly with dictionaries.

6 Letter-by-letter dictation

• Play the recording (on which words are spelt out) or spell the words. Stop after each word and check the answers.

The words are: *name, your, hello, right, what, is, yes, no, my, one, five, three.*

• Continue the exercise with other words, or get students to continue in groups.

7 Spelling names

• Point out the use of *double* in the examples.
• Ask students to look at their lists from Exercise 2.
• Call out a number and ask a student to spell the name.
• This can be done as a team game, with team members taking turns trying to spell the names chosen by the other team; or after practice with you, it can be done in small groups.
• The names give practice on the commonly confused letters of the English alphabet.

8 Students spell their names

• Make sure each student learns to spell his or her own first name and surname.
• Then let them practise: a student spells his or her name, and then calls out the name of another student. The second student must spell back the name correctly, and then spell his or her own name and choose someone else to continue.

Practice Book exercises: choose two or more
1. Revision of *my* and *your*.
2. Revision of *his* and *her*.
3. Distinguishing first names and surnames.
4. Translation of expressions and sentences from the lesson.
5. Crossword puzzle using words from Lessons 1A and 1B.
6. Student's Cassette exercise (Student's Book Exercise 5). Practising the pronunciation of the letters of the alphabet.

1B His name's James Wharton

People's names; spelling; *his, her.*

1 Match the people and the names.

'1. Her name's Denise Quinton.'

1 one

2 two

3 three

4 four

5 five

6 six

2 Copy and complete the table.

	FIRST NAME	SURNAME
1.	Denise	Quinton
2.		
3.		
4.		
5.		
6.		

3 Write sentences and read to other students.
Examples:

1. Her first name is Denise.

1. Her surname is Quinton.

2. His name is Gavin Jowitt.

'Her first name's Gillian.'   'Six.'   'That's right.'
'His surname's Jowitt.'   'One.'   'No, two.'

4 Ask about other students.

'What's his surname?'   'I don't know.'
'Is her first name Anne?'   'Yes, that's right.'
'Is her name Barbara?'   'No, it isn't.'

ABCDEFGHIJKLMNOPQRSTUVWXYZ
abcdefghijklmnopqrstuvwxyz

5 Listen and practise.

AHJK   IY   UQW   R
EBCDGPTV   O   FLMNSXZ

6 Listen and write the words.

name   yo   h   r

7 Ask other students to spell a name from
Exercise 2.

'Five.'   'J, A, M, E, S, W, H, A, R, T, O, N.'

'Six.'   'G, I, double L, I, A, N, S, H, A, R, P, E.'

8 Spell your name, and choose another student to
spell it back to you.

Learn: four; five; six; his; her; first name;
surname; I; I don't know; that's right; double;
ABCDEFGHIJKLMNOPQRSTUVWXYZ.

7

1C How are you?

Saying hello and goodbye; *I am*; *I'm*; *are you?*

1 Listen, and practise the conversation.

2 Close your books. Can you remember the conversation?

3 Listen to the recording and complete the conversations.

ALICE: Excuse me. ....
Fred Andrews?
JAKE: ...., I'm sorry, ... It's Jake
Barker.
ALICE: .... sorry.

ALICE: Excuse me. Are .... Fred Andrews?
FRED: ...., I am.
ALICE: Oh, ... Alice Watson.
FRED: Oh, yes. How do you do?
ALICE: ....?

4 Practise the conversations.

5 Listen to the recording and answer.

6 Choose a person to be, and a person to look for, from the list on page 132. Walk round until you find your person.

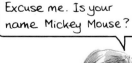 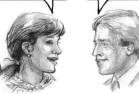

I am (I'm)	am I?
you are (you're)	are you?
he/she/it is (he's / she's / it's)	is he/she/it?

Learn: you; Hi; How are you?; and; Fine, thanks; Goodbye; Bye; See you; Oh; Here's . . . ; me; Excuse me; I'm sorry; How do you do?

Unit 1: Lesson C

Students learn simple ways of greeting and saying goodbye.
Structures: first and second persons of *be* (*I am, I'm, are you?*).

Language notes and possible problems

1. **How do you do?** Students are likely to confuse *How are you?* and *How do you do?* unless the difference is made clear.
2. **Excuse me.** They may also confuse *Excuse me* (used in British English mostly when interrupting people or asking strangers for help etc.) and *(I'm) sorry* (used for apologising).

Optional extra materials

A set of prompts for Exercise 6, one for each student in the class. (See Exercise 6.)

1 Presentation of new material

- Play the recording while students follow in their books.
- Explain any difficulties.
- Practise the sentences with the students. Note the 'linking' in *How are you?*
- Get them to practise the conversation in pairs.

2 Recall

- Ask students to close their books and see how much of the conversation they can remember. Build it up on the blackboard.

3 Listening practice

- Play the first sentence (two or three times if necessary) and ask students to write the missing words.
- Tell them to compare notes with their neighbours.
- Tell them the answer. (*Is your name . . . ?*)
- Play the rest of the first conversation (stopping for students to write).
- Let them compare notes.
- Tell them the answers (see below).
- Explain any difficult points.
- Do the second conversation in the same way.
- Point out the relationship between *I'm* (unstressed) and *I am* (stressed).

Tapescript and answers to Exercise 3

ALICE: Excuse me. *Is your name* Fred Andrews?
JAKE: *No,* I'm sorry, *it isn't.* It's Jake Barker.
ALICE: *I'm* sorry.

         *   *   *

ALICE: Excuse me. Are *you* Fred Andrews?
FRED: *Yes,* I am.
ALICE: Oh, *hello.* I'm Alice Watson.
FRED: Oh, yes. How do you do?
ALICE: *How do you do?*

4 Speaking practice

- Get students to write out the complete conversations.
- Practise the pronunciation, paying careful attention to intonation and rhythm.
- Get students to practise the conversations in pairs, changing the names if they wish.

Optional activity

- The dialogues in Exercise 1 and Exercise 3 can be practised further by a 'walk-round' activity in which students stop when they meet somebody else and improvise brief conversations like the ones in the exercises.

5 Conversational responses

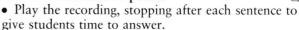

- Play the recording, stopping after each sentence to give students time to answer.
- Repeat the exercise several times until students are fluent.

Tapescript and answers to Exercise 5

Hello. (Answer 'Hello' or 'Hi'.)
Is your name Margaret? (Answer presumably 'No, it isn't'.)
What's your name?
How do you do? (Answer 'How do you do?')
How are you? (Answer 'Fine, thanks'.)
Goodbye. (Answer 'Goodbye', 'Bye' or 'See you'.)

6 Looking for someone

- You can make this exercise more interesting for the students by taking a few minutes before class to write up prompts for them. Each student will need a piece of paper that says *(Name 1): Look for (Name 2).* Instead of the names in the back of the book, use names of pop stars, movie stars, or other people in the news who will interest your own students.
- After giving out the prompts (or asking each student to choose a person to be and a person to look for from page 132 in their book), demonstrate with a volunteer. (*'Excuse me. Is your name Minnie Mouse?' 'No, I'm sorry, it isn't. It's Annie Oakley.'* and so on.)
- Then let students walk round looking for their person.

Practice Book exercises: choose two or more

1. and 2. Revision of expressions from the lesson.
3. Calculations to practise numbers *one* to *six*.
4. Practising the difference between *Excuse me* and *I'm sorry.*
5. Translation of sentences from the lesson.

Greetings and goodbyes
From this lesson onwards, you may like to make a habit of getting students to greet you and each other in English at the beginning of the class and to say goodbye in English at the end. When you greet students yourself, make it clear that *you* (in *How are you?*) can refer to one or more people.

Unit 1: Lesson D

Students learn to say where they come from, and to ask where other people are from.
Structures: *he* and *she.*
Phonology: weak and strong forms of *from*; word stress and /ə/; linking /r/.

Language notes and possible problems
1. *England* and *Britain* Many students are likely to think that *England* and *English* refer to the whole of Britain.
2. Gender In Exercise 3, you may need to point out to some students that English adjectives do not have different masculine and feminine forms.
3. Stress Not all languages have stressed and unstressed syllables: Exercise 4 will be difficult (and important) for some students.

Optional extra materials
Pictures of famous people from different countries. (Pictures of) things from different countries (e.g. a Swiss watch). Flashcards with the names of countries on them.

1 *Where's he from? Where's she from?*
• Practise saying *he*, *she*, and the names of countries. As you practise *Australia*, *India*, *Japan*, *Scotland* and *Italy*, point out the /ə/ in unstressed syllables.
• Practise *Where's he from?* and *Where's she from?*
• Ask students to make questions for the other pictures.
• Then go through the pictures getting them to say where the people are from.
• They should say '*He's/She's from . . .*' Encourage them to pronounce *from* as /frəm/ here, and not as /frɒm/.
• Consolidate by asking them to write about one or two of the pictures, using uncontracted forms (*he is*; *she is*).

Optional activity
• Use pictures of famous living people from different countries to get more examples of *He/She's from . . .*

2 Personalisation
• Practise the question and answer. *From* is pronounced /frɒm/ (stressed) in the question and /frəm/ in the answer. Practise the linking in *Where are* (/ˈweərə/).
• In a one-nationality class, get students to choose new countries from those in Exercise 1.
• Students walk round asking where people are from.
• If additional practice is needed, let them choose new countries and walk round again.

Optional activity
• Give students cards with the names of countries.
• Get them to say, in turn, '*I'm from . . .*' (with the name of their 'new' country). Do this twice.
• See how well the class can remember people's new nationalities, by asking '*Where's he/she from?*'

3 Dictionary work (national adjectives)
• Let students use dictionaries to fill in the lists.
• Then let them compare notes with their neighbours.
• When you give them the answers, point out that national adjectives always have capital letters.
• Ask students if they know (or want to know) any more words to add to the lists, but don't add too many.
• They can look up more nationality words at home.
• Practise saying nationalities and countries, paying attention to /ə/ in unstressed syllables.

Optional activity
• (Pictures of) things from different countries can give additional practice in using national adjectives.

4 Word stress
• Play the recording, or say the words for the students; get them to repeat with the correct stress.
• There are no simple rules for word stress in English. However, this exercise will help to sensitise students to the existence of stress differences.
• Pay attention to /ə/ in unstressed syllables.

5 Revision of numbers and letters
• Tell the students they must write down the numbers and the letters that they hear. You may have to play the recording more than once.

Tapescript and answers to Exercise 5

Part One:
One; Germany	Four; Britain
Two; Italian	Five; Scotland
Three; Japanese	Six; Greece

Part Two:
A, E, I, O, U, G, H, K, Q, J,
V, W, E, I, A, R, J, G, W, V.

6 Languages; fluency practice
• Go over what Susie says and make sure students understand. You may want to practise some words and phrases, such as *speak*, *a little*, and unstressed *and* (/ənd/) in '*French and a little English*'.
• Ask students to choose foreign roles for themselves, and make sentences like Susie's.
• Point out that in many cases the name of the language is the same as the national adjective.
• Teach the formula *Do you speak . . . ?*
• Ask the students to write their sentences.
• If there is time, they can then choose another foreign role and walk round introducing themselves to one another.

Practice Book exercises: choose two or more
1. Saying country and nationality words with the right stress.
2. Writing full forms from contractions.
3. National adjectives.
4. Translation of sentences from the lesson.
5. Student's Cassette exercise (Student's Book Exercise 4). Students read the words and check their pronunciation with the recording.
6. Crossword puzzle.

Dictionary use
A bilingual dictionary is a very useful learning aid, particularly when used under a teacher's supervision. Students need bilingual dictionaries for some exercises in the course (e.g. Exercise 3 in this lesson), and for autonomous work outside the classroom. They should buy good-sized dictionaries (not pocket editions): suggest titles if you can. To begin with, students may need help to make the best use of their dictionaries. Show how the entries are organised and what kinds of information they can provide. Make sure students understand that words have different translations in different contexts, and that one can only discover meanings with a dictionary by learning to select the appropriate translation from among the several that are offered.

1D Where are you from?

Asking and saying where people are from; nationalities; *he* and *she*.

1 Where's she from? Where's he from?

Australia   Egypt   India   Japan   Scotland
Italy   the United States   Russia

1

2

3

4

5

6

7

8

2 Where are you from? Ask and answer.

3 Use your dictionary.

COUNTRY	NATIONALITY
Carla's from Italy.	She's Italian.
Manuel's from Spain.	He's Spanish.
Shu-Fang's from China.	He's ....
Rob's from	He's Australian.
Kenji's from	He's Japanese.
Joyce is from the United States.	She's American.
Sally's from Britain.	She's ....
Rosa's from	She's Argentinian.
Fiona's from	She's Scottish.
Mohammed's from	He's Algerian.
Lakshmi's from India.	She's ....
Milton's from	He's Nigerian.
Sarah's from England.	She's ....

4 [cassette] Pronunciation: stress.
Listen and repeat.

☐☐
England
English
Britain
British
German
China
Spanish

☐☐☐
Japanese

☐☐
Japan
Chinese

☐☐☐☐
Italian
American
Australian

☐☐☐
Italy
Germany
Switzerland

5 Listen to the recordings.
1. Write the numbers and the words.
2. Write the letters.

6 Use your real name or invent a person. Answer Susie.

My name's Susie. I'm from Switzerland. I speak German, French and a little English. And you?

I	—	my
you	—	your
he	—	his
she	—	her

Learn: he; she; where; from; speak; a little; Britain; British; the United States; American; English; Where (are you) from?

Learn some more words for countries and nationalities if you want to.

Unit 2 You

2A What do you do?

Jobs; *a* and *an*.

1 Complete the sentences.

artist
doctor
electrician
housewife
secretary
shop assistant

1. He's an *artist*_____. 2. He's a _____. 3. She's a _____.

4. She's a _____. 5. He's an _____. 6. She's a _____.

2 Choose a job or use your job. Say what you do.

'I'm an engineer.'
'I'm a medical student.'
'I'm a photographer.'
'I'm between jobs.'

3 Ask and answer.

'What do you do?'
'I'm a dentist.'
'I'm an artist.'
'I'm a housewife.'

4 Say what other students do.

'She's a doctor.'
'He's an electrician.'

5 🔊 Listen and practise.

What do you do?

I'm a secretary.

Are you a doctor?

No, I'm an artist. She's a doctor.

Are you a photographer?

Yes, I am. Are you an artist?

No, I'm not. I'm a doctor. He's an artist.

6 Choose jobs and work in pairs. Ask and answer.

'Are you a doctor?'
'Yes, I am.' / 'No, I'm not.'

7 Find another pair; ask and answer.

'Is she an artist?'
'Yes, she is.' / 'No, she isn't.'

'Is he an engineer?'
'Yes, he is.' / 'No, he isn't.'

Learn: What do you do?; do; a; an; student; between jobs.

Learn four or more: doctor; secretary; electrician; housewife; shop assistant; artist; engineer; dentist; photographer; medical student.

Unit 2: Lesson A

Students learn to talk about professions.
Structures: *a/an* with professions.
Phonology: rhythm, intonation and linking in questions and statements.

Language notes and possible problems

1. Gender You may need to tell students that English does not have 'masculine' and 'feminine' nouns, articles, etc.
2. Articles Students whose languages do not have articles will need extra help and explanations. See *Appendix* page 135.
3. *What do you do?* is best treated as a formula at this stage, without explaining the grammar. But students should learn the meaning of the lexical verb *do*.

Optional extra materials

Five or more pictures of people cut out of magazines (Exercise 1).
Cards or slips of paper with professions written on them (Exercises 2 and 6).

1 Matching (vocabulary presentation)

• Get the students to look at the six pictures in Exercise 1.
• They try to match words and pictures.
• Students can work in small groups.
• When they have finished, try to elicit the difference between *a* and *an*. Then write on the board:

an	a
a, e, i, o, u	b, c, d, f, g, h, j, k, l, m, . . .

Optional activity

• You can do further practice by asking students to guess the professions of people in suitably chosen pictures cut out of magazines.

2 *I'm a teacher*

• If your students are too young to have jobs yet, ask them to choose jobs, or hand out cards or slips of paper with the names of jobs on them.
• Otherwise, students can do this exercise using their own jobs. Unemployed people can say *'I'm between jobs'*.
• Say *'I'm a teacher'*; write on the board:
  I am a teacher.
  I'm a teacher.
• Ask students *'What do you do?'* and help them with answers.
• Aid with pronunciation, stress and rhythm.
• Don't let them forget *a/an*.

3 Practice (walk-round)

• Practise *What do you do?*; write it on the board.
• Get students to walk round asking one another's occupations and answering.

4 *He's/She's a doctor*

• Choose a female student and tell the class what her job is (or what job she's chosen): for example, *'She's a doctor'*.
• Write on the board, for example:
  She is a doctor.
  She's a doctor.
• Demonstrate *He* with a male student. Make sure the students notice that *She's a* and *He's a* are linked so as to sound like single words.

• Point at a few students and ask the class what they do, to check that they have understood and are linking the words properly.
• Put the students in pairs and get them to tell each other what everyone else in the class does; walk round to help when needed.

5 Pronunciation

• Get the students to look at the conversation while you play the recording.
• Help them to practise the pronunciation.
• Points to remember (you may want to write them up):
– **Intonation:** rising in *yes/no* questions, falling in the answers.
  Are you a doctor?   No, I'm not.
– **Rhythm:** articles are unstressed.
  *Are you a **doctor**?*
– **Linking:** *you a* and *I am* are pronounced almost like *you wa* and *I yam*.

6 Guessing: questions and short answers (*you, I*)

• Ask students to choose another profession, or write the names of the professions learnt on cards or pieces of paper.
• Students work in pairs.
• Give each student a card/slip of paper with a profession written on it.
• Partners must not look at each other's cards.
• They try to guess each other's occupations by asking *'Are you a . . . ?'* and answering *'No, I'm not'* or *'Yes, I am'*.
• When students have finished they can exchange cards with other students (or change partners) and start again.

7 More questions and short answers: *he* and *she*

• When students have had enough practice with *you* and *I*, get each pair to find another pair.
• Demonstrate with two pairs: the people from the first pair ask one of the members of the second pair about the other one's job until they guess it: *'Is he/she a . . . ?' 'No, he/she isn't.' / 'Yes, he/she is.'*
• Help students with linking: almost like *he yis, she yisn't*, etc.
• Get the students to practise until they are fluent.

Practice Book exercises: choose two or more

1. Personal pronouns and possessives.
2. Pronunciation: stress.
3. *A* and *an*.
4. Dialogue completion.
5. Translation of sentences from the lesson (and some contrasting sentences from earlier lessons).
6. Student's Cassette exercise (Student's Book Exercise 5). Students say the sentences from their books and check their pronunciation with the recording.

Rhythm and stress
English is 'stress-timed'. Stressed syllables are slower and clearer than unstressed syllables; they come at roughly equal intervals. Unstressed syllables are fitted in quickly so as not to interrupt the rhythm. *There was a man in the garden* (eight syllables, two stresses) doesn't take much longer to say than *back door* (two syllables, two stresses). Speakers of 'syllable-timed' languages need practice in this area if they are to understand English speech and to be understood.

Unit 2: Lesson B

Students learn formal and informal ways of greeting.
Structures: no new structures.
Phonology: intonation of greetings and replies.

Possible problem

Register Some of the exercises concentrate on the difference in level of formality between the first and the second dialogue. Presenting this concept in a class where you do not speak the students' language(s) requires care.

Optional extra materials

A set of cards or slips of paper (one per student plus a few extras) with names of well-known people on them (extension of Exercise 5).

1 Times of day (presentation, practice)

- Get the students to look at the labelled pictures before Exercise 1. If you think it will be clearer for them, write times on the board to define the four parts of the day.
- Then let them do the exercise, preferably in small groups.
- Practise the pronunciation of the words with them, paying special attention to stress in **morning**, **after*noon*** and **evening**.
- When they have finished, call for the answers, paying attention to pronunciation once more.

Answers to Exercise 1

1. morning or evening   2. afternoon or evening   3. night
4. morning or afternoon   5. morning   6. morning or afternoon

2 Greetings (presentation, practice)

- Get the students to look at the two pictures.
- Get them to notice that the same woman is in both pictures. They might be able to tell you where she is each time if they have a little English from before the course.
- Establish that the woman is about 35, the man in the first picture 60+, and the man in the second picture about 35.
- Then get the students to close their books and listen to the recording. Stop after the first dialogue and see if they can remember any words. Do the same with the second dialogue.
- Play the recording again with books open. Explain or demonstrate new words or let students find them in their dictionaries.
- Play the recording once more, stopping after these phrases to let the students practise them (pay special attention to intonation):

Good morning.	*Hello.*
How are you?	*Hi.*
I'm very well, thank	*Fine thanks.*
* you. And you?*	*Not bad.*
I'm fine, thank you.	

- Try to get the students saying the phrases from the first dialogue in a formal or respectful way. (It will help if you demonstrate.) The phrases from the second dialogue should sound (and look) much more informal.

3 Differences in formality

- Ask students to decide (preferably in small groups) which greeting is probably being used in each picture.
- Check the answers with the whole class.
- Follow up by asking how they would greet people they know or have heard of (another student; a pop star; the Pope; etc.).
- If you speak the students' language, you may want to talk about the different factors which cause British people to choose between formal and informal language (familiarity, age, social class, relative status).
- While going over the answers with the students, practise the pronunciation of *Good afternoon*, *Good evening*, and *Good night*. Note that in modern British and American usage *Good morning/afternoon/evening* mean 'Hello', while *Good night* means 'Goodbye'.

4 Formality (continued)

- Now that students have understood the difference between the two dialogues, they can complete the table giving formal and informal equivalents. The completed table will look like this:

CONVERSATION 1	CONVERSATION 2
1. Good morning	Hello/Hi
2. *Dr Wagner*	Mary
3. How are you?	How are you?
4. *I'm fine / I'm very well*	Fine / Not bad
5. *thank you*	thanks
6. *And you?*	And you?

5 Practising greetings

- If possible, get students to walk round the room greeting as many other people as they can.
- Alternatively, get them to stand up and turn to greet as many others as possible.
- You will presumably want them to use informal greetings.
- To extend the exercise, hand out cards with names of famous people on them. The students hold their cards in front of themselves and go round greeting once again, deciding whether to be formal or informal.

Practice Book exercises: choose two or more
1. Parts of *be*, affirmative and negative.
2. Vocabulary practice: distinguishing *morning*, *afternoon*, *evening*, and *night*.
3. Dialogue completion.
4. Vocabulary revision.
5. Grammar: completing paradigm of *be*, singular.
6. Translation of sentences from the lesson.
7. Student's Cassette exercise (Student's Book Exercise 2). Students read the sentences from their Student's Books and check their pronunciation with the recording.

2B I'm very well, thank you

Formal and informal greetings.

morning   *afternoon*

evening   *night*

1 Morning, afternoon, evening or night?
Example:

1. morning or night

2 [cassette] Listen. Learn the new words from a dictionary or from your teacher. Listen again and practise.

WOMAN: Good morning, Mr Roberts. How are you?
MAN: Oh, good morning, Dr Wagner. I'm very well, thank you. And you?
WOMAN: I'm fine, thank you.

MAN: Hello, Mary.
WOMAN: Hi, Tom. How are you?
MAN: Fine, thanks. And you?
WOMAN: Not bad – but my daughter's not well today.
MAN: Oh, I'm sorry to hear that.

3 *Good morning* or *Hello*?

1   2   3

Good afternoon or *Hello*?

4   5   6

Good evening or *Hello*?

7   8   9

4 Differences. Read the conversations again and complete the table.

CONVERSATION 1	CONVERSATION 2
1. Good morning	Hello/Hi
2.	Mary
3. How are you?	How are you?
4.	Fine / Not bad
5.	thanks
6.	And you?

5 Stand up, walk around if you can, and greet other students.

Learn: morning; afternoon; evening; night; Good morning; Good afternoon; Good evening; Good night; very; well; I'm very well; not well; not bad; or; man; woman; Dr; Mr.

11

2C I'm an actress. And you?

More personal information.

1 🔊 Listen and practise.

1	one	11	eleven
2	two	12	twelve
3	three	13	thirteen
4	four	14	fourteen
5	five	15	fifteen
6	six	16	sixteen
7	seven	17	seventeen
8	eight	18	eighteen
9	nine	19	nineteen
10	ten	20	twenty

2 What number? What letter?
Test other students.

1.	R	11.	B
2.	E	12.	W
3.	N	13.	L
4.	J	14.	P
5.	A	15.	H
6.	V	16.	U
7.	I	17.	O
8.	M	18.	Y
9.	Z	19.	Q
10.	G	20.	S

3 Listening for information. Copy the table; then listen, and fill it in.

NAME	NATIONALITY	JOB	MARRIED/SINGLE	ADDRESS
Bill			don't know	14 Church Street
Lucy			married	.......Sutton Road
Jane Webb				.......Hirst Close
Gérard	French			.......Ross Street
Annie		photographer		.......Cedar Avenue
Philip				.......Evans Lane

4 Complete the dialogue and practise it.

VIRGINIA: Hello, I'm Virginia. What's your name?
YOU: ....
VIRGINIA: Is that an English name?
YOU: .... ,
.... ?
VIRGINIA: No, I'm not. I'm Argentinian.
YOU: .... , Virginia?
VIRGINIA: I'm an actress. And you?
YOU: ....
VIRGINIA: That's interesting. Are you married?
YOU: ....
.... ?
VIRGINIA: Yes, I am.

Learn: seven; eight; nine; ten; eleven; twelve;
thirteen; fourteen; fifteen; sixteen; seventeen;
eighteen; nineteen; twenty; married; single; address;
number; letter; (That's) interesting.

12

Unit 2: Lesson C

Students practise self-identification. They learn the numbers *seven* to *twenty*.
Structures: no new structures.
Phonology: word stress.

Optional extra materials
Slips of paper or cards with names of famous real or imaginary people (see Optional activity).

---

1 Numbers *one* to *twenty*
- Students have already seen numbers *one* to *six*. Ask them to close their books while you write these on the board one by one for identification and practice.
- Continue with numbers *seven* to *twenty*.
- False beginners may be able to name the numbers; beginners can repeat after you or the recording.
- Make sure students stress the last syllable in *thirteen*, *fourteen*, etc.
- Go round the class having each student say one number; count forwards/backwards, even numbers forwards/backwards, odd numbers forwards/backwards, by threes forwards/backwards.

2 Number and letter practice
- Open books; divide the class into two teams.
- Demonstrate: give the first member of Team A a letter and ask for the corresponding number. Then give the same student a number, to get its letter.
- Go on to the first member of Team B. Keep score.
- Finally, add the scores and declare winners.
- Then get the students to work in pairs playing the same game. Give a three-minute time limit.

3 Listening for information
- Get the students to copy the table.
- Use the examples to show what *nationality* and *address* mean. Explain *married* and *single*.
- Play the first section (Bill) once or twice.
- Make sure all students have written correct answers.
- Play the rest, more than once if necessary.
- Students compare answers before checking with you.

Tapescript and answers to Exercise 3

Hello. My name's Bill. I'm British. I'm a doctor. My address is 14 Church Street.

She's an artist. She's American. Her name's Lucy. She's married, and her address is 10 Sutton Road.

'Hello. Come in and sit down. What's your name?'
'Jane Webb.'
'And where do you come from, Ms Webb?'
'I'm British.'
'Are you married?'
'No, I'm not.'
'And what's your job, Ms Webb? What do you do?'
'I'm a teacher. I, I teach in a primary school.'
'I see. And can I have your address, please?'

'It's 16 Hirst Close.'
'16 Hirst Close. Thank you. Now, tell me, how do you think . . .'

He's a French electrician. His name's Gérard. He's single. His address is 119 Ross Street.

I'm a photographer. I'm Greek. My name's Annie, and my address is 17 Cedar Avenue.

'Hello. What's your name?'
'Philip.'
'What's your job, Philip?'
'I'm a secretary.'
'Are you American?'
'No, I'm not. I'm Australian. But I'm married to an American.'
'OK. And do you mind giving me your address?'
'Not at all. It's 8 Evans Lane.'
'8 Evans Lane. Fine. Now . . .'

Answers to Exercise 3: see below

4 Dialogue completion (revision)

- Get the students to read the sentences Virginia says.
- They should ask you or consult their dictionaries for new words (*actress*, *interesting*).
- Write Virginia's first line on the board.
- Ask the students for suggestions for the first reply, writing up the one you decide on.
- Write up Virginia's second line, and point out that they must now supply two sentences – one following the question and one preceding Virginia's next answer.
- Continue through the entire dialogue.
- Play the recording and let them answer.
- Clean the board and try the recording again.
- Follow up by practising *married* and *single* (talking about the students themselves or people they know).

Optional activity: inventing dialogues
- Put the students into pairs.
- Each pair should write another dialogue, either using their own identities or choosing other identities.
- You may want to have suggested names ready.
- Students look at the 'Virginia' dialogue, and try and invent their own dialogue (ten to twelve lines).
- They practise, and find other pairs to perform for.
- Volunteers can perform their dialogues for everyone.

Practice Book exercises: choose two or more
1. Subject pronouns and *be* (blank filling).
2. Writing questions for answers.
3. Vocabulary revision (blank filling).
4. First names and surnames.
5. Translation of material from the lesson.
6. Student's Cassette exercise (Student's Book Exercise 1). Students read the numbers from their books and check their pronunciation with the recording. Note stress on *teen* in *thirteen*, etc.
7. Jumbled stories (with a few unknown words which students need not know in order to complete the exercise). The stories are in order, but are mixed up with one another.

Answers to Exercise 3

NAME	NATIONALITY	JOB	MARRIED/SINGLE	ADDRESS
Bill	*British*	*doctor*	don't know	14 Church Street
Lucy	*American*	*artist*	married	10 Sutton Road
Jane Webb	*British*	*teacher*	single	16 Hirst Close
Gérard	French	*electrician*	single	119 Ross Street
Annie	*Greek*	photographer	*don't know*	17 Cedar Avenue
Philip	*Australian*	*secretary*	married	8 Evans Lane

Unit 2: Lesson D

Students learn more numbers and learn to talk about age.
Structures: *be* in questions and statements about age.
Phonology: word stress.

Possible problem
In some languages, the equivalent of *have*, not *be*, is used in talking about age. Students may have trouble on this point.

Optional extra materials
Flashcards for counting exercises.

1 Presentation: numbers *twenty* to *a hundred*
- Students should have their books closed.
- Write the numbers from the book on the board, getting students to repeat each one after you or the recording as you do so.

2 Teens and tens
- Practise the difference between *thirteen* (stressed at the end when in isolation) and *thirty* (stressed at the beginning).
- Then say the following numbers (or play the recording) and get the students to write what they hear.
- Let them compare notes before giving them the answers.

Answers to Exercise 2
thirteen	fifty	seventy	fourteen	forty
nineteen	seventeen	sixteen	ninety	eighty

3 Practice with numbers: counting
- Get students to do the four counting tasks as quickly as they can, each student saying a number in turn.
- If you go around the class once or twice for each task this should give ample practice – no need to count all the way down to 1 from 99!

4 Group and pair work on numbers
- Call one student to the board and dictate a few numbers to write. Get volunteers from the class to dictate a few more.
- Then divide the class into pairs or small groups and let them dictate numbers to one another.
- Write $38 + 7 = ?$ on the board.
- Say *'Thirty-eight and seven?'* and let the class answer.
- Call out a few more sums, and then put the students back into their pairs/groups to do the same.
- Write $6 \times 7 = ?$ on the board and say *'Six sevens?'*
- Once again, call out a few more multiplications and put students back into group/pair work.

5 Ages
- If your students are of different ages, and if you think they will not be embarrassed, begin by asking them to guess each other's ages (and yours).
- Get them to say *'I think you're (about) . . .'*
- If you think they will be embarrassed, just give them your own age and then ask them to look at picture A. Help them to express their guesses with *I think* and *about*.
- Ask them to work individually writing down their guesses of the ages of the ten people.
- Then put them in groups of about four to agree on best guesses for the ten ages. Demonstrate with one of the pictures with one group before beginning. Walk round while they are working to give any help that is needed.

- When they are finished, ask for the results. Say *'How old is A?'* and so on. When you have all the guesses for picture A, give them the right answer, and so on.

Answers to Exercise 5
A 51, B 26, C 8, D 66, E 35, F 2, G 33, H 19

6 Filling in a form
- Go over the form explaining new vocabulary.
- You will probably want to point out that while *Miss* and *Mrs* are traditional forms, some women now prefer the title *Ms* (pronounced /mɪz/ or /məz/), which like *Mr* gives no information about the marital status of the person.
- Get students to copy the form before filling it in with their own details.
- Meanwhile write your own form on the board and fill it in.
- If students are likely to be unhappy about revealing personal information, tell them that they don't have to show what they have written to you or anyone else.
- Walk round to check they have understood.

7 Role play
- Get the students to copy the form again and invent a new identity to complete it with. You may want to demonstrate on the board first, inventing a far-fetched identity for yourself.
- Get students to question one another on their new identities, if possible walking round the room to interview a maximum number of other students.

Practice Book exercises: choose two or more
1. Capitalisation and punctuation.
2. Practice in matching words and numbers.
3. Writing numbers in words.
4. Odd word out. You will have to explain to students that in each group of words there is one that is different in some way. Books closed, write on the board: *morning, evening, night, name* and ask students to decide which one is different. (You will probably need to teach the word *different*.)
5. Dialogue completion.
6. Translation of material from the lesson, and some contrasting material from earlier lessons.
7. Student's Cassette exercise (Student's Book Exercise 1). Students read the numbers from their Student's Books and check their pronunciation with the recording.
8. Extensive reading: the first part of *It's a Long Story*, a rather frivolous serial. There will be one episode in each unit.

Answers to Practice Book Exercise 4
1. name   2. Hi   3. Japan   4. Good morning (formal)
5. good (not an answer to 'How are you?')   6. seven (odd number)   7. eighty-two (not divisible by five)

Role play and movement
If students are not used to playing parts or moving around the classroom, they may take a little time to get used to exercises that require this. It may be better with some classes (particularly with teenagers) to avoid full-scale walk-round exercises at the beginning, until students are used to working in pairs and groups. Instead, get students to talk to as many people as they can without moving from their seats.

2D How old are you?

Numbers; ages; titles.

1 🔊 Listen and practise.

20	twenty	30	thirty	40	forty
21	twenty-one	34	thirty-four	50	fifty
22	twenty-two	35	thirty-five	60	sixty
23	twenty-three	36	thirty-six	70	seventy
24	twenty-four	37	thirty-seven	80	eighty
25	twenty-five	38	thirty-eight	90	ninety
26	twenty-six	39	thirty-nine	100	a hundred

2 Thir*teen* or *thir*ty? Four*teen* or *for*ty?
Listen and write what you hear.

3 Practise with numbers.

1. Count: '1, 2, 3, . . .'
2. Count in twos: '2, 4, 6, 8, . . .'
3. Count in fives: '5, 10, 15, . . .'
4. Count backwards: '99, 98, 97, . . .'

4 Work in groups or pairs.
1. Say numbers for other students to write.
   'Fifty-six.' 56
2. Say numbers for other students to add.
   'Thirty-eight and seven?' *'Forty-five.'*
3. Say numbers for other students to multiply.
   'Six sevens?' *'Forty-two.'*

5 How old?
1. Write down an age for each person.
2. Talk to some other students and agree on the ages.

'I think A is about 50.'
'I think she's about 60.'
'No, 55.'
'OK, 55.'

 A
 B
 C
 D

 E
 F
 G
 H

HARRIS AND SANDERS
Photographic Supplies
13 Old High Street, Wembley

Job Application

Mr/Mrs/Miss/Ms ....

First name ....

Surname ....

Age ....

Marital status: single ☐
      married ☐
      divorced ☐
      separated ☐
      widow(er) ☐

Nationality ....

Address ....

....

6 Copy and fill in the form.

7 Copy the form again and fill it in with a new identity. Then work with a partner. Ask each other these questions.

1. Mr, Mrs, Miss or Ms?
2. What's your first name?
3. How do you spell it?
4. What's your surname?
5. How do you spell it?
6. How old are you?
7. Where are you from?
8. Are you married?
9. What's your address?

Learn: *numbers* 21 to 100; How old are you?;
divorced; separated; widow; widower; Miss; Mrs; Ms;
I think; about; OK; How do you spell it?

Unit 3 People

3A Andrew's bag's under the table

Prepositions; possessive *'s*; *Where* questions.

1 Under, on, in or near ?

1 2 3 4 5 6 7 8

2 Describe the picture. Example:

'His coat's on the chair.'

3 Look at the picture for one minute. Then turn to page 132 and say where things are.

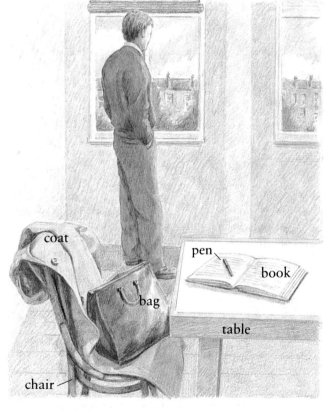

coat
pen
book
bag
table
chair

Polly   Ann   Andrew

4 Turn to the page your teacher tells you. Describe your picture for your partner to draw. Example:

'Andrew's bag's under the chair.'

5 Work in groups. Move things around, and let another group say where things are.

'Annie's book's under her chair.'

'Where's Ana's coat?'
'It's on Antonio's chair.'

'Where's Guido's pen?'
'It's on the table near Carla.'

Learn: pen; hat; book; coat; bag; table; chair; on; in; under; near; the.

14

Unit 3: Lesson A

Students learn to talk about place and possession.
Structures: possessive *'s*; some prepositions of place; *Where* questions.

Language notes and possible problems
1. Word order Students often have difficulty with the word order in possessive expressions. (A typical mistake is *bag's Andrew* instead of *Andrew's bag*.) False beginners may also add articles (*the Andrew's bag*).
2. *The* is introduced here as a vocabulary item. The grammar of the definite article is dealt with in Unit 5.

1 Presentation of prepositions
• In this exercise students have only to decide which preposition is used in each situation.
• Demonstrate the prepositions with an object, e.g. your pen, getting the students to repeat *under, on, in* and *near* after you.
• Then get them to do the exercise, telling you in each case which preposition is used.

2 Saying where things are
• Use objects from the classroom or drawings on the board to demonstrate the meanings of *chair, table, coat, bag, book,* and *pen,* and help students practise the pronunciation of the words.
• Ask students to look at the picture, and tell them *'His coat's on the chair'*.
• Get students to give you other sentences about the picture (using *His*).
• Write one or more of the sentences on the board, and remind the students that *'s* means *is*.

3 Possessive *'s*
• Ask students to look at the picture in their books and help them with the pronunciation of *Polly, Ann* and *Andrew*.
• Then give them exactly one minute to look at the picture again.
• Ask them to turn to page 132 and look at the picture there.
• Say *'Andrew's bag's under the table'*.
• Write on the board:
  Andrew's bag's under the table.
  His bag is under the table.
and point out the difference between the two *'s* constructions.
• Get students to try and say where Andrew's, Polly's and Ann's things are. Try to make sure they don't look back; don't correct them if they say something is in the wrong place.
• When they have said as much as they can, let them look back at page 132 and check their answers.

Answers to Exercise 3
Andrew's bag's under the table.
Andrew's hat's in his bag.
Andrew's book's on his bag.
Andrew's pen's on the table.
Ann's bag's near the chair.
Ann's book's in her bag.
Ann's coat's on the chair.
Ann's hat's on the chair.
Polly's coat's on the table (near her hat).
Polly's hat's near her coat.
Polly's book's under her bag / on the table.
Polly's bag's on her book.

4 Pair work: possessive *'s*
• Tell the students to take out a piece of paper.
• Get them to count themselves off around the classroom: *'1, 2, 3, 4, 5 . . . ,'* and to remember their numbers.
• Tell all the students with even numbers (translate or demonstrate what *even* means) to look at page 132 in their books, and all the students with odd numbers to look at page 134.
• Without looking at each other's pages, the students work in pairs. Each person tries to describe his picture so a partner can draw it.
• Give them a start by telling the even-numbered students: *'Andrew's bag's near the chair'*.
• Walk round while they are working to give any help that is needed.

5 Group work
• Ask the students to look very carefully at all the students around them.
• Then divide the class into groups of three or four. Each group must change the position of some things.
• Then a neighbouring group must try and guess where things are.
• Demonstrate with the examples in the book.
• Walk round while students are working to help with any problems.
• Give the students a few extra words if they need them, but be careful not to introduce too much new vocabulary.

Practice Book exercises: choose two or more
1. Distinguishing between possessive *'s* and *'s* for contracted *is*.
2. Writing questions (revision from this and previous lessons).
3. Revision of names of professions, with possessive *'s*.
4. Writing answers to questions (revision from this and previous lessons).
5. Translation of sentences from the lesson.
6. Student's Cassette exercise (Student's Book Lesson 2B, Exercise 2). Dictation: students listen and try to write down the conversations.

Pair and group work
In activities where more than one student is speaking at a time, teachers sometimes worry about the fact that they cannot listen to and correct everybody. This loss of control should not be seen as a problem. It is very important to do practice which bridges the gap between totally controlled exercises (where everything is checked) and real-life communication (where nothing is checked). In pair work and group work, you can supervise just as many people as you can in fully controlled exercises (i.e., one at a time); meanwhile, the people you are not supervising also get useful fluency practice. Even if some students take the opportunity to waste time or lapse into their own language, there will still be far more people practising English during group work than when students answer questions one at a time.

Unit 3: Lesson B

Students learn to give simple descriptions of people.
Structures: *we/you/they are*; more work on possessive *'s*.
Phonology: pronunciation of *'s*.

Language notes and possible problems

1. Are The weak pronunciation of *are* (/ə(r)/) will need attention.

2. Pretty Students will need help to realise that *pretty* is used for women but not for men, while *good-looking* can be used for both sexes.

3. Fat Make sure students realise that this is an unflattering or pejorative word. If necessary teach *plump* for more polite use.

4. Quite is taught here with its 'gradable' meaning (similar to *relatively* or *fairly*). Note that *quite* is not generally used in this way in American English.

5. We In English, *we* can mean *you and I*, *he/she and I*, or *they and I*. Some languages have different pronouns for these different cases.

6. You Make sure students realise that *you* can be both singular and plural. Tell them that this is also true of *your*.

7. Dictionaries will be needed for Exercise 3 and possibly Exercise 1. Students should make a habit of bringing dictionaries to class – they are necessary for many of the exercises in the course.

Optional extra materials

Pictures of people for additional descriptions (Exercises 1 and 3).

1 Guided composition

• Go through the description of Judy, getting students to guess the new words, look them up or tell each other their meanings.

• The descriptions of Sam and Eric can be done on the board with the students suggesting words for the gaps.

• Get them to write the description of Alice (working individually). Let them compare notes in groups before you give them your version.

• *This is* is extremely difficult to pronounce. Don't be too perfectionist at this stage.

Answers to Exercise 1

SAM
This is Sam. He is Judy's boyfriend. He is not very *tall*. *He is* dark. *He is* quite good-looking.

ERIC
This is Sam's friend, Eric. He is *tall* and *dark*. He is Alice's *boyfriend*. He is *not very* good-looking.

ALICE (possible answer)
This is Eric's girlfriend, *Alice. She is fair, and not very tall. She is not very pretty.*

Optional activity

• Use pictures of suitable-looking people to give further practice.

• Show the pictures and let students describe them.

• Describe one of the pictures and let students guess which one you are talking about.

• Let students do the same in groups.

2 Pronunciation of possessive *'s*

• If students want a very good standard of pronunciation, you may wish to work on the three different pronunciations of possessive *'s* (/z/ after a vowel or voiced consonant; /s/ after an unvoiced consonant; /ɪz/ after /s/, /z/ and other sibilants). If you don't need to be perfectionist, drop the exercise – but make sure *Alice's* is pronounced correctly.

3 More adjectives

• This exercise adds some more common adjectives and gives students practice in using dictionaries.

• Ask them to write the numbers 1–9, and to put the correct adjectives against them.

• Let them compare notes in groups before giving them the answers. In some cases more than one correct answer is possible.

• Practise the pronunciation of the new words.

Optional exercise

• Use pictures for a guessing game to practise the new words.

• Show several pictures (all of males or all of females).

• Students have to guess which picture you are thinking of – they are allowed to ask three questions beginning *Is he/she . . . ?* before guessing.

4 We and plural *you*

• Demonstrate or explain the meaning of *we*. Depending on the students' mother tongue, it may be important to show both the inclusive meaning (*you and I*) and the exclusive meaning (*he/she/they and I*) – see *Language notes*.

• Practise the pronunciation of *we are* and *we're* (/wɪə(r)/).

• Start the exercise by talking about yourself and a student with whom you have something in common (e.g. height, hair colour, age, nationality, profession).

• Make at least one untrue statement, and get the class to say 'No, you aren't' (as in the example).

• Point out the plural meaning of *you* here.

• Put the students in pairs and get them to continue making examples in turn (including one or two untrue examples). Encourage them to use *quite* and *not very*.

5 They

• Make a few examples with *they*. If possible, make one example about two men and one about two women, so that it's clear that *they* is the plural of both *he* and *she*.

• Practise the pronunciation of *they are* and *they're* (/ðeə(r)/).

• Ask for more examples from the class.

• Pick out two students who have several things in common and ask students to write about them.

• When they have finished, get them to read out what they have written (or to put it up on the class notice board for everybody to look at).

Practice Book exercises: choose two or more

1. Singular and plural forms of *be*.
2. Singular and plural personal pronouns.
3. Questions.
4. Translation of sentences from the lesson.
5. Writing descriptions.

3B This is Judy

Possessive *'s*; *we are, you are, they are*; descriptions; *This is . . .*

JUDY
This is Judy.
She is tall and fair.
She is very pretty.

SAM
This is Sam.
He is Judy's boyfriend.
He is not very ....
.... dark.
.... quite
   good-looking.

ERIC
.... Sam's
   friend, Eric.
He is .... and
....
He is Alice's ....
He is ....
   good-looking.

ALICE
.... Eric's
   girlfriend, ...
....
....

1 Look at the pictures and complete the descriptions.

2 Pronunciation. Practise:

Judy's	Mary's	Joe's	Harry's	(/z/)
Sam's	Bob's	Anne's	Susan's	(/z/)
Eric's	Margaret's	Jeff's	Kate's	(/s/)
Alice's	Joyce's	Ross's	Des's	(/ɪz/)

3 Use your dictionary. Match the words and the pictures.

dark	fair	fat	intelligent	old
slim	strong	tall	young	

1   2   3   4   5   6   7   8   9

4 Work with another student. Make sentences about the two of you. Tell the class:

> We're not very tall. We're young. We're English.

> No, you aren't. You're Mexican.

5 Write about two other students. Example:

Mario and Carla are tall, slim and dark. They are quite young.

we are (we're)	are we?	we are not (aren't)
you are (you're)	are you?	you are not (aren't)
they are (they're)	are they?	they are not (aren't)

Learn: dark; fair; fat; good-looking; intelligent; old; pretty; slim; tall; strong; young; friend; boyfriend; girlfriend; they; we; quite; not very; this.

15

3C I've got three children

Families; noun plurals; plural *s'*; *Who* questions; *have got*; *their*.

1 Look at the 'family tree' and complete the sentences. Use your dictionary.

his	her	wife	husband	brother	sister

1. John is Polly's .... Polly is John's ....
2. Andrew is Joyce's .... Joyce is Andrew's ....
3. Polly and John are Joyce's parents. Polly is her mother, and John is .... father.
4. Andrew and Joyce are John's children. Andrew is his son, and Joyce is .... daughter.

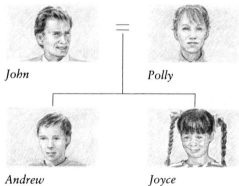

John *Polly*

Andrew *Joyce*

2 Now look at this family tree. Read the sentences and put in the names.

Eric	Lucy	Ann	Harry
Pat	Fred	Alice	Joe

1. Joe 2. ....

3. .... 4. .... 5. .... 6. ....

7. .... 8. ....

Joe's wife's name is Ann. Joe and Ann have got three children: two daughters and a son. Their daughters' names are Alice and Lucy, and their son's name is Fred. Fred and Lucy are not married. Alice's husband's name is Harry. Harry and Alice have got two children: a boy and a girl. Their daughter's name is Pat, and their son's name is Eric.

3 Listening. Look at the family tree in Exercise 1. Listen to the sentences and say *Yes* or *No.* Then look at Exercise 2. Make some sentences for other students. Examples:

'Ann has got two sons.' *'No.'*
'Alice's husband's name is Harry.' *'Yes.'*

4 Write five or more true sentences about your family. Use some of these words.

boy(s)   brother(s)   girl(s)   mother
parents   child(ren)   father   daughter(s)
husband   son(s)   wife   sister(s)   married
divorced   separated   widow   widower

Examples:

I've got three children, two girls and a boy.
My sister and I are dark, but our brother is fair.
My mother has got four sisters and a brother.
I've got no children.

5 Talk about your family. Say three things, and then answer one question. Examples:

'We've got one child, a daughter. Her name's Helen. She's short and fair.'
'How old is she?'
'Two.'

'My mother's sister has got three sons. They're sixteen, thirteen and twelve. They're in Barcelona.'
'What are their names?'
'Antonio, Juan and Carlos.'

'My sister and I are quite tall, and my brothers are very tall. Our mother isn't very tall.'
'Is your father tall?'
'Yes, very tall.'

Regular plurals		**Irregular plurals**	
daughter	daughters	child	children
parent	parents	man	men
		woman	women
family	families	wife	wives
secretary	secretaries		
address	addresses		
six	sixes		

Possessive *s*

Helen(s)name = (her)name

my daughter(s')names = (their)names

Learn: father; mother; wife; husband; brother; sister; son; daughter; parent; child; boy; girl; family; I've / they've / he's / she's got; who; their; our.

Unit 3: Lesson C

Students learn to talk about family relationships.
Structures: regular and irregular noun plurals; plural possessive (s'); questions with *Who*; *have got*; *their*.

Language notes and possible problems
1. *No* It is common in English to use a plural noun after *no* (e.g. *no children*). This may cause difficulty.
2. *Their* (Exercise 2) is pronounced in the same way as *they're*. This may cause problems for some students.

1 Vocabulary learning
• Ask students to use their dictionaries to fill in the first blank. Check the answer.
• Let them continue individually or in groups.
• Note that some students may need help in learning to use dictionaries effectively.
• Get students to read out their answers.
• Then point out the formation of plurals. Write on the board:

1	2, 3, 4 . . .
brother	brothers
sister	sisters
parent	parents
son	sons
daughter	daughters
family	families
address	addresses
child	children
wife	wives

• If you can speak the students' language(s), explain that most plurals in English are regular, but that a few irregular plurals must be learnt.
• Show the rules for regular plural formation: words ending in consonant + *y* drop the *y* and add *ies*; words ending in *s*, *x*, *sh* or *ch* add *es*; all other words add *s*.
• Practise the pronunciation of the plurals; the pronunciation rules are the same as those for possessives (see Lesson 3B, Exercise 2).

2 Comprehension practice
• Copy the family tree onto the board. Read the first sentence and ask students where you should put *Ann*.
• Ask students to carry on by themselves. Let them compare notes before you put the answers on the board.

Answers: 1. Joe 2. Ann 3. Fred 4. Lucy 5. Alice 6. Harry 7. Eric 8. Pat

• Explain what *their* means. You may want to warn students that it is pronounced in the same way as *they're*.
• Explain the contrast between 's and s':

his son	his son's name
his sons	his sons' names
their daughter	their daughter's name
their daughters	their daughters' names

• Finally, ask students to close their books and see if they can remember any of the sentences from the text.

3 Listening: true or false?
• Tell students to look at the family tree.
• Play the recording or say the following sentences:
Andrew is Joyce's sister. (*No*)
John is Polly's son. (*No*)
Polly is John's wife. (*Yes*)
Joyce is Andrew's sister. (*Yes*)
Joyce is John's father. (*No*)
Polly is Andrew's mother. (*Yes*)
Andrew and Joyce are John and Polly's parents. (*No*)
John is Polly's husband. (*Yes*)
• Students should answer 'Yes' or 'No'.
• Ask them to try to correct the false statements.
• Go over the examples and point out the use of *has got* in the third person.
• Then ask them to look at the text and family tree in Exercise 2 and make up 'true or false' statements and try them on each other.

4 Writing about families
• Go over the examples. Explain the use of *our*.
• Ask each student to write five or more true sentences about his or her family.
• You may want to put an example on the board yourself, or get a volunteer to do so.
• Walk round while the students are working to give any help that is needed.

5 Talking about families
• Tell the students about part of your family, as in the examples. Get them to ask you questions. (Teach *Have you got . . . ?* at this point only if the students need it to ask their questions.)
• Point out the examples in the book, and explain or demonstrate that each student must say three things about his or her family to a partner, and then answer one question.
• When students have finished they should change partners; if it is convenient they can move round the classroom.
• Walk round while they are working to give any help that is needed.
• You can give them a few extra words (*grandmother*, *cousin*, etc.), but try to limit these.

Optional activities
1. Two students give information about their families (as in Exercise 4). They repeat the information. The rest of the class or group then have to remember what they were told. (Teach *He's got* and *She's got*.)
2. Students bring family photos to class and tell each other about them.

Practice Book exercises: choose two or more
1. Practice with *his*, *her*, *their*, *is* and *are*.
2. Pronunciation of possessive 's and s'.
3. Writing possessives in sentences.
4. Students write about their families (five sentences).
5. Writing plurals.
6. Translation of sentences from the lesson.

Unit 3: Lesson D

Students practise understanding conversational spoken English.
Structures: *Have you got . . . ?*; *Yes, I have*; *No, I haven't*; *any* in questions; preview of *to*-infinitive.
Phonology: stress, intonation and linking.

Possible problems
Real beginners will find this lesson more difficult than the work they have done so far. They should not try to learn all of the new material if they find this too hard. False beginners should learn all or most of the new vocabulary.

Extra materials
Role-cards for dialogues (see Optional activity).

Prediction exercise (before Exercise 1)
• If your class are 'false beginners' with some knowledge of English, ask them to look at the picture (while covering up the conversation) and to try to guess what is going on.
   Possible questions:
   Where are the two men?
   Whose office is it? How do you know?
   What does the man on the left want?
   What do you think the other man will say?
• Real beginners will not be able to do this, and should go straight on to Exercise 1.

1 Presentation
• Play the recording twice, while the students listen with their books closed.
• Ask them to tell you what they can remember (any words or expressions at all from the dialogue).
• See if you can build up some of the conversation on the board with the students' help.
• Tell them to open their books; replay the recording.
• Go through the text explaining words and expressions that students don't know. This is a good moment to teach the formula *What does . . . mean?* With real beginners you may wish to explain selected items only.
• Point out that *any* is used in front of plural nouns in questions, in the same way that *a/an* is used in front of singular nouns.
• You may wish to draw students' attention to the following points:
1. The form of the article (*a* not *an*) in *a university teacher* (/ə ju:nɪˈvɜːsəti/).
2. The use of *aren't you?* etc. to ask for confirmation of something the speaker is not sure of.
3. The contrast between *Excuse me* and *(I'm) sorry* (already seen in Lesson 1C).
• The *to*-infinitive is previewed here; it will be studied in detail later.

2 Rhythm and linking
• Practise the expressions – perhaps in chorus first of all and then individually round the class.
• Pay special attention to rhythm – the alternation between slow stressed syllables (printed in bold type) and quicker unstressed syllables.
• Pay attention, also, to linking.
• The customer has a Canadian accent.

3 Dialogue practice
• Divide the dialogue into short sections of between four and eight lines.

• Work on one or more of these sections (depending on students' level, interest and time available) as follows.
• Practise the section together. Pay attention to rhythm and linking, and to intonation.
• Get students to practise the section in pairs, working simultaneously. They should act it, not just say the lines.
• If this works well, get them to memorise the section so that they can act it out without the book.

4 Have you got . . . ?
• Students do more practice on *have got*.
• In older classes, you may want to add *Have you got any children?*
• *Some* and *any* are studied in detail in Unit 7.

5 Mini-interviews
• Get students to write role-cards for themselves, choosing personal details from the box or inventing them.
• Divide the students into pairs. They take turns to interview each other.
• If you wish, they can report back to the class.

Optional activity
• This may be too difficult for complete beginners, but should work well with false beginners.
• Prepare a number of role-cards (suggestions below).
• Divide the students into pairs: one is a bank manager, the other is a customer.
• Give the customers each a role-card.
• Tell the bank managers to interview the customers, asking more or less the same questions as in the dialogue.
• Demonstrate yourself first with a good student if necessary.

Suggested role-cards:

MR CARTER Age: 22. Married.
Wife's name: Anne. Wife's age: 20.
One child: a boy (John, age 1).
Job: shop assistant.
You want £100,000 to buy a house.

MRS BULL Age: 40. Divorced.
One child: a girl (Jane, age 15).
Job: secretary.
You want £50,000 to buy a flat.

DR ALLEN Age: 27. Single.
Job: doctor.
You want £150,000 to buy a house.

MR ROBINSON Age: 34. Married.
Wife's name: Helen. Wife's age: 36.
Four children: three girls and a boy (Sally, age 12; Mary, age 10; Margaret, age 5; Joe, age 3).
Job: businessman.
You want £100,000 to buy a house for your mother.

MRS LANE Age: 27. Married.
Husband's name: Peter. Husband's age: 29.
Two children: a boy (Robert, age 4) and a girl (Emily, age 3).
Job: writer of children's books.
You want £10,000 to buy a car.

Practice Book exercises: choose two or more
1. Consolidation of *have got*.
2. Revision of lesson material: dialogue completion.
3. Translation of sentences from the lesson.
4. Student's Cassette exercise (Student's Book Exercise 1). Further practice on pronunciation of sentences in dialogue.
5. Reading: Part 2 of *It's a Long Story*.
6. Revision crossword puzzle.

3D An interview

Conversation practice; *Have you got . . . ?*; *Yes, I have*; *No, I haven't.*

BANK MANAGER: Good morning,
    Mr Harris.
CUSTOMER: Good morning.
BM: Please sit down.
C: Thank you.
BM: Now, one or two questions . . .
C: Yes, of course.
BM: How old are you, Mr Harris?
C: Thirty-two.
BM: And you're Canadian, aren't you?

C: Yes, that's right.
BM: Are you married?
C: Yes, I am.
BM: What is your wife's name?
C: Monica.
BM: And your wife's age, Mr Harris?
C: Pardon?
BM: How old is Mrs Harris?
C: Oh, she's thirty.
BM: Thirty. And is she Canadian, too?

C: No, she's British.
BM: British, yes. Have you got any
    children?
C: Yes, three. Two boys and a girl.

(Phone rings)

BM: Excuse me a moment. Hello,
    Anne. Yes? Yes? Yes, I am. No.
    Yes. No, I'm sorry, I don't know.
    No. Yes, all right. Thank you.
    Goodbye. I'm sorry, Mr Harris.
    Now, two girls and a boy, you said?
C: No, two boys and a girl.
BM: Oh, yes, I'm sorry. And what are
    their names?
C: Alan, Jane and Max.
BM: And their ages?
C: Twelve, ten and six.
BM: I see. Now one more question, Mr
    Harris. What is your job?
C: I'm a university teacher.
BM: A university teacher. Right. Thank
    you. Now, you want £100,000 to
    buy a house.
C: That's right.
BM: And how much . . . ?

1 Listen to the conversation. Then see how much you can remember.

2 Pronunciation. Practise these expressions.

one or two questions   Yes, of course.
How old are you?   How old is Mrs Harris?
What is your wife's name?   Yes, I am.
two boys and a girl   What are their names?
Twelve, ten and six.

3 Practise part of the conversation.

4 Ask and answer. Examples:

'Have you got any brothers or sisters?'
'Yes, I have. I've got two brothers.' / 'No, I haven't.'

5 Choose a new name, age, nationality, job, etc. Then work with another student, and interview him or her.

'What is your husband's name, Ms Carter?'   *'Eric.'*

> NAME: Mr Harris / Mr Gordon / Mrs Shaw /
>   Ms Carter / . . .
> AGE: 22 / 30 / 41 / 67 / . . .
> NATIONALITY: English/Scottish/Australian/ . . .
> JOB: teacher/doctor/engineer/secretary/ . . .
> WIFE'S/HUSBAND'S NAME: Mary/Alice/Sam/
>   Eric/ . . .
> CHILDREN: a boy and a girl
>   two boys and a girl
>   two girls and a boy
> ....
> CHILDREN'S NAMES: ....
> CHILDREN'S AGES: ....

I have (I've) got	have I got?	I have not (haven't) got
you have (you've) got	have you got?	you have not (haven't) got
he/she/it has (he's *etc.*) got	has he *etc.* got?	she *etc.* has not (hasn't) got
we have (we've) got	have we got?	we have not (haven't) got
you have (you've) got	have you got?	you have not (haven't) got
they have (they've) got	have they got?	they have not (haven't) got

> **Learn:** age; (a) moment; aren't you?; any; job; of course; Pardon?;
> please; question; sit down; teacher; too; What does . . . mean?;
> Have you got . . . ?; Yes, I have; No, I haven't.

17

Unit 4 Consolidation

4A Things to remember: Units 1, 2 and 3

I am

I am (I'm)	am I?	I am (I'm) not
you are (you're)	are you?	you are not (aren't)
he is (he's)	is he?	he is not (isn't)
she is (she's)	is she?	she is not (isn't)
it is (it's)	is it?	it is not (isn't)
her name is (her name's)	is her name?	her name is not (isn't)
we are (we're)	are we?	we are not (aren't)
you are (you're)	are you?	you are not (aren't)
they are (they're)	are they?	they are not (aren't)

Examples:
I'm sixteen. (~~I have sixteen.~~)
'Are you English?' 'Yes, I **am**.' (~~'Yes, I'm.'~~)
'Is Susan an engineer?' 'Yes, she **is**.' (~~'Yes, she's.'~~ ~~'Yes, Susan is.'~~)
Are John and his father doctors? (~~Are doctors John and his father?~~)
'You're Canadian, **aren't** you?' 'Yes, **that's** right.'

I've got

I have (I've) got	have I got?	I have not (haven't) got
you have (you've) got	have you got?	you have not (haven't) got
he/she/it has (he's *etc.*) got	has he *etc.* got?	she *etc.* has not (hasn't) got
we have (we've) got	have we got?	we have not (haven't) got
you have (you've) got	have you got?	you have not (haven't) got
they have (they've) got	have they got?	they have not (haven't) got

Examples:
'**Have** you **got** any sisters or brothers?' 'Yes, I **have**. I've **got** two sisters.' / 'No, I **haven't**.'
'**Has** your mother **got** any sisters?' 'Yes, she **has**. She's **got** two.' / 'No, she **hasn't**.'

A and an

an + a....., e....., i....., o....., u..... (/ʌ/): an engineer, an artist, an architect
a + u..... (/juː/), other letters: a university teacher, a secretary, a name

A, B, C, . . . : pronunciation

/eɪ/: A, H, J, K
/iː/: E, B, C, D, G, P, T, V
/aɪ/: I, Y
/əʊ/: O
/juː/: U, Q, W
/e/: F, L, M, N, S, X, Z
/ɑː(r)/: R

Remember:
A (/eɪ/) and R (/ɑː(r)/)
E (/iː/) and I (/aɪ/)
G (/dʒiː/) and J (/dʒeɪ/)
V (/viː/) and W (/ˈdʌbljuː/)

Nouns: singular and plural

Regular

boy ———→ boys
girl ———→ girls
name ———→ names
parent ———→ parents
family ———→ families
secretary ———→ secretaries
address ———→ addresses
six ———→ sixes

Irregular

child ———→ children
man ———→ men
woman ———→ women
wife ———→ wives
housewife ———→ housewives

Prepositions

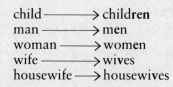

Adjectives

John is quite **tall**. Mary is very **tall**.
My daughters are quite **tall**.
  (~~My daughters are quite talls.~~)

Unit 4: Lesson A

Summary of language taught in Units 1, 2 and 3.

Consolidation units: structure

The structure of the consolidation units (Units 4, 8, 12, 16, 20 and 24) is as follows:

Lesson A The language that students should have learnt in the past three units is displayed. Teachers can spend a short amount of time going over these pages with the students, and students should look at them at home. Note that words in the functional sections (in this lesson, *Questions and answers*, *Excuse me*, *Hello/Goodbye*) are not always repeated in the vocabulary section.

Lessons B and C The language displayed in Lesson A is revised; speaking, listening, reading and writing skills are practised.

Lesson D The language displayed in Lesson A and practised in Lessons B and C is tested.

Student's Book Lesson 4A

No detailed teacher's instructions are provided for this section, nor for any of the A sections of the other consolidation units. Teachers can choose the most appropriate way of going over this section quickly with their students. The material displayed here is revised in Lessons B and C, and tested in Lesson D.

Practice Book Lesson 4A

It is suggested that the students do the Practice Book exercises in the following way:
1. Look over the Student's Book, either on their own or with the teacher.
2. Try to do the Practice Book exercises without looking back at the Student's Book.
3. Consult the Student's Book if there are difficulties, and/or to check answers.

Practice Book exercises: choose two or more
1. Students insert kinship terms on a family tree.
2. *Where*, *Who*, *What*, or *How*: students must choose the correct word.
3. Students look at pictures and choose *Excuse me*, *Pardon* or *I'm sorry*.
4. Making plurals.
5. Writing the names of numbers.
6. Crossword.

Practice Book work

Students' progress through the course will depend very much on the amount of work they do outside the lessons. However successful the lessons appear to be, most students will forget much of what they have learnt unless they do more practice, revision and reading in their own time. Try to make sure that your students do regular work from the Practice Book. Most of this can be self-corrected if your students have the *with Key* edition of the Practice Book, so Practice Book work need not involve a very heavy correction load for the teacher.

Video

The New Cambridge English Course 1 Video revises and expands on the language taught in Level 1 of the course. There are a variety of video sequences: some documentary, some dramatised. Each sequence or pair of sequences is designed to be used at the same point in the course as a consolidation unit (Units 4, 8, 12, 16, 20 and 24). Sequences are followed by *Language Review* sections which highlight key language and provide opportunities for language production.

The *Teacher's Guide* to the video gives detailed guidance on using the sequences in the classroom.

Sequence 1, **Arrivals**, can be used around this point in the book, as it relates to Units 1–3 in the coursebook. The topics are names; nationalities; jobs. Language focus is on *I'm*, *he's*, *she's*, *they're*, and on the questions *What do you do? Where are you from?*

My, your, his, her . . .

I ————————→ my
you ————————→ your
he ————————→ his
John ————————→ John's
she ————————→ her
Susan ————————→ Susan's
it ————————→ (its)
we ————————→ our
you ————————→ your
they ————————→ their
my sons ————————→ my sons'

Examples:
My bag is on the chair.
Susan's surname is Perkins.
    (The Susan's surname is Perkins.)

Where, who, what, how: questions and answers

'Where are you from?' 'Egypt.'
'Where's my pen?' 'It's under your book.'
'Who's your doctor?' 'Doctor Wagner.'
'What does *coat* mean?'
'What's your name?' 'Denise Quinton.'
'What do you do?' | 'I'm an artist/electrician/engineer.' ('I'm artist.')
                   | 'I'm a student/teacher/doctor.' ('I'm student.')
'How do you do?' 'How do you do?'
'How are you?' | 'Very well, thank you. And you?' 'Fine, thank you.'
               | 'Not bad, thanks. And you?' 'Fine, thanks.'
               | 'Not very well.' 'I'm sorry to hear that.'
'How old are you?' 'I'm thirty-five.' ('I've got thirty-five.')
'How do you spell it?' 'J, O, W, I, double T.'
'What's your address?' '17 Church Street.'

Excuse me, I'm sorry, Pardon

'Excuse me, is your name Fred
    Andrews?'
'No, I'm sorry, it's not. It's Jake
    Barker.'
'Pardon?'
'It's Jake Barker.'
'Oh, I'm sorry.'

Numbers

1	one	11	eleven	20	twenty	30	thirty
2	two	12	twelve	21	twenty-one	40	forty
3	three	13	thirteen	22	twenty-two	50	fifty
4	four	14	fourteen	23	twenty-three	60	sixty
5	five	15	fifteen	24	twenty-four	70	seventy
6	six	16	sixteen	25	twenty-five	80	eighty
7	seven	17	seventeen	26	twenty-six	90	ninety
8	eight	18	eighteen	27	twenty-seven	100	a hundred
9	nine	19	nineteen	28	twenty-eight		
10	ten			29	twenty-nine		

Hello and goodbye

Formal
Good morning/afternoon/evening.
Goodbye / Good night.

Informal
Hi / Hello.
Bye / Goodbye / See you / Good night.

Words and expressions

Nouns			Adjectives	Other words and expressions	
name	man (men)	number	double	not	this
first name	woman	letter	British	yes	a little
surname	(women)	pen	American	no	please
address	boy	hat	English	a	between jobs
age	girl	book	well	an	very
job	friend	coat	married	the	not very
widow	boyfriend	bag	single	any	quite
widower	girlfriend	table	divorced	and	not well
Britain	father	chair	separated	or	too
the United States	mother	question	dark	Oh	Here's . . .
student	wife (wives)		fair	from	I don't know
teacher	husband		fat	speak	That's right
morning	brother		slim	do	That's interesting
afternoon	sister		young	sit down	I think
evening	son		old	about	a moment
night	daughter		good-looking	OK	of course
moment	parent		intelligent	Dr	. . . aren't you?
	child		pretty	Miss	
	(children)		tall	Mr	
	family		strong	Mrs	
				Ms	

Optional words to learn

doctor; secretary; electrician; housewife (housewives); shop assistant;
artist; engineer; medical student; photographer; dentist.

4B Please write

1 Copy the form and put the right words in the coloured blanks. Then check your answers with a partner. If you have difficulty, you can look at the word list in Lesson 4A.

Mr / ▆▆▆ / Miss / ▆▆▆ /(Dr)

▆▆▆ JACKSON

First name MIRIAM

▆▆▆ 28

▆▆▆ /(▆▆▆▆▆) / separated / ▆▆▆▆ / widow / ▆▆▆

▆▆▆ DOCTOR

▆▆▆▆ 17 CHURCH STREET,

UPTON

▆▆▆▆ / husband's name and ▆▆ STEPHEN JACKSON, 28

▆▆▆▆ name(s) and ▆▆▆ MARK (2), SARAH (1)

2 Work with a partner. Change the questions on the form into spoken questions. Then listen and check your answers. Example:

Surname: *'What is your surname?'*

20

Unit 4: Lesson B

Students revise vocabulary and question forms and practise reading and writing.

1 Vocabulary: backwards form-filling

- Here students are given a form with the answers filled in and most of the items in the headings missing.
- Make sure that they understand what is missing from the form. Do the first three items with them (*Ms* or *Mrs*; *Mrs* or *Ms*; *Surname*).
- Then ask them to work individually to complete the other eleven items.
- When most of them have finished, ask them to compare answers in pairs before checking with you.
- Encourage them to look at the vocabulary list on page 19 if they have difficulty remembering any words.
- When the pairs have finished, check the answers with the class.

Answers to Exercise 1

Mr/Ms(Mrs)/Miss/Mrs(Ms)/(Dr)

Surname JACKSON

First name MIRIAM

Age 28

Single/married/separated/divorced/widow/widower

Job (occupation/profession) DOCTOR

Address 17 CHURCH STREET, UPTON

Wife's/husband's name and age
STEPHEN JACKSON, 28

Child's/children's names(s) and age(s) MARK (2), SARAH (1)

2 Forming questions and listening to check

- In this revision activity students should be encouraged to look back at pages 13 and 19 if they have trouble remembering.
- Ask them to work in pairs to write down the questions that correspond to the headings on the form.
- Do the first few questions with them to make sure that they understand the task, and then walk round while they are working to give any help that is needed.
- When they are ready, play the recording so they can check their questions. Note that the recording contains first the dialogue in its entirety, and then the questions in isolation.
- Play the recording more than once if students have not caught all the questions the first time.
- Note that in some cases more than one correct question form is possible.

Tapescript and answers to Exercise 2

Dialogue

BANK MANAGER: Good morning. Do sit down.
MIRIAM JACKSON: Thank you.
BM: Now, you want to buy a house.
MJ: That's right.
BM: Just one or two questions, then, please.
MJ: Of course.
BM: Is it Miss or Mrs?
MJ: It's Dr, actually.
BM: Oh, I see. And what is your surname?
MJ: Jackson.
BM: What is your first name, Dr Jackson?

MJ: Miriam.
BM: How old are you, please?
MJ: 28.
BM: Fine. Are you married?
MJ: Yes, I am.
BM: What is your address?
MJ: 17 Church Street, Upton.
BM: 17 Church Street, Upton. And what do you do?
MJ: I'm a doctor, a medical doctor.
BM: What is your husband's name?
MJ: Stephen Jackson.
BM: And how old is he?
MJ: He's 28, too.
BM: Have you got any children?
MJ: Yes, two.
BM: What are their names?
MJ: Mark and Sarah.
BM: And how old are they?
MJ: Mark's two and Sarah's one.
BM: Fine. Now, about this house . . . (*Fade*)

Questions
Is it Miss or Mrs?
And what is your surname?
What is your first name, Dr Jackson?
How old are you, please?
Are you married?
What is your address?
And what do you do?
What is your husband's name?
And how old is he?
Have you got any children?
What are their names?
And how old are they?

3 A scrambled letter

- Students' task is to put the sentences in order to make a letter, and then to decide which picture represents Teresa's family.
- If you speak the students' language(s), you can tell them that it is a first letter from a pen pal.
- Let them look over the exercise and ask you about any new vocabulary.
- Then ask them to tell you how they think the letter begins. If they are from a language group that is not too distant from English, they should have no trouble with the first sentence. Write it up on the board, first writing the date and *Dear Miriam*.
- If their language has very different rhetorical conventions from English, you may need to listen to their guesses and then tell them what the first sentence is.
- Continue with the other sentences in the same way; or if you think students will find it relatively easy, let them work individually or in groups to put the letter in order before checking with you.
- Make sure that they copy the letter out, not just number the sentences and put the numbers in order.
- If you speak the students' language(s), it is good to discuss why some orders are acceptable and some not.
- Point out the punctuation as you go along.
- Note that there is more than one acceptable order.

Possible answer to Exercise 3

(*Date*)
Dear Miriam,
My name is Teresa Riera. I'm Spanish, from Barcelona. I'm a photographer for a fashion magazine, and my husband Patricio is an artist. I am tall and dark, and Patricio is tall and fair. We've got two children: our daughter Rosa is four, and our son Antonio is two. They are dark and very good-looking, and very intelligent too. I speak Catalan, Spanish, and a little French. I am an English student at a language school. Here's a photograph. Please write.
Yours sincerely,
Teresa

The second picture shows Teresa's family.

4 Writing: Miriam's answer

- Ask the students to work individually to write an answer from Miriam to Teresa, using the information from Exercise 1.
- As they finish, get them to compare answers in groups of three or four; walk round while they are doing this to give advice where necessary.
- Do not bother at this point with problems of spelling, capitalisation, punctuation, or verb forms; these areas can be dealt with later. If you speak the students' language(s), tell them that for this exercise it is their thoughts, and their ideas about ordering those thoughts, that interest you.
- Just make sure that the letters are comprehensible and that the order is acceptable.
- (If you, or the students, wish, you can collect the letters and mark them later for mistakes of form.)

5 Writing game: imaginary pen pals

- Tell the students they are to choose another personality, and write a pen pal letter to one of the (real) people in the class. (In cases where you do not speak the students' language(s), use the illustration, and yourself as an example, to demonstrate.)
- Walk round while students are writing to give any help that is needed. You may want to make sure that the letters are more or less well distributed and do not all go to the same person.

- As students finish, you should act as a letter carrier, taking the completed letters to the students they are addressed to.
- Each student who receives a letter must try and guess who has written it.
- Some students (with the permission of the writers) can read out the letters they have received.
- Alternatively, if there is time, students can answer the letters they have received; you can collect the answers and then call out the names of the imaginary addressees so students can see who wrote which letters.

Practice Book exercises: choose two or more
Make sure that students understand that they are free to consult Student's Book Lesson 4A while they do these exercises: the purpose is revision, not testing.
1. Writing questions for answers.
2. Vocabulary: revision of some common words.
3. Stress: grouping words according to stress patterns.
4. Vocabulary: revision of some easily confused items.
5. Reading: ordering a scrambled text.
6. Writing a short descriptive text. (Exercises 5 and 6 should be done one after the other.)

3 Put the letter in the right order. Which picture is Teresa's family?

Dear Miriam,

and very intelligent, too.
They are dark and very good-looking,
We've got two children:
I'm Spanish, from Barcelona.
Here's a photograph.
I am tall and dark,
our daughter Rosa is four,
My name is Teresa Riera.
I speak Catalan, Spanish, and a little French.
and my husband Patricio is an artist.
I am an English student at a language school.
I'm a photographer for a fashion magazine,
Please write.
and Patricio is tall and fair.
and our son Antonio is two.

Yours sincerely,

Teresa

1

2

3

4

4 Write Miriam's answer to Teresa.
Begin: *Dear Teresa,*
    Thank you for . . .

5 Imagine you are someone else. Write a letter to someone in your class. When you receive a letter, try and guess who it is from.

4C I've got a new girlfriend

Social chat; /θ/ and /ð/; questions; role play.

1 What do you think they say next? Your teacher will help. Listen to check.

2 Listen to these two words from the dialogue:

thanks   mother

Can you say them correctly? And how about these words:

th like *thanks* (/θ/):
think   thirteen   thirty   three

th like *mother* (/ð/):
brother   father   that's   the   their   they

3 Make as many questions as you can.

What		Is		John		an engineer	
Who		is		Ann and her mother		photographers	
How			Are	they		English	
How old		are		your sister		do	
Where		Have		your name		spell it	?
		do		you		got any children	
		does			he	got any sisters	
				rapid		your brother	
				she		from	
						mean	

4 Who's who? Get your role from the teacher, and find . . .
Example:

Have you got any brothers?

Yes, I have.

What are their names?

I don't know. They're 34 and 38. One's an engineer.

Are you an engineer?

Yes, I am.

How old are you?

38.

What's your name?

Unit 4: Lesson C

Students revise social English and question forms; they participate in a role play for fluency practice.
Phonology: pronunciation of /θ/ and /ð/.

Possible problems
Note that the role play in Exercise 4 will only work:
1. if you have four or more students in the class
2. if you copy the role descriptions beforehand
3. in the case of a class with fewer than twenty students, if you give out the role descriptions in order; e.g., for ten students, give out descriptions 1 to 10.
This role play will take about twenty to thirty minutes.

NOTE THAT YOU MUST COPY THE ROLE DESCRIPTIONS FOR EXERCISE 4 BEFORE THE LESSON BEGINS.

1 Building a dialogue

• This dialogue revises structures, functions and vocabulary from the first three units.
• Ask students to look at the picture and tell you what they think the man on the right is saying.
• Get as many suggestions as you can, and accept anything that sounds plausible.
• Play the first line of the dialogue and get students to decipher it before writing it on the board.
• Then ask them to tell you what they think the second line is, and treat it in the same way.
• Go on, line by line, to the end of the dialogue.
• Teach the meaning of *new* when it occurs.
• Note the use of *Yeah*, a common way of saying *Yes*; and of *has got* (for recognition only).
• When all of the dialogue is on the board, play it through again as students read it from page 132 in the Student's Book.

Tapescript for Exercise 1: see page 140

Optional activity
• Before erasing the dialogue, ask for a volunteer to come to the board and quickly erase five words (you may need to demonstrate first yourself).
• The other students must try and remember what words are missing.
• Another student erases another five words, and so on.
• Let a total of five or six students erase words.
• Then play the recording again as students look at the gapped version of the dialogue.

2 Pronunciation /θ/ and /ð/

• Demonstrate to students how the *th* sounds in *thanks* and *mother* are pronounced, pointing out the position of the tongue and the difference between voiced and unvoiced sounds.
• Pronounce the words yourself or play the recording for the students to repeat.
• Then list the words on the board, and point to them randomly, for individual students to pronounce.

3 Question practice
• Give students three minutes working individually to write as many questions as they can using the balloon table in their books.
• Walk round to give any help that is needed.
• Let them compare their questions in small groups.
• Then get students to call out one question each.
• Make sure '*Is John your brother?*' is included in the

questions; the form is important for the next exercise.
• Ask students to think of any more questions they know how to make in English.

4 Who's who?
• This is a role play exercise in which each student must find someone else by asking questions.
• It will work if there are four or more students in the class.
• We have provided role descriptions for twenty students; if there are fewer students in your class, use the descriptions in order from the top of the list. *If you do not, the exercise will not work.*
• If there are more than twenty students, you can use some descriptions twice.
• If you have a large class that is not very confident, you may wish to divide them into groups, and use only the first ten or so descriptions for each group.
• Copy the descriptions pages (Teacher's Book pages 138 and 139) and cut them into individual descriptions. Count out just enough descriptions for the students in your class, *starting with number 1.*
• Shuffle the descriptions and hand them out.
• Make sure that students understand the task: each student will walk round asking questions like the ones in Exercise 3, in order to find the person or information in their description.
• Go over the examples in the book, pointing out that they may have to ask several people before they find the answers to their individual questions.
• Explain the meanings of *ex-wife*, *ex-husband*, and *at school*; then get them to stand up and begin working.
• Walk round while they are working, but do not interfere unless communication breaks down.
• You may need to remind them that they will have to ask around a bit to find their answers.
• Students should not stop working when they find the answers to their questions, but should find out more about their (role) families, by listening to other people and asking more questions.

Role descriptions, answers and family tree for Exercise 4: see pages 138 and 139

Optional activity: building a family tree
• When everyone has found the answer to their question, get the students to help you put their family tree on the board (only that part of the whole family tree that your own class has used).
• Begin by writing *James* on the board, and asking who his wife is; gradually build the family tree up by asking questions.

Practice Book exercises: choose two or more
Make sure students understand that they can consult Student's Book Lesson 4A while they do these exercises.
1. Completing a grammatical table (subject pronouns, possessives, and the present of the verb *be*).
2. Writing the full forms of contractions.
3. Distinguishing between *'s* possessive and *'s* as a contraction of *is*.
4. Singular and plural possessive (*'s* and *s'*).
5. Gap-filling (based on common mistakes; taken from the crossed-out sections of Student's Book Lesson 4A).
6. Reading: a logic puzzle based on careful reading.
7. Student's Cassette exercise (Student's Book Exercise 1). Students listen to each of Andrew's lines of the dialogue, then pause and try to remember Dan's part before playing it.
8. Reading: Part 3 of *It's a Long Story.*

The purpose of the test

This test, and the others in the book, are provided for teachers who feel that they will be useful. Each test covers several different areas: it is not of course necessary to do all of the sections, and teachers should select according to their students' needs. Teachers who do not feel a test will be useful should simply drop it altogether.

The tests have three main functions:
1. To show you and the students whether there are any points that have not been properly learnt for any reason.
2. To identify any students who are having serious difficulty with the course, if this is not already evident.
3. To motivate the students to look back over the work they have done and do some serious revision before they move on.

If possible, try to make the students feel that they are 'testing themselves', rather than 'being tested'. It is not intended that students should 'pass' or 'fail' the test, and it is not particularly useful to give marks (though some education systems may require that this be done). But students should of course be told whether you feel their performance is satisfactory. In principle, most students ought to get most answers right. If this does not happen, efficient learning is not taking place (because of poor motivation, too rapid a pace, absenteeism, failure to do Practice Book work or follow-up study outside class, or for some other reason).

Administration

The test can be administered in various ways, depending on how strictly you want to control students' performance; whether you want to collect the answers and mark them, or allow the students to correct them in class; and so on.

In the listening sections, you may wish to play the recordings twice; the recording for Section 1 will need to be played with pauses to give students time to write.

If you are not collecting students' scripts, correction can be done by class discussion when everybody has finished. Answers are given below to facilitate correction.

LISTENING

1 Tapescript

Her name's Ann Harris. She's 30, and she's a photographer. She lives at number 17 York Gardens, Perth, in Scotland. She's married; her husband's name is John Harris, and he's 26. He's a dentist. They've got two children, Mary and Sam. Mary's four and Sam's two.

Answers

FIRST NAME: *Ann.*
SURNAME: Harris
AGE: *30.*
JOB: *Photographer.*
ADDRESS: *17* York Gardens, Perth.
HUSBAND'S NAME: *John* Harris.
HUSBAND'S AGE: *26.*
HUSBAND'S JOB: *Dentist.*
NUMBER OF CHILDREN: *2.*
CHILDREN'S NAMES AND AGES: Mary (*4*), *Sam (2).*

2 Tapescript
1. Hi!
2. Where's she from?
3. How do you do?

4. Is your name Ann Carter?
5. What's his address?

Answers
1A, 2B, 3C, 4A, 5C

3 The letters on the recording are:
Q, R, E, Y, A, U, K, X, G, W, J, I, H, V.

VOCABULARY

1 seventeen, thirty, fifty-one, twelve, twenty-six, ninety-nine, eight, fifteen, eleven, a (one) hundred

2 Various answers possible: see vocabulary lists in Lesson 4A, page 19.

GRAMMAR

1 1. Have you got any brothers?
2. Excuse me, is your name Ann Smith?
3. Are Lucy and her brother students?
4. Where is Catherine's father from?
5. How do you spell your first name?

2 1. I've got three *brothers*.
2. My *brothers* are very *tall*.
3. My *sister's husband's* name's Steve.
4. My *parents'* surname is Webb, but my *name's* Watson.
5. How *old* are *your children*?

3 1. My wife and *her* brother are in America.
2. My *wife's* parents are artists.
3. Her brother's *a* teacher.
4. We've got two children; *they* are very tall.
5. My wife and I are dark, but *our* children are fair.

PRONUNCIATION

1 1. that (/ðæt/)
2. think (/θɪŋk/)
3. father (/fɑːðə(r)/)

2 1. married (the only word normally stressed on the first syllable)
2. afternoon (the only word normally stressed on the third syllable)
3. hello (the only word normally stressed on the second syllable)

Practice Book
Note that there are no Practice Book exercises for the test lessons (4D, 8D, 12D etc.).

Test Book recordings
A recording for Test 1 in the Test Book follows this lesson on the Class Cassette.

4D Test yourself

LISTENING

1 Copy the form. Then listen, and fill it in.

```
FIRST NAME: ................
SURNAME: Harris.
AGE: ................
JOB: ................
ADDRESS: ................ York Gardens, Perth.
HUSBAND'S NAME: ................ Harris.
HUSBAND'S AGE: ................
HUSBAND'S JOB: ................
NUMBER OF CHILDREN: ................
CHILDREN'S NAMES AND AGES: Mary (................),
................................................................
```

2 Listen and choose the best answer.

1. A. Hi!
   B. Good morning.
   C. Goodbye.

2. A. Thanks.
   B. China.
   C. I'm a teacher.

3. A. Very well, thank you.
   B. I'm thirty-two.
   C. How do you do?

4. A. No, I'm sorry, it's not.
   B. He's an engineer.
   C. It's under your book.

5. A. Not very well.
   B. In America.
   C. 17 Church Street.

3 Listen and write the letters.

VOCABULARY

1 Write the numbers in words. Example:

13 thirteen

17   30   51   12   26
99   8   15   11   100

2 Add five more words to each list.

1. student, teacher, secretary, . . .
2. British, Egyptian, Indian, . . .
3. Japan, Spain, the USSR, . . .

GRAMMAR

1 Put the words in the right order.

1. got you brothers any have ?
2. me is Ann name excuse your Smith ?
3. Lucy are her students and brother ?
4. from where Catherine's is father ?
5. spell name your how do first you ?

2 Add s, 's, s' or – .

1. I've got three brother........
2. My brother........ are very tall........
3. My sister........ husband........ name........ Steve.
4. My parent........ surname is Webb, but my name........ Watson.
5. How old........ are your........ children........?

3 Choose the correct word.

1. My wife and *his/her* brother are in America.
2. My *wife/wife's/wives'* parents are artists.
3. Her brother's *a/an* teacher.
4. We've got two children; *they/their* are very tall.
5. My wife and I are dark, but *our/your/their* children are fair.

PRONUNCIATION

1 Which *th* is different?

1. think, that, three, thanks
2. brother, they, the, think
3. father, thanks, think, thirteen

2 Which word has a different stress? Example:

husband, letter, teacher, address

1. married, excuse, goodbye, address
2. family, interesting, secretary, afternoon
3. doctor, hello, double, woman

Unit 5 Where?

5A Home

Houses and flats; *there is* and *there are*.

1 Look at the picture, and put the words with the right letters. Use your dictionary or work with other students. Example:

A. bathroom

bedroom	kitchen	toilet
bathroom	living room	hall

2 Now put these words with the right numbers.

chair	bed	toilet	door
window	stairs	cooker	
sofa	fridge	armchair	
television (TV)	cupboard		
wardrobe	sink	washbasin	
bath			

3 The teacher's home. Listen.

4 Complete the sentences, and make some more sentences about the house in the picture.

1. There are .... bedrooms in the house.
2. There is (There's) an armchair .... the living room.
3. .... is not (isn't) a garage.
4. There .... bathroom.
5. There .... two toilets.
6. .... fridge in the kitchen.

5 Work in pairs.
1. Both students copy the plan.
2. One student furnishes his or her rooms.
3. The other asks questions beginning *Is there a . . . ?* or *Are there any . . . ?*
4. He or she listens to the answers and tries to put the right furniture etc. into the rooms.

Examples:

'*Is there a table in the living room?*' '*Yes, there is.*'
'*Is it near the hall?*' '*Yes, it is.*'
'*Is it under the window?*' '*No, it isn't.*'

'*Are there any chairs in the bathroom?*' '*Yes, there are.*' (Or '*Yes, there are two.*')

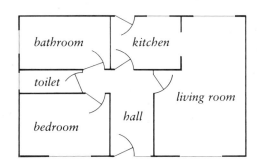

there is (there's)	is there?	there is not (isn't)
there are (–)	are there?	there are not (aren't)

Learn: there is/are; house; window; door; stairs; room.

Learn three or more: bedroom; kitchen; bathroom; toilet; living room; wall; garage.

Learn three or more: furniture; bed; cooker; sofa; fridge; armchair; television; TV; cupboard; bath; wardrobe.

Unit 5: Lesson A

Students learn to talk about houses and flats.
Structures: *there is/are*; *the* before a clearly identified noun.
Phonology: weak forms, linking and rhythm in sentences with *there is/are*.

Language notes and possible problems

1. Articles The definite article is introduced here. It is used to signal the fact that a noun has a precisely defined reference. For example, *the house* is the one the students can see in the picture; *the living room* is the one in that house. It contrasts with the indefinite article, which is used in descriptions and definitions (*She's a doctor; He's a tall man*), and when we are talking about any one of a class or making existential statements (*There's an armchair in the living room*).

Students who speak western European languages will have little difficulty with the difference between *the* and *a/an* in sentences like *There's a big table in the kitchen*. Others will probably need extra help: see *Appendix* page 135.

2. *Any* in questions *Any* was used in questions with plural nouns in Lesson 3D. Here, in Exercise 5, it is practised more fully. Point out that in questions *any* is used with plural nouns in the same way that *a* and *an* are used with singular nouns.

3. Vocabulary Real beginners will find the vocabulary load in this lesson rather heavy. They should only learn some of the words now – help them decide what is most important.

Optional extra materials

Pictures of rooms and/or furniture would be useful.

1 Presentation of vocabulary: rooms

- False beginners can do the exercise in groups, pooling their knowledge. Let real beginners use dictionaries.
- When students are ready, give them the answers and practise the pronunciation of the new words. Note *house* (/haʊs/) but *houses* (/'haʊzɪz/).

2 More vocabulary: furniture

- This can be done in the same way as Exercise 1.
- If students want to ask for new words, teach them to say '*What's this?*' and '*How do you say . . . in English?*'
- But don't let this go on too long, or students will write down a lot of words which they will not learn.

3 Describing your own home (*there is/are*)

- Start by sketching a plan of your house/flat on the board (or the house/flat of somebody you know).
- Tell the students whose home it is and where it is.
- Describe the house/flat in a few simple sentences. Include examples of *there is/are*. Use a chatty style. Students needn't understand every word. Example:
  '*This is my flat. It's in Via Marconi, and it's small but nice. There are two rooms: there's a living room and a bedroom. And oh, yes – there's a kitchen, and there's a bathroom. The living room is pleasant: there are two big windows; there's a comfortable sofa, and there are three armchairs.*'
- Don't ask questions – just let students enjoy understanding a piece of real communication in English.

4 *There is*: practice

- Do the first two sample sentences with the class.
- Practise the pronunciation. Work on:
  Weak forms and linking
  there's a = /ðəzə/   *there is* = /ðərɪz/
  there are = /ðərə(r)/

Rhythm
*There are **two bed**rooms in the **house**.*
*There's an **arm**chair in the **living room**.*

- Do the exercise orally. Make sure that each student makes at least one sentence.
- After a minute or two, ask students to close their books and continue from memory.

5 Information-gap work

- Before starting, practise the pronunciation of *Is there a . . . ?* (/'ɪzðərə/) and *Are there any . . . ?* (/'ɑːðəreni/).
- Demonstrate the exercise first with a student. Make sure students realise they should not see each other's sketches. Those who can't draw can write the words (*bed* etc.) in the various rooms.
- The exercise works best if each student has *two* plans – one to fill with furniture, and one to use when asking questions. You can save time by handing out copies of the plan, if this is feasible.
- When students have finished, they should compare plans to see if the questioner has got an accurate copy of his or her partner's plan.

Optional activities

1. Use magazine pictures of rooms for extra practice.
2. Hand out pairs of pictures showing rooms which are similar but not the same. (Advertisements are a good source.) Students look for differences.
3. Exercise 5 can be extended as follows:
   - Students draw plans of their homes or dream homes, without writing their names.
   - On a separate paper, they write their names and five sentences about the homes.
   - You collect plans and descriptions.
   - Shuffle and number the plans; put them on the class notice board or lay them out on tables.
   - Shuffle the descriptions and give them out again.
   - Students come and look at the plans and try to find the one that matches their description.
   - When they find one, they note the name and number and exchange descriptions with somebody else.
   - After five minutes or so, compare notes and see how accurate the guesses were.
4. Students sit round a big sheet of paper and draw a flat in which they each have a room. They talk to decide where doors, toilet, telephone, living room etc. are. Then they tell each other about their own rooms. Can be done in groups of four to six.

Practice Book exercises: choose two or more

1. Writing: answering questions (*there is/are*).
2. Students write five questions about a picture of a room (from a magazine). In class they exchange papers and answer each other's questions.
3. Pronunciation: stress in sentences with *there is/are*.
4. Articles: discrimination between *a/an* and *the*.
5. Guided writing: students get information about two flats in note and picture form. They complete the description of one flat and then write the description of the second flat. Ideally students should then do Exercise 6.
6. Freer writing: students write about a real or imaginary house or flat. Explain *dream house*.
7. Recreational reading: *Believe it or not*.

Unit 5: Lesson B

Students learn to say where people live and work, and to ask for and give telephone numbers.
Structures: introduction to Simple Present affirmative and interrogative of lexical verbs; prepositions of place in addresses.
Phonology: /θ/ in ordinals; linking; /ɪ/.

Language notes and possible problems
1. Simple Present affirmatives and second-person question forms are introduced here. (You will probably want to emphasize final -s in the third person singular; some students may drop it when they are not concentrating.) The Simple Present is studied in more detail in Unit 6.
2. Ground floor, etc. Note that the British *ground floor* is the American *first floor*, the British *first floor* is the American *second floor*, and so on.
3. Street and **road** can be treated as synonyms for the moment.

Optional extra materials
Cards with British or American-type addresses on (Exercise 2).

1 Presentation
• Explain the first sentence to the students. Ask where it should go in the picture.
• Give them a few minutes to decide where the other sentences should go.
• Ask what sentence goes with each number. Practise the pronunciation and explain any problems.
• Practise the pronunciation of the ordinal numbers, but don't be too perfectionist: *fifth* and *sixth* are difficult.
• You may also like to practise the vowel /ɪ/ in *live*.

2 Prepositions in addresses
• Do the exercise orally, then consolidate in writing.
• In this and the following exercises, pay attention to linking in *live at*, *live in* and *live on*.
• Help students to see the rules:
– *at* is used before exact addresses
– *in* is used before the names of streets and larger places
– *on* is used before *the first/second/ . . . floor*.
• The order of elements in addresses is 'smallest first' (house number, then street name, then town).

Optional activity
• Give out slips of paper with English-language addresses on. Tell students to memorise the addresses and put the papers away. Memorise an address yourself.
• Get a volunteer to help you build up a sample dialogue, e.g.:
    'Excuse me. What's your address?'
    '16 Grange Road. Where do you live?'
    'At 17 Queen's Drive.'
• Help students to practise '**What's your address?**' and '**Where do you live?**'; pay special attention to rhythm and stress, including contrastive stress on *you*.
• Without leaving their seats, students should find out and write down as many addresses as possible. Put *How do you spell that?* on the board, and encourage them to use this question if necessary.

3 Listening for information
• Students will not understand everything they hear. This does not matter; their job is just to listen for specific information and fill in the table.
• They will hear six pieces of conversation or

monologue (not in the same order as the names in the table). In each, there is an address; in three, there are telephone numbers.
• Their task is to pick out the addresses and phone numbers they hear from the lists in their books, and enter the letters in the table.
• Note that there are too many addresses and phone numbers: they don't all occur in the recording.
• Tell students to copy the table from their books.
• Play the recording once without stopping. (Students don't write this time.)
• Play the first conversation again, and ask students to fill in the answer. Check that it's right.
• Play the other extracts, pausing after each for students to write the answer.
• Let them compare notes.
• Play the recording once more.
• Give them the answers.

Tapescripts for Exercise 3: see page 140

Answers to Exercise 3

NAME	LIVES	PHONE NUMBER
John	D	X
Peter Matthews	F	–
Alice's mother	C	–
Mr Billows	E	–
Mrs Webber	G	Y
Mrs Simon	A	W

4 Questions and answers
• Copy this list as many times as you need to in order to give each student one job, floor and phone number; hand them out.
    shop assistant, ground floor, 472 1099
    electrician, first floor, 783 3574
    architect, second floor, 604 7575
    doctor, third floor, 226 8345
    engineer, fourth floor, 633 4945
    English teacher, fifth floor, 531 3588
    dentist, sixth floor, 701 7236
    photographer, seventh floor, 858 9137
• Try and make sure students do not show their information to one another.
• Students should try to memorise their information, but they might need to refer back to the telephone numbers.
• Tell them how to say telephone numbers: say the figures one by one; say *oh* for zero; and say *double* for double numbers. For example: *three oh six double two double seven.*
• Practise the questions and answers with a volunteer.
• Ask students to walk round (or ask as many people as possible from their seats) to try and find one person who works on each of the floors from the ground floor to the seventh floor; and to write down their job, the floor they work on, and their telephone number.
• When everyone has finished, ask the students to work in groups writing out the sentences; point out the use of the third person -s. Check the answers with the whole class when they have finished.

Practice Book exercises: choose two or more
1. Choosing the right preposition (*at*, *in*, or *on*).
2. Third person singular -s.
3. Revision of names of letters.
4. Reading: a logic problem.
5. Student's Cassette exercise (Student's Book Exercise 3, first conversation). Students listen and write the conversation.

25

5B Where do you work?

Where people live and work; Simple Present tense; *at*, *in* and *on*; phone numbers; *first, second,* . . .

1 Look at the pictures. Put the words in the right places.

> The Prime Minister lives at 10 Downing Street.
> My sister works in Edinburgh.
> 'Where do you live, Mary?' 'In Aston Street.'
> 'What's your address?' '39 Morrison Avenue.'
> We live in a small flat on the fourth floor.
>
> Mrs L. Williams
> 17 Harcourt Road
> Coventry
> West Midlands CY2 4BJ

ninth (9th) floor
eighth (8th) floor
seventh (7th) floor
sixth (6th) floor
fifth (5th) floor
fourth (4th) floor
third (3rd) floor
second (2nd) floor
first (1st) floor
ground floor

2 *At, in* or *on*?

1. I live .... 37 Valley Road.
2. 'Where do you work?' '............... New York.'
3. My office is .... the fourteenth floor.
4. Jake lives .... a big old house ....
   Washington.
5. 'Where do you live?' '............... 116 New Street.'

3 🔊 Listening for information. Copy the table. Then listen to the conversations, and write the correct letters after the names. (There are only three phone numbers.)

NAME	LIVES	PHONE NUMBER
John		✗
Peter Matthews		
Alice's mother		
Mr Billows		
Mrs Webber	G	
Mrs Simon		

A at 16 Norris Road, Bedford.   V 314 6928
B in a small flat in North London. W 41632
C in Birmingham.   X 314 6829
D at 116 Market Street.   Y 41785
E in New York.   Z 41758
F on the fourth floor.
G at 60 Hamilton Road, Gloucester.

4 You all work in the same building; it has got eight floors. Your teacher will tell you your jobs and phone numbers and what floor you work on. Find out who works where; ask for phone numbers.
Example:

'What do you do?'   'What's your phone
'I'm an engineer.'   number?'
'And where do you work?'   '633 4945.'
'I work on the fourth floor.' 'Thanks.'

Now look at the example and complete the sentences.

An engineer works (or *Two engineers work*) *on the fourth floor, and his/her/their phone number is 633 4945.*

1. .... work(s) on the ground floor, and ....
   phone number is ....
2. .... work(s) on the first floor, and ....
3. .... work(s) on the .... , and ....
4. .... on the .... , and ....
5. .... , and ....
6. ....
7. ....

I live	we live
you live	you live
he/she/it lives	they live

> **Learn:** work; live; at; big; small; flat; street; road; floor; ground floor; first; second; third; fourth; fifth; sixth; seventh; eighth; ninth; phone number.

5C   Where's the nearest post office?

Asking for and giving directions.

1 Put the words with the correct pictures.

phone box   supermarket   bank   post office
police station   car park   bus stop   station

1 post office

2

3

4

5

6

7

8

2 Listen and practise these dialogues.

A: Excuse me. Where's the nearest post office, please?

B: It's over there on the [right] / [left.]

A: Oh, thank you very much.
B: Not at all.

*   *   *

A: Excuse me. Where's the nearest bank, please?
B: I'm sorry, I don't know.
A: Thank you anyway.

3 Complete these dialogues and practise them.

A: .... the manager's office, ...?

B: .... by the reception desk.
A: ....

*   *   *

A: .... the toilets, ...?

B: Upstairs .... the first floor, first door .... left.

A: .... much.

4 Make up similar conversations in pairs and practise them. You are: a person who lives in your town and a foreign tourist; or a visitor to your school and a student; or a visitor to the planet Mars and a Martian.

Learn: there; over there; right; left; on the right/left; Thank you anyway; Not at all; by; upstairs; downstairs.

Learn four or more: phone box; supermarket; bank; post office; police; police station; car park; bus stop; station.

Unit 5: Lesson C

Students learn to ask for and give directions.
Structures: no new structures.
Phonology: intonation of polite questions.

Language notes and possible problems
1. Intonation Intonation is difficult to describe by precise rules. It is best to teach it by imitation exercises in well-defined situations. In Exercise 2 help students to hear how the question-word *where* is pronounced on a high pitch and how the voice falls and rises at the end of the sentence. It is this (even more than the use of *Excuse me* and *please*) that makes a question or request sound polite.
2. Answer to *Thank you* Students should realise that *Not at all* is not an automatic answer to *Thank you* – it doesn't come in all of these dialogues. British people often make no reply when they are thanked for small things.
3. Additional vocabulary Students may want to learn the words for some more of the places that one might ask one's way to (e.g. *swimming pool, pub, restaurant*). Teach more words at your discretion, but don't allow the students to become overloaded with vocabulary.

Optional extra materials
Cards with names of places for Optional activities after Exercise 4.

1 Presentation of vocabulary
• This can be done in small groups, with students pooling their knowledge. (With real beginners who don't know any of the words, and who don't have cognate words in their languages which would help them to guess, tell them the answers or get them to use their dictionaries.)
• Practise the pronunciation of the new vocabulary.

2 Dialogues
• Play the dialogues once or twice while students listen with their books closed.
• Ask them to recall words and expressions.
• Get the class to help you build up the dialogues on the board.
• Open books and play again while students follow the text.
• Explain new words and expressions.
• Practise the sentences, paying special attention to intonation, linking and rhythm.
• Ask students to practise in pairs until they can do it without the books (changing over so that each student plays both parts).

3 Dialogue completion
• Students can do this in groups – the missing expressions can be found in the dialogues in Exercise 2.
• Explain any difficulties. Teach *downstairs*.
• Get students to practise the new dialogues once or twice.

Answers to Exercise 3
A: *Excuse me. Where's* the manager's office, *please?*
B: *It's over there* by the reception desk.
A: *Thank you.*

               ✳   ✳   ✳

A: *Excuse me. Where are* the toilets, *please?*
B: Upstairs *on the* first floor, first door *on the* left.
A: *Thank you very* much.

4 Students' dialogues
• Ask students to work in pairs and to choose one of the options in the exercise: native and tourist, visitor and student, visitor and Martian.
• Get them to make up conversations, using words and expressions from the dialogues they have just studied, but varying and combining elements so as to make something a little different.
• You might like to do one on the board with the students first of all to give them the idea.
• Tell them to practise their conversations.
• If there is time, and you think they would enjoy it, you can ask for volunteers to perform their conversations for the class.

Optional activities
1. Divide the class into two groups: 'strangers' and 'natives'. Tell them to imagine that they are in a particular well-known place (e.g. the town centre; the entrance to the school). 'Strangers' stop 'natives' and ask them the way to various places; 'natives' improvise their answers.
2. Develop the previous activity by taking students out into the street or into other parts of the building – this gives much more realistic practice.
3. If necessary, give 'strangers' cards with the names of places that they have to ask the way to.
4. Another approach is to draw a simple town plan on the board and ask students to copy it, filling in the station, car park etc. where they want to. Then do a 'walk-round' exercise as above; 'natives' use their maps to work out their answers.

Practice Book exercises: choose two or more
1. Dialogue completion (revision of lesson material).
2. Giving true answers to questions, using *Yes, there is/are, No, there isn't/aren't,* and *I don't know.*
3. Reading: true or false questions. Tell students that they can use their dictionaries if they need to.
4. Making questions with *Is there* and *Are there.*
5. Student's Cassette exercise (Student's Book Exercise 3). Explain to students that they are to listen to the conversation one line at a time, trying to remember what the next line is before they play it.
6. Authentic text for reading practice.

Students' dialogues: fluency and accuracy
In activities like Exercise 4, the emphasis is on fluency. It is very important for students to practise talking at reasonable speed without stopping to think everything out. In exercises of this kind, it is best not to interrupt students with corrections unless there is a real breakdown in communication. Any serious mistakes can be noted and dealt with in another lesson.

Unit 5: Lesson D

Students learn more ways of giving and asking for directions.
Structures: imperatives; *for* with expressions of distance.

Language notes and possible problems

1. Imperatives are introduced here. They present no problem, but you may wish to comment explicitly on the use of the 'base form' of a verb for making suggestions, giving orders, giving instructions, etc.
2. Vocabulary Exercise 5 introduces some new vocabulary which might overload weaker students. Drop the exercise if you think they will find it too daunting.
3. *Yards* occurs in Exercise 1 – this is the word students will hear if they ask for directions in Britain, and they must know it. (For practical purposes, a yard is close to a metre.) Students may prefer to use *metre* in their own practice (for instance in Exercise 4). In the USA, *feet* is often used in directions; a foot is a third of a yard, or about 30cm.

Optional extra materials

Photocopies of the local town plan, or of a plan of some other place students know, would be useful. (See Alternative to Exercise 4.)

1 Completing and ordering dialogues

• This is quite a demanding exercise. It can be done in groups, or (with weaker classes) as a whole-class activity.
• Students will need to ask you about the meaning of some of the new words and expressions as they do the exercise. Remind them to say *'What does . . . mean?'*
• When they are ready, let them compare notes and check their answers.
• You may like to get students to practise the conversations in pairs – standing up and acting out the conversations if possible.

Answers to Exercise 1

'Excuse me. *Where's* the nearest car park, *please?*'
'*First* on the right, then second *on the left.* It's next to the post office.'
'*How far* is it?'
'About five hundred yards.'
'Thank you very much.'
'*Not at all.*'

*   *   *

'Excuse me. Is there a *swimming pool* near here?'
'Yes. It's *opposite* the car park. Go *straight* on for about three hundred *yards.*'
'Thanks very much.'

2 Memory test

• Give students a couple of minutes to memorise the map. Then put them in groups of four or so. One questions the others, looking at the map if necessary.

Alternative to Exercise 2

• As a variant, you can get students to test each other on their knowledge of the town where they are studying.

3 Listening practice

• Before playing the first section (which starts 'You are at A'), point out A, B, C and D on the map.

Tapescript and answers to Exercise 3

1. You are at A. Go straight on, take the second street on the left and the first on the right. Where are you? (**Answer:** in Wood Street.)
2. You are at C. Go down Park Road, turn right, turn left into Station Road, go straight on for about 200 yards. Where are you? (**Answer:** by the railway station and the police station.)
3. You are at D. Take the first left, second right and first left. Where are you? (**Answer:** near the bus stop in Wood Street.)

4 Giving directions

• This can be done in small groups, with students taking turns to give directions. The others follow on the map, as in Exercise 3.

Alternative to Exercise 4

• A variant of this exercise can be done with copies of the local town/city map.
• Give students fixed starting points (e.g. *'You are at the end of rue Leblanc facing north'*); this avoids confusion.

5 Extension

• This exercise introduces some new vocabulary (which will need explaining).
• In each pair, one student should take list A and the other list B.
• Each student should fill in the new places where he or she wants to (on a copy of the map if you don't want students to write in their books).
• Then students work in pairs as in the example.

Optional activity

• If there is room, pretend the classroom is a central place in a town or city the students know.
• Divide them into 'tourists' and 'natives'.
• Students walk round.
• 'Tourists' stop 'natives' and ask them the way to various places.
• (It is advisable to make sure that everybody knows which way the classroom is supposed to be facing – for instance, the blackboard could be the north side of the square.)

Practice Book exercises: choose two or more

1. Giving directions.
2. Choosing the correct preposition.
3. Pronunciation: stress.
4. Vocabulary recall.
5. Translation of material from the unit.
6. Student's Cassette exercise (Student's Book Exercise 3, first set of directions). Students should listen to the directions and try to write them down, pausing where necessary, and playing the recording as many times as they need to.
7. Reading: Part 4 of *It's a Long Story.*

5D   First on the right, second on the left

More asking for and giving directions.

1 Put in the missing words, and put the sentences in the right order in each conversation.

'Thank you very much.'
'............... on the right, then second .... It's next to the post office.'
'............... is it?'
'Excuse me. .... the nearest car park, ...?'
'About five hundred yards.'
'.................?'

*   *   *

'Yes. It's .... the car park. Go .... for about three hundred ....'
'Thanks very much.'
'................. Is there a .... near here?'

excuse me	first	how far		not at all
on the left	opposite	please		straight on
swimming pool	where's	yards		

2 Look at the map. Then work with another student and test his or her memory.

'Where's the police station?'   'Opposite the railway station.'
'Where's the car park?'   'I don't remember.'

3 📼 Listen and follow the directions on the map. Then say where you are.

4 Give directions to other students. Example:

'You are at A. Take the first left, second right, first right, second right, and go straight on for about three hundred metres. Where are you?'

5 Copy the map. Then put in *either* the places in list A *or* the places in list B.

A.		B.	
a supermarket		a church	
a swimming pool		a good restaurant	
a bookshop		a good hotel	
a phone box		a chemist's	
a cheap restaurant		a public toilet	
a cheap hotel			

Work in pairs. Ask and give directions (you are at A on the map). Example:

'Excuse me. Is there a bookshop near here, please?'
'Yes. First left, second right, in Station Road.'
'Thank you.'

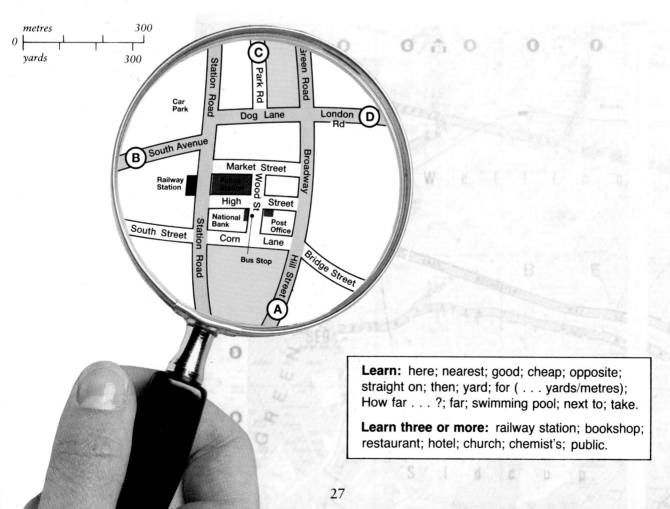

Learn: here; nearest; good; cheap; opposite; straight on; then; yard; for (. . . yards/metres); How far . . . ?; far; swimming pool; next to; take.

Learn three or more: railway station; bookshop; restaurant; hotel; church; chemist's; public.

Unit 6 Habits

6A What do you like?

Likes and dislikes; Simple Present tense; *him, her, it* and *them.*

Jackson Pollock: Yellow Island

1 Look at the pictures and statue. Which one do you like? Examples:

'I like the Greek statue very much.'
'I quite like the mask.'
'The mask is OK.'
'I don't like the Vermeer picture much.'
'I hate the Pollock picture. I don't like it at all.'
'I like the Greek statue the best.'

Vermeer: Young Girl

Mexican mask

Greek statue

2 Listen to the music and sounds and say whether you like them or not.

I like it very much.

I don't like it at all.

3 Put in *like, likes, it, them, him* or *her.*

1. I don't .... cats, but my brother .... them very much.
2. 'Do you .... dogs?' 'Yes, I love ....'
3. George .... Mary, but Mary doesn't like ....
4. Mary .... dancing and travelling.
5. 'Do you .... orange juice?' 'No, I don't like .... at all.'
6. I don't dislike opera, but I don't really ....
7. 'Your husband .... cooking, doesn't he?' 'Yes, he does.'
8. My wife hates big dogs, but I love ....
9. My wife and I .... the sea, but our children don't – they .... climbing mountains.
10. 'Do you .... Anne?' 'Yes, I .... very much.'

4 Do you like these? Ask other students about one of them.

big dogs	maths	whisky	mountains	the sea	cats
shopping	watching TV	cooking	dancing	writing letters
travelling

'Do you like cooking?'   'Yes, I do.'
'Do you like big dogs?'   'No, I don't.'
                          'I hate it/them.'
                          'I love it/them.'
                          'It depends.'

5 Report to the class. Examples:

'Seven students like cats.'   'Jean-Claude likes whisky very much.'
'Five people like big dogs.'   'Nobody likes cooking.'
'Only two people like shopping.'   'Everybody likes the sea.'
'Only one person likes maths.'

Pronouns

Subject	Object	Subject	Object
I ⟶	me	we ⟶	us
you ⟶	you	you ⟶	you
he ⟶	him	they ⟶	them
she ⟶	her		
it ⟶	it		

Learn: like; hate; love; dislike; him; her; them; it depends; only; nobody; everybody; very much; not much; not at all.

28

Unit 6: Lesson A

Students learn to talk about likes and dislikes.
Structures: Simple Present tense; object pronouns *him*,
her, *it* and *them*; no article before nouns used in a
general sense; -*ing* form for activities.

Language notes and possible problems

1. Simple Present   Here students mainly use forms that
they have met: affirmatives, second person singular
interrogative and first person singular negative.
2. Word order   Note the position of *very much* in, for
example, *I like the statue very much*.
3. Articles   In Exercises 3 and 4, note the use of
uncountable and plural nouns without articles to express a
general meaning (e.g. *I like **cats***). Some students will find
this difficult; look out for mistakes like **I like the cats*, and
explain the point briefly if necessary.
4. -*ing* forms   Note also the use of -*ing* forms to refer to
activities, after *like, love, dislike, hate*. There is no need to
comment specifically on this at this stage unless students
have difficulty with it.
5. *Him* and *her* are most often pronounced in their 'weak
forms', /ɪm/ and /ə(r)/. You will want to point this out to
students.
6. *Maths* (Exercise 4)   Note that this word is a singular.
7. Vocabulary   False beginners should be encouraged to
choose five or six extra vocabulary items to learn from the
lesson.

Optional extra materials
Postcards (reproductions of works of art, or pictures of
singers or film stars) for Exercise 1.
Short pieces of recorded music for Exercise 2.

1 Reacting to pictures
• Ask students to look at the pictures for a minute or
two.
• Try to get spontaneous reactions: refer to a picture
and help students to say '*I like it*' or '*I don't like it*'.
• Then look over the different ways of expressing likes
and dislikes in the examples. Explain any difficulties.
• Ask for more sentences about the pictures. Give help
with pronunciation of the artists' names as needed.
• Ask students to tell you about other artists they like
or dislike.
• Get students to ask you (and each other) questions
about your artistic preferences (e.g. '*Do you like
Picasso?*'). Practise *Do you . . . ?* (/djʊ/), *Yes, I do* (not
*Yes, I like), *No, I don't*.
• Finally, ask them to write one or two sentences about
their reactions to the pictures.

Alternative to Exercise 1
• Instead of using the pictures in the book, bring in art
postcards, pictures of singers, or anything else about
which students can express likes and dislikes.

2 Music and sounds
• This is a similar activity, but this time students react
to things they hear.
• Play the recording, stopping after each item to ask for
reactions. Students will need to use the pronoun *it* (e.g.
I like it).
• If reactions are strong, teach *love*.

Students will hear:
1. Several short extracts from pieces of music in very different
styles.
2. a pneumatic drill; traffic; birdsong; church bells; children
playing; a jet.

3 Grammar
• Before starting the exercise, put on the board:
I like   we like
you like   you like
he/she likes   they like
• Remind students about the -*s* on the third person
singular.
• Put on the board:
I like music.   I like it.
I like dogs.   I like them.
• Practise the pronunciation, being careful not to stress
it and *them* (/ðəm/).
• Do the exercise, explaining vocabulary as you go
along.
• You may like to get students to do some sentences
orally and others in writing.
• Practise the pronunciation of *do, don't, does* and
doesn't as they come up.
• Point out the two object forms *him* and *her*, and tell
students to learn them. Get them to say the tenth
sentence, and make sure they pronounce *her* as /ə/. Tell
them that *him* and *her* are usually pronounced /ɪm/ and
/ə(r)/, unless there is some reason to emphasize them.
• Students may want to ask you about the structure of
the third person negative (*doesn't like*), which is
previewed in Question 3.

4 Class survey
• Run over the vocabulary, and practise the
pronunciation of the questions and answers in the
examples.
• Ask some students whether or not they like some of
the things in the list. Get them to ask you. (Note that
maths is singular – they will need to say *I like / don't
like it*).
• Then ask each student to choose one thing from the
list, and to walk round asking the others whether they
like it or not. They must keep a record of the answers,
perhaps by writing down a list of the expressions from
Exercise 1 (*like, quite like*, etc.) and putting ticks beside
them as people answer.

5 Reporting the survey
• When students have finished their survey they should
report to the class (or to members of a group) saying
how many people love/like/dislike/*etc.* their item.
• Before starting, look at the examples: remind students
that third person singular subjects (including *everybody*
and *nobody*) take a verb form with -*s*.
• You may need to teach *doesn't* for singular negative
examples like *Maria doesn't like cats*.

Practice Book exercises: choose two or more
1. Blank-filling with Simple Present forms from the
lesson.
2. Choosing the correct third person subject or object
pronoun.
3. Pronunciation: stress in sentences from the lesson.
4. Reading: a logic puzzle.
5. Writing: students write poems. This exercise is
simple to do, and very satisfying for students.

Unit 6: Lesson B

Students learn to tell the time in English.
Structures: no article in expressions like *at home, in bed,* etc.
Phonology: /ɪ/; 'weak' pronunciation of *at; the* before a vowel.

Language notes and possible problems

1. Three fifteen, etc. Some students may be familiar with the other way of telling the time (*three fifteen,* etc.). If necessary, explain that this is slightly less common in conversation, and easy to understand if students do run across it.
2. 24-hour clock You may also need to explain that the 24-hour clock is not normally used except when talking about travel arrangements.
3. Half six, etc. In English *half six* is a colloquial way of saying *half past six.* You may need to point this out to speakers of certain languages (such as German), for whom *half six* means *half past five.*
4. Pronunciation You may need to practise /ɪ/ in *it's* (Exercise 1). *Half* and *quarter* will also need practice. Note the 'weak' pronunciation of *at* (/ət/) in Exercise 5. In Exercise 6, *the* (/ðiː/) occurs before a vowel in *the afternoon* and *the evening.* This may need attention.

Optional extra materials

A toy clock is useful for practice in telling the time.

1 Telling the time ('past')

● Practise the pronunciation of the five examples. Then ask students to tell you what time it is on each of the eight small dials.
● Consolidate by asking them to write the times.

2 Telling the time ('to')

● Do this in the same way as Exercise 1.

3 Listening practice

● Play the recording (or read the text at normal speed) more than once if necessary.
● Tell students to write down *only* the times they hear in each extract. (They won't understand much else, but this is *not* important.)
● Let them compare notes before giving the answers.
● If necessary, explain that *four twenty* means 'twenty past four' and *seven twenty-five* means 'twenty-five past seven'.
● Don't explain everything in the conversation (see *Introduction* page VIII).

Tapescript and answers to Exercise 3

1. 'Excuse me. I wonder if you could tell me the time.'
   'Er, yes. It's *half past ten.*'
   'Thank you very much.'

2. 'Got the time?'
   'Yeah. *Twenty to eleven.*'

3. 'What time is your train?'
   'Pardon?'
   'I said, what time did you say your train was?'
   'Oh, just a second. It's . . . er . . . *twenty-five past seven.*'
   'Oh, that's all right, then. Adrian can take you.'

4. 'What time do you think you'll be getting home?'
   'Well, it depends on how long the play lasts, but I should think about *eleven o'clock.* Is that all right?'
   'Oh yes, that's fine. I just wanted to have an idea.'

5. 'When are the meetings?'
   'Well, we meet on Thursdays at *a quarter to eight* officially, but things don't really get started until *eight o'clock.*'

6. 'The next train from platform one will be the *four twenty* for Hereford, calling at . . . '

7. 'At the third stroke, it will be *seven twenty-five* precisely.'

4 Asking the time

● Practise the question, '*What time is it?*', and the two ways of answering.
● Ask the students to set their watches to new times.
● Do a 'walk-round' exercise: half the class ask and the others answer, and then they change over.

5 At home etc.

● Go over the expressions in the box with the students, explaining where necessary.
● Then ask the students to look at the chart and work individually to try and complete the sentences.
● When most of them have finished, ask them to compare their answers in pairs or small groups before checking with you.
● Make sure students pronounce *at* correctly (/ət/), without stressing it.

Answers to Exercise 5

1. At half past six in the morning, Ingrid is *in bed.*
2. At a quarter to eight, George is still *in bed.*
3. At nine o'clock, Ingrid is *on her way to school,* but George is still *at home.*
4. At five past ten, George is *on his way to work,* and Ingrid is *at school.*
5. At five past one, Ingrid *is at lunch,* but George is still *at work.*
6. At a quarter to two, George is *at lunch,* and Ingrid is *at school.*
7. At five o'clock, Ingrid is *on her way back from school, but* George is *still at work.*
8. At eight o'clock in the evening, George *is on his way home from work.*
9. At half past nine in the evening, George is *at home* or *out.*
10. At ten to eleven in the evening, Ingrid is *at home or out.*

6 Where are you?

● Look at the job names in the box with students, and explain any new words.
● Ask each student to choose a job, without telling anyone else, and imagine what his/her working day is like.
● Show students the examples: students work in pairs, each asking the other four questions beginning '*Where are you . . .*' and then trying to guess what job the other has chosen.
● Practise the pronunciation of *the afternoon* and *the evening* – this is the first time students have met *the* before a vowel.

Practice Book exercises: choose two or more

1. Questions requiring answers with *in bed, at home,* etc.
2. Writing down times from clocks.
3. Revision: pronunciation of letters of the alphabet.
4. Student's Cassette exercise (Student's Book Exercise 3, numbers 1–4). Students have a list of sentences. They must listen to numbers 1–4 of the recording and decide which sentences from the list occur.
   Answers: sentences A, B, and D occur in the recording.
5. Crossword.

6B Where are you at seven o'clock?

1

It's three o'clock.   It's ten past three.

It's a quarter past three.   It's half past three.

What time is it?

2

It's twenty-five to four.   It's a quarter to four.

It's ten to four.   It's five to four.

What time is it?

3 📼 Listening for information. Listen and write down the times you hear.

4 Set your watch to a new time. Ask and answer:

'What time is it?'   'A quarter past twelve.'
'What time is it?'   'Erm, about a quarter to four.'

5 Look at the chart. Complete the sentences. You can use words from the box.

Ingrid (student)

George (architect)

> on his/her way to school/work   at home   at lunch   at school
> at work   but   out   on his/her way back from school/work
> in bed

1. At half past six in the morning, Ingrid is ....
2. At a quarter to eight, George is still ....
3. At nine o'clock, Ingrid is ...., but George is still ....
4. At five past ten, George is ...., and Ingrid is ....
5. At five past one, Ingrid ...., ... George is still ....
6. At a quarter to two, George is ...., and Ingrid is ....
7. At five o'clock, Ingrid is ...., ... George is ....
8. At eight o'clock in the evening, George ....
9. At half past nine in the evening, George is at home or ....
10. At ten to eleven in the evening, Ingrid is ....

6 Work in pairs. Each person chooses a job. Ask the other person four questions about time and try to guess their job. Example:

'Where are you at a quarter to seven in the morning?'
'At work.'
'Where are you at a quarter past eleven in the morning?'
'In bed.'
'Where are you at four o'clock in the afternoon?'

'At home.'
'Where are you at twenty past nine in the evening?'
'At work.'
'Are you a nurse?'
'Yes.'

> JOBS
> nurse   jazz singer   waiter/waitress   baker   bank manager
> school teacher   postman/postwoman

6C Work

Routines; more Simple Present tense; *Does he/she . . . ?*; *he/she doesn't*; *at, from* and *until* with times.

1 Put the words into the text.

Stan Dixon is a shop assistant. He sells men's clothes in a small shop. It is a tiring job.

Stan .... at seven o'clock. After ...., he .... to work by .... He .... work at a quarter past nine; the shop .... at half past. Stan .... lunch at twelve, and then .... from 12.45 until 5.45.

On Saturdays, Stan .... work at one o'clock. On Sundays he .... cycling or .... tennis.

Stan does not .... his job much.

has	like	breakfast	goes	works	bus
gets up	opens	stops	plays	starts	
goes					

2 Do it yourself. Ask the teacher questions, and write the text about Karen Miller.

Karen Miller is a mechanic. She repairs cars in a garage . . .

What time does she get up?
How .... she go to work?
Does she *have/has* breakfast?
What time .... she start work?
.... time does she *stop/stops* work?
What .... does .... have lunch?
.... supper?
.... work on Saturdays?
What .... do at the weekend?
.... like her job?

3 Learn the days of the week.

MARCH

Monday	5	12	19	26
Tuesday	6	13	20	27
Wednesday	7	14	21	28
Thursday	1	8	15	22	29
Friday	2	9	16	23	30
Saturday	3	10	17	24	31
Sunday	4	11	18	25

4 Write four sentences about yourself using words or expressions from the box.

get up	have breakfast	have lunch	go to school	go to work
on Saturdays	on Sundays	at the weekend	

Now talk to other students. Ask questions as in the examples. Have you written the same sentences?

'*What time do you get up?*' '*Seven o'clock.*'
'*What do you do on Saturdays?*' '*I play tennis.*'

I work	do I work?
you work	do you work?
he/she works	does he/she work?
we work	do we work?
you work	do you work?
they work	do they work?

Learn: have; get up; go; start; stop; breakfast; lunch; supper; from; until; at; (by) bus; (by) car; Monday; Tuesday; Wednesday; Thursday; Friday; Saturday; Sunday; (at the) weekend.

Unit 6: Lesson C

Students learn to talk and ask about daily work routines.

Stuctures: Simple Present third person singular interrogatives and negatives; *at* with times; *by bus, car* etc.; *from . . . until . . .* ; *has.*

Language notes and possible problems

1. Simple Present tense: forms Here, students have to learn that the third person singular has *-s* on the main verb in affirmatives, but on the auxiliary in questions and negatives. This is likely to cause problems for some time. The pronunciation and spelling rules for the third person ending are the same as those for plurals.

2. Simple Present tense: use Students will now have learnt two characteristic uses of the Simple Present: to talk about states (e.g. likes and dislikes) and routines. Until they have learnt the Present Progressive, however, they are likely to over-generalise the Simple Present: look out for mistakes like **Do you work now?*

3. *Have* The 'dynamic' use of *have* (as in *have breakfast, have a rest*) is peculiar to English, and students may find it difficult to learn at the beginning. It shouldn't be confused with *have got.*

4. (At) What time . . . ? Note that the preposition is normally dropped.

---

1 Text completion

● This is a suitable exercise for 'false beginners', or for others who know a little more English than they have learnt from the lessons.
● Put the students in groups of five or six, and let them pool their knowledge to complete the text.
● Get groups to compare notes before giving them the answers.
● With complete beginners who don't know any of the new words, you will of course have to get them to use their dictionaries, or pre-teach the vocabulary.
● Give whatever explanations are necessary.

2 Guided composition

● In order to write the text about Karen Miller, students have to ask you for information.
● And in order to do this they must be able to ask third-person questions.
● Start by practising the pronunciation of the first question in the list.
● Tell students the answer and get them to start writing the text. They should work individually.
● As they need more information, they will ask you the rest of the questions. The facts about Karen are as follows:
– Karen gets up at half past six.
– She doesn't have breakfast. (Write *does not* on the board.)
– She goes to work by car.
– She starts work at eight o'clock.
– She stops work at a quarter to six.
– She has lunch at twelve o'clock.
– She has supper at half past six.
– She doesn't work on Saturdays. (Write *does not* on the board.)
– At the weekend she goes to see friends or plays tennis.
– She likes her job.

● When students are ready, put an agreed version of the text on the board.
● Finish by asking students to look at the table in their books. Point out how the third-person *-s* appears on the auxiliary verb in questions, and on the main verb in affirmative sentences.
● Mention the irregular forms *has, goes.*
● Remind students that *be* and *have got* form questions without *do.*

3 The days of the week

● These can be learnt by practising round the class.
● If you want, teach the meanings of *after* and *before* so you can ask questions like *What day is after Tuesday?* and *What day is before Sunday?*
● Note the pronunciation (/ˈmʌndi/, /ˈtjuːzdi/ etc.).

4 Personalisation

● Each student should write four sentences about himself or herself, using phrases from the box.
● Then they should walk round asking each other questions, as in the examples, to try and find one other person who has written one of the same sentences.
● Demonstrate with a volunteer before they begin, and walk round while they are working to give any help that is needed.

Practice Book exercises: choose two or more
1. Choosing between *do* and *does.*
2. Choosing Simple Present forms with and without *-s.*
3. Making questions in the Simple Present.
4. Pronunciation: words and sentences with /ɪ/.
5. Reading: students read texts to decide which jobs they describe.

Unit 6: Lesson D

Students learn to talk about their leisure occupations and interests.
Structures: more practice on Simple Present forms, especially interrogatives, negatives and short answers; introduction to frequency adverbs.
Phonology: sentence stress and weak forms in questions and short answers.

Language notes and possible problems
Frequency adverbs are introduced here in pre-verb position. (More complicated problems of word order are left until later.) Some students may tend to put these adverbs between the verb and the object (e.g. *I read never newspapers*).

If you are short of time
Get students to do Exercise 6 for homework.

1 Students' interests
• Look at the diagram of frequency adverbs with the students and make sure they understand the meanings of the words.
• Ask them to copy the form and fill in the first entry.
• Then ask what sort of books they read; supply vocabulary as necessary. Make sure they tell you about a *category* of book – they shouldn't give you the name of a particular book they are reading at the moment. Try to bring the term *science fiction* into the discussion; this will be needed for the next exercise.
• Students continue filling in the form, asking you for words or using dictionaries as necessary.
• They may want to learn a good deal of new vocabulary. This is *preview* vocabulary (see *Introduction* page VII), and students don't need to learn it now.
• Make sure the words *fish, beer, football,* and *politics* come up – students will need to recognise these in the next exercise.

2 Interrogation
• The tape recorder 'interrogates' the students, asking them questions about themselves.
• Explain vocabulary in advance if necessary.
• Alternate between chorus and individual replies. You may like to get written answers to some questions. There is a pause after each question, but you must stop the recording if you want written replies.
• You may like to go through the exercise twice or more so that students can increase their fluency.
• Check that short answers (*Yes, I do; No, I'm not;* etc.) are correct.

Tapescript for Exercise 2

Hello. How are you?
What's your name?
Where are you from?
What do you do?
Are you married?
Have you got any brothers or
  sisters?
Where do you live?
What's your address?
What's your phone number?
How old are you?
Pardon?
Do you speak English?
What newspapers do you read?
Do you like music?
What sort of music do you like?

Do you play football?
Do you watch football?
Do you like reading?
Do you read science
  fiction?
What sort of books do
  you like?
Do you like fish?
Do you like beer?
What drinks do you like?
Where do you go on
  holiday?
Are you interested in
  politics?
Are you interested in
  maths?

3 Pronunciation: sentence stress
• Ask students to work individually, copying the sentences and underlining the stressed syllables.
• Then play the recording so that they listen for the stresses before checking the answers with you.
• Help them practise the sentences, paying attention to the stresses and pronouncing /ə/ where it occurs.

Tapescript and answers to Exercise 3
1. **What** do you **do**? **Where** do you **live**? **How** do you travel to **work**? What **time** do you **start work**? What **time** do you **stop work**? **What sort** of **food** do you **like**?
2. **What** does she **do**? **Where** does she **work**? **How** does she **go** to **work**?
3. **Yes**, I **do**. **No**, I **don't**. **Yes**, he **does**. **No**, he **doesn't**.

4 Interviewing the teacher
• A list of questions is given in the Student's Book for reference, but it is much better if students can make up the questions for themselves.
• Ask them to close their books and work in groups to prepare a list of questions to ask you about yourself. (Like the questions the recording has just asked them.)
• When they are ready, they can open their books and compare their lists with the list in the book, making any corrections or adjustments that they wish to.
• Get them to ask you their questions. They don't need to note the answers.

5 Interviewing another student
• Put students in pairs. Each student has five minutes to interview the other.
• They can use the same questions as they used for Exercise 4.
• When they have finished, ask them to report some of the negative facts and things in common that they have found out, either to another student or to the class.
• You will have to teach the use of *both* as in the example sentence; students may tend to put this in the wrong place in the sentence.

Optional activities
1. Exercise 5 can be done as a role play, with students taking parts such as Cleopatra, the President, etc., and answering appropriately.
2. False beginners who have some extra vocabulary can play a variant of 'Twenty questions' called 'Who am I?' A volunteer student is a famous person. The others have to find out his or her identity by asking questions that can be answered *Yes* or *No*.

6 Writing
• If time allows, this can be done as a supervised class writing exercise. Otherwise students can do it for homework.
• Encourage students to join sentences with *and* and *but*.

Practice Book exercises: choose two or more
1. Writing Simple Present third person singular forms.
2. Third person object pronouns.
3. Frequency adverbs.
4. Translation of material from the unit.
5. Student's Cassette exercise (Student's Book Exercise 2, first sixteen questions). Students listen to the recording and write down five or more of the questions.
6. Writing about how an imaginary person spends his or her day.
7. Reading: Part 5 of *It's a Long Story*.

6D What newspaper do you read?

More Simple Present tense; frequency adverbs; talking about interests.

never	sometimes	often	usually	always
0%				→ 100%

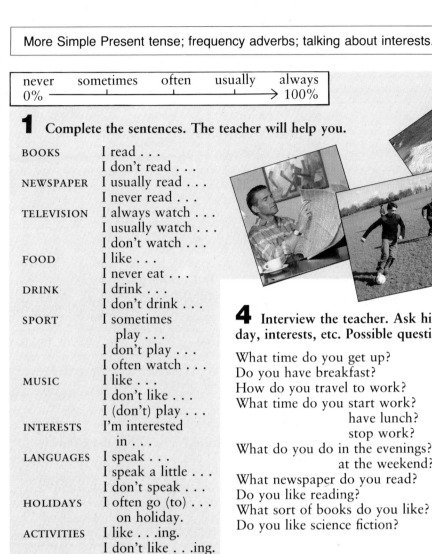

1 Complete the sentences. The teacher will help you.

BOOKS	I read . . .
	I don't read . . .
NEWSPAPER	I usually read . . .
	I never read . . .
TELEVISION	I always watch . . .
	I usually watch . . .
	I don't watch . . .
FOOD	I like . . .
	I never eat . . .
DRINK	I drink . . .
	I don't drink . . .
SPORT	I sometimes play . . .
	I don't play . . .
	I often watch . . .
MUSIC	I like . . .
	I don't like . . .
	I (don't) play . . .
INTERESTS	I'm interested in . . .
LANGUAGES	I speak . . .
	I speak a little . . .
	I don't speak . . .
HOLIDAYS	I often go (to) . . . on holiday.
ACTIVITIES	I like . . .ing.
	I don't like . . .ing.

2 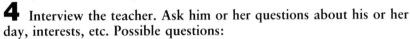 Listen to the recording. Answer the questions. Examples:

'Are you married?' 'Yes, I am.' / 'No, I'm not.'
'Do you like music?' 'Yes, I do.' / 'No, I don't.'
'What sort of music do you like?' 'Rock.'

3 Where are the stresses?

1. What do you do?
   Where do you live?
   How do you travel to work?
   What time do you start work?
   What time do you stop work?
   What sort of food do you like?
2. What does she do?
   Where does she work?
   How does she go to work?
3. Yes, I do. No, I don't.
   Yes, he does. No, he doesn't.

4 Interview the teacher. Ask him or her questions about his or her day, interests, etc. Possible questions:

What time do you get up?
Do you have breakfast?
How do you travel to work?
What time do you start work?
       have lunch?
       stop work?
What do you do in the evenings?
       at the weekend?
What newspaper do you read?
Do you like reading?
What sort of books do you like?
Do you like science fiction?

Do you like fish?
What sort of food do you like?
Do you like beer?
Do you play tennis?
Do you like skiing?
Do you watch football?
Do you like music?
Do you play an instrument?
Are you interested in politics?
What languages do you speak?
Where do you go on holiday?

5 Interview another student. Spend five minutes with him or her, and try to find:

1. Five negative facts (for example, 'He doesn't play tennis.').
2. Five things that you both have in common (for example, 'We both like the sea.').

6 Write about the student you interviewed.

Simple Present tense		
I play	do I play?	I do not (don't) play
you play	do you play?	you do not (don't) play
he/she/it plays	does she etc. play?	he etc. does not (doesn't) play
we play	do we play?	we do not (don't) play
you play	do you play?	you do not (don't) play
they play	do they play?	they do not (don't) play

Learn: newspaper; language; travel; read; play; watch; both; never; sometimes; often; usually; always; interested in; (on) holiday; What sort of . . . ?

Learn three or more: maths; music; rock; science fiction; fish; beer; tennis; skiing; football; instrument; politics.

Unit 7 Counting and measuring

7A How many calories?

Two sorts of nouns (countable and uncountable); food and drink.

2. *a litre of* .... *calories*

1. *100ml of* .... *calories*

3. *500g of* .... *calories*

4. *an* .... *calories*

5. *half a litre of* .... *calories*

6. *100ml of* .... *calories*

7. *a* .... *calories*

8. *a* .... *calories*

9. *a* .... *calories*

10. *500g of* .... *calories*

11. *an* .... *calories*

12. *150g of* .... *calories*

13. *50g of* .... *calories*

1 What are the names of the things in the picture? Try to put the words in the right places.

banana	bread	cheese	coffee	egg
ice cream	milk	orange	orange juice	
potato	rump steak	tomato	water	

2 How many calories? Try to put the numbers with the pictures.

0	7	40	40	50	80	90
	115	175	320	636	850	893

3 Listen to the recording of people guessing how many calories there are. Write down the calories they guess for: ice cream, orange, milk, coffee and potato.

4 Can you complete the lists?

C: an egg, a tomato, . . .
U: orange juice, cheese, . . .

5 Two students take turns choosing food from Exercise 1, and adding up the calories. The person who can total closest to 1,500 calories wins.

Learn: gram; litre; money; listen to; try; of; half a . . . of . . .

Learn five or more: banana; bread; cheese; coffee; egg; ice cream; milk; orange; (orange) juice; potato; rump steak; tomato; water.

Unit 7: Lesson A

Students begin work on quantification, in the context of food and drink.
Structures: the difference between countable and uncountable nouns; no indefinite article with uncountables; *of* in expressions of quantity; *half a . . .*
Phonology: word stress.

Language notes and possible problems
Countable and uncountable nouns   This terminology is adopted (in preference to 'count and mass nouns') because of its widespread use in standard dictionaries.

The distinction between countable and uncountable nouns is important for correct use of articles and quantifiers. It is, however, a difficult and abstract concept, and some students may take time to grasp it, especially if it does not correspond to a grammatical distinction in their languages. Even where a student's language does have the same distinction, certain nouns may be countable in English and uncountable in another language, or vice versa (the word for *hair* is plural in many languages, for instance).

The distinction is often arbitrary (compare *lentils* and *rice*, or *soot* and *ashes*, or *wheat* and *oats*). Note also that many nouns have both countable and uncountable uses (e.g. *paper*, *glass*); this area will be dealt with in Lesson 7C.

Optional extra materials
You may wish to bring concrete examples of countable and uncountable things into the classroom, for additional practice. Suggestions: salt, sugar, tea, polish, make-up, a brush, a stamp, a toy, a photo, a ring. Avoid 'grainy' things like rice, peas, grapes, unground coffee – usage here is inconsistent.

1 Presentation of vocabulary
• Ask students to look at the picture and to try to write the answers. They can do this in groups, pooling their knowledge – or it can be a dictionary exercise.
• Give the answers and practise the pronunciation.

2 Guessing the number of calories
• Make it clear that students are not expected to *know* the number of calories – they have to see how many they can guess right. They may get some surprises.
• The exercise can be done individually, or in groups (with each group giving an agreed group answer after discussion).
• Teach the students how to say the numbers with hundreds correctly, e.g. *eight hundred and ninety-three*.
• You may have to teach *a thousand* here.

Answers to Exercise 2
1. orange juice 40
2. water 0
3. ice cream 893
4. orange 40
5. milk 320
6. coffee (with 5ml sugar) 50
7. potato 175
8. banana 80
9. tomato 7
10. rump steak 850
11. egg 90
12. cheese 636
13. bread 115

3 Listening: other people's guesses
• This is a recording of native English speakers doing the same task the students have just done.
• The students must write down the numbers of calories they hear. This gives them practice in listening for numbers, and a chance to hear some 'real' English whose gist they will understand, even if they do not catch every word.
• Ask students to take a piece of paper and write column headings: *ice cream, orange, milk, coffee, potato.*

• Then play the recording through. The students should write down the number of each speaker, and the calories he or she guessed for each item.
• Pause the recording at appropriate moments; and you will probably want to play the recording more than once, until students are satisfied that they have written down all the numbers they can.

Answers to Exercise 3

SPEAKER	1	2	3	4
ice cream	80	850	893	893
orange	50	40	40	50
milk	115	90	320	320
coffee	320	80	50	80
potato	40	175	175	40

Tapescript for Exercise 3: see page 140

4 Countable and uncountable nouns
• Don't tell students what is meant by 'C' and 'U'. Ask them what words from Exercise 1 they think can be put in each list.
• If they have trouble in deciding, put on the board: *Is . . . C or U?* and get them to ask you questions about the various words they have learnt.
• They should see sooner or later that the top list contains words with *a/an*, and the other has words with no article.
• Explain that the words with *a/an* are the names of things you can count; the other words are the names of things you can't count – they have no plurals. (You can say *three tomatoes* but not *three milks*.)
• Tell them that *a/an* means *one*.
• Teach *countable* and *uncountable*.
• Help them pronounce the words, paying special attention to the stress.

Optional activity
• Divide the class into groups of three or four. Give the groups four minutes to draw a suitable symbol for 'countable' and 'uncountable.' When the four minutes is over, show the symbols around and let the class vote on the best ones.

5 Game: adding up calories
• Demonstrate with two volunteers. They come to the front of the room, with their lists of how many calories there are in each food.
• They choose items from the list in turn, while the class helps you write up the calorie content of each food chosen.
• Explain or demonstrate *I'll have*, and help them practise saying, *'I'll have 500g of rump steak.'* Make sure that they do not stress *of*.
• The aim is to get as close as possible to 1,500 calories. (If you have not taught *a thousand* earlier in the lesson, you will need to do so now.)
• One player can stop while the other continues to add items on.
• When the game is finished, divide the class into small groups to play the game for 1,200, 1,000 and 800 calories.

Practice Book exercises: choose two or more
1. Changing contractions to full forms.
2. Revision of pronouns and possessives.
3. Revision of short answers.
4. Revision of third person singular forms.
5. Revision of *do* and *does*.
6. Revision of ordinal numbers.
7. Reading for information.

Unit 7: Lesson B

Students learn to talk about prices.
Structures: no article with plural and uncountable nouns used in a general sense; *be* used for prices; *80p a kilo*, etc.; *I was, you were, it was, they were*.
Phonology: practice in rhythm, stress, linking and intonation.

Language notes and possible problems

1. Money You may want to explain the British monetary system. Note the common use of *p* (/piː/) instead of *pence*. (The singular of *pence* is *penny*. But this word is going out of use in Britain today; people tend to say *1p* (*one pee*) or even *one pence*. So we have not listed *penny* as an item for students to learn.)

2. No article before nouns used in a general sense Even students whose languages have roughly the same article system as English may have difficulty here; in some languages, the equivalent of *the* comes before uncountable and plural nouns used in a general sense.

3. *Was* and *were* are introduced here in the singular, and in the plural of the third person. A full treatment of this tense comes later in the course.

4. Improvisation Exercise 6 involves some simple improvisation. If your students are not yet able to manage this sort of work, let them prepare their conversations instead.

Optional extra materials

A few shopping bags will add realism to the improvisation in Exercise 6.

1 Listening for information

• Ask students to close their books, and play the conversation while they listen.
• Play it again, and ask them to write down the names of any items of food or drink they recognise.
• Play it again, and ask them to listen for the prices of potatoes (two prices), tomatoes (two prices), milk, rump steak, oranges, cheese and bananas.
• Play it one more time, and ask students to note down any uncountable nouns they hear.
• Tell students to open their books. Go through the dialogue checking the answers and explaining any difficulties.
• Point out the irregular spelling of the plurals *tomatoes* and *potatoes*.
• You may also want to point out that *a/an* is not used with plurals, and that *the* is not used with plurals when they have a general sense.

2 Rhythm, stress and linking

• Practise the words and expressions.
Note:
1. Weak pronunciation of *a*, *are* and *was* (/wəz/).
2. Pronunciation of *Do you know?* (/djəˈnəʊ/).
3. Syllables in bold type are stressed.
4. Words beginning with a vowel should not be separated from preceding words in the same phrase.

3 No articles with nouns used in a general sense

• Point out some of the sentences in the dialogue where uncountable and plural nouns are used in a general sense without articles.
• If you speak your students' language(s), elicit or explain the rule that is operating.
• Look at the first two sentences in Exercise 3; elicit or point out that in the second sentence, the fridge is a specific fridge.
• Then let the students do the exercise individually while you walk round to see who is having difficulty, and help them; or continue to do the exercise orally.
• Students should do Exercise 1 in the Practice Book if they need any consolidation of this point.

4 Am/is/are/was/were

• Ask students to look at the last nine lines of the dialogue. Put on the board:

I was
you
he/she/it
they

and get students to help you fill in the correct verbs.
• If you and your students feel it is helpful, you can complete the paradigm with *we* and plural *you*, but these will not be focused on until later in the course.
• Ask students to do the exercise individually, and then compare answers in groups before checking with you.
• Walk round while they are working to give any help that is necessary.

5 Pronunciation practice

• Get the students to say some of the sentences after you or after the recording. Concentrate on getting the stress and intonation reasonably correct.
• Then ask them to practise in pairs, going through the dialogue.

6 Improvisation

• Get a volunteer group of good students (four or five), give them shopping bags if you have brought them, and ask them to act out a conversation between shoppers who meet in the street. It doesn't need to go on longer than 30 seconds.
• Put the other students in groups and get them to do the same. They can change groups once or twice and begin again, but do not let the exercise go on too long.
• You can walk around while they are working, to help if anybody really gets stuck.
• Real beginners may find this too difficult. They can prepare six- to eight-line conversations in groups of three, and perform them for the class or another group.
• The emphasis here is on fluency, and it is a bad idea to correct any grammar or pronunciation mistakes unless they make understanding impossible.

Practice Book exercises: choose two or more
1. Choosing *the* versus no article.
2. Choosing *am/is/are/was/were*.
3. Writing: giving prices of some things.
4. Revision of negative short answers.
5. Student's Cassette exercise (Student's Book Exercise 1, last part of dialogue). Students listen to the exercise and write down five or more sentences.
6. Reading for information.

7B It's terrible

Prices; nouns without articles; *was* and *were*.

- It's terrible.
- The prices.
- Oh dear.
- Do you know potatoes are eighty pence a kilo?
- Eighty pence a kilo? In our supermarket they're eighty-five.
- It's terrible.
- Oh dear.
- Everything's so expensive.
- Do you know tomatoes are £6.00 a kilo?
- £6.00? In our supermarket they're £6.25.
- No!!!
- Yes!
- It's terrible.
- Milk's seventy-five pence a litre.
- Half a kilo of rump steak is £7.50.
- An orange costs 60p. One orange!
- And cheese!
- I know!
- Do you know, yesterday I was in Patterson's.
- Were you?
- Yes, and cheese was £8.30 a kilo.
- £8.30?
- Yes, and bananas were £2.25.
- It's terrible.

1 🔊 **Listen to the conversation (books closed) and answer the teacher's questions.**

2 **Say these words and expressions.**

It's terrible
eighty pence a kilo
Potatoes are eighty pence a kilo.
In our supermarket they're eighty-five.
expensive
Everything's so expensive.
tomatoes are six pounds
six pounds a kilo
half a kilo
an orange
I was in Patterson's
Do you know?
bananas were two pounds twenty-five

3 **Put in *the* where necessary.**

1. There are 424 calories in 100g of ....--......... cheese.
2. Your tomatoes are in .....*the*..... fridge.
3. .... potatoes are not very expensive.
4. There are no calories in .... water.
5. 'Where are .... bananas?' 'On .... table.'
6. .... wine is expensive in Britain.
7. 'We've got one orange and one banana.' 'I'll have .... orange.'
8. Do you like .... tomatoes?

4 **Put in *am, is, are, was* or *were*.**

1. Yesterday I .... in London.
2. Steak .... very expensive.
3. Yesterday my mother and father .... in Manchester.
4. Oranges .... £1.40 a kilo.
5. In 1960, oranges .... 20p a kilo and a bottle of wine .... 60p.
6. When I .... a child, bananas .... very expensive.
7. My daughter's name .... Helen.
8. .... you American?
9. Where .... you yesterday?
10. 'What do you do?' 'I .... a teacher.'

5 **Practise the conversation.**

6 **Make short conversations in groups of four or five. Begin: *'It's terrible.'***

Learn: price; terrible; Do you know?; pound (£); pence (p); I know; yesterday; kilo; cost; was; were; Oh dear; expensive.

> More countables and uncountables; *there is/are*; *some* and *any*.

1 Countable or uncountable? Put *a/an* before the countable nouns.

car   chair   music

light   lamp   apple

snow   rain   cup

horse   money   ice

potato   glass   lamb

potato   glass   lamb

2 Look at the picture for two minutes. Then close your book. Work with a partner, and make as many sentences as you can with *some*. Examples:

There are some books on the tables.

There's some ice outside the window.

3 Show your sentences to the other students. Then open your book and check. Were any of your sentences wrong? Examples:

'There aren't any horses on the tables. There are some horses on a bed.'
'There isn't any snow on the television; there's some rain.'

Now make four more sentences about things that *aren't* in the picture.

4 🔊 Listen to the questions and write the answers:

Yes, there is.   No, there isn't.
Yes, there's one.   No, there aren't.
Yes, there are.

    I don't know.
    I don't understand.

5 Class survey. Choose one countable and one uncountable. Ask other students: *'Are there any . . . ?' / 'Is there any . . . ?'* Keep account of the results.

fair people in your family	cheese in your kitchen
books under your chair	money in your bag
chairs in your bathroom	rain in your country today
horses near your home	snow in your country today
apples in your kitchen	ice in your fridge
doctors in your street	ice cream in your fridge

Yes	?	No
There is some rain.	Is there any rain?	There isn't any rain.
There are some horses.	Are there any horses?	There aren't any horses.

Learn: music; snow; ice; light; rain; lamp; cup; apple; horse; glass; people; outside; some; (I don't) understand.

Unit 7: Lesson C

Students learn more about quantification.
Structures: *some* and *any* with uncountables and plurals.
Phonology: practice of weak forms (e.g. *There are some . . .* /ðərəsəm/).

Language notes and possible problems

1. Some/any The meaning of *some/any* may be difficult to get across (they are used to talk about a limited but indefinite quantity or number). Here students learn to use *some* in affirmative and *any* in questions and negative sentences. The use of *some* in questions, and the use of *any* to mean 'no matter which', will be studied later in the course.

2. Singular countables Some students may try to make examples using *some* or *any* with singular countable nouns (e.g. **There isn't any TV in my house*). Get them to keep to uncountables and plurals for the moment.

3. Unstress Students will find it hard to pronounce a string of unstressed weak forms as in *There are some . . .* Don't be too perfectionist about this.

1 Countables and uncountables

● Go over the first twelve pictures with the students, getting them to tell you whether they think the things are countable or uncountable. Help them with pronunciation as they go along.
● If they have difficulty with *money*, you can tell them that *pound, peseta, dollar*, etc. are countable, but *money* is not.
● Then go on to the last six pictures. If you speak the students' language(s), explain that some words can be countable or uncountable, according to their use.
● Finally, ask students to copy the words, adding *a* or *an* in front of the countable nouns.

2 Memory game: *some*

● Ask the students to look at the picture. Write the beginnings of two lists on the board:
  There are some books on the tables.
  There's some ice outside the window.
● Explain that *there's* means *there is*.
● Then give students two minutes to look at the picture and try to remember everything they can.
● Ask them to work in pairs, writing sentences beginning with *There are some* or *There's some*.
● If your students enjoy competition, you may want to ask them to see which pair can write the most true sentences.

3 Correcting the game: *some* and *any*

● Tell the students to keep their books closed.
● Get volunteers to come up and write *There are* and *There's* sentences under your example sentences on the board.
● Do not comment on the truth or falsity of the sentences, and discourage the other students from doing so.
● Each volunteer should write one sentence that has not been written before, reading it out before writing it. Help them practise the pronunciation, encouraging weak forms (*There are some* is pronounced /ðərəsəm/).
● Help with vocabulary if needed; for example, someone may want to say *'There are some people in the room'*.

● When no more new sentences are forthcoming, ask the students to open their books and check their own sentences and the ones on the board to see if they correspond to the picture.
● There are very likely to be some mistakes. Get students to tell you about them, using *There aren't/isn't any . . .* as in the examples.
● Then ask them to work individually to make four more sentences about things that are not in the picture.
● Walk round while they are working to check comprehension, and to give any help that is needed.

4 Listening: personalisation

● Tell students that they are going to hear some questions and they must write the answers.
● Go over the possible answers with them.
● Then play each question, more than once if necessary (but without 'translating' the question into slower English for the students). Pause the cassette to give students time to write their answers.
● If students request it, write any questions they have had problems with on the board for them.

Tapescript for Exercise 4
Is there any water in this room?
Is there any cheese in your house?
Are there any doctors in the class?
Is there any money on your table?
Is there any apple juice in your fridge?
Are there any eggs in your fridge?
Are there any chairs in your bedroom?
Are there any horses near your home?
Is there any bread in your kitchen?

5 Oral practice: class survey

● Go over the two lists with the students. You may have to explain *people* if it has not come up in Exercise 3.
● Each student has to choose one item from each list, and walk round asking everybody else about those two items and noting the answers.
● Practise the pronunciation of the question and answer forms so that students are comfortable with them.
● You can participate in the survey yourself, or just walk round helping when needed.
● If there is time, students may want to report on the survey. If so, encourage them to use the forms:
  'Are there any fair people in your family?' *'Two yeses, 14 nos.'*

Grammar table

● Draw students' attention to the table, which summarises the grammar studied in the lesson; and answer any related questions.

Practice Book exercises: choose two or more
1. Distinguishing between countables and uncountables.
2. Distinguishing between countable and uncountable uses of the same words.
3. Choosing *some* or *any*.
4. Writing true sentences with structures from the lesson.
5. Revision of Simple Present structures.
6. Student's Cassette exercise (Student's Book Exercise 4). Students listen to the exercise and write down five or more questions.

34

Unit 7: Lesson D

Students continue their work on quantification.
Structures: *how much* and *how many*; *too much, too many* and *enough*; *not much, not many* and *a lot of*.

Language notes and possible problems

1. *Much* and *many* Some students will find it difficult to distinguish between these at first.

2. *A lot of* Note that *much* and *many* are unusual in affirmative sentences in an informal style except after *too, so* and sometimes *very*. Students should be encouraged to say, for instance, *I've got a lot of friends* or *There is a lot of noise* rather than *I've got many friends* or *There is much noise*, which sound unnatural.

3. *Hair, money* and *people* may cause problems – the equivalents of *hair* and *money* are plural countables in some languages; *people* looks like a singular, and has a singular equivalent in some languages. Look out for mistakes like **many hairs, *many money, *much people.*

Note

This is a long lesson which deals with a relatively complicated area of grammar. For weaker students, it may be better to divide the material into two separate lessons (for example, Exercises 1–2 and the rest).

1 Presentation: quantifiers with uncountables and plurals

• Go over the table with the students, and see if any of them can tell you the meanings of *how much/many*; *too much/many* etc.

• Ask them which columns the words in the box should go in. Help them to see the differences between the two lists (uncountables and plurals).

• *Hair, people* and *money* may cause problems – see *Language notes*.

• Make sure students finish the exercise by understanding clearly that *much* is used with uncountables and *many* with plurals.

2 Quiz: *How much/many*

• Let students work on this in groups, using dictionaries if necessary.

• Give the answers and discuss any problems. (Note that in question 7 *How much* is used as a pronoun, without a following noun.)

• Get students to make up a few more quiz questions for each other (perhaps four new questions per group).

• Questions should of course begin *How much/many*.

Answers to Exercise 2

1. 50 (though European atlases often count the District of Columbia, making a total of 51).
2. 110 million bottles.
3. Nine (Mercury, Venus, Earth, Mars, Jupiter, Saturn, Uranus, Neptune, Pluto).
4. Usually 88.
5. After breathing in, between one and a half and two litres.
6. Four.
7. 60%.

3 Listening: *not much/many; a lot of*

• Students will hear a series of conversations and sounds – their job is to say or write appropriate phrases to describe what they hear.

• Before starting, practise the pronunciation of *a lot of* (/əˈlɒtəv/).

• Explain that it means the same as *much/many*, but that *a lot of* is more common in affirmative sentences in spoken English.

Answers to Exercise 3

Suitable descriptions of the situations are:
1. not many people
2. a lot of people
3. not much money
4. a lot of cats
5. a lot of food
6. not much time
7. not many students
8. a lot of girlfriends
9. a lot of money
10. a lot of water
11. not much food

4 The classroom

• Students should be able to think of several examples (you may need to help with vocabulary).

• The exercise can be extended by looking out of the window; thinking about the whole building; about the students' homes; about the town.

• Encourage correct pronunciation of *a lot of*.

5 *Not enough; too much/many*

• Translate or demonstrate *not enough, enough,* and *too much/many*.

• Practise the pronunciation of *enough*.

• Do the first two or three examples together.

• Get students to do the exercise individually or in small groups, comparing notes when they have finished.

6 Personalisation

• Ask students to write one or two sentences first.

• Get them to tell you what they have written, and see if they can make more examples orally.

Practice Book exercises: choose two or more

1. Choosing between *How much* and *How many*.
2. Making true sentences with *enough, too much, too many* and *a lot of*.
3. Pronunciation (stress).
4. Translation of material from the unit.
5. Reading and punctuation.
6. Writing: a holiday postcard.
7. Reading: Part 6 of *It's a Long Story*.

7D Not enough money

Much and many; too and enough; a lot of.

1 Put the words from the box in the right columns. What kind of words go in each column?

How much?	How many?
Too much	Too many?
Not much	Not many
Enough	Enough
A lot of	A lot of
water	cars
light	houses
air	children

milk	tomatoes	potatoes	cheese	bread
wine	rain	hair	men	chairs	people
snow	money			

2 Quiz. Put in *How much* or *How many*. Can you answer any of the questions? Make some questions yourself.

1. .... states are there in the USA – 36, 49, 50 or 60?
2. .... Coca-Cola is drunk in the world in one day – one million bottles, 11 million bottles or 110 million bottles?
3. .... planets (Mercury, Venus etc.) are there – 7, 9, 11 or 13?
4. .... keys are there on a piano – 70, 82 or 88?
5. .... air is there in our lungs – half a litre, one and a half litres or two and a half litres?
6. .... Beatles were there – 3, 4 or 5?
7. .... of a person is water – 40%, 60% or 90%?

3 Listen, and choose the right words for each situation. Example:

1. 'not many people'

not much	people	cats	cigarettes
not many	students	food	money
a lot of	time	water	girlfriends

4 Talk about the classroom. Begin:

'There isn't much . . .'
'There aren't many . . .'
'There is/are a lot of . . .'

5 Look at the pictures and choose the right words.

not enough	people	toothpaste	hair
too much		perfume	light
too many	money	cars	toilets
	children	chips	hair
	shaving cream	numbers	

6 Talk about yourself.

'I've got enough / too much / too many . . .'
'I haven't got enough . . .'

Learn: much; many; how much/many; not much/many; too much/many; a lot of; enough; word; person (people); toothpaste; hair; wine; food; cat.

Learn if you want: shaving cream; perfume; chips.

35

Unit 8 Consolidation

8A Things to remember: Units 5, 6 and 7

There is, there are . . .

there is (there's)	is there?	there is not (isn't)
there are (−)	are there?	there are not (aren't)

Examples:

There's a big table in my kitchen.
There's some coffee on the table.
Is there a bathroom on the first floor?
'Is there any milk in the fridge?'
  'Yes, there is.' / 'No, there isn't.'
There isn't a garage.
There isn't any ice in your glass.

There are two chairs in the hall.
There are some apples here.
'Are there any oranges?' 'Yes, there are.' /
  'Yes, there's one.' / 'No, there aren't.'
There aren't enough eggs.
There aren't any potatoes.

Stress
There's a **big ta**ble in my **kit**chen.
'Is there a (/ɪzðərə/) **bath**room on the **first floor**?'
  'Yes, there **is**.' / 'No, there **isn't**.'
There **isn't** any **ice** in your **glass**.
There are (/ðərə/) **two chairs** in the **hall**.
There are some (/ðərəsəm/) **apples** here.
'Are there any **oranges**?' 'Yes, there **are**.' / 'No, there **aren't**.'
There **aren't enough eggs**.

Was and were

I was
you were
he/she/it was
we were
you were
they were

Simple Present tense

I play	do I play?	I do not (don't) play
you play	do you play?	you do not (don't) play
he/she/it plays	does he *etc.* play?	she *etc.* does not (doesn't) play
we play	do we play?	we do not (don't) play
you play	do you play?	you do not (don't) play
they play	do they play?	they do not (don't) play

Examples:
'I **live** in Curzon Street.' 'Oh? I **do**, too.'
'**Do** you **like** orange juice?' 'Yes, I **do**.' ('Yes, I like.')
'What time **does** Karen **get up**?' 'Half past seven.'
'**Does** she **have** breakfast?' 'No, she **doesn't**.' ('No, she hasn't.')
'**Does** she **go** to work by car?' 'Yes, she **does**.' ('Yes, she goes.')
'**Do** Sam and Virginia **live** near you?' 'No, they **don't**.'

Spelling of *he/she/it* forms

Regular		Irregular	
get	→gets	have got	→has got
play	→plays	do	→does
live	→lives	go	→goes
try	→tries		
watch	→watches		

Stress
'**Do** you (/djʊ/) **like** orange **juice**?'
  'Yes, I **do**.' / 'No, I **don't**.'
What time does (/dəz/) **Karen get up**?
'**Does** she **have** (/dəʃiˈhæv/) **breakfast**?'
  'Yes, she **does**.' / 'No, she **doesn't**.'

Frequency adverbs

I **never** read science fiction. (I read never science fiction.)
I **sometimes** watch television in the evening.
She **often** goes to work by bus.
They **usually** have supper at six on Sundays.
John **always** goes to work by car.

Both

We **both** like rock music. (We like both rock music. We like rock music both.)

This lesson displays the language that students should have learnt in the last three units. Spend a short time going over the lesson pages with the students. Point out that they are expected to learn not only the vocabulary in the *Words and expressions* section, but also that in the sections *Prepositions, Days, First, second . . . , Time, Likes and dislikes, Questions and answers* and *Directions*.

Ask the students to look over the lesson again at home before trying the Practice Book exercises. They should try to do the Practice Book exercises with the Student's Book closed, unless they have difficulties. Once they have finished the Practice Book exercises, they can look back at the Student's Book to check their work.

Note that *us* has been included in the list of object pronouns, and *its* in the list of possessives, although they have not yet been taught, since some students are likely to want the complete table. For the same reason, first and second person plural forms have been included in the *was/were* table.

Practice Book exercises: choose two or more
1. Choosing the right preposition (note that in some cases more than one answer is acceptable).
2. Making questions for answers (more than one question often acceptable).
3. *There is/are*; quantifiers with uncountable and plural nouns.
4. Frequency adverbs.
5. Recreational reading: *Believe it or not*.
6. Crossword.

Video

Sequences 2A and 2B in *The New Cambridge English Course 1 Video* can be used around this point in the book, as they relate to Units 5–7 of the coursebook.

In Sequence 2A, **A day in the life of Nick Hill**, the topics are daily routines; commuting; leisure activities; likes and dislikes. Language focus is on Simple Present tense forms; telling the time; frequency adverbs.

In Sequence 2B, **The move**, the topics are houses; rooms; furniture. Language focus is on prepositions of place; *too* and *enough*; Simple Present tense forms; negative forms.

Pronouns and possessives

Subject		Object		Possessive
I	→	me	→	my
you	→	you	→	your
he	→	him	→	his
she	→	her	→	her
it	→	it	→	its
we	→	us	→	our
you	→	you	→	your
they	→	them	→	their

Articles

a/an: There's **an** apple on the table.
There's **a** book under your chair.

a/an and *some*: There's **a** woman at the reception desk.
There's **some** milk in the fridge.
(There's a milk . . .)
There are **some** books on the table.

no article: **Oranges** were expensive when I was young.
(The oranges were expensive when I was young.)

a and *the*: There's **a** chair in **the** bathroom.   Where's **the** car?

Quantifiers with plurals and uncountables

Much with uncountables;
many with plurals

There **isn't much light** in this room.
How **much air** is there in our lungs?
There **was** too **much snow** at St Moritz.
There **aren't many cars** in the street.
How **many brothers** and **sisters** have you got?
I've got too **many students** in my class.

Enough and *a lot (of)*

We haven't got **enough** ice cream. (. . . enough of . . .)
We've got **a lot of** potatoes. (. . . a lot potatoes.)
'How much would you like?'   '**A lot**.' ('A lot of.')

Some in affirmatives; *any* in negatives and questions

There are **some** oranges on the table. (. . . any oranges . . .)
I haven't got **any** time this morning. (. . . some time . . .)
Is there **any** ice in the fridge? (. . . some ice . . .)

Prepositions

Places: by the reception desk
opposite the railway station
next to the post office
on his way **to** work
on her way back **from** school
outside the window
in England; **in** New York; **in** Park Street, **in** a flat; **in** a big house; **in** the living room
at 23 Park Street
on the second floor

Special expressions: at home, **at** work, **at** school, **in** bed

Time: at half **past** seven
from nine o'clock **until** a quarter **to** six
on Saturdays
at the weekend
in the morning/afternoon/evening

Travel: by bus; **by** car; **on** holiday

Days

Monday (/'mʌndi/), Tuesday (/'tjuːzdi/),
Wednesday (/'wenzdi/), Thursday (/'θɜːzdi/),
Friday (/'fraɪdi/), Saturday (/'sætədi/),
Sunday (/'sʌndi/)   **Note** the s in 'On Sundays'.

First, second . . .

1st	first	4th	fourth	7th	seventh
2nd	second	5th	fifth	8th	eighth
3rd	third	6th	sixth	9th	ninth

Time

What time is it? Where are you at seven o'clock?
five past six; a quarter past six; half past six
twenty to seven; a quarter to seven; seven o'clock
What time do you get up? (At what time do you get up?)
I have lunch from 12.30 to 1.15.

Likes and dislikes

I like the Greek statue very much.
I quite like the mask.   The mask is OK.
I like the Vermeer best.
I hate shopping.
I don't like classical music at all.
'Do you like travelling?'   'It depends.'
Everybody likes music.   Nobody likes rain.

Questions and answers

'Where do you live?'   'In Barcelona.'
'Where do you work?'   'In a shop in George Street.'
'What's your phone number?'   'Seven six two, four three eight five.'
'What newspaper do you read?'   '*The Independent*.'

'How do you travel to work?'   'By bus.'
'What sort of books do you like?'   'Science fiction.'
'Are you interested in politics?'   'Yes, I am.'
'Would you like some fruit juice?'   'I'm sorry, I don't understand.'

Directions

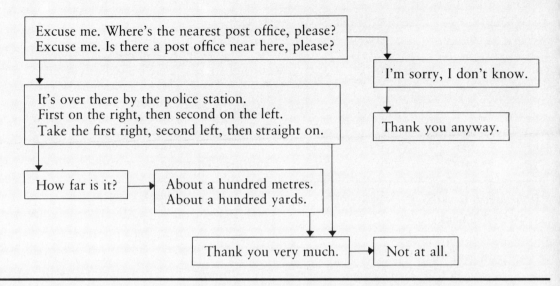

Excuse me. Where's the nearest post office, please?
Excuse me. Is there a post office near here, please?

I'm sorry, I don't know.

It's over there by the police station.
First on the right, then second on the left.
Take the first right, second left, then straight on.

Thank you anyway.

How far is it?

About a hundred metres.
About a hundred yards.

Thank you very much.

Not at all.

Words and expressions

Countable nouns

house	phone number	car	kilo
window	yard	weekend	lamp
door	swimming pool	newspaper	cup
stairs	home	language	apple
room	school	holiday	horse
flat	bed	gram	person (people)
street	breakfast	litre	word
road	lunch	price	cat
floor	supper	pound (£)	
ground floor	bus	pence (p)	

Uncountable nouns

time	light
work	rain
money	toothpaste
music	hair
snow	wine
ice	food

Countable or uncountable noun

glass

Verbs

work	stop
live	travel
take	read
like	play
hate	watch
love	listen to
dislike	try
have	understand
get up	cost
go	was/were
start	

Adjectives

big
small
nearest
good
cheap
expensive
terrible

Adverbs

upstairs	not much
downstairs	not at all
there	never
here	sometimes
right	often
left	usually
straight on	always
then	out
far	still
only	yesterday
very much	

Prepositions

for	by
next to	past
opposite	to
from	of
until	outside
at	

Other words and expressions

nobody	It depends	Do you know?	any
everybody	interested in	I know	(too) much/many
both	but	Oh dear	enough
for . . . yards/metres	half a . . . of . . .	some	a lot of

Optional words to learn

Rooms: bedroom; kitchen; bathroom; toilet; living room; wall; garage.
Furniture: furniture (*uncountable*); cooker; sofa; fridge; armchair; television; TV; cupboard; bath; wardrobe.
Places: phone box; supermarket; bank; post office; police station; car park; bus stop; station; railway station; bookshop; restaurant; hotel; church; chemist's.
Interests: maths; rock; science fiction; tennis; skiing; football; instrument; politics.
Food – countable: banana; egg; orange; tomato; chips.
     – uncountable: fish; beer; bread; cheese; coffee; ice cream; milk; juice; rump steak; water.
     – countable or uncountable: potato.
Other: police (*plural*); public; shaving cream; perfume.

Unit 8: Lesson B

Students revise vocabulary and work on writing and listening skills.
Structures: Simple Present; telling time.

If you are short of time
Divide Exercise 2 into sections (see instructions for exercise). Give the writing part of Exercise 3 for homework.

---

1 Vocabulary revision
• Ask students to work individually to write down as many words as they can remember to add to the three lists.
• Then get them to work in groups of three or four to combine their lists.
• Let students volunteer words for class lists; a student should write each list on the board as classmates call the words out.

2 Filling in a letter
• All students should copy the letter and fill in the picture words; but they can work in pairs to try and decide what the picture words are.
• Ask them to write numbers out in letters, and times out in words.
• Walk round while they are working to give any help that is needed.
• When they have finished, check the answers with the class as a whole.
• If you want to save time, divide the letter into sections and get different students to work on different parts.

Answers to Exercise 2
Dear Miriam,
Thank you for writing, and thank you for the photographs. Mark and Sarah are very pretty!

What sort of *house* do we live in? Well, it's not a *house*, it's a *flat*. It's got 4 *bedrooms*, 2 *bathrooms*, a big *living room* and a big *kitchen*. There is a *park* just opposite our building where the *children* play.

You know Patricio and I both work. We *get up* at *ten past eight*, and go to work by *bus*. Patricio *works* (or *paints*) *from a quarter to nine to half past one* and then *has lunch*. He works again in the afternoon, and *comes home* at about *ten to five*. I start *work* at *nine o'clock*, and (I) *have lunch* at about *a quarter past two*. I stop *work* at *half past five*.

A young *woman* comes to look after the *children*. They *get up* at about *twenty to nine*, and say *goodbye* to us. Then they have *breakfast*, and go to *play* in the *park*. They have *lunch* at about *a quarter to two*, and after *lunch* they go to *bed* until *half past four*. Then they have a bit of *bread* and *jam*. When Patricio and I get home we *play* with them for a while. We have *supper* at about *a quarter to nine*, and the children go to *bed* at *twenty past ten*. When they are *in bed*, Patricio and I *read* or *watch television*, or talk.

3 Listening and writing
• Play the recording of Miriam talking to the researcher one or more times while students take any notes they wish.
• Ask them to tell you anything they have noted or can remember.
• Then play the tape again. This should be enough unless students are having great difficulty; they are not meant to write down or even understand every word, just to get the main points.
• They should gather the following information:

– Miriam lives in a house.
– It has got 4 bedrooms, a small kitchen, and a big living room.
– On Saturdays and Sundays she: reads, plays tennis, listens to music.
– On Saturday evenings she watches TV.
– On Sunday morning she plays with the children (goes to the zoo or something).

• When the students have gathered the information, ask them to work individually to write Miriam's answer to Teresa's letter. (This can be done at home if you want to save time.)
• If you speak the students' language(s), ask them to concentrate on content, not form; it is better in the first instance if they are not too worried about getting the spelling, etc. right.
• If you have a small class, you may be able to look over the papers while the students are doing Exercise 4; otherwise you will have to take them home and return them in the next lesson.
• In either case, check the papers, not for grammar and spelling, but by answering the following questions:
1. Would the letter be comprehensible to an English-speaking person who did not speak the student's language?
2. Are there any positive points to be noted in the areas of organisation or expression of ideas?
• When you hand the papers back, tell students (if you speak their language) how you have corrected them, trying to be as positive as possible.
• Tell them that if anyone wants to rewrite their letter, this time paying attention to spelling and grammar, you will be happy to correct them again.

Tapescript for Exercise 3
RESEARCHER: Excuse me, I wonder if you could answer a few questions.
MIRIAM: Well, yes, I suppose so.
R: Do you own your own home?
M: Yes.
R: And is it a house or a flat?
M: It's a detached house.
R: How many bedrooms has it got?
M: There are three, no, four bedrooms.
R: And would you classify your kitchen as big or small?
M: Oh, it's a small kitchen.
R: And your living room?
M: A big living room.
R: A big living room. OK. Now, which of these do you do on a typical Sunday or Saturday: read?
M: Yes.
R: Do you play some sport?
M: Yes, tennis, usually.
R: Do you listen to music?
M: Yes.
R: How about television?
M: I watch TV on Saturday evenings, usually.
R: Does your family do things together?
M: We usually play with the children, go to the zoo or something, on Sunday morning.
R: And what do you . . . *(Fade)*

Practice Book exercises: choose two or more
1. Putting verbs into correct Simple Present forms.
2. Pronunciation: stress in Simple Present sentences.
3. Spelling of third person singular forms of the Simple Present.
4. Student's Cassette exercise (Student's Book Exercise 3, first part of conversation). Students compare a list of questions in their books with the questions on the tape; they must decide which are the same.
5. Writing about habits; spelling of days of the week.
6. Applying for penfriends.

8B What sort of house do you live in?

Vocabulary (homes, habits); writing; listening.

1 How many words and expressions can you add to these lists?

1. kitchen, bedroom, . . .
2. chair, table, . . .
3. get up, have breakfast, . . .

Now practise the pronunciation of the words and expressions you have written.

2 Write out Teresa's letter.

Dear Miriam,

Thank you for writing, and thank you for the photographs. Mark and Sarah are very pretty!

What sort of ___ do we live in? Well, it's not a ___, it's a ___. It's got 4 ___, 2 ___, a big ___ and a big ___. There is a ___ just opposite our building where the ___ play.

You know Patricio and I both work. We ___ at ___, and go to work by ___. Patricio ___ ___ and then ___. He works again in the afternoon, and ___ at about ___. I start ___ at ___, and ___ at about ___. I stop ___ at ___.

A young ___ comes to look after the ___. They ___ at about ___, and say ___ to us. Then they have ___, and go to ___ in the ___. They have ___ at about ___, and after ___ they go to ___ until ___. Then they have a bit of ___ and ___. When Patricio and I get home we ___ with them for a while. We have ___ at about ___, and the children go to ___ at ___. When they are ___, Patricio and I ___ or ___, or talk.

What sort of house do you live in? What do you do on Saturdays and Sundays? Please write soon.

All the best, *Teresa*

3 Listen and take notes. Then write Miriam's answer to Teresa.

8C Choose

A choice of pronunciation, grammar, speaking and listening exercises.

Look at the exercises, decide which ones are useful to you, and do two or more.

PRONUNCIATION

1 Listen. How many words? (Contractions like *isn't* count as two words.)

2 Stress. A lot of words are stressed on the first syllable:

armchair   **any**way   **super**market

but some words are stressed on the second syllable:

a**bout**   ba**na**na

and some words are stressed on the third syllable:

under**stand**

How are these words stressed? Copy the box patterns and see if there are words for each pattern. Then pronounce the words.

cupboard   everybody   excuse   expensive
holiday   interested   kilo   language
newspaper   nobody   opposite   people
person   police   post office   potato
quarter   Saturday   second   seventh
tomato   Wednesday

3 Copy the sentences and underline the stressed syllables, check your answers with the recording, and pronounce the sentences.

1. There are some people at the reception desk.
2. There's some water on your book.
3. Are there any potatoes?
4. Is there any orange juice in the fridge?
5. How many people are there?
6. How much time is there?

GRAMMAR

1 Do you know the names of the things in the bags? Choose a bag; try to find out which bag another student has chosen. Examples:

'Are there any apples in your bag?'
'No, there aren't. Is there any milk in your bag?'
'Yes, there is.'
'How much?'
'A litre.'

first bag

second bag

third bag

fourth bag

2 Survey. Write three questions: one using *many*, one using *much* and one using *enough*. Walk round asking your questions and noting the answers. Report back to the class, or write the results down and ask your teacher to put them up where everybody can read them. Examples:

'How much television do you watch every week?' 'About three hours.'
'Do you think there are too many cars in this city?' 'No, I think there are too many bicycles.'
'Do you usually have enough time to read the newspaper?' 'Yes, I do.'

Unit 8: Lesson C

Students and teacher choose which revision exercises they need the most, and do as many as they have time for.

Note

There is much more than 45 minutes' work in this lesson, and most classes will probably not have time to do everything. Help the students to decide which areas they need to work on; you may like to do this by asking the students to vote.

PRONUNCIATION

1 How many words?

• This exercise trains students to hear unstressed words in fast natural speech.
• Play the first sentence, and ask everybody to decide how many words there are in it.
• Count contractions (e.g. *There's*) as two words.
• Play the sentence more than once if students are not sure.
• Then ask what the words are. Put the correct sentence on the board.
• Do the other sentences in the same way.

Tapescript for Exercise 1
1. There are some apples here. (5)
2. There isn't a lot of cheese in the cupboard. (10)
3. Have you got enough potatoes? (5)
4. A lot of my friends play tennis. (7)
5. There isn't much light in this room. (8)
6. What time does Karen get up? (6)
7. Does she have breakfast? (4)
8. Do you like orange juice? (5)
9. Oranges were expensive when I was young. (7)
10. What time do you get up? (6)
11. Where's the nearest post office, please? (7)
12. What sort of books do you like? (7)

2 Word stress

• Go over the instructions with the students, making sure that they understand the different stress patterns.
• Ask them to work individually; they should put the six patterns on a piece of paper, and then list the words under the patterns they follow.
• When they finish, go over the lists with them and help them pronounce the words, paying special attention to reduced /ə/ and /ɪ/ sounds.

Answers to Exercise 2

☐☐	☐☐☐	☐☐☐☐
cupboard	**hol**iday	**ev**erybody
kilo	**in**terested	
language	**news**paper	
people	**op**posite	
person	**no**body	
quarter	**post** office	
second	**Sat**urday	
seventh		
Wednesday		

☐☐	☐☐☐	☐☐☐
ex**cuse**	ex**pen**sive	(no words)
po**lice**	po**ta**to	
	to**ma**to	

3 Stress in *there is/are* sentences

• Look at the example with the students. Then ask them to copy the sentences and to work individually underlining the stressed syllables.
• Walk round while they are working to note if anyone is having particular difficulty.
• When they have finished, play the recording for them to check their answers, pausing after each sentence.
• If they are not confident of having heard the stress correctly, you may have to go over the answers with them.

Tapescript and answers to Exercise 3
1. There are some **people** at the reception **desk**.
2. There's some **water** on your **book**.
3. Are there any po**ta**toes?
4. Is there any **orange juice** in the **fridge**?
5. **How** many **people** are there?
6. **How** much **time** is there?

GRAMMAR

1 Game: 'Which bag?'

• Check that students know the names of all the things in the bags. Help them work out the quantities of milk, orange juice, etc. from the labels visible on some of the containers.
• Explain or demonstrate that each student should choose one bag without telling anyone which one it is.
• Students then walk round asking *Is there any / Are there any* and *How much / How many* questions, to try and deduce which bags people have chosen.
• You can demonstrate with a quick student (who must then choose a new bag for the actual game).
• Each student should try to talk to as many others as possible.

2 Survey: *much/many/enough*

• Go over examples with students, making sure everyone remembers when and how to use each of the quantifiers.
• Then get each one to write a question with *much*, a question with *many* and a question with *enough*.
• Walk round while they are working to give any help that is needed and to check the forms.
• Ask them to walk round asking their questions of everyone else; or if this is impossible, to ask as many people as they can without moving from their desks.
• If there is time, they can report their results to the class or to a group; otherwise post them up where everyone can read them.

SPEAKING AND LISTENING

1 Things in common

• Ask students for the names of as many sports as they can think of and note them on the board (help them with translations where necessary, if this is possible).
• Do the same for different sorts of music and newspapers.
• Then ask each student to choose a sport, a sort of music and a newspaper. They need not be the ones they really play, listen to and read!
• Get a confident student to demonstrate the questions and answers with you, and then to choose another three things for the game.

- Students should stand up and walk round where possible, and try to find someone with as many things in common with them as they can.

2 Listening: Where are you?

- Ask the students to match the abbreviations and their meanings, and to practise the pronunciation (this is so they will be able to follow the spoken directions).
- Let them look at the map for a minute or so, and make sure that they understand what the *You Are Here* sign means.
- Then play the recording while they try to follow the directions. Ask them to write down the name of the street they are in.
- Play the recording a second time so they can check their answers, and so those who were unsure the first time can have another chance.

Answer to Exercise 2: Boxhill Walk

Tapescript for Exercise 2
Let's see, you go straight on, don't take the first left into Park Road. Take the second left, that's Bath Street. Go on past the side of Abingdon School, and take the first turning on your right. I think it's Letcombe Street, or Avenue, or something. Anyway, go on up past Nuneham Square to the T-junction, and turn left. That's left into Fitzharry's Road. The school is just across the first street you come to, opposite Fitzharry's Road.

3 Listening: Which directions are wrong?

- Ask the students to look at the map again, and to locate Clifton Drive (which is about halfway across the map, and about a third of the way from the top).
- Then tell them that they are going to hear directions starting from the same place as in Exercise 2.
- The students' task is to decide if any of the directions does not lead to Clifton Drive.
- Play the recording, more than once if necessary, pausing between each set of directions.

Answer to Exercise 3: Number 2 is incorrect.

Tapescript for Exercise 3

1. Well, erm, go straight on up Stratton Way, and take the first, no, not the first, the second left. That's Bath Street. Keep straight on to Letcombe Avenue, and turn right, I think that's the first right. Then take the second right, and the first left. It's on the right.

2. Er, what's the best way to tell you? Erm, go on up here, take the first left. Walk along the side of the Abingdon School. Take the first right, Letcombe Avenue, and then the first left. That's Clifton Drive. The house is on the right.

3. Er, let's see, go straight on here up Stratton Way, second left, first right, second right, first left. It's on the right.

4. Erm, do you know where the big supermarket is? No, oh, well, just go on straight up here, don't take Park Road, where the park is, take the second left, that's Bath Street, don't know why it's called Bath Street. Anyway, take the first, yeah, the first right, and the first right again. Then turn left into Stanford Drive, and it's just across Fitzharry's Road. It's on the right.

4 Oral fluency: misleading directions

- Before beginning this exercise, you may want students to look over the section on directions on page 38, to refresh their memories.
- Establish that you will all be giving one another directions to places in the town or city where you are studying.

- Everyone should imagine they are starting from the same central place, facing the same way.
- Each student must decide whether to give correct or misleading directions, and should walk round exchanging directions with as many other students as possible, and noting how many can tell if the directions are correct or misleading.
- At the end they can reveal which directions were misleading.

5 Song: If You Can Keep A Secret

- Ask students to work individually or in small groups, using their dictionaries to understand the words of the song and to decide which words go into the blanks.
- You will want to explain briefly what *can* means, and say that it will be studied later in the course.
- If their bilingual dictionaries do not give a definition for *jive*, you will have to explain that it can be a noun or a verb, meaning '(dance to) a sort of popular music with a strong regular beat'.
- When they have filled as many of the blanks as they can, do not go over the answers with them until you have played the recording so that they can check the answers they do have and try to hear the ones they missed.
- You will probably want to play the recording more than once.

Answers to Exercise 5

1. go	8. place
2. many	9. secret
3. go	10. find
4. feet	11. secret
5. everybody	12. dance
6. know	13. everybody
7. everybody	14. go

Practice Book exercises: choose two or more

1. Sentence stress.
2. Quantifiers: students look at a picture and write an appropriate sentence.
3. Choosing the right article (or no article).
4. Vocabulary: public places.
5. Students write directions to places on the map in the Student's Book.
6. Student's Cassette exercise (Student's Book Speaking and Listening Exercise 3). Students listen, and try to write down the directions in numbers 1 and 3.
7. Reading: Part 7 of *It's a Long Story*.

'Untidy' listening and reading material
At one time, it was considered wrong to give elementary students reading and listening material which had not been very carefully 'graded' by removing unusual words and difficult structures. Clearly such material can be very useful, but it is also important to expose learners to suitable authentic, ungraded material from time to time. This gets them used to the flavour and texture of real-life language, and also provides valuable 'preview' of words and structures which they will be learning later on. When working with this kind of material, encourage students to listen or read for overall meaning or for specific information; they should not worry if they don't understand every single word and structure.

---

1 Choose: a sport, a sort of music, and a newspaper. Try to find somebody else in the class who has chosen the same things. Examples:

'Do you play football?'
'No, I don't. Do you like rock music?'
'Yes, I do. Do you read "Le Monde"?'
'Yes, I do.'

2 Match the abbreviations with their meanings, and practise their pronunciation.

Ave   Street
Dr   Road
Rd   Avenue
Sq   Square
St   Drive

Now look at the map and listen. What is the name of the street you arrive in at the end?

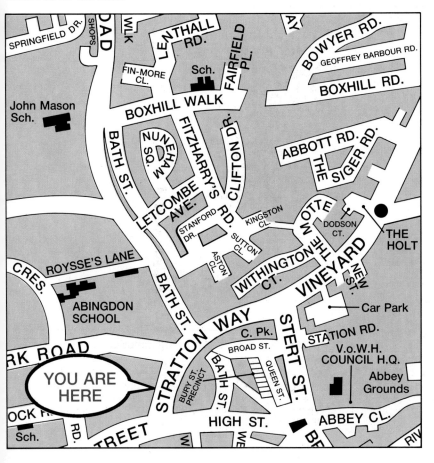

3 🔊 Look at the map again; listen to four people giving directions to 2 Clifton Drive. Are any of them wrong?

4 How many people can you fool? Give correct *or* wrong directions to a place in the town. Look at page 38 if you need help in giving directions.

5 🔊 Put a word or expression from the box into each blank in the song (you can use your dictionary). Then listen to see if you were right.

dance	everybody	feet
find	go go go	know
place	secret	secret
there's a	many	everybody
everybody	want	

IF YOU CAN KEEP A SECRET

There's a club where I ......1...... dancing,
So ......2...... people you can meet.
There's a club where I ......3...... dancing,
I get rhythm in my ......4.......

Oh, ...5...... wants to dance there,
But they don't ......6...... where to go.
Oh, ...7...... wants to jive there,
It's the very best ......8...... I know.

If you can keep a ......9......,
I'll tell tell you where to ......10...... the place.
If you can keep a ......11......,
We're going to ......12...... the night away.

Well, ...13...... wants to dance there . . .
There's a club where I ......14...... dancing . . .

8D Test yourself

LISTENING

1 Dictation: listen and write down the conversation.

GRAMMAR

1 Make questions. Example:

where | you | live?

Where do you live ?

1. you | like | classical music?
2. where | your mother | work?

2 Complete the sentences.

1. My father always .... to work by bus. (*go*)
2. Both my parents .... on Saturdays. (*work*)
3. Have you got .... apples? (*some/any*)

3 Write the object pronouns and possessives. Example:

I *me, my*

you, he, she, we, they

4 Put in the correct words.

1. I live .... 17 Hazel Avenue, Dundee.
2. I live .... the fourth floor.
3. I usually get up .... six o'clock.
4. How .... people are there in your class?
5. How .... money have you got?
6. John and .... wife live in the next house to Marianne and .... husband.

5 Give the plurals. Example:

cat *cats*

man, woman, child, boy, secretary, person, name, address, wife, house

6 Give the *he/she/it* forms. Example:

get *gets*

play, live, try, watch, do

7 Put in *a, an, the, some* or – (= no article).

1. There's .... orange on the table.
2. There's .... cheese in the fridge.
3. My sister's .... student.
4. What time do you have .... lunch?
5. .... food is expensive.
6. Where's .... nearest post office, please?

VOCABULARY

1 Put four more words in each of these lists.

1. father, brother, . . .
2. Monday, . . .
3. first, second, . . .

2 Write the names of:

1. two big things
2. two small things
3. two cheap things
4. two expensive things

LANGUAGE IN USE

1 Write questions for these answers. Example:

Jean Sheppard. *What's your name ?*

1. Japan.
2. I'm 35.
3. 42 Feynman Road.
4. Twenty past seven.
5. First on the right, then second on the left.
6. About a hundred metres.
7. Seven six two, four three eight five.
8. I'm sorry, I don't know.

PRONUNCIATION

1 Which sound is different? Example:

like   by   ninth   (live)

1. door   floor   start   small
2. bread   reads   pence   very
3. work   third   person   hair

2 Which syllable is stressed? Example:

breakfast

opposite, Saturday, sometimes, newspaper, understand

42

Unit 8: Lesson D

Students do a simple revision test.

The purpose of the test

This test, like the others in the book, is provided for teachers who feel that it will be useful. It covers several different areas: it is not of course necessary to do all of the sections, and teachers should select according to their students' needs. Teachers who do not feel the test will be useful should simply drop it altogether.

The test has three main functions:
1. To show you and the students whether there are any points that have not been properly learnt for any reason.
2. To identify any students who are having serious difficulty with the course, if this is not already evident.
3. To motivate the students to look back over the work they have done and do some serious revision before they move on.

If possible, try to make the students feel that they are 'testing themselves', rather than 'being tested'. It is not intended that students should 'pass' or 'fail' the test, and it is not particularly useful to give marks. (If the school or education system requires that this be done, you will need to work out a simple marking scheme.) But students should of course be told whether you feel their performance is satisfactory. In principle, most students ought to get most answers right. If this does not happen, efficient learning is not taking place (because of poor motivation, too rapid a pace, absenteeism, failure to do Practice Book work or follow-up study outside class, or for some other reason).

Administration

The test can be administered in various ways, depending on how strictly you want to control students' performance; whether you want to collect the answers and mark them, or allow the students to correct them in class; and so on.

If you use the recording for the dictation test in the 'listening' section, you will need to pause the recorder to give students time to write.

The 'speaking' tests will need to be done individually, with students interrupting their work on the other tests to come and talk to you one at a time. You may wish to photocopy the interview form so that students don't have to copy it by hand.

If you are not collecting students' scripts, correction can be done by class discussion when everybody has finished.

Notes, tapescript and answers are given below.

LISTENING

1 **The text for the dictation test is as follows. You will probably want to play the recording twice.**

'Excuse me. Where's the nearest post office, please?'
'First on the right, then second on the left. Then straight on for about a hundred metres, and it's on your right.'
'Thanks very much.'
'Not at all.'

GRAMMAR

1 1. Do you like classical music?
   2. Where does your mother work?

2 1. goes
   2. work
   3. any

3 you, your; him, his; her, her; us, our; them, their.

4 1. at
   2. on
   3. at
   4. many
   5. much
   6. his, her

5 men, women, children, boys, secretaries, people, names, addresses, wives, houses

6 plays, lives, tries, watches, does

7 1. an
   2. some
   3. a
   4. –
   5. –
   6. the

VOCABULARY

1 (Various possible answers.)

2 (Various possible answers.)

LANGUAGE IN USE

1 (Alternatives may be possible in some cases.)
   1. Where are you from?
   2. How old are you?
   3. What's your address? / Where do you live?
   4. What time is it?
   5. (Various possible answers.)
   6. Is it far? / How far is it?
   7. What's your (tele)phone number?
   8. (Various possible answers.)

PRONUNCIATION

1 1. start
   2. reads
   3. hair

2 opposite, Saturday, sometimes, newspaper, understand

WRITING

You may need to explain *penfriend*. Students should provide most of the information asked for in reasonably correct English, but don't look for perfection at this stage. (A real penfriend wouldn't.)

SPEAKING

In the first part of the test, students should produce reasonably correct questions in order to obtain the specified information. Many of the questions can be put in more than one way (e.g. *What's your address? / Where do you live?*). It is up to you to decide whether the students' production is sufficiently correct and fluent.

In the second section, you should ask the students simple questions at normal speed, and check whether they are able to answer with reasonable fluency and correctness. Some suggestions are given below, but you may wish to add to or change the list.

What time is it?
How old are you?
Have you got any brothers or sisters?
What sort of music do you like?
What newspaper do you read?
How many rooms are there in your house?
Where's the nearest post office / bus stop / etc.?
Spell your name and address.

Test Book recordings
A recording for Test 2 in the Test Book follows this lesson on the Class Cassette.

WRITING

1 Read the advertisement and write a short letter
to Anna Schultz. Tell her:
– your name, nationality and age
– what you do
– where you are from
– about your home and family
– about your interests.
Begin:

Dear Anna Schultz,
I am ...

SPEAKING

1 Interview the teacher. Ask him/her questions and
fill in the form.

UNIVERSAL IMPORT/EXPORT

PERSONAL DETAILS

Name ....

Address ....

....

Telephone ....

Age ....

Married/Single/Divorced/Widowed ....

Children ....

Languages ....

House/Flat ....

Floor ....

How many bedrooms ....

How many people ....

2 Answer the teacher's questions.

Unit 9 Appearances

9A Sheila has got long dark hair

Have got; describing people.

1   Read the sentences in the box and complete the descriptions. Use your dictionary. Which name goes with which picture?

Sheila has got long dark hair.	Mary has not got grey hair.
Lucy has got short hair.	Sheila has not got blue eyes.
Mary has got green eyes.	Lucy has not got brown eyes or fair hair.

Sheila has got .... hair and .... eyes.
Mary .... got .... hair and ....
Lucy .... and ....

2   Copy and complete the table.

I .... got
You have ....
He/She/It ....
We ....
They ....

3   Ask the teacher questions.

What's this ?
It's your mouth.
What are these ?
Ears.

4   Do what the teacher tells you. Then test other students. Do they know these words?

arm   ears   eyes   face   foot   hair   hand
left   leg   mouth   nose   right

Touch your right eye.
Touch your left ear.

5   Talk about yourself and other people. Example:

'I've got small hands. My mother's got pretty hair.'

Can you remember what other students said?
Example:

'Maria's got brown eyes. Her father's got small ears.'

6   Write three sentences with *and*, and three with *but*. Ask the teacher for words. Examples:

I have got blue eyes, and my mother has, too. I have got straight hair, but Chris has got curly hair.

Learn: eye; nose; ear; mouth; face; arm; hand; foot (feet); leg; long; short; brown; green; blue; grey; these; What's this?; What are these?

Unit 9: Lesson A

Students learn to describe people's physical appearances.
Structures: more work on *have got* (affirmative).

Language notes and possible problems

1. *Have got* Note that the forms of *have* are not the same in British and American English. In British English, the *have-got* forms are generally used in speech to talk about possession and related ideas, especially in the present tense; forms without *got* can sound very unnatural. In American English, forms without *got* are much more common in this context.

Some students may get worried about the meaning of *got* and try to find it in their dictionaries. Help them to understand that *got* means nothing here, and that *have got* simply means the same as 'have'.

2. *Hair* Remind students that *hair* is uncountable (and has a singular verb). You may need to teach *red hair*; if so, try to make it clear that this is a special use of *red* (the normal use is taught in Lesson 9B).

3. Adjectives with nouns Some students may be inclined to put adjectives after nouns. Look out for mistakes like **eyes green, *hair dark long*.

4. *And* with adjectives Students have learnt to join adjectives with *and* (e.g. *She is tall and fair*). Here they will learn that adjectives are not usually joined with *and* before a noun (e.g. *long dark hair*).

5. Vocabulary Students will probably want to ask for a lot of words referring to parts of the body and physical description. Use your discretion about how long to spend on Exercise 3: this lesson has a heavy vocabulary load, and there's no value in students noting large numbers of extra words that they won't have time to learn.

1 Presentation

• Give students a few minutes to look at the pictures and solve the problem, working individually at first and then comparing notes. Explain the new vocabulary or (preferably) let them use their dictionaries.
• Go over the answers (see below). Practise the pronunciation of the new words, especially *eyes*; pay attention to the unstressed weak forms of *has* (/(h)əz/) and *and* (/ənd/).
• Point out that adjectives before a noun are not usually joined with *and*.

Answers to Exercise 1
Sheila (No 3) has got long dark hair and brown eyes.
Mary (No 1) has got long fair hair and green eyes.
Lucy (No 2) has got short grey hair and blue eyes.

2 *Have got*: revision of forms

• This will give you a chance to check briefly that all students are clear about the present tense forms of *have got*.
• Ask students, working individually, to complete the phrases.

3 Student-directed vocabulary learning

• This exercise gives students a chance to learn words of their choice.
• Practise the questions *What's this?* and *What are these?* (/ˈwɒt ə ˈðiːz/).
• Let students ask you questions.
• Put the new words on the board and practise their pronunciation.
• When *tooth* and *foot* come up, make sure students understand that they have irregular plurals.

• Don't let the exercise go on too long. When you decide to finish, give students a minute or two to look over the new words and consolidate them.

4 Testing each other on vocabulary

• Start by testing the students yourself.
• Practise the pronunciation of *touch* and let the students continue in groups.

Alternative to Exercise 4: 'Simon says'
• This is a (rather childish) game which can make the practice more amusing.
• Give commands as in Exercise 4, but put the words 'Simon says' before some of them. (For example: *Simon says touch your nose.*)
• Students must only do what 'Simon says'. If they hear a command without these words, they should do nothing.
• Give the commands more and more quickly.

5 Spoken descriptions

• Revise the contracted forms *I've got* etc. If possible, make sure students understand that contracted forms are less formal than non-contracted forms, and therefore common in conversation.
• Ask students for descriptions of themselves and other people. Get examples from everybody.

6 Written descriptions

• Go over the examples. Make sure students understand the structure of the first one, with *has* used elliptically for *has got blue eyes*. Explain *straight* and *curly* if these have not already come up.
• Go round looking at students' sentences, and get some of them read aloud. Encourage students to pronounce the weak forms of *and* (/ənd/) and *but* (/bət/) correctly.

Practice Book exercises: choose two or more
1. Revision of the forms of *have got*.
2. The use or omission of *and* between adjectives.
3. Revision of interrogators *what, where, who* and *how*.
4. Revision of 'short answers'.
5. Pronunciation of *-(e)s* endings.
6. Some simple authentic reading material.

Unit 9: Lesson B

Students learn to talk about clothing and colours.
Structures: preview of Present Progressive tense.

Language notes and possible problems

1. The Present Progressive tense is previewed here, but will not be studied in detail until Unit 15. You may want to give a short explanation, telling students that we say something *is happening* to talk about a present action, rather than a habitual or repeated one.

2. Vocabulary problems Students may take a little time to grasp that *trousers, jeans, tights* and *pants* are plural.

Note: we don't say somebody *is wearing* a beard.

3. Colours Unlike most other adjectives, colour-words are joined with *and* before nouns (*a red and white dress*). They come after most other adjectives (*a long red dress*).

Purple may be a 'false friend': in many European languages there is a similar-looking word which refers to a kind of dark red; *purple* is close to violet.

4. Vocabulary load A lot of new words are introduced in this lesson. Don't insist on students learning more than they can easily manage.

Optional extra materials

Pictures of clothes cut from magazines (Exercise 2).

1 Colours

- Look at the colours and practise the pronunciation of the words.
- Demonstrate the meanings of *this* and *that*; then get students to find examples of coloured things, at first for the whole class and then in pairs.
- Walk round while they are working to make sure they are using *this* and *that* correctly.

2 Descriptions

- Go over the names of the articles of clothing with the students.
- Look at the sample sentence and practise the pronunciation of *Pat is wearing*.
- Ask students to say what Keith and Annie are wearing.
- Ask them to write down what Robert is wearing.
- Let them compare notes and check the answers.
- Use pictures from magazines for more practice.

3 Student-directed vocabulary learning

- Practise the questions and then let students ask you for words, spellings and pronunciations.
- If you think it will be too difficult for your students to learn '*What's this called?*' and '*What are these called?*', just get them to say '*What's this?*' / '*What are these?*'
- Don't let this go on too long: if students get overloaded with new words they will get discouraged.

4 Answering questions

- The questions follow each other quickly, and the recording will not wait for a slow answer; so students must think fast in order to keep up.
- The *yes/no* questions can be answered by everybody simultaneously, or by individuals.
- You may like to play through the recording two or three times until students can answer fluently.

5 Memory test

- This can be done in various ways.
1. A student comes to the front. The others observe him/her. He/she goes to the back and the others try to remember what he/she is wearing.
2. A student comes to the front and observes the class for a minute or two. He/she closes his/her eyes and somebody asks '*What am I wearing?*' The student tries to give an accurate description.
3. Students stand in pairs observing each other for one minute. They then close their eyes, or stand back to back, and each says what the other is wearing.

6 Eight questions

- Demonstrate yourself first of all with a volunteer.
- Make sure that the person who answers starts by saying '*It's a man/woman/boy/girl*'; otherwise the questioner doesn't know whether to say *he* or *she*.
- This can also be done in small groups.

Optional activity: observation game

- Two teams of five to eight students stand facing each other about ten feet apart. (In big classes, you will have more than one pair of teams.)
- The students have three minutes to observe the opposite team without speaking. Each student must try to memorise the appearance of all the people opposite – clothes, appearance and position.
- Separate the teams. If possible, put one team outside the classroom or in another room. One person in each team acts as secretary; with everybody's help, he or she writes down everything the team can remember.
- Tell each team to change their appearance as much as possible, exchanging glasses, jewellery, etc.
- Tell teams to come back and stand opposite each other again, but to line up *in a different order*.
- Students now speak in turn. Each student tries to get one thing put right. They might say, for instance:
  '*Juan, go and stand next to Fritz.*'
  '*Yasuko, that's Rosita's watch.*'
  '*Brigitte, you've got Olga's shoes on.*'
Put a few examples on the board (using these structures) to help students make their sentences.
- If possible, students should get the opposite team back in the original order, dressed as before.

(Game taken from *Drama Techniques in Language Learning* by Alan Maley and Alan Duff, Cambridge University Press, 1982.)

Practice Book exercises: choose two or more

1. Colour words.
2. Labelling magazine pictures of clothing.
3. Revision of *be* and *have got*.
4. Re-ordering jumbled sentences.
5. Revision of subject and object pronouns and possessives (with preview of *us*).
6. Student's Cassette exercise (Student's Book Exercise 4, first 7 questions). Students try to write down the questions.
7. Authentic reading: contact ads.

9B A red sweater and blue jeans

Clothes and colours; Present Progressive tense; asking about language.

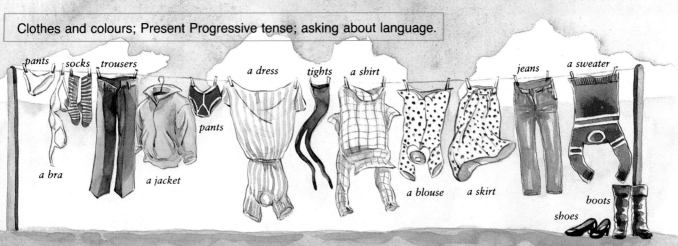

Red

Orange

Pink

Yellow

Green

Blue

Purple

Brown

Light Green

Dark Green

Light Blue

Dark Blue

Black

White

1 Can you find something red in the classroom? Something blue? Something orange? . . . Examples:

'This is red.' 'That's blue.'
'These are orange.' 'My book is red.'

2 Look at the pictures.

Pat is wearing a white sweater, a green blouse, and a red and black skirt.

Make some more sentences about Keith, Annie and Robert.

'Keith is wearing . . .'

Pat   Keith   Annie   Robert

3 Ask the teacher questions.

'What's this called in English?'
'What are these called?'
'How do you say boucles d'oreille in English?' 'Ear-rings.'
'How do you say rosa?' 'Pink.'
'How do you pronounce b-l-o-u-s-e?'

4 Listen to the recording and answer the questions.

'Are you wearing a sweater?' 'Yes, I am.'
'Who's wearing brown shoes?' 'I am.'

5 Look at another student. Then close your eyes and describe him/her. Example:

'Carlos is wearing blue jeans and a black shirt. I can't remember the colour of his shoes.'

6 Work with another student. One of you thinks of another person in the class. The other tries to find out who it is, in eight questions beginning *'Is he/she wearing . . . ?'* Example:

'It's a man.'
'Is he wearing jeans?' 'No, he isn't.'
'Is he wearing glasses?' 'Yes, he is.'

I am wearing	we are wearing
you are wearing	you are wearing
he/she is wearing	they are wearing

| are you wearing? |
| is he/she wearing? *etc.* |

Learn: *the names of the colours*; light; dark; colour; wear; something; that (= not this); (I can't) remember; What's this called?; What are these called?; How do you say . . . ?; How do you pronounce . . . ?

Learn four or more: pants; bra; sock; jeans; jacket; dress; tights; shirt; blouse; skirt; trousers; sweater; boot; shoe; glasses; bow tie; ear-rings.

45

9C I look like my father

Simple Present questions, negatives; resemblances; *all* and *both*; skills practice.

1	2	3	4	5	6	7	8

1 Listen to the recording. Who is speaking? Read the text and put the names with the pictures.

Alice	Ann	Joe	Philip	Alice's father	Alice's mother
Uncle George and family		Uncle Edward			

My name's Alice. I've got a sister (her name's Ann), and two brothers, Joe and Philip. We've all got fair hair and blue eyes, and we're all slim except Joe – he's very fat. Ann's very pretty, and she's got lots of boyfriends. I've only got one boyfriend: his name's Kevin, and he's very nice.

I look a bit like my father – I've got his long nose and big mouth – but I've got my mother's personality. Joe and Phil both look more like Mum.

We've got two uncles and an aunt. Uncle George and Aunt Agnes have got three young children. Uncle Edward is only thirteen, so he hasn't got any children, but he's got a rabbit.

2 What are your family like? Who looks like who? Examples:

'In my family we're all tall, and we all wear glasses.'
'Carlos and I have both got dark hair.'
'I look a bit like my father.'
'My brother looks very like me.'
'Ana looks quite like Aunt Maria.'
'I've got my mother's eyes, but I've got my father's personality.'

3 🔲 Listening for information. Copy the table. Then listen to the recording and fill in the table.

	HEIGHT	HAIR COLOUR	FACE	EYES	GOOD-LOOKING?
Steve's wife	5 ft 8				don't know
Lorna's mum			pale		
Ruth's friend					
Katy's son					
Sue's husband					

4 Prepare questions and answers for an interview. Examples:

How many people are there in your family?

Have you got any . . . ?   Yes, I have. / No, I haven't.
How many . . . have you got?
Has your . . . got any . . . ?   Yes, she has. / No, he hasn't.
How many . . . has your . . . got?

Do you look like . . . ?   Yes, I do. / No, I don't.
Who do you look like?
Does . . . look like . . . ?   Yes, he does. / No, she doesn't.

What colour is/are your . . .'s . . . ?
How old is . . . ?
Is . . . good-looking?   Yes, she is. / No, he isn't.

5 Interview another student and report to the class. Example:

'Carlos has got three brothers. They all look like their mother, but they've got their father's personality. His brother Diego has got four children . . .'

> **Learn:** uncle; aunt; look like; like; all; nice; except; a bit; more; lots of; What colour is/are . . . ?

Unit 9: Lesson C

Students learn to talk about resemblances between people.
Structures: revision of *have got* (questions and short answers); Simple Present of *look like* (affirmatives, questions, negatives and short answers); position of *both* and *all*; *What colour is/are . . . ?*
Phonology: practice in linking words together.

Language notes and possible problems

1. *Both* **and** *all* (Exercise 2)   The exact rules for the placing of these two words (which come in the same position as mid-verb adverbs) are quite complicated. For the purposes of this lesson, it is enough to get students to put them after *are* and *have*, and before other verbs such as *look*.

2. Timing   This is a long lesson. Exercise 3 can be dropped if time is short.

1 Listening and identifying

- Ask students to cover the text and look at the picture for a minute or so.
- Tell the students they are going to hear one of the people in the picture speaking; they must try to decide which one.
- Play the recording once without stopping. See if the students can tell you which person is Alice.
- Play it again once or twice, and see if they can identify some of the other people, using the names in the box.
- Let students look at the text and finish working out the solution.
- Discuss the answers with them. Go over the text and explain any difficulties.
- Put the negative forms of *have got* on the board:
  I have not (haven't) got
  you have not (haven't) got
  he/she/it has not (hasn't) got
  we have not (haven't) got
  you have not (haven't) got
  they have not (haven't) got
- Practise the pronunciation of *haven't* and *hasn't*.

Answers to Exercise 1
1. Alice's mother   2. Joe   3. Uncle Edward   4. Ann
5. Alice   6. Philip   7. Alice's father   8. Uncle George and family

2 Personalisation: *both* and *all*

- Practise the example sentences.
- Ask students to write one or two similar sentences, and to talk about resemblances in their families, or between people they know.
- Encourage them to use *both* and *all* in some of their sentences, as well as the modifiers *very*, *quite*, *a bit*. Pay attention to linking in expressions like *we're all*, *we all*, *brothers are*, *sister and I*.
- If they are interested in the subject, they can go on to talk about resemblances between people in the class.

- You can also talk about what types people fall into (e.g. *Alfonso looks like a teacher*).

3 Listening for specific information

- Tell students that they are going to hear a recording in which five people describe other people that they know well. There is some background noise, but the recording is reasonably clear. Students will not understand every word, but they should be able to pick out most of the necessary information.
- Get them to copy the table from the book; make sure they understand all the words.
- Preteach *thin* and *round*, which they will need for the 'faces' column.
- Explain that all the heights except one are given in feet and inches: *five foot eight* or *five feet eight* means 'five feet eight inches'. (An inch is about 2½cm; a foot is about 30cm.)
- Play the recording right through once.
- Then play it again, stopping after each description so that students can fill in their tables.
- Play it a third time if necessary.
- Let students compare notes; then go over the answers with them.
- Students may ask you to go over the text in detail explaining every word. It is probably better not to do this; it is not the purpose of the exercise, and would almost certainly be an inefficient use of your time.
- For your own reference, the tapescript is on page 140.

Answers to Exercise 3: see below

4 Preparing for an interview

- This is a good moment to revise question forms and short answers.
- Go over the questions in the examples, making sure students know the words and structures.
- Students will need practice on *How many people are there in your family?* (They are likely to use *How many are you . . . ?* instead – this is less natural in standard English.)
- Tell students to prepare several questions to ask other students.

5 Interview and reporting

- Get students to work in pairs, asking their questions in turn and noting the answers.
- Then get some or all of the students to report to the class.

Practice Book exercises: choose two or more
1. Writing contracted forms.
2. Writing questions with *have/has got*.
3. Writing negative sentences with *have/has got*.
4. Writing about resemblances with *look like*.
5. Student's Cassette exercise (Student's Book Exercise 3, first two speakers). Students listen to the recording and try to write down five or more words.
6. Guided composition: writing descriptions.

Answers to Exercise 3

	HEIGHT	HAIR COLOUR	FACE	EYES	GOOD-LOOKING?
Steve's wife	5ft 8	*fair*	*thin*	*don't know*	don't know
Lorna's mum	*5ft 5*	*dark brown*	pale	*dark brown*	*fairly pretty*
Ruth's friend	*5ft 10/11*	*dark brown*	nice	*blue*	yes
Katy's son	*105cm*	*fair*	*don't know*	*blue*	*yes (very)*
Sue's husband	*5ft 8*	*fair/white*	*round*	*blue*	*don't know*

Unit 9: Lesson D

Students learn letter-writing conventions; they practise listening and speaking. They consolidate the language of personal descriptions and greeting.
Structures: preview of various structures, including Present Progressive referring to future; *will*; *can*; Simple Past question forms (*Did you have . . . ?*).
Phonology: rising intonation to signal questions; high pitch for emphasis.

Language notes and possible problems
Previewed structures   Several new structures are previewed here (see list above). It is probably best to leave them at a 'phrase-book' level for the moment. That is to say, get students to treat *Did you have a good journey?*, *Can you meet me?* etc. as fixed formulae, without giving more grammatical explanations than necessary.

1 Presentation: reading the letter
• Give students a few minutes to read the letter, using dictionaries or not, as you think best.
• When they think they have found the two differences, let them compare notes.
• Check that they have the right answers. (In the picture, Paul Sanders has a *big* beard and a *light* blue sweater; in the letter, he has a *small* beard and a *dark* blue sweater.)
• Go over the letter clearing up any difficulties, but don't spend too much time on the 'previewed' grammar points (see *Language notes*). These will be dealt with in detail later in the course. When you explain *a.m.*, teach *p.m.* at the same time.
• Pay special attention to the fixed phrases and layout conventions typical of English letters. Make sure students learn where to put the address, date and salutation, and how to open and close letters to strangers.

2 Listening: choosing the correct recording
• Get students to read the conversations, and clear up any problems.
• Tell them to close their books.
• Play the recording, and see if the students can pick out the version which is exactly the same as the one in their books. (It is 'Version 2'.)
• Play the recording again and let students follow with their books open.

Tapescript for Exercise 2

VERSION 1
'Paul Sanders?'
'Yes. Hello. Mr Bell?'
'Yes, I'm John Bell. How was your journey?'
'Fine, thanks.'
'Oh, good. Well, my car's outside. Let's go . . . '

VERSION 2
'Hello, Mr Sanders. I'm John Bell. Did you have a good journey?'
'Not bad, thanks. But I'm not Mr Sanders.'
'Oh, I am sorry.'

'Paul Sanders?'
'Sorry.'

'Paul Sanders?'
'Yes. Hello. Mr Bell?'
'Yes, I'm John Bell. How was your journey?'
'Terrible.'
'Oh, I am sorry. Well, my car's outside. Let's go . . . '

VERSION 3
'Hello, Mr Sanders, I'm John Bell. How was your journey?'
'Fine, thanks. But I'm not Mr Sanders.'
'Oh, I am sorry.'

'Mr Sanders?'
'Sorry.'

'Paul Sanders?'
'Yes. Hello. Mr Bell?'
'Yes, I'm John Bell. How was your journey?'
'Not bad. Not bad at all.'
'Fine. Well, my car's outside. Let's go . . . '

3 Intonation practice
• Practise the examples of rising intonation and emphatic intonation. Use the recording of 'Version 2' of the conversations as a model if you wish.
• Then get students to practise all three versions of the conversations several times in groups of four, taking the different parts in turn.

4 Writing letters
• Give students fifteen minutes or so to write their letters. Go round helping as required.
• Make sure they describe themselves as they are now, at the time of writing.
• They must put false names, not their real names.
• Don't let them show each other their letters.

5 Role play: meeting people
• When students are ready, collect the letters from one half of the class.
• Shuffle the letters, and give them out to the other half of the class.
• Give students a minute or two to read the letters they have received.
• Then get everybody to stand up, and tell them they are at the station or airport.
• People who have received letters should try to find the people who wrote them.
• The resulting conversations should be similar to the ones practised in Exercises 2 and 3.
• When everybody has found the people they are supposed to be meeting, get them to sit down again.
• Collect the letters that were written by the other half of the class, and do the same thing again.

Practice Book exercises: choose two or more
1. Simple Present questions.
2. Simple Present questions.
3. Completing a dialogue.
4. Word stress.
5. Check on revision vocabulary.
6. Translation of material from the unit.
7. Student's Cassette exercise (Student's Book Exercise 2, second conversation). Pronunciation practice. Tell students to try to predict the intonation of the sentences in the Practice Book before listening to them.
8. Reading: Part 8 of *It's a Long Story*.

Preview
In 'real-life' language learning, people often come across a word or structure a number of times before they fully understand it and are ready to use it. This is why the course often exposes students to language which is a little above their present level. Many of the exercise instructions in the Student's Book and Practice Book are deliberately phrased so as to give students preview of language that they will learn later.

47

9D Dear Mr Bell . . .

1 Read the letter and look at the picture of Paul Sanders. Can you find two differences?

Flat 6
Monument House
Castle Street
Newcastle NE1 2HH

September 12, 1990

Dear Mr Bell,

I am coming to Edinburgh by train next Tuesday, arriving at Waverley Station at 11.40 a.m. Can you meet me?

I am sorry that I have not got a photograph, but here is a description. I am 32, quite short, with dark hair and a small beard. I have got blue eyes. I will be wearing a white shirt, a dark blue sweater and light grey trousers.

I look forward to seeing you.

Yours sincerely,
Paul Sanders.

Mr J.C.Bell
366 Ulster Drive
Edinburgh EH8 7BJ

2 🔊 Read the conversations and then listen to the three recordings with your books closed. Which is the correct recording?

'Hello, Mr Sanders. I'm John Bell. Did you have a good journey?'
'Not bad, thanks. But I'm not Mr Sanders.'
'Oh, I am sorry.'

'Paul Sanders?'
'Sorry.'

'Paul Sanders?'
'Yes. Hello. Mr Bell?'
'Yes, I'm John Bell. How was your journey?'
'Terrible.'
'Oh, I am sorry. Well, my car's outside. Let's go . . . '

3 Practise these sentences.

Paul Sanders?
Mr Bell?
Oh, I am sorry.

Now practise the conversations in groups of four.

4 You are going on a holiday or a business trip. Write a letter to a person you don't know, asking him/her to meet you at the station or airport, and giving a description of yourself. Sign the letter with a false name. Give your letter to the teacher.

5 The teacher will give you a letter. Read it, then go and meet the person who wrote it.

Learn: letter; train; station; journey; look (at); arrive (at); meet; next; short; bad; with; a.m.; p.m.; Dear . . . ; Yours sincerely; Let's go.

Unit 10 Wanting things

10A I'm hungry

1 Put the adjectives with the right pictures. Use your dictionary.

hungry   tired   ill   happy   cold   dirty   bored   unhappy   thirsty   hot

1. She is .... 2. He is .... 3. She is .... 4. He is .... 5. She is ....

    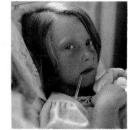

6. He is .... 7. She is .... 8. He is .... 9. She is .... 10. She is ....

2 Say how you feel now. Examples:

'I'm very hungry.'
'I'm quite tired.'
'I'm a bit cold.'
'I'm not very happy.'
'I'm not at all thirsty.'

3 Mime one of the adjectives for the class.

You're unhappy.

4 Say these words and expressions.

hungry   happy   unhappy
house   home   at home
hotel   Hilton Hotel   holiday
on holiday   hair   have   half
hundred   a hundred   him
her

5 Have you got a good memory? Look at the sentences for two minutes. Then close your book and answer the teacher's questions.

When Fred's hungry he goes to a restaurant.
When Lucy's hungry she has bread and cheese.
When Fred's thirsty he has a beer.
When Lucy's thirsty she has a drink of water.
When Fred's bored he goes to the cinema.
When Lucy's bored she goes to see friends.
When Fred's hot he goes to the swimming pool.
When Lucy's hot she has a drink of water.
When Fred's dirty he has a bath.
When Lucy's dirty she has a shower.
When Fred's happy he goes shopping.
When Lucy's happy she telephones all her friends.
When Fred's unhappy he goes to bed.
When Lucy's unhappy she goes shopping.
When Fred's ill he goes to the doctor.
When Lucy's ill she goes to bed.

6 What do you do when you're happy, unhappy, tired, bored, etc.?

7 You're in one of these places. Do a mime; the class will say where you are.

at a swimming pool   at a disco   at a restaurant
in bed   in the bathroom   at a car park
at the doctor's   at the dentist's   at a supermarket
at a clothes shop   at home   at school
at a bus stop   at a station   at a hotel

Learn: water; hungry; thirsty; hot; cold; happy; unhappy; bored; tired; ill; dirty; not at all (*with adjectives*); when (*conjunction*); (have a) bath; (have a) shower; go shopping.

Learn some of these if you want: restaurant; hotel; cinema.

48

Unit 10: Lesson A

Students learn to talk about some physical and emotional states.
Structures: *be* with adjectives like *hungry*, *cold*; *at* with places; *when*-clauses.
Phonology: /h/; strong form of *have*; voiced *s* in verb endings.

Language notes and possible problems

1. *Hungry, cold* etc. For some students it may be surprising that the verb *be* is used to express these ideas. Look out for mistakes like *I have cold*.

2. *To, at* and *in* (Exercises 5 and 7) It may be necessary to explain the difference between *to* (movement) and *at* or *in* (position). (Note that students have already come across *arrive at*, which is an apparent exception.)

The difference between *at* and *in* is not easy to explain in simple terms. Get students to note which preposition is used in which expression. Note that *at* is pronounced /ət/ unless stressed.

3. *Have* So far, students have mainly practised the 'static' use of *have* (*got*) (meaning 'possess', 'be related to', and similar ideas). In Exercise 5, there are a number of examples of the 'dynamic' use of *have* (meaning 'consume', 'experience' etc.). You will need to remind students that *have*, in this sense, is used without *got* and has no weak pronunciation.

4. 'Voiced' final *s* Exercise 5 gives an opportunity to focus on the 'voiced' pronunciation of third-person *-s* after a vowel or voiced consonant, if this is important for your students. The words involved are *goes* (/gəʊz/), *has* (/hæz/) and *telephones* (/'telɪfəʊnz/). Note that this *-s* is not really very 'voiced', especially in *goes to*, where it is followed by an unvoiced sound. It is distinguished from 'unvoiced' *-s* (as in *stops*) mainly by being lighter, and by the fact that vowels are longer before 'voiced' endings.

5. Mime Mime can be a useful stimulus for speech. However, students may need time to get used to it. In very shy or self-conscious classes, Exercises 3 and 7 may not work as suggested, and you may need to do all the miming yourself. If you don't feel able to do this, just teach the vocabulary and move on.

1 Matching

• False beginners can try this exercise in groups without dictionaries, pooling their knowledge.
• With real beginners who don't know any of the words, you will need to teach them the words or let them use their dictionaries.
• Get students to write out or say the ten sentences, not just the adjectives.
• Practise the pronunciation of the adjectives. Pay special attention to the /h/ in *hungry*, *happy* and *unhappy* if this is a problem for your students.

2 Personalisation

• Get students to tell you how they feel – and tell them how you feel.
• If you want more practice, ask questions and elicit short answers ('*Are you hungry?*' '*No, I'm not.*').

3 Miming adjectives

• Start by miming one of the adjectives yourself and getting students to say, for instance, '*You're cold.*'
• Ask for volunteers to mime one or two of the other adjectives.

4 Pronunciation: /h/

• This exercise is obviously only necessary for students who have difficulty pronouncing /h/ correctly.

5 Memory game

• Besides giving further practice in the adjectives that have just been taught, this exercise introduces *when*-clauses, as well as examples of the 'dynamic' use of *have* (see *Language notes*).
• Ask students to look over the sentences for just two minutes (time them carefully), and then tell them to close their books.
• Ask them to write (or tell you) the answers to the following questions.
– What does Lucy do when she's thirsty?
– What does Fred do when he's unhappy?
– What does Fred do when he's hot?
– What does Lucy do when she's bored?
– What does Fred do when he's hungry?
– What does Lucy do when she's hungry?
– What does Lucy do when she's unhappy?
– What does Lucy do when she's happy?
– What does Fred do when he's bored?
– What does Lucy do when she's hot?
– What does Fred do when he's ill?
• Point out the irregular spelling of *goes*. You may want to practise the pronunciation of *go* and of 'voiced' third-person *-s* (see *Language notes*), and/or to comment on the use of *have* in *have a drink*, *have a bath* etc. (see *Language notes*).

6 Personalisation

• Ask students to volunteer answers. Follow up by getting everybody to write one or two sentences.

Optional exercise

• Get two volunteers to tell the class in turn what they do when they are hungry, tired etc., using similar structures to those in Exercise 5. They should produce about ten sentences each.
• The class should try to remember what each one does, as in Exercise 5.

7 Mime (places)

• This can be done in groups. Each group chooses a phrase and mimes it collectively; the rest of the class try to say where the group is.
• Encourage correct stress and rhythm (e.g. *at a cinema* /ət ə 'sɪnəmə/).

Practice Book exercises: choose two or more

1. Vocabulary from the lesson; discriminating *be* and *have*.
2. Vocabulary from the lesson; combining clauses with *when*.
3. Stress and rhythm.
4. Vocabulary from the lesson; *at/in* + place.
5. Crossword.

Unit 10: Lesson B

Students learn to buy clothing and shoes.
Structures: *a . . . one*; preview of *can*.

Language notes and possible problems
1. *Suit* and *fit*   Students may confuse these: some languages use the same word for both ideas.
2. *Can* is previewed here (in *Can I help you?* and *Can I try them on?*). These can just be learnt as fixed phrases at this stage.

Optional extra materials
Copies of the lists given in the instructions for the optional activity after Exercise 3, cut into strips – enough so that each student can have at least one strip.

1 Presentation: matching
• Ask students to match the first two sentences to the numbered speech balloons in the first cartoon strip.
• Check that everyone has understood and done the task correctly.
• Then ask them to do the second strip.
• Students can compare notes before you check the correct order with them (1e, 2c, 3b, 5a, 6d, 7g, 8j, 9h, 10f, 11i; or . . . 7g, 8f, 9i, 10j, 11h).
• Write the dialogue on the board as the students give you the correct order.
• Do the third dialogue in the same way as the second. (Correct order: 1a, 2d, 3c, 4e, 5b.)

2 Consolidation and practice
• Work on each dialogue as follows:
• Play the dialogue once while the students look at the strip.
• Allow students to ask questions (*'What does . . . mean?'*) or give them practice in using their dictionaries to look up words and expressions.
• Then wipe the dialogue off the board, ask students to close their books, and get them to recall any words or expressions they can.
• With their help, reconstruct the dialogue on the board, playing the recording again if necessary.
• Get the students to practise the customer's part in the dialogue, using the recording as a model if you wish.
• Don't erase the second dialogue once you have got it back on the board; you will need it for Exercise 3.

3 Extension
• You have already written the second dialogue on the board.
• Now erase the word *sweater* and ask students to suggest other words that might go there e.g. *trousers*, *skirt* etc. Do the same with *fourteen*, *yellow*, *blue*.
• Get the students to pair off and make up their own dialogues to practise, reading from the board and changing the words.
• They may want to make use of the size charts at the bottom of the page.

Optional activity
• Before class, copy the following items and cut each item out on a separate strip of paper.
• If there are more than sixteen students in the class, copy the lists twice or more.
• Try to have a few more items than there are students.

a. You've got red, blue and green sweaters, all sizes, £21.
b. You've got blue sweaters and red sweaters, all sizes, £19.50.
c. You've got men's and women's trousers, all sizes, brown or black, £20.99.
d. You've got men's and women's trousers, all sizes, all colours, £22.49.
e. You've got blue, pink and white shirts for men, £19.99.
f. You've got white shirts for men and women, £18.95.
g. You've got shoes, all colours, sizes 3 to 11, £25.45.
h. You've got shoes, all colours, sizes 3 to 11, £29.99.

1. A red sweater; you've got £20.
2. A blue sweater for a friend; you've got £22.
3. Trousers; you've got £22.
4. Blue trousers; you've got £25.
5. A shirt for your mother or father; you've got £20.
6. A white shirt for your uncle; you've got £22.
7. Black shoes; you've got £35.
8. Brown shoes; you've got £30.

• Get half the students to stand on one side of the room.
• Tell them they are shop assistants and give each of them one or more lettered sentences.
• Distribute all the lettered sentences.
• The other students, the customers, each get a numbered sentence.
• Leftover numbered sentences are put in a pile on your desk.
• Customers walk round and try to find what they want at a price they can pay.
• You may wish to demonstrate with one pair before the exercise begins.
• When a student has found the item on the slip of paper, he or she can exchange slips with another customer or with the pile of leftovers.
• If there is time, the 'shoppers' can become 'shop assistants' and vice versa; they can use the same items.

Practice Book exercises: choose two or more
1. Revision of lesson material.
2. Grammar from the lesson: *a . . . one*.
3. Revision of third person pronouns.
4. Revision of articles.
5. Student's Cassette exercise (Student's Book Exercise 2, third conversation). Students listen and try to write down the conversation.

10B Have you got anything in blue?

How to buy clothes and shoes; *a . . . one.*

1 Here are three conversations (two in clothes shops, one in a shoe shop). Match the sentences to their places in the conversations.

a. I'm just looking.
b. Can I help you?

a. Here's a lovely one.
b. What size?
c. Yes, I'm looking for a sweater.
d. Well, yellow doesn't really suit me. Have you got anything in blue?
e. Can I help you?

f. Can I try them on?
g. Here's a nice one in blue. And here's another one.
h. £23.99.
i. Yes, of course.
j. How much are they?

a. These are a bit small. Have you got them in a larger size?
b. Yes, these fit very well. I'll take them, please.
c. No, I'm afraid I haven't. Would you like to try these?
d. I'll just see.
e. Yes, please.

2 🔊 Listen to the three conversations. Use your dictionary or ask your teacher about the new words. Then practise the customer's part in each conversation.

3 Change things (clothes, colours, sizes) in the second conversation and practise the new conversation with another student.

Men's clothes				
British	37–38	39–40	41–42	43–44
Continental	94–97	99–102	104–107	109–112
American	38	40	42	44

Women's clothes						
British	10	12	14	16	18	20	22
Continental	38	40	42	44	46	48	50
American	8	10	12	14	16	18	20

Men's shoes							
British	7	8	9	10	11	12	13
Continental	41	42	43	44	45½	47	48
American	8	9	10	11	12	13	14

Women's shoes							
British	3	4	5	6	7	8	9
Continental	35½	36½	38	39½	40½	42	43
American	4½	5½	6½	7½	8½	9½	10½

Learn: size; shop (*noun*); clothes; help; look for; try (on); take; large; other; another; anything; really; I'm afraid; well; Can I . . . ?; a . . . one; Would you like?

Choose two or more other words or expressions from the lesson to learn.

10C Buying things

Prepositions; *this*, *that*, *these*, *those*; the language of shopping.

1 Look at the picture on page 133 for three minutes. Then:
a. write down the names of all the things you can remember (time limit two minutes).
b. look at the picture again and complete the following sentences.
c. write two more sentences about the picture.

1. There is a .... in front of the ....
2. There is a .... on the ....
3. There are some .... under the ....
4. There is a .... outside the ....
5. The .... is by the ....
6. The .... is behind the ....
7. The .... is in the ....
8. The .... is between the .... and the ....

2 Practise saying these sentences. Put them with the right pictures.

How much is this?   This is nice.
How much are these?   I like these.
How much is that?   I don't like that very
How much are those?   much.
                           Those aren't very nice.

1   2

3   4

5   6

7   8

3 Listening to fast speech. How many words are there in each sentence? What are they? (Contractions like *there's* count as two words.)

4 Can you put the beginnings and ends of the sentences together? Do you know all the expressions?

How much is   for some coffee.
How much are   nice colour!
I'm looking   looking.
I'm just   you?
Can I look   these shoes?
What a   round?
What nice   that dictionary?
Can I help   size?
Sorry – we've got   trousers!
What   nothing in blue.

        *   *   *

I'd like to look   us, please?
Would you like   grams of blue cheese.
Can I   colour.
I'd like 500   try it on?
I like this   at some watches.
I'll take   to try it on?
Have you got anything   them.
Can you help   a red one.
I'd like   in blue?

5 Work with one or two other students. Prepare a conversation in a shop, in which somebody tries to buy something unusual. Use some of the expressions from Exercises 2 and 4.

Learn: thing; watch (*noun*); buy; those; behind; between; in front of; us; nothing; Can I look round?; How much is/are . . . ?; What (a) nice . . . !; I'd like (to).

Choose two or more other words or expressions from the lesson to learn.

50

Students work on the language of shopping.
Structures: demonstratives; prepositions of place; exclamations with *What (a)*; *I'd like*.
Phonology: hearing unstressed syllables.

Language notes and possible problems

1. Demonstratives Not all languages have demonstratives that work like the English system. Look out for confusions (*this/that, these/those*).

Point out their double use as determiners (e.g. *Read this book*) and pronouns (e.g. *Read this*).

Some students may use demonstratives with articles (**the this . . .*). Explain that articles, demonstratives and possessives are not normally used together.

Pronunciation of *this* and *these* is a problem. Practise them alone and in phrases like *this is*.

2. Exclamations with *what* Some students may tend to drop the article with singular countable nouns after *what*. Look out for mistakes like **What nice blouse!*.

3. *Would like* Students are coming across examples of *would like*. For now, you can treat these as fixed phrases. But make sure students understand clearly the difference between *would like* and *like*.

Optional extra materials

Exercise 5 involves 'playing shops'. Bring in (or have students bring in) things to 'buy' and 'sell'.

1 Language revision: memory game

- The main purpose of this exercise is to revise *there is/are*, *some* and prepositions of place.
- First of all, teach *in front of*, *behind* and *between*.
- Get students to turn to page 133. Make sure they know the names of all the things in the picture and give them three minutes to memorise the picture.
- Then go back to the exercise and do the first part.
- Let them compare notes and check with the picture.
- Then get them to do the rest of the exercise.

2 Demonstratives

- Check that students all understand the differences between the four demonstratives.
- Practise the pronunciation, using the recording if you wish.
- Ask students which picture each sentence goes with.
- You might ask students to make up a similar exercise (e.g. four pictures and four sentences).

Answers to Exercise 2

1. How much is that?
2. How much are these?
3. How much is this?
4. How much are those?
5. This is nice.
6. Those aren't very nice.
7. I like these.
8. I don't like that very much.

3 Hearing unstressed syllables

- Play each sentence once, and ask students to write down the number of words they think they hear.
- Play the sentence again until students agree on the number of words and (more or less) what they are.
- Move on to the next sentence.

Answers to Exercise 3

There are some apples in the fridge. (7)
There's a clock between the fridge and the door. (10)
How much are those bananas? (5)
Do you like that table? (5)
I don't like these shoes very much. (8)
I'm looking for a blouse. (6)

Have you got anything in green? (6)
These are a bit small. (5)
Would you like to try this one? (7)
Have you got them in a larger size? (8)

4 Expressions used for shopping

- This exercise contains a number of expressions that students already know, plus some new material.
- Get them to try to put together the first group of sentences (working individually or in groups).
- Explain any difficulties, and then do the second group of sentences in the same way.
- The expressions exemplify quite a number of grammatical structures, some known, some to be studied later. Without going into too much detail, you may wish to comment briefly on:
  – *how much is/are* for asking prices
  – the difference between *look*, *look at* and *look for*
  – the infinitive without *to* (after *can*) and with *to* (after *would like*)
  – exclamations: *What a . . . !* + singular countable nouns; *What . . . !* + uncountables and plurals
  – *us* (completing the list of object personal pronouns)
  – *like* and *would like*.

Answers to Exercise 4

How much is that dictionary?
How much are these shoes?
I'm looking for some coffee.
I'm just looking.
Can I look round?
What a nice colour!
What nice trousers!
Can I help you?
Sorry – we've got nothing in blue.
What size?

         *   *   *

I'd like to look at some watches.
Would you like to try it on?
Can I try it on?
I'd like 500 grams of blue cheese.
I like this colour.
I'll take them.
Have you got anything in blue?
Can you help us, please?
I'd like a red one.

5 Prepared conversations

- Give students ten to fifteen minutes to work in groups preparing and practising 'shop' conversations, using expressions from the last two lessons.
- Go round helping as necessary.
- Let students perform their conversations for the rest of the class.

Optional extension

- Divide the class into shopkeepers and customers.
- The shopkeepers should have objects (or pictures of objects) to sell.
- The customers wander round and buy things.

Practice Book exercises: choose two or more

1. Stress and rhythm.
2. Revision of material from the lesson.
3. Revision of prepositions.
4. Grammar revision: *much* and *many*.
5. Authentic reading text: scanning.

Unit 10: Lesson D

Students learn some of the language used for train travel, changing money and booking hotel rooms.

Language notes and possible problems

1. Choice If students are likely to be using English while travelling in the reasonably near future, it is probably worth studying all four dialogues. If not, choose one or two, depending on the students' level of interest. If they feel they have had enough dialogue work for the moment, drop the lesson and come back to it later.

2. *Can* and *could* If you study the fourth conversation with your students, you will probably want to teach *Can I* and *Could you* as fixed phrases used for polite requests, without going into their grammar for the moment.

1 Introductory exercise: matching

- See how quickly students can match the dialogues with the pictures.
- What words and expressions helped them to decide?

2 Completing a dialogue

- Get students to choose one of the dialogues for more detailed study.
- If different students want to study different dialogues, you may like to divide them into groups.
- Let students work together in small groups on the dialogue(s) of their choice. They should use dictionaries or ask you for words they don't know. Tell them to try to decide what some of the missing words might be.
- Play the dialogue two or three times, so that students can check their guesses.
- Go through the dialogue, putting the complete text on the board. Clear up any problems.

Tapescript and answers to Exercise 2

1. TRAVELLER: I'd like *two* singles to Norwich, *please.*
   CLERK: *That's* £26.40, *please.*
   TRAVELLER: Twenty-six pounds, ten, twenty, *thirty,* forty.
   CLERK: *Thank you.*
   TRAVELLER: *Thank you.*

2. TRAVELLER: *What* time is the *next* train to Oxford, please?
   CLERK: Erm, there's one *at* 3.45, change *at* Didcot, arriving *at* Oxford *at* 5.04, or there's a direct one *at* 3.49, arriving *at* 4.50.
   TRAVELLER: *Which* platform for the 3.49?
   CLERK: *Platform* 6.
   TRAVELLER: *Thank you very* much.

3. CLERK: How would you like it?
   TRAVELLER: *Pardon?*
   CLERK: How would you like it?
   TRAVELLER: I'm *sorry,* I don't *understand.* Could you *speak* more slowly, please?
   CLERK: How would you *like* your money? In tens?
   TRAVELLER: Oh, er, four fives and the rest *in* tens, *please.*
   CLERK: Fifty, one, two, three and twenty pence. And here's your receipt.
   TRAVELLER: Thank you.

4. RECEPTIONIST: Can I *help* you?
   TRAVELLER: Yes, I'd *like* a room, please.
   RECEPT.: Single or double?
   TRAVELLER: Single, please.
   RECEPT.: For *one* night?
   TRAVELLER: No, two nights.
   RECEPT.: With bath *or* with shower?
   TRAVELLER: With bath, please, How much *is* the room?
   RECEPT.: £68 a night, including breakfast.
   TRAVELLER: Can I pay by credit card?
   RECEPT.: Yes, of *course.* We take American Express, Access or Visa. Could you register, please?
   TRAVELLER: *Pardon?*
   RECEPT.: Could you fill in the form, *please?*
   TRAVELLER: Oh, yes.
   RECEPT.: Your room *number* is 403. Have a good stay.
   TRAVELLER: *Thank you.*

3 Practising the dialogue

- Give students a few minutes to practise the dialogue aloud in pairs.
- Play the recording again if necessary to provide a pronunciation model.
- Pay special attention to rhythm, intonation and linking.

4 Exploring the language of the situation

- Get students to think of other things that might be said in the same situation. Tell them (or find out if anybody else in the class knows) how these things are normally said in English.

5 Students' conversations

- Tell students to work in pairs.
- They should keep to the same situation as the original dialogue, and use plenty of the language they have just learnt, but make as many changes of detail as possible.
- You may like to introduce a 'problem' element to make the situation more interesting – for instance, put them in groups of three and have two travellers who keep disagreeing; or one of the people could be deaf; or the traveller could be running away from the police. Ask the class for ideas.
- Help groups to write and practise their new dialogues.
- Let them perform their dialogues for the rest of the class, preferably acting them out.
- You may like to tape- or video-record the performances. If so, warn students in advance – this will give them an incentive to do well.

Practice Book exercises: choose two or more
1. Revision of quantifiers (*how/too/not much/many*).
2. Stress and rhythm.
3. Check on revision vocabulary.
4. Translation of material from the unit.
5. Student's Cassette exercise (Student's Book Exercise 2, third conversation). Students listen and try to write down the conversation.
6. Constructing dialogues from notes.
7. Reading: Part 9 of *It's a Long Story.*

The language of travelling.

1 Look at the four conversations. Which conversation goes with which picture?

1. TRAVELLER: I'd like .... singles to Norwich, ...
   CLERK: .... £26.40, ...
   TRAVELLER: Twenty-six pounds, ten, twenty, ..., forty.
   CLERK: ....
   TRAVELLER: ....

2. TRAVELLER: .... time is the .... train to Oxford, please?
   CLERK: There's one .... 3.45, change .... Didcot, arriving .... Oxford .... 5.04, or there's a direct .... at 3.49, arriving .... 4.50.
   TRAVELLER: .... platform for the 3.49?
   CLERK: .... 6.
   TRAVELLER: .... much.

3. CLERK: How would you like it?
   TRAVELLER: ....?
   CLERK: How would you like it?
   TRAVELLER: I'm ...., I don't .... Could you .... more slowly, please?
   CLERK: How would you .... your money? In tens?
   TRAVELLER: Oh, er, four fives and the rest .... tens, ...
   CLERK: Fifty, one, two, three and twenty pence. And here's your receipt.
   TRAVELLER: Thank you.

4. RECEPTIONIST: Can I .... you?
   TRAVELLER: Yes, I'd .... a room, please.
   RECEPT.: Single or double?
   TRAVELLER: Single, please.
   RECEPT.: For .... night?
   TRAVELLER: No, two nights.
   RECEPT.: With bath .... with shower?
   TRAVELLER: With bath, please. How much .... the room?
   RECEPT.: £68 a night, including breakfast.
   TRAVELLER: Can I pay by credit card?
   RECEPT.: Yes, of .... We take American Express, Access or Visa. Could you register, please?
   TRAVELLER: ....?
   RECEPT.: Could you fill in the form, ...?
   TRAVELLER: Oh, yes.
   RECEPT.: Your room .... is 403. Have a good stay.
   TRAVELLER: ....

A

B

C

D

2 Choose one or more of the conversations to study. What are the missing words, do you think? Listen to the recording and complete the conversation with your teacher's help. Then ask the teacher about the new words, or find them in a dictionary.

3 Practise your conversation with another student.

4 Think of some other things to say in the same situation. Ask the teacher.

5 Change as many things as possible in your conversation; write and practise a new conversation for the same situation.

Learn: which; Could you speak more slowly, please?

Choose ten or more other words and expressions to learn.

Unit 11 People's pasts

11A She never studied . . .

	ANGELA	SARAH
school	✗ 4 schools ages 11–16	♥ one school ages 11–16
studied	before exams until age 14	every day
music	rock	classical
instrument	guitar	violin
TV	science fiction, cartoons	news, historical dramas
sport	snooker	tennis
age 16	rock group	bank, string quartet
ages 16–20	4 different rock groups	the same bank, the same string quartet
now	rock star	deputy manager at bank, string quartet
income	£1,000,000/year	£22,000/year

1 🔘 Look at the chart and find any new words in your dictionary. Then try to complete the text; use the chart, and the words in the box. Listen to check your answers.

changed	hated	listened	played
started	stopped	studied	watched

When Angela was younger, she ....1.... school. She ....2.... schools three times between the ages of 11 and 16. She never ....3.... except before exams, and she ....4.... studying altogether when she was fourteen. At home, she ....5.... to rock music and ....6.... science fiction and cartoons on TV. In the evenings and at weekends, she ....7.... the guitar, or ....8.... snooker with friends.

When she was sixteen, she ....9.... a rock group. She was in four different rock groups in the next four years.

Now Angela is a rock star, and she earns £1,000,000 a year. She says, 'I love my work, but I'm sorry I ....10.... studying at school.'

2 Look at the way to write regular past tenses:

1. Most regular verbs:
   listen + ed = listened
2. Verb ending in e:
   hate + d = hated
3. Short verbs ending in consonant + vowel + consonant:
   stop + ped = stopped
4. Verbs ending in consonant + y:
   study + ied = studied

Now write about Sarah's past, working from the chart. Your teacher can help you with any new words you need.

3 Say these regular past tense verbs.

1. arrived   lived   listened   played   studied
2. disliked   helped   liked   pronounced   watched
3. depended   hated   started

4 Copy the grid in Exercise 1 and write notes about some of your own past. You can change things, or add different notes and pictures if you want.

5 Take another student's notes and tell the class about his or her past. Don't say the student's name!

> When this person was younger, she quite liked school, except for languages. She started a job in a hospital in 1985 ...

> Is it Dolores?

Learn: thousand; million; news (*uncountable*); income; day; sport; earn; study; change; different; the same; before; every.

Unit 11: Lesson A

Students learn to speak about people's pasts.
Structures: Simple Past tense of regular verbs.
Phonology: pronunciation of regular Simple Past tense endings.

Language notes and possible problems

1. Timing   This lesson may be a bit long for some classes. Students can do Exercise 4 for homework, and do Exercise 5 at the beginning of the next class; or simply stop the lesson after Exercise 3.

2. Younger classes will have difficulty doing Exercises 4 and 5; see Optional activity.

3. Spelling of regular past tense   The rules in Exercise 2 will help students deal with most verbs. Point out that final *y* is considered as a vowel, not a consonant (and so does not fall under rule 3). Verbs like *open* where the last syllable is unstressed do not double the final consonant, but don't mention this unless students bring it up; they can learn it later.

4. Pronunciation of -ed   In the first line of Exercise 3, *-ed* is pronounced /d/, because it follows a 'voiced' sound in each case. In the second line, *-ed* is pronounced /t/, because it follows an 'unvoiced' sound. And in the third line, *-ed* comes after *d* or *t* and is pronounced /ɪd/.

The most important thing is for the students to know when to pronounce /ɪd/ and when not to. The difference between /t/ and /d/ is less important.

5. Past narrative   In some European languages, the tense used for past narrative is formed like the Present Perfect in English: a 'have' verb + past participle. Point out to speakers of these languages that it is the Simple Past which is the normal tense for narrative in English.

---

1 Completing the story

- Ask students to look at the chart, and to look up any unfamiliar words in the dictionary (or ask you for their meanings).
- Then let them work individually on trying to complete the story.
- Ask them to compare their answers in small groups.
- Play the recording once or more so thay can check their answers.
- Point out that the verbs in the box are regular. Make sure that they notice that there is no third-person inflection in past tense verbs.

Answers to Exercise 1

1. hated
2. changed
3. studied
4. stopped
5. listened
6. watched
7. played
8. played
9. started
10. stopped

Tapescript for Exercise 1: see page 140

2 Writing Sarah's story

- Go over the spelling rules with the students to make sure they understand.
- Let them work individually or in small groups, consulting the chart to write a story for Sarah.
- Walk round while they are working to give any help that is needed; you will need to let them know whether the verbs they want to use are regular.
- If your students want to use irregular verbs, don't stop them. Just point out that the verbs are irregular and that the Simple Past forms are in the table on the inside back cover of the book.
- Students can read one another's stories.

Optional preparation for Exercise 3: voicing

- Write these two groups of letters on the board:
  ay m n v r ee d
  s sh ch f p k x t
- Get the students to pronounce them after you (without putting /ə/ after any of the consonants).
- Get them to do the same thing again, but with the palms of their hands tight over their ears. They will hear that in the first group (but not the second) there is a loud buzzing vibration.
- Explain or demonstrate that the vibration comes from the vocal cords in the throat.
- Rub the *d* and the *t* out of the lists and show what happens when *d* or *ed* follows the sounds:
  ay m n v r ee + ed/d = /d/
  s sh ch f p k x + ed/d = /t/

3 Pronouncing -ed

- Go over each line of the exercise; students say the past tense forms after you or the recording.
- Make sure they don't pronounce /ɪd/ in either of the first two lines.
- See if they can tell you why *-ed* is pronounced /ɪd/ in the third line (because it isn't possible in English to pronounce /dd/ or /tt/).

4 Students write notes about their own past

- Get students to copy the categories from the left-hand side of the chart.
- Ask them to write notes about their own past lives for some or all of the categories. They can delete, add, or change categories as they wish.
- Write notes for yourself as well; if all of your students are much younger than you, make sure you don't give this away in your notes.
- Walk round while they are working to give any help that is needed.

Optional activity: invented pasts

(This activity would replace Exercises 4 and 5.)
- Ask students to copy the grid in Exercise 1 and invent imaginary personalities and lives for themselves.
- They should make notes about their lives, and then work in pairs to tell each other about their pasts.
- Walk round while they are working to give any help that is needed. Encourage them to use vocabulary they have already learnt, but give them new words if they need them.

5 A guessing game

- Take up all the papers and shuffle them. Include your own paper.
- Give the papers back out, making sure that no one has his or her own paper.
- Demonstrate by taking the paper you are left with and giving the students the information from it. Begin: *This person liked/disliked/hated school . . .* Then let the students guess who it is.
- Each student in turn relates the information on his or her sheet and the others try to guess who wrote it.
- In a large class, you may do this in groups.

Practice Book exercises: choose two or more

1. Writing regular past tenses.
2. Students write about their own pasts.
3. Revision: telling the time.
4. Revision: pronunciation of letters of the alphabet and common words.

Unit 11: Lesson B

Students continue to speak about people's pasts.
Structures: past tense of *be*; sentences with *when*-clauses.
Phonology: stress in sentences with *was* and *were*; strong and weak forms.

Language notes and possible problems
1. Dictionary work   Note that students are asked to use their dictionaries in Exercise 1. If for some reason this presents difficulties, you can help them with the new words.
2. *Was* and *were*   Students have had some exposure to the past tense of *be*; in this lesson the rest of the forms are learnt. You may want to point out that this is the only verb whose past tense forms change for the different persons.
3. Stress and weak forms   Students who speak syllable-timed languages may need special help with the pronunciation of sentences containing weak forms of *was* and *were*.

1 Presentation: *was* and *were*
• Ask students to read the first story, and to look up any unfamiliar words in the dictionary (or ask you for their meanings).
• Then ask them to do the same for the second story, filling in the verb forms in the blanks. They can look at the table at the bottom of the page for help in choosing *was* or *were*. This can be done as a whole-class activity or individually with checking afterwards.
• For the third story, students must supply some other words in addition to the verb forms. Ask them to work individually for a few minutes, and then to compare answers in groups of three or four before checking with you.
• When you have checked the answers to the third story, choose, or let the students choose, one sentence from the three stories with *was* and one sentence with *were*, for pronunciation practice.
• Make sure that they use the correct stress, and pronounce the 'weak forms' of *was* (/wəz/) and *were* (/wə(r)/).

Possible answers to Exercise 1, Question 3
A Dakota Indian speaks: *I was born* in a cloth tipi near Sisseton, South Dakota *in the* United States. *We were* poor. *My mother and father were* farmers. *I was* sometimes hungry *when I was* a small child, but *I was very* happy. My mother *was* a good cook, and my father *was* a good teacher. *Life* was hard, and white people *were* not usually *kind* to us.

2 Listening for information

• Students will hear three people speaking about themselves. They will not understand every word, but they will grasp enough to do the exercise.
• Go over the table with the students. Make sure they understand everything; you will have to explain some of the vocabulary.
• Tell them to copy the grid, with the names and the headings.
• Tell them that when they listen to the recording, they should write each person's age, the number of his/her brothers and sisters, the place of birth (chosen from the alternatives in the Student's Book), and an appropriate phrase about the person's childhood (chosen from the alternatives given).
• When they are ready, play the recording, pausing after each extract so that students can write their answers.

• Play the recording two or three times if necessary.
• Let students compare notes before going over the answers.
• The tapescript is given for reference, but it is not useful to spend time going over everything that is said.

Answers to Exercise 2
Adrian Webber: Age 42; a sister; born in India; childhood varied and quite happy.
Lorna Higgs: Age 19; two brothers; born in Oxford; childhood 'quite mixed, really'.
Sue Ward: Age not given; three brothers and a sister; born in Tadcaster, very happy childhood.

Tapescript for Exercise 2: see page 141

3 Questions with *was* and *were*
• Put students into groups of three or four and give them three minutes to write as many questions as they can, using the words given.
• When you are checking the questions, help students to pronounce them with the correct stress, and weak forms of the verbs.

4 Class survey
• Each student should choose one question from Exercise 3, or make up another question beginning *'When you were a small child, was/were . . .'*
• Then students should walk round and ask their questions of everyone else in the class; or if it is very inconvenient to walk round, they should ask everyone they can without moving from their seats.
• Ask them to note the answers they get; if there is time when they finish, they can report the results back to the class, e.g. *'Four people were sometimes hungry, and twelve people were never hungry when they were children.'*
• Give them a few minutes to look at the table with the verb forms, and/or ask them to look at it at home.

Practice Book exercises: choose two or more
1. Making questions with *was/were*.
2. Vocabulary revision: 'odd one out'.
3. Word stress.
4. Student's Cassette exercise (Student's Book Exercise 2, first section). Students listen and try to write down what they hear.
5. Guided writing (follow-up to Student's Book Exercise 1). Writing from notes.

11B When I was a small child . . .

People's childhoods; *was* and *were*.

1 Use your dictionary to read the first text and complete the other texts (blanks can mean one or more words). Practise reading some of the sentences.

1. A Zulu speaks:
'I was born in a brick house in Soweto, near Johannesburg in South Africa. We were poor. My mother was a maid and my father was a factory worker. He died when I was six. I was always hungry, and nearly always unhappy, when I was a small child. Life was very hard. White people were terrible to us.'

2. A Maori speaks:
'I .... born in a wooden house in a village near Rotorua in New Zealand. We .... not poor, but we .... not rich. My mother and father .... farmers. I .... never hungry when I .... a small child; I .... quite happy, really. Life .... not hard, but white people .... not always kind to me.'

3. A Dakota Indian speaks:
'................ in a cloth *tipi* near Sisseton, South Dakota .... United States. .... poor. .... farmers. .... sometimes hungry .... a small child, but .... happy. My mother .... good cook, and my father .... good teacher. .... hard, and white people .... not usually .... us.'

2 🔊 Copy the grid; then listen to the three people and complete it.

NAME	AGE	BROTHERS	SISTERS	PLACE OF BIRTH	CHILDHOOD
Adrian Webber				India England Edinburgh	varied and quite happy very unhappy very happy
Lorna Higgs				Austria Oslo Oxford	quite miserable quite interesting quite mixed, really
Sue Ward				Tadcaster Manchester Hong Kong	very unhappy very happy varied and happy

3 How many questions can you make?

> When you were a small child,

was were

you your parents life you and your family your mother your father your school other people

happy ever hungry hard poor rich at home from 9 to 5 out a lot good kind to you

?

4 Choose one question from Exercise 3, and ask as many people as you can; or make up your own question. Begin: '*When you were a small child, was/were . . .*' Examples:

'*When you were a small child, were you happy?*'
'*Yes, I was.*' / '*No, I wasn't.*' / '*I was quite happy.*'

Past tense of *be*

I was	was I?	I was not (wasn't)
you were	were you?	you were not (weren't)
he/she/it was	was he/she/it?	he/she/it was not (wasn't)
we were	were we?	we were not (weren't)
you were	were you?	you were not (weren't)
they were	were they?	they were not (weren't)

Learn: life; village; (was/were) born; die; poor; rich; hard; kind (to); nearly.

11C They didn't drink tea

Life in the past; Simple Past tense negatives and questions; *ago*.

1 These pictures show life in the country in
Europe 500 years ago. Make fifteen sentences about
people who lived in Europe, or in your country, at
that time; use *didn't, wasn't* and *weren't*. Examples:

'Five hundred years ago, they didn't drink tea.'
'They didn't have passports.'
'They didn't know about America five hundred years
    ago.'
'Most people weren't very tall.'
'There wasn't any paper money.'

2 Write seven sentences about changes in your life.
Read one or two of them to the class. Examples:

I didn't like cheese when I was a small child, but
    now I do.
I played tennis when I was ten, but now I don't.
We didn't have a television then, but now we've got
    one.
There weren't any pocket calculators then, but now
    there are millions of them.

3 Work in groups. Write a questionnaire to find out about life forty
or fifty years ago in the country where you are studying. Then find some
older people and get answers to your questions. Examples:

1. *How did children travel to school fifty years ago?*
2. *Did your family have a television?*
3. *What was your favourite sport?*

Report the results of your questionnaire back to the class.

Simple Past tense		
I changed	did I change?	I did not (didn't) change
you changed	did you change?	you did not (didn't) change
he/she/it changed	did she *etc.* change?	he *etc.* did not (didn't) change
we changed	did we change?	we did not (didn't) change
you changed	did you change?	you did not (didn't) change
they changed	did they change?	they did not (didn't) change

Learn: tea; passport; paper; pocket; calculator; year; America; Europe;
know about (knew); most; favourite; then; now; ago.

54

Unit 11: Lesson C

Students continue to speak about people's pasts.
Structures: negative and interrogative of the Simple Past tense; *ago*.
Phonology: stress in negative sentences; stress for contrast.

Language notes and possible problems

1. Exercise 1   Some students may feel that they do not know enough about history to do Exercise 1. A way of modifying the exercise to make it easier for them is given below.

2. Ago   Students may take a little time to get used to the word order with *ago*. Look out for mistakes like **ago 500 years* or **before 500 years*. If they have real difficulty, you may like to do Practice Book Exercise 1 in class, adding some more examples yourself if necessary.

3. Past of have/has got   You will want to point out that *had/didn't have* are the most common past tense forms of *have/has got*.

4. One as a substitute word occurs in one of the examples for Exercise 2. You may wish to comment on it (and the plural *some*) if opportunities come up in the students' own sentences.

5. Long sentences   Students may have difficulty with the long sentences in Exercise 2. They can be helped by emphasis on correct stress and rhythm, and with 'backchaining' (first they repeat only the last stress group of the sentence, then the last two stress groups, etc.).

6. Project work   Exercise 3 is a small project requiring students to find people over 55 years of age who will answer questions about their childhood. Although this is somewhat more time-consuming than the general run of homework, it can be a very motivating activity. Students who are studying in their own country will of course have to translate the questions into their own language and the answers into English; students who are studying in an English-speaking country may need help in finding volunteers to answer their questions.

---

1 Life five hundred years ago

• Get students to look at the pictures at the top of the page (covering up the rest of the text). Ask them when they think people lived like that.

• One of the students may see '*500 years*' in Exercise 1: otherwise write this on the board and explain the meaning of *ago*.

• Ask the class where they think the pictures are of. You will probably get answers like *France, Germany*, etc.; say that it is somewhere in Europe.

• Go over the sample sentences with the students, getting them to repeat them after you or the recording. Explain the meanings of new words, including *most* in the phrase *most people*.

• Pay special attention to stress and rhythm, and point out that the word carrying the negative (*didn't, wasn't, weren't*) is usually stressed.

• Divide the class into groups of three or four and ask each group to write fifteen negative sentences about Europe, or their own country, about five hundred years ago.

• Walk round the room as they are working, and help with any problems that come up. Encourage them to use the vocabulary they know, but give them a few new words if they ask for them.

• When the exercise is finished get each group to read out or write on the board one or two of their sentences.

Alternative Exercise 1 procedure

• If students feel daunted by the task, you can put the following words on the board to help them. They will still get practice using the forms, though the exercise will not be as interesting for them as if they had thought of the examples themselves.

Coca-Cola	hospitals	travel
cigarettes	banks	read
shaving cream	central heating	write
toothpaste	Australia	supermarkets
buses	electricity	school
cars	telephones	bookshops
fridges	machines	Eskimos
aeroplanes	trousers	jazz

2 Personalisation

• Go over the examples with the class, explaining how the pro-verbs (*do, does, don't, doesn't*) work.

• Then ask each student to write seven true sentences on the same model.

• Tell them they can ask you for help: give them any vocabulary or irregular past forms they need.

• (You may want to teach them to say '*Is . . . a regular verb?*')

• Ask for volunteers to read out some of their sentences to the class.

3 Project: questionnaire

• Put the students into groups of three or four, and explain the task.

• Each group must produce a questionnaire to get an idea of what life was like fifty years ago in the country where they are studying.

• Look at the sample questions with the students and point out how questions are formed in the Simple Past tense.

• Give the groups three minutes for each one to elect a chairperson, who must make sure that everyone speaks and that the group meets the deadline.

• Tell them what their time limit is for producing a questionnaire; you may also want to give them a minimum number of questions to write. Point out that every member of the group must write down the questions that they decide on.

• Walk round while they are working to give any language help that is requested, but as far as possible let the students manage the task themselves.

• Only correct the language in the questionnaires if you are asked to, or if you really think they will/would be incomprehensible to ordinary native speakers.

• Spend a few minutes discussing with the whole class where they can find people to answer their questionnaires.

• Each student should administer the questionnaire to at least one older person (over 55) and note down the answers.

• If the students are not studying in their own country, you may need to help organise contacts with older people, for example through a local day centre.

• Results of the questionnaires can be reported a few days later.

Practice Book exercises: choose two or more
1. *Ago* with expressions of time.
2. Making past negative sentences.
3. Making past questions.
4. Punctuation and capitalisation.
5. Sentence stress and rhythm.

Unit 11: Lesson D

Students learn to speak about the recent past.
Stuctures: irregular Simple Past verb forms.
Phonology: rhythm and stress in questions.

Language notes and possible problems

1. Reported speech   When we are reporting things that people have said about the recent past, we do not always make all the 'tense changes' that are described in grammars. For instance, instead of 'June said that she *had* gone to a folk concert,' it is quite all right to say 'June said that she *went* to a folk concert.' In Exercise 3, students can use this structure; a more detailed study of 'reported speech' will come later.

2. *Say* and *tell*   You will need to explain the difference between *say* (which does not need to have an indirect object) and *tell* (which normally must have one).

3. *That*   Note that the conjunction *that* is often left out after common verbs of reporting in an informal style. You may wish students to practise sentences with and without *that*.

4. *Go* and *come*   Students may need to be shown the difference between *go* (movement away from the speaker or unrelated to the speaker) and *come* (movement towards the speaker).

5. *Actually* (Exercise 3)   The meaning of *actually* should be clear from the context – it is very often used in this way to correct mistakes or misunderstandings. Note, though, that it is a 'false friend' for many students: similar words in other European languages tend to mean 'at present'.

6. *Got* is encountered for the first time as the past of *get* (rather than as part of *have got*).

1 Irregular verbs

• Get the students to do the matching exercise. This should not be difficult.
• The exercise will prepare students for the new verb forms in the next exercises.
• Explain the meanings of the new words, and make sure students know how to find and use the irregular verb lists in their dictionaries. (There is also a list of common irregular verbs at the back of the Student's Book.)

2 Listening

• Set the scene by getting the students to look at the picture.
• Elicit the information that the people are a father and a daughter; get the students to guess their approximate ages.
• Then get them to close their books.
• Explain or demonstrate the meanings of *quietly*, *concert*, *late*, *midnight*, *hear* and *disco*.
• Play the recording once.
• Ask questions to see if students have got the gist of the dialogue, e.g.
  'What time did June come home?'
  'Did she go to a disco or a concert?'
• You may have to play the recording again if students have not understood much the first time.
• When you are satisfied that they have got the gist of the dialogue, play it again, stopping after these sentences for the students to repeat them:
  What time did you come home last night, then, June?
  Oh, I don't know. About half past twelve, I think.
  Half past twelve? I didn't hear you.
  You know I don't like loud music.
  Why did you come back so late?
• Pay special attention to stress and rhythm.

• Ask the students to open their books and read the dialogue as you play it again.
• Get them to ask you about any words they don't know, using the *What does . . . mean?* form.
• Get them to read the diary entry, once again asking you for the meanings of new words.

3 Find the differences (reported speech)

• Point out the distinction between *say* and *tell*, and the meaning of *actually*.
• Get each student to write down one difference, following the models in the book.
• Ask a few volunteers to read their sentences. Help them with pronunciation, paying special attention to rhythm and intonation. Point out the pronunciation of *said* (/sed/).
• Make sure you have examples of both *say* and *tell*; or you may wish to ask each student to give his or her answer in both forms.
• Ask the class if there are any more differences (i.e. let them complete the exercise orally).

4 Writing half-dialogues

• Tell the right-hand half of the class to turn to page 133, and the left-hand half of the class to turn to page 134, and to find the exercise for Lesson 11D.
• Students should work quietly in pairs or threes, trying not to let the other side of the class hear much of what they say.
• Get them to look through their half-dialogues without showing them to the students on the other side of the room. They can use their dictionaries or ask you about new words.
• Then they should write the other half of their dialogue. They work in pairs or threes, but EACH student should write ONLY the new sentences on a piece of paper (so that each student ends up with a new half-dialogue that s/he has just helped to write).
• Walk round while they are working to give any help that is needed. Do not worry too much about perfect grammar, but try and check, where possible, that the sentences they have written fit logically into the half-dialogue they have been given.
• When everyone has finished and closed their books, each student should find someone from the other side of the class to combine half-dialogues with.
• Ask them to read their dialogues to each other a couple of times, trying for good pronunciation.
• If there is time, some students may want to read their dialogues out for the class.

Practice Book exercises: choose two or more
1. Writing regular and irregular pasts.
2. Writing infinitives of regular and irregular verbs.
3. Writing sentences: comparing the past and the present.
4. Students write about what they did yesterday or last weekend.
5. Check on revision vocabulary.
6. Translation of material from the unit.
7. Student's Cassette exercise (Student's Book Exercise 2). Students listen for discrepancies between sentences in the recording and those in their book.
8. Reading: Part 10 of *It's a Long Story*.

11D   Danced till half past one

Talking about past events; Simple Past of irregular verbs.

1 Match the present and past forms of these irregular verbs.

go   tell   get   can   do   come   hear   (wake)   have   say   know
(woke)   could   went   heard   said   told   came   had   did   got   knew

2 Close your book and listen to the dialogue. See how much you can remember. Then read the dialogue and the text. Ask your teacher about new words.

May 14 Tuesday

Lovely time with Frank at the disco. Danced till half past one. Then went to his place for a drink. We kissed a bit. Got home at 3 a.m. again. Couldn't find my key, so climbed in through a window. V. tired this morning. Daddy asked a lot of stupid questions, as usual.

FATHER: What time did you come home last night, then, June?
JUNE: Oh, I don't know. About half past twelve, I think.
FATHER: Half past twelve? I didn't hear you.
JUNE: Well, I came in quietly. I didn't want to wake you up.
FATHER: You didn't go to that damned disco, did you?
JUNE: Disco, Daddy? Oh, no. You know I don't like loud music. No, I went to a folk concert with Alice and

Mary. It was very good. There was one singer . . .
FATHER: Why did you come back so late? The concert didn't go on till midnight, did it?
JUNE: No, but we went to Alice's place and had coffee, and then we started talking about politics, you know. Alice's boyfriend – he's the President of the Students' Union Conservative Club . . .

3 Find the differences. Example:

June said (that) she went to a folk concert, but actually she went to a disco.
OR: June told her father (that) she...

4 Turn to the page that your teacher tells you. Write ONLY the other half of the conversation. Then find a partner and practise the new conversation.

Learn: tell (told); come (came); say (said); ask; kiss; want; get (got); get home; hear (heard); wake up (woke); talk; last night; late; again; actually; this morning; why.

Unit 12 Consolidation

12A Things to remember: Units 9, 10 and 11

Present Progressive tense
I'**m looking** for a blue sweater.
'**Are** George and Tom **wearing** their blue jackets?'
   'Yes, they **are**.' / 'No, they **aren't**.'

Simple Past tense

I stopped	did I stop?	I did not (didn't) stop
you stopped	did you stop?	you did not (didn't) stop
he/she/it stopped	did she *etc.* stop?	he *etc.* did not (didn't) stop
we stopped	did we stop?	we did not (didn't) stop
you stopped	did you stop?	you did not (didn't) stop
they stopped	did they stop?	they did not (didn't) stop
the cars stopped	did the cars stop?	the cars did not (didn't) stop

Examples:
When Angela was younger, she **hated** school.
I **didn't like** cheese when I was a small child, but I do now.
   (I liked not cheese . . . I not liked cheese . . . I didn't liked cheese . . .)
'**Did** your family **have** a television when you were a child?' 'Yes, we **did**.' / 'No, we **didn't**.'
'**Did** you **like** school when you were a child?' 'Yes, I **did**.' ('Yes, I liked.')

Spelling of regular verbs
1. Most regular verbs:
   listen + ed = listened
2. Verbs ending in *-e*:
   hate + d = hated
3. Short verbs ending in one vowel + one consonant:
   stop + ped = stopped
4. Verbs ending in consonant + *-y*:
   study + ied = studied

Pronunciation of regular verbs
1. /d/ after vowels and /b/, /l/, /g/, /v/, /ð/, /z/, /ʒ/, /m/, /n/, /ŋ/, /dʒ/
2. /t/ after /p/, /k/, /tʃ/, /f/, /θ/, /s/, /ʃ/
3. /ɪd/ after /t/ and /d/

Which verbs learnt so far are irregular?

Infinitive	Past tense	Infinitive	Past tense	Infinitive	Past tense
be	was, were	have got	had	sit down	sat down
can	could	know	knew (/njuː/)	speak	spoke
come	came	mean	meant (/ment/)	take	took
cost	cost	meet	met	tell	told
do	did	read	read (/red/)	think	thought (/θɔːt/)
get	got	say	said (/sed/)	understand	understood
go	went	see	saw (/sɔː/)	wear	wore
have	had				

The past tense of *be*: *was* and *were*

I was	was I?	I was not (wasn't)
you were	were you?	you were not (weren't)
he/she/it was	was she *etc.*?	he *etc.* was not (wasn't)
we were	were we?	we were not (weren't)
you were	were you?	you were not (weren't)
they were	were they?	they were not (weren't)

Examples:
'When you **were** a small child, **were** you happy?'
   'Yes, I **was**.' / 'No, I **wasn't**.' / 'I **was** quite happy.'
We **weren't** poor, but we **weren't** rich.
My mother **was** a good cook.
It **was** very good. There **was** one singer . . .

Pronunciation
We were (/wə/) **poor**. I was (/wəz/) always **hungry**.
Were (/wə/) you ever **hungry**?
Yes, I was (/wɒz/). No, I wasn't (/'wɒznt/).
Were (/wə/) your parents **poor**?
Yes, they were (/wɜː/). No, they weren't (/wɜːnt/).

This lesson displays the language that students should have learnt in the last three units. Spend a short time going over the lesson pages with the students. Point out that they are expected to learn not only the vocabulary in the *Words and expressions* section, but also that in the functional sections (*Asking about English, Appearances and clothes, Shopping* and *Writing formal letters*).

Note

Student's Book Lesson 12C contains a number of activities to choose from. In one of these (Speaking Exercise 2), students will need to bring along pictures of their family and friends; you will have to tell them about this in advance. If students are studying in their own country they can probably collect quite a number of family photos, photos of themselves when younger, etc. Even students studying abroad are likely to have some photos with them. Bring along some photos of your family and friends as well.

Practice Book exercises: choose two or more
1. Completing a story by writing the past tense forms of verbs.
2. Writing past tense questions.
3. Choosing *be, have*, or *have got.*
4. Writing sentences for pictured dialogues.
5. Writing a formal letter describing oneself.
6. Reading an authentic text for specific information.
7. Crossword.

Video

Sequences 3A and 3B in *The New Cambridge English Course 1 Video* can be used around this point in the book, as they relate to Units 9–11 of the coursebook.

In Sequence 3A, **In the market**, the topics are shopping for food and clothes; prices; colours; heights; likes and dislikes. Language focus is on asking for things; countables and uncountables; *a bit (big)*; *have got.*

In Sequence 3B, **First meeting**, the topics are physical descriptions of people; describing clothes; forms of transport. Language focus is on *s/he's got*, e.g. *She's got brown hair*; Present Progressive tense, e.g. *I'm wearing a brown jacket.*

Have and *has*; *be* and *have*

I have
you have
she/he/it has
we have
you have
they have

Examples:
When Lucy **is** hungry she **has** bread and cheese.
~~(When Lucy has hungry . . .   . . . she takes bread . . .)~~
When I**'m** thirsty I **have** a glass of orange juice.
~~(When I have thirsty . . .   . . . I've a glass . . .)~~
When I**'m** dirty I **have** a bath / a shower.
What colour **are** her eyes?

Examples:
This cheese is terrible.
These tomatoes are very nice.
'I like **those** ear-rings.'   'Thank you!'
How much is **that**?

When

When Fred's hungry he goes to a restaurant.
When Lucy's dirty she has a shower.

Tell and *say*

June **told** her father she went to a folk concert.
OR June **told** her father that she went to a folk
concert.
~~(June said her father she went to a folk concert.)~~
June **said** she went to Alice's place.
OR June **said** that she went to Alice's place.
~~(June told that she went to Alice's place.)~~

Both and *all*

We **both** wear glasses.
We've **both** got red cars.
We're **all** tall.
They've **all** got dark hair.

Asking about English

'What's this?'   'It's an umbrella.'
'What are these?'   'Train tickets.'
What's this called in English?
'How do you say *arroyo* in English?'   'I can't
remember.'
How do you pronounce k-n-e-w?
Could you speak more slowly, please?

Appearances and clothes

Lucy has got short grey hair and blue eyes.
Pat is wearing a white sweater and a green blouse.
My sister looks very like my mother; I look more like
my aunt.
What colour eyes has your mother got?
'Who do you look like?'   'I look a bit like my
father.'
I've got my mother's eyes, but I've got my father's
personality.

Shopping

'Can I help you?'   'I'm just looking.'
'I'm looking for a sweater.'   'Here's a lovely one.'
What a lovely sweater! ~~(What lovely sweater!)~~
What nice shoes!
Those aren't very nice.   I don't like that very much.
Can I look round?
Can I try them on?
'Have you got anything in black?'   'I'll just see.'
'No, I'm afraid I haven't. Would you like to try
these?' ~~(Would you like try these?)~~
How much are they?   How much is it?
I'll take them, please.
I'd like a red one.
I'd like to look at some watches.
~~(I'd like look at some watches.)~~

Writing formal letters

Castle Street
Newcastle NE1 2HH
September 12, 1990

Dear Mr Bell,

I am arriving at Waverley Station, Edinburgh . . .

. . .

I look forward to seeing you.

Yours sincerely,

Paul Sanders

12A continued

Words and expressions

Countable nouns
eye	aunt	watch
nose	letter	income
ear	train	day
mouth	station	life
face	journey	village
arm	bath	passport
hand	shower	pocket
foot (feet)	size	calculator
leg	shop	year
colour	clothes	America
uncle	thing	Europe

Uncountable nouns
water
news
tea

Countable or uncountable nouns
paper
sport

Adjectives
long	white	tired
short	nice	ill
brown	next	dirty
green	short	large
blue	bad	different
grey	hungry	the same
red	thirsty	poor
pink	hot	rich
orange	cold	hard
yellow	happy	kind (to)
purple	unhappy	favourite
black	bored	

Verbs
wear (wore)	buy (bought)	say (said)
remember	earn	ask
look like	study	kiss
look (at)	change	want
arrive (at)	was/were born	get (got)
meet (met)	die	get home
help	know about (knew)	hear (heard)
look for	tell (told)	wake up (woke)
try (on)	come (came)	talk
take (took)		

Adverbs
light	then
dark	now
more	ago
a bit	last night
not at all	this morning
really	late
well	again
nearly	actually

Prepositions
like
except
with
behind
between
in front of
before

Other words and expressions
us	those	million	have a shower
something	lots of	What colour is/are . . . ?	go shopping
anything	other	a.m.	Let's go
nothing	another	p.m.	a . . . one
all	every	when	which
that	most	have a bath	why
these	thousand		

Optional words and expressions to learn
pants; bra; sock; jeans; jacket; dress; tights; shirt; blouse; skirt; trousers; sweater; boot; shoe; glasses; bow tie; ear-rings; restaurant; hotel; cinema.

Unit 12: Lesson B

Students develop writing skills.
Structures: Simple Past tense; use of conjunctions and adverbials to structure narrative.

Language notes and possible problems

1. Students' reservations   Students may wonder about the importance of developing writing skills in English. You may want to tell them that you are not hoping to make novelists of them, but aiming to give them the means of writing clearly in order to communicate with people. Of course, the writing practice is also valuable revision of past tense verb forms and of vocabulary.

2. The structure of the lesson   You will notice that the lesson starts with an unguided writing exercise. You and your students may be more accustomed to writing lessons which begin with a very controlled exercise and only gradually move towards more freedom. We have put an unguided exercise first to allow students to concentrate on the ideas they wish to communicate, and to focus on the problems they encounter before working towards solutions to the problems. After writing without guidance, students are given a sample of how a native speaker approached the same task; they look at the structuring devices used, and then try writing new texts of the same sort.

1 *On Saturday . . . :* introduction and sensitisation

- On the board, write notes (true or imaginary) about how you spent last Saturday. Talk the students through the notes as you write them.
- Ask each student to make his or her own notes; give them no longer than five minutes for this.
- Then they should work individually, using the notes to write connected texts about how they spent their Saturday. Write your own brief narrative as well.
- When most of the students have finished, call a confident student up to the front and exchange stories with him or her.
- Read each other's stories silently; find something nice to say about the ideas (not the spelling or the grammar!) in your partner's story, and ask a 'follow-up' question about the contents. Get your partner to do the same for you.
- Then let students work in pairs for a short time reading each other's stories and commenting on them as you have done.

2 Presentation of narrative form

- Ask students to turn to page 133 and read the story there. While they are doing so, write the words and expressions in the panel (*and, and then* etc.) on the board and ask them to read the text again, paying special attention to how they are used.
- If you speak their language(s), discuss with them how these words and expressions make the text easier to read.
- Then ask them to work individually to see if they can use any of these words and expressions to rewrite their texts from Exercise 1.
- When they have finished, collect the papers. When you mark them, write positive comments about what interests you in the stories, or questions about content, as well as corrections of form.
- Be careful not to put too many corrections; if a paper is returned as a network of red ink, the student will learn nothing from it. In choosing which mistakes to mark, it is probably best to give priority to those that tend to make communication break down.

3 Writing from notes and pictures

- Let students look at the notes and the pictures.
- Then ask them to work in pairs or threes to write a story from the notes.
- Make it clear that you expect them to write more than one draft, and tell them not to worry about getting the words from the box into the first draft.
- They can use their imagination to add any details they wish.
- When they are satisfied with the general shape of the story, they should try to include some of the words and expressions from Exercise 2.
- If there is time, they can exchange texts between groups and do the same sort of 'appreciation and question' activity as they did for Exercise 1.
- Collect the papers if they wish you to, and mark them in the same way that you mark the individually written texts.

Practice Book exercises: choose two or more
1. Vocabulary revision (various lexical fields).
2. Choosing between *here* and *there*, *this* and *that*, *these* and *those*, *come* and *go*.
3. Pronunciation: odd one out.
4. Writing questions: revision of tenses learnt so far.
5. Matching beginnings and ends of past tense sentences about historical figures.
6. Guided writing: writing a story from notes.
7. Writing about the student's own life, or the life of a famous man or woman.

Developing writing skills
Research done in the past few years indicates that good writers (both native speakers and non-native speakers) do not initially pay too much attention to the sentence-level details of their texts. Their first concern is to get their ideas organised and written down; they then revise, perhaps more than once, before worrying about things like spelling or finding just the word that they are looking for in a particular sentence. In fact, writers who pay a lot of attention to grammar and spelling at the beginning of the writing process produce consistently poorer texts than those who do not. So there is some justification in encouraging in learners of English the same sort of writing behaviour that successful writers use.

This is why we have asked students to begin by writing their own stories, before concentrating on a model which can help them approach standard English narrative form more closely. This is also why students and teacher are encouraged to make positive and interested remarks about the contents of one another's writing.

Writing.

1 Write about what you did on Saturday. Then read another student's writing; say one good thing about it and ask one question. Examples:

'You play tennis – that's interesting. Where did you go shopping?'

'Where do you work on Saturdays? I liked that film, too.'

2 Turn to page 133 and look at the story. Notice how these words and expressions are used.

and	and then	but	in the afternoon
in the evening		until	when

Now look at your own text (from Exercise 1) and see if you can put in any words from the box.

3 Look at the pictures and notes, and write a story. Use your imagination; and put in some words from the box in Exercise 2.

woke up at 8
didn't get up until 9
shower, breakfast, newspaper
met friend in park
post office, lunch with friend
television
swimming pool
cinema

12C Choose

A choice of pronunciation, listening and speaking exercises.

Look at the exercises, decide which ones are useful to you, and do two or more.

PRONUNCIATION

1 Difficult words. Can you pronounce all of these?

/ð/: the there then mother brother with this that these those

/θ/: thank thirty thirsty Thursday third three thousand

/ɪz/: watches oranges languages villages buses houses

/ʌ/: brother son mother love money some once young touch cupboard

/ɪ/: English women orange village

/e/: many any friend sweater breakfast

/aɪ/: night light right write eye quiet

/ɔː/: daughter quarter water you're sure

(l): half could

(various problems): child woman people tired wrong watch year enough aunt listen

Ask your teacher how to pronounce other words.

> How do you pronounce t-h-r-o-u-g-h?

> Is this correct: "Zaturday"?

LISTENING

1 [cassette] Listening for information. Listen to the telephone conversations.

Who do you think saw Peter Anderson – the first caller (Mrs Collins), the second (Mr Sands), or the third (Mr Harris)?

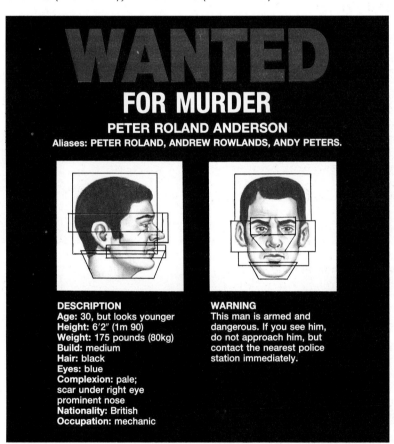

WANTED
FOR MURDER
PETER ROLAND ANDERSON
Aliases: PETER ROLAND, ANDREW ROWLANDS, ANDY PETERS.

DESCRIPTION
Age: 30, but looks younger
Height: 6'2" (1m 90)
Weight: 175 pounds (80kg)
Build: medium
Hair: black
Eyes: blue
Complexion: pale; scar under right eye prominent nose
Nationality: British
Occupation: mechanic

WARNING
This man is armed and dangerous. If you see him, do not approach him, but contact the nearest police station immediately.

2 [cassette] Put *I*, *I'm*, *I've*, *you*, *your* or *me* into each blank in the song; listen to the song. Close your book and try to remember.

PLEASE WRITE

.... wonder what you're doing now.
Are .... making a new friend?
.... got to see .... again somehow.
.... don't want this love to end.

Oh baby, please write.
Why don't .... write?
.... waiting to get .... letter, baby.

Please write.
Why don't .... write?
It means so much to ....

.... tried to call .... on the phone,
But nobody knew .... name.
Oh, ... can feel .... love run cold.
But listen to what I'm saying, baby.

Unit 12: Lesson C

Students and teacher choose from a selection of pronunciation, listening and speaking exercises.

Note
There is enough work in this lesson for 3–4 hours. You may like to get the students to vote for the exercises they consider most useful.

Extra materials
Student's family photos for Speaking Exercise 2.

PRONUNCIATION

1 Difficulties with particular sounds and words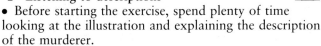
● Go through the list section by section, getting the students to try the words. The recording can be used as a guide if you wish.
● Then encourage the students to ask about the pronunciation of other words they are not sure of.

LISTENING

1 Listening to descriptions
● Before starting the exercise, spend plenty of time looking at the illustration and explaining the description of the murderer.
● Tell the students they will hear three telephone conversations with people who *think* they have seen Anderson.
● Only one person has seen the real Peter Anderson. Which one?
● Students will not understand everything that is said, and they should not worry about this. Get them to concentrate on the descriptions, particularly age, hair colour, eye colour and the scar.
● Play the recording two or three times.

Answer: Mrs Collins saw the murderer.

Tapescript for Exercise 1

– North Yorkshire Police.
– Hello. Listen. I've just seen Peter Anderson! In the . . .
– One moment, please.
– Peter Anderson! The murderer! He's here in Newtown! I saw him in the street! He . . .
– One moment, please.
– He's a big man, with short black hair and a scar on his face. He's 25 or . . .
– What is your name, please?
– Mrs Collins. He's 25 or 26. He's got . . .
– Your address, Mrs Collins?
– blue eyes, I think. And what a big nose he's got! I know it's him. He's wearing a black jacket and green trousers . . .

– Thames Valley Police.
– Hello. I've seen Peter Anderson.
– One moment, please.
– Hello. Detective Sergeant Callan speaking. Can I help you?
– Yes. I've just seen Peter Anderson. In the post office. Here in Chilton.
– Can I have your name and address, please, sir?
– Robert Sands. 17 High Street, Chilton. I'm sure it was Anderson. He's very tall, with long dark hair, a big nose, green eyes, and a scar on the left-hand side of his face. About 35 years old.
– What was he wearing?

– . . . and can you describe the man, Mr Harris?
– Yes. He's quite tall, about 25 or 30, with long fair hair, big ears, and a scar under his left eye. Oh, and he's got a big nose.
– Colour of eyes?
– I've no idea.
– What was he wearing?
– A blue jacket and brown trousers . . .

2 Song: *Please Write*
● Get students to work individually, trying to put the words into the blanks. They can use their dictionaries or ask you for help with unfamiliar words.
● Let them compare their answers in small groups before you play the recording so they can check.
● You may want to play the recording more than once.
● When you go over the answers with them, be sure they understand why each blank is filled as it is.

Tapescript and answers to Exercise 2

PLEASE WRITE

I wonder what you're doing now.
Are *you* making a new friend?
I've got to see *you* again somehow.
I don't want this love to end.

Oh, baby, please write.
Why don't *you* write?
I'm waiting to get *your* letter, baby.
Please write.
Why don't *you* write?
It means so much to *me*.

I tried to call *you* on the phone,
But nobody knew *your* name.
Oh, *I* can feel *your* love run cold.
But listen to what I'm saying, baby.

SPEAKING

1 Talking about the recent past

• Give students five minutes to prepare a short talk about what they did yesterday evening or last weekend. Explain that they must include one lie.
• Help with vocabulary if necessary, but encourage students to use language that the others will understand easily.
• When students are ready, put them in groups of 3–4 and let them talk in turn. The group must try to decide which is the untrue statement.
• One member of each group should time the talks – they should go on for at least two minutes, and not more than three.

2 Talking about personal photos

• Students should have been warned in advance to bring photos to class.
• If students are studying in their own countries they can probably collect quite a number of family photos, photos of themselves when younger, etc. Even students studying abroad are likely to have some photos with them.
• Before starting, bring out one or two of your own photos and show them around.
• Get students to make comments and ask some questions about them.
• Write the questions (corrected if necessary) on the board.
• Possible questions:
  Who's that?
  How old is he/she?
  Where is it?
  When was that?
• Talk about what else it is possible to say about the photos (people's appearance, what they do, where they live and so on).
• Get students showing their photos in groups – not too many groups, so that you can get round to each one to help with vocabulary.
• If the activity goes well, it can be done more than once, with students showing their photos to several different groups.

3 Memory game: names of clothes

• It may be useful to do revision work on the names of articles of clothing – Lesson 9B contained a lot of new vocabulary, and students may not have learnt everything thoroughly.
• This exercise is a repeat of Lesson 9B Exercise 5. See the lesson notes for detailed suggestions. You may also like to try the suggested 'optional activity' from the same lesson, if you have not already done this.

4 Sketches

Introductory note

As this is the first time that students have done full-scale dramatisations, the quality will probably be uneven: some groups will succeed in completing and performing sketches, others may not. This doesn't matter: the purpose is not to put on a polished theatrical performance, but to revise some language points in a new and interesting way.

Not all students will be used to doing this sort of work in school, and there are always one or two students who really dislike acting. Some gentle pressure will be necessary to get everybody working, but once the initial resistance is overcome students will enjoy the activity. (Anybody who is really very shy, however, should not be forced to take part.)

Give lots of encouragement, and be generous with praise for good ideas and successful performances.

If possible you may like to record the final sketches on tape or video – this encourages students to aim at a high standard.

Presentation

Divide the students into groups of four to six. Try to mix strong and weak students.

Go through the instructions with them, helping them to understand what they have to do. (Note that Alex can be a boy's or a girl's name.)

Tell the students if they are going to be recorded when they perform their sketches.

Set a time-limit for the work.

Explain the listed words and expressions where necessary and practise pronunciation.

Preparation

If necessary, work with one group at the front of the class for a minute or two, demonstrating how to start. ('*OK. Mr and Mrs Harris and Alex are going into the bank. Who's Mr Harris? . . . What does the manager say?*')

In groups of less than six, not all the roles need to be included in the sketch.

Students usually spend the first five or ten minutes in despair because they can't think of anything, and then get going. If a group gets really stuck, help out with suggestions.

Discourage groups from writing over-complicated material which will be full of mistakes, and which only they will understand. They should use a maximum of material from the previous lessons (tell them to look back in their books) and a minimum of new vocabulary.

Practice

When groups are ready, ask them to practise their sketches a few times. Correct grammar and pronunciation where necessary.

Practice should be done with appropriate actions and movements (where space allows), so that when they perform their sketches for the class they will know how to position themselves.

Performance

When groups perform their sketches, make sure that the others keep quiet and listen. (Groups who have not yet performed will be tempted to discuss last-minute changes to their own sketches.)

Don't take the best group first (they will make the others feel they can't compete), but start with a group that is likely to do a reasonable job without breaking down (panic is infectious).

It's nice if the class applauds each performance.

If time allows, it's good to get students to try to learn their parts so that they can act them without scripts.

If you have recorded the sketches, don't be over-critical when you play them back – this is a vulnerable moment for students.

Practice Book exercises: choose two or more
1. Vocabulary revision (clothes).
2. Word stress.
3. Writing questions.
4. Third-person and plural -*s*.
5. *Some* and *any*.
6. Student's Cassette exercise (Student's Book Listening Exercise 1, third conversation). Students listen to the conversation and try to write it down.
7. Reading: students separate two mixed-up stories.
8. Reading: Part 11 of *It's a Long Story*.

SPEAKING

1 Work in groups of 3–4 people. Tell the others what you did yesterday evening or last weekend. You must speak for two minutes. You must tell the group one thing that is not true. See if they can tell you what it is.

Then I went to see my old friend the President ...

Not true !!!

2 Work in groups. Show the other students photos of your family and friends, and talk about them.

This is my sister. She's 23.

This is my mother.

What nice eyes!

She's very pretty.

This is my brother. He's got blue eyes.

Who's that?

3 What are you wearing?
1. Do you know the names of all the different clothes you are wearing? Check up.
2. Observe another student for one minute. Then turn your back and try to say everything that he/she is wearing.

4 Revision sketch. Work in groups of 4–6.
Roles:

Mr Harris
Mrs Harris
Their child Alex
Bank manager
Wanted man or woman
Policeman or policewoman

Write and practise a sketch, using the English you have learnt in Units 1–11. In your sketch, you must use five or more of these sentences:

First on the right, second on the left.
It's terrible.
I'm hungry.
Two boys and a girl.
I quite like it.
Tall, dark and good-looking.
What time is the next train?
Hands up!

12D Test yourself

LISTENING

1 Listen to the conversation and choose the correct answers.

1. Phone number: (a) 67482   (b) 64482   (c) 61483
2. Caller's name: (a) Mary   (b) Helen   (c) Sally
3. Caller asks for: (a) Mary   (b) Helen   (c) Sally
4. Film is at: (a) 7.15   (b) 7.45   (c) 7.00
5. Name of film: (a) *Gone with the Wind*   (b) *Ben Hur*
   (c) *King Kong*
6. Cinema is in: (a) Oxford   (b) Cambridge   (c) London
7. Meet at: (a) station   (b) cinema   (c) pub

2 Listen to the conversation and answer the questions.

1. What colour are the woman's ear-rings?
2. What colour are her eyes?
3. Is her hair short or long?

GRAMMAR

1 Put the words in order. Example:

school where you to go did ?

Where did you go to school ?

1. brother got blue has your eyes ?
2. glasses wear we both .
3. tired they very are all .

2 Choose the correct word.

1. My sister *is/has* got very long hair.
2. What colour *are/have* your eyes?
3. *Are/Have* you cold?
4. When I *am/have* dirty I *am/have* a bath.

3 Give the past of these verbs. Examples:

like liked   go went
1. stop, play, hate, study, work, live
2. come, know, say, see, speak, take

4 Make these sentences negative. Example:

I hated my school.

I did not hate my school.

1. I liked cheese when I was a child.
2. Peter got up at ten o'clock yesterday.
3. My mother was a teacher.

5 Make questions. Example:

They lived in Ireland. (*Where . . . ?*)

Where did they live ?

1. She got up at six o'clock. (*What time . . . ?*)
2. We played football at school. (*Did . . . ?*)

6 Ask for more information. Example:

Chris likes music. (*What sort . . . ?*)

What sort (of music) does she like ?

1. I saw Alice yesterday. (*Where . . . ?*)
2. I've got two brothers. (*. . . sisters?*)
3. Lucy's coming to see us. (*When . . . ?*)

7 Put in *this*, *that*, *these* or *those*.

1. 'Which ones do you want?' '................. blue ones over there.'
2. Look at .... new car in front of Anne's house.
3. Are you at home .... evening?

Unit 12: Lesson D

Students do a simple revision test.

The purpose of the test

This test, like the others in the book, is provided for teachers who feel that it will be useful. It covers several different areas: it is not of course necessary to do all of the sections, and teachers should select according to their students' needs. Teachers who do not feel the test will be useful should simply drop it altogether.

The test has three main functions:
1. To show you and the students whether there are any points that have not been properly learnt for any reason.
2. To identify any students who are having serious difficulty with the course, if this is not already evident.
3. To motivate the students to look back over the work they have done and do some serious revision before they move on.

If possible, try to make the students feel that they are 'testing themselves', rather than 'being tested'. It is not intended that students should 'pass' or 'fail' the test, and it is not particularly useful to give marks. (If the school or education system requires that this be done, you will need to work out a simple marking scheme.) But students should of course be told whether you feel their performance is satisfactory. In principle, most students ought to get most answers right. If this does not happen, efficient learning is not taking place (because of poor motivation, too rapid a pace, absenteeism, failure to do Practice Book work or follow-up study outside class, or for some other reason).

Administration

The test can be administered in various ways, depending on how strictly you want to control students' performance; whether you want to collect the answers and mark them, or allow the students to correct them in class; and so on.

The 'speaking' tests will need to be done individually, with students interrupting their work on the other tests to come and talk to you one at a time.

If you are not collecting students' scripts, correction can be done by class discussion when everybody has finished.

Notes, tapescripts and answers are given below.

LISTENING

• Tapescripts and answers are as follows. Before starting, go over the instructions and questions and clear up any problems.
• A possible approach is to play each conversation two or three times, pausing after each playing for students to write answers.

1 Tapescript
MARY: Hello, 64482.
HELEN: Hello, Mary. Can I speak to Sally?
MARY: Hi, Helen. Just a moment.
SALLY: Hello, Helen. How are you?
HELEN: Hi, Sally. Do you want to go and see *Ben Hur* in London tonight?
SALLY: Yes, OK. Which cinema is it on at?
HELEN: The Paramount, in Oxford Street.
SALLY: What time?
HELEN: Quarter to eight.
SALLY: OK. Let's meet at the station at 7.15.
HELEN: Right. Bye.
SALLY: See you. Bye.

Answers
1. 64482
2. Helen
3. Sally
4. 7.45
5. *Ben Hur*
6. London
7. station

2 Tapescript
MAN: I do like your ear-rings.
WOMAN: Oh, thank you.
MAN: They're such a lovely blue. Turquoise, aren't they?
WOMAN: Yes.
MAN: The same colour as your eyes. Really pretty. Your hair's nice, too.
WOMAN: Oh, do you think so?
MAN: Yes, I like it short. It suits you . . .

Answers
1. blue (turquoise)
2. blue
3. short

GRAMMAR

1 1. Has your brother got blue eyes?
2. We both wear glasses.
3. They are all very tired.

2 1. has
2. are
3. Are
4. am; have

3 1. stopped, played, hated, studied, worked, lived
2. came, knew, said, saw, spoke, took

4 1. I did not (didn't) like cheese when I was a child.
2. Peter did not (didn't) get up at ten o'clock yesterday.
3. My mother was not (wasn't) a teacher.

5 1. What time did she get up?
2. Did you/we play football at school?

6 1. Where did you see her?
2. Have you got any sisters?
3. When is (When's) she coming (to see us)?

7 1. Those
2. that
3. this

VOCABULARY

1 (Various possible answers.)

2 (Various possible answers.)

LANGUAGE IN USE

1 (Suggested questions. Other questions are possible in most cases.)
  1. How much is it / is that / are they?
  2. What's this/that?
  3. What are those?
  4. (Various possible answers.)
  5. Can I help you?
  6–9. (Various possible answers.)

PRONUNCIATION

1 1. grey
  2. rich
  3. wear
  4. where
  5. there

2 **colour**; **in**come; **vill**age; **pass**port; **cal**culator; A**mer**ica; **Eu**rope; re**mem**ber; a**rrive**; **or**ange; **diff**erent; **fav**ourite; ex**cept**; be**hind**; be**tween**; be**fore**; **some**thing; a**noth**er; **thou**sand; **act**ually.

WRITING

37 Lucerne Road
Edinburgh EH9 7BK

14 January 1990

Dear Mrs Anderson,

Thank you very much for your letter. I am arriving at Newton Station at 9.35 a.m. next Saturday. Can you meet me?

Yours sincerely,

Peter Morris

SPEAKING

Go over the instructions with the whole class and make sure they understand what they have to do. Then test the students one by one. The conversation should run more or less as follows, but all sorts of variations are possible.

YOU: Can I help you?
STUDENT: How much is the/that (blue) sweater in the window?
YOU: £19.50.
STUDENT: Can I try it on?
YOU: Of course.
STUDENT: (I'm afraid) it's too big. Can I try another one?
YOU: Yes, of course.
STUDENT: This one's OK. Have you got any other colours?
YOU: Yes. I've got it in red, green, yellow or black.
STUDENT: I'd like a red one . . . Yes, that's OK. I'll take it, please.

Test Book recordings
A recording for Test 3 in the Test Book follows this lesson on the Class Cassette.

VOCABULARY

1 Put four more words in each of these lists.

1. tall, nice, . . .
2. red, green, . . .
3. trousers, shirt, . . .
4. living room, . . .
5. eye, foot, . . .
6. station, bank, . . .

2 Write the names of:

1. four things that you like
2. four things that you don't like

LANGUAGE IN USE

1 Write questions for these answers. Example:

Mary Lewis. *What's your name ?*

1. £3.75
2. It's an umbrella.
3. They're train tickets.
4. Blue.
5. I'm just looking.
6. Yes, of course.
7. I'm afraid I haven't.
8. No, I don't.
9. I'm sorry, I can't remember.

PRONUNCIATION

1 Which word is different? Example:

like   by   ninth   (live)

1. size   grey   life   eye
2. buy   tired   rich   kind
3. wear   ear   hear   nearly
4. earn   third   where   dirty
5. purple   thirsty journey there

2 Which syllable is stressed? Example:

breakfast

colour; income; village; passport; calculator;
America; Europe; remember; arrive; orange;
different; favourite; except; behind; between; before;
something; another; thousand; actually.

WRITING

1 Write this letter with all the lines in the right places.

Yours sincerely,
Can you meet me?
Dear Mrs Anderson,
37 Lucerne Road
Thank you very much for your letter.
Peter Morris
Edinburgh EH9 7BK
I am arriving at Newton Station
    at 9.35 a.m. next Saturday.
14 January 1990

SPEAKING

1 Act out this conversation. Your teacher will take the other part.

CLOTHES SHOP
Go into a clothes shop and ask the price of the blue
sweater in the shop window. Ask to try it on. It is
too big. Try another one. It's OK. Ask if they have
any other colours. Choose a colour and buy
the sweater.

Unit 13 Differences

13A I can sing, but I can't draw

Can and *can't* for abilities.

1 Which of these things can you do? Which of them can't you do? Example:

'*I can sing, but I can't draw.*'

> draw   drive   make cakes
> play chess   play tennis
> play the violin   run a mile
> see well without glasses
> sing   speak Chinese
> speak German   type

2 🔲 Say these sentences after the recording.

1. I can sing.
2. I can't draw.
3. I can **type**.
4. Yes, I **can**.
5. No, I **can't**.

3 Can you swim / cook / play the piano / dance / go without sleep / sleep in the daytime? Ask two other people, and report their answers to the class. Make sentences with *but*.

'*Can you dance?*' '*Yes, I can.*' /
   '*No, I can't.*'
'*Diego can dance, but Alice can't.*'
'*Solange can dance, but she can't
   cook.*'

4 Listen, and write *can* or *can't*.

5 In groups: find a person for each job. Tell the class about it. Example:

'*Preeda can do the first job. He can't play the guitar, but he can play the flute. He can cook and drive, and he likes children.*'

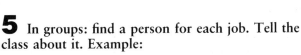

Telex machine operator wanted for a period of 9 months, must have had at least 2 years experience – if interested phone Milton Harbord on 01 621 5511.

Help us with our children and travel around the world. If you can play the guitar or another instrument, cook, and drive, phone Whitfield at 689 6328.

Typist required, excellent pay, one week nights, two weeks days. Musician appreciated. Write to Box 635, Oxford OX6 82J.

Please Help! We are moving to India in six months time and need a good home for our parrot Leroy. He's well behaved and very clean. Loves classical music. If interested please contact Richard Tilt 01 521 5558

urgently. Telephone 2014 01759 now!

Travelling companion/driver required for American writer; speaking English, other languages. Chess player appreciated. Excellent pay. Write to Box 492, Newton Tribune.

Take 2 Italian boys, 8 and 10, on holiday in June. Some cooking but no cleaning. Swimming, tennis, windsurfing. Very good pay. Phone Guidotti 2783440 evenings.

Expert tree surgeon required to remove four oak trees damaged by storm. Very difficult job. Phone Mrs Relton-Smithe 625 112.

Help wanted for old people's home in only

Can	
I can go (~~I can to go~~)	
you can go	
he/she/it can go (~~he/she/it cans go~~)	
we can go	
you can go	
they can go	
can I go? (~~do I can go?~~)	
I cannot (can't) go	

Learn: sleep (*noun*); glasses; can (could); cook; dance; drive (drove); make (made); run (ran); see (saw); sleep (slept); swim (swam); write (wrote); without.

Learn some of these if you want: cake; chess; piano; tennis; violin; type; in the daytime; go without sleep.

Unit 13: Lesson A

Students learn to talk about abilities.
Structure: *can* (affirmative, negative, question).
Phonology: /kən/, /kæn/ and /kɑ:nt/ (recognition and production); American /kænt/ (recognition).

Language notes and possible problems

1. Pronunciation When *can* is followed by another verb (as in *I can swim*), it is normally pronounced like *c'n* (/kən/); the strong pronunciation /kæn/ is mostly heard in short answers (*Yes, I can*). In questions (*Can you swim? What can you see?*), both pronunciations are possible.

In standard British English, *can't* is pronounced /kɑ:nt/. Exercise 4 also includes some examples of the American pronunciation /kænt/, for students to recognise.

2. Spelling You may wish to tell students that *cannot* is written as one word.

3. Grammar Point out that there is no *-s* on the third-person singular *can*, and that *can* is followed by an infinitive without *to*.

4. Articles Note the difference between *to play **the** piano* and *to play football/chess*.

Optional extra materials

Cards with *can*-questions (see Optional activity after Exercise 3).

1 *I can / I can't . . .*

- Let the students look at the words in the box and ask you if there are any that they don't understand.
- Then make a true sentence about yourself in the form *I can . . . but I can't . . .*
- Point out the pronunciations /kən/ and /kɑ:nt/, and make sure students notice the stress pattern of the sentence.
- Get them to practise the sample sentence, stressing as follows:
  '*I can **sing**, but I can't **draw**.*'
- Then let the students make sentences about themselves, using the words in the box.
- You could do this as a 'ball game': crumple a sheet of paper and roll it into a ball, and say your sentence again: '*I can . . . but I can't . . . And you?*'
- At the last words throw the ball to someone else, who must give their sentence and throw the ball again.

Optional activity
- Students mime things they can do; the others watch them and say '*You can cook*', or whatever they think it is.

2 Pronunciation of *can* and *can't*

- Ask students to look at the sentences and notice where the stress comes.
- Then play the recording or read the sentences for students to repeat. If you read the sentences yourself, be very careful not to stress *can* (/kən/) in sentences 1 and 3.

3 Survey

- Go over the vocabulary with the students.
- Demonstrate and help the students practise the pronunciation of the question and answer forms.
- Then divide the class into threes. Each group asks one another the questions, and notes the answers.
- When the questioning is finished, each person should report to the class with at least two sentences about the other people in the group. The sentences should all contain *but*.

Optional activity
- Prepare a large number of cards. Each card should tell students to find a person who can do one thing. Examples:
  Find a person who can speak Chinese (or some other appropriate language).
  Find a person who can stand on his/her head.
  Find a person who can solve this equation:
  $3x = 75 - 2x.$
- There should be several times as many cards as students – but some can be duplicated.
- Students take a card from you, and go round asking '*Can you . . . ?*' When they find a person who can, they write down his/her name and take another card.
- The winner is the one who collects the most names.

4 Listening for *can't* and unstressed *can*

- Students will hear eleven fragments (six of British speech followed by five of American speech).
- They simply have to note down whether they hear *can* or *can't* in each one.

Tapescript and answers to Exercise 4
1. I *can* type.
2. I *can't* type.
3. Well, Mr Wharton, I'd like to help, but I'm afraid I *can't* do it right now.
4. 'What are you doing?' 'It's all right, Dad, I *can* explain everything.'
5. Jane's eight years old, and she still *can't* swim.
6. You *can* have the cheese that's in the fridge, but please don't eat the eggs.
7. I *can* type.
8. I *can't* type.
9. I *can't* understand what she wants.
10. Young Robert *can't* talk very well.
11. I *can* eat anything I like.

5 Small ads

- Divide the class into groups of three or four.
- Let them read the small ads with their dictionaries or ask you for unknown words.
- Each group must find the best person in the group for each job, given the requirements and the abilities and tastes of the people in the group.
- The groups then report to the class, with the reasons for their choices.
- The class can vote on the best candidate for each job.

Optional activity
- Students can write a letter of application for the job they have been chosen for. Suggest something like:

Dear Sir/Madam,

I should like to apply for the job of .... which you advertised in yesterday's paper. I can .... and .... I like ....

I look forward to your reply.

Yours faithfully,

....

Practice Book exercises: choose two or more
1. Saying sentences with *can* and *can't* with correct stress.
2. Writing about things students can and can't do.
3. Vocabulary revision of words from Units 1 to 8.
4. Student's Cassette exercise (Student's Book Exercise 2). Listen and repeat.
5. Recreational reading: *Believe it or not.*

Unit 13: Lesson B

Students learn to compare how well things are done.
Structures: *I can . . . better than you; good at* + noun/gerund.
Phonology: different pronunciations of the letter *a*: /eɪ/, /æ/, /ɑː/, and /ɔː/.

1 True or false?
• Go over the table and explain vocabulary, or let the students use their dictionaries.
• Explain what *true* and *false* mean.
• Then get them to answer the questions, comparing notes with their neighbours.

Answers to Exercise 1

1. True	4. False	7. True
2. False	5. False	8. False
3. False	6. True	9. True

2 Listening: true or false?
• Get students to write the numbers 1–6 down the side of a sheet of paper.
• Then play the recording, pausing for them to write *T* or *F* for each sentence.

Tapescript and answers to Exercise 2
1. I'm the Queen. I can spell very well. (*T*)
2. I can draw better than the Prime Minister. (*F*)
3. The Minister of Finance can run faster than me. (*T*)
4. I'm the Minister of Education. I can run very fast. (*F*)
5. I can draw better than all the others. (*T*)
6. I can count better than all the others. (*F*)

3 Pronunciations of *a*
• Get the students to repeat the words after you or the recording.
• Point out that each row contains words where *a* is pronounced the same.
• Then let students work individually for a few minutes to see if they can classify the lettered words according to the pronunciations they have practised in the numbered rows.
• Let them compare answers in small groups.
• Rather than giving the answers (e.g. 1 or 3) right away, simply play the recording or say the words yourself.
• Then check which numbers they have put, and see if they can offer any rules.
• The rules are:
  /eɪ/ before consonant + *e*, or before *i* + consonant
  /æ/ before final consonant or double consonant
  /ɑː/ before (mute) *r*; before *f*, *s* + consonant, final *th*
  /ɔː/ before final *w*, double *l*, *lk*

Answers to Exercise 3

a. past 3	e. call 4	i. law 4
b. age 1	f. artist 3	j. paper 1
c. apple 2	g. pass 3	
d. bag 2	h. Spain 1	

4 *. . . when I was younger*
• Go over the sample sentences with the students, pointing out:
1. the use of *good at* + noun or gerund
2. ellipsis (omission of words) after *than* and *but*: e.g. '. . . than I can (swim) now.' '. . . but I'm not (good at maths) now.'
• You may wish to write the sentences up on the board and get the students to help you mark the stressed syllables before practising the sentences.
• Then ask each student to write two sentences about now and when he/she was younger.
• You can walk round while students are working to help with any problems.
• Then get each student to say one of his or her sentences to the class.

5 Memory test
• Divide the class into two teams.
• Each team must try to remember what the members of the other team said in Exercise 4.
• The person in question should answer '*You're right*' or '*I'm afraid you're wrong*'.
• Give one point for each correct answer.

Optional activity: boasting and confessing
• Students compete to produce the most impressive piece of boasting or confession.
• *Either* they tell the class what they can do, what they are good at, what they do well;
  Or they tell the class what they can't do, what they are bad at, what they do badly.
• Emphasize that they do not have to tell the truth.

Practice Book exercises: choose two or more
1. Marking stresses and /ə/ in sentences with *can* and *can't*.
2. Pronunciation of words with *a* in them.
3. Writing questions with *can*, Simple Past, Simple Present, and *have got*.
4. Writing a 'circle' with *can . . . faster/better* etc. *than*.
5. Recreational reading: a logic puzzle.

'Role' and 'real' communication
Some students enjoy role play, and may indeed be more articulate when acting a part than when expressing their own views and feelings. (Shy people are sometimes 'liberated' by being given a role to play.) Other students prefer to be themselves, and do best in exercises where they can say what they really think. It is important to provide exercises that are suitable for both kinds of personality, and to remember that there is not necessarily something wrong if some of one's students are unenthusiastic about role play or if others don't want to talk about themselves.

13B Better than all the others

I can ... better than ... ; good at + ...ing.

WHAT CAN THEY DO?	PLAY TENNIS	DRAW	COUNT	SPELL	RUN 100m	MAKE CAKES	SPEAK ENGLISH
The Queen			1 2 3	abcde	43 secs		3 words
The Prime Minister			1 2	ab	35 secs		10 words
The Foreign Minister			1	abc	5 mins	–	–
The Minister of Education			3 1 4 2	a	–		1 word
The Minister of Finance			0	abcd	22 secs		400 words

1 True or false? Look at the table.

1. The Queen can spell very well.
2. The Foreign Minister can count quite well.
3. The Minister of Finance can't speak English.
4. The Prime Minister can't count.
5. The Queen can make cakes better than the Minister of Finance.
6. The Minister of Education can draw better than the Queen.
7. The Prime Minister can run faster than the Minister of Education.
8. The Minister of Education can spell better than the Foreign Minister.
9. The Queen can spell better than all the others.

2 True or false? Listen to the recording.

3 Pronunciations of the letter *a*. Say these words after the recording or your teacher.

1. make   cake   play   late   rain
2. finance   am   cat   back   hand
3. faster   glasses   car   bath   half
4. draw   all   walk   saw   tall   talk

Now look at these words: 1, 2, 3 or 4? Decide how to pronounce them and then check with your teacher or the recording.

a. past ...3...   f. artist
b. age   g. pass
c. apple   h. Spain
d. bag   i. law
e. call   j. paper

4 Talk about now and when you were younger; use *than* and *but*.

'My father can speak Spanish better now than he could when I was younger.'
'I could swim better when I was younger than I can now.'
'I was good at maths when I was younger, but I'm not now.'
'I'm better at running now than I was when I was younger.'
'When I was younger I couldn't cook at all, but now I can cook quite well.'

5 In teams: try to remember other students' sentences. One point for each correct one.

Michel can ski better now than he could when he was younger.

You're right. / I'm afraid you're wrong.

Learn: count; draw (drew); sing (sang); ski; foreign; better; fast; faster; than; good at ...ing.

13C I'm much taller than my mother

Comparative and superlative adjectives.

More beautiful slimmer fatter OLDER

1 Look at the list of adjectives. Can you see any rules? Which adjectives are irregular? What are the comparative and superlative of these words?

long _longer longest_

dark   near   hungry   intelligent
cold   big   nice   expensive

ADJECTIVE	COMPARATIVE	SUPERLATIVE
1. old	older	oldest
short	shorter	shortest
cheap	cheaper	cheapest
fair	fairer	fairest
2. fat	fatter	fattest
slim	slimmer	slimmest
3. happy	happier	happiest
easy	easier	easiest
4. late	later	latest
fine	finer	finest
5. good	better	best
bad	worse	worst
far	farther	farthest
6. interesting	more interesting	most interesting
beautiful	more beautiful	most beautiful
difficult	more difficult	most difficult

2 Compare people you know.

A is (much)	taller shorter older younger slimmer etc.	than B.

'I'm much taller than my mother.'
'Mario's a bit older than his brother.'

In your family, who is the oldest / the youngest / the shortest / the best at English?

3 Compare countries (warm/cold/big/small/ cheap/expensive/noisy/quiet) or cars (big/small/fast/ slow/expensive/cheap/comfortable/economical/good). Examples:

'Japan is much more expensive than Greece.'
'A Volkswagen is much cheaper than a Mercedes.'

4 Choose a question, and ask as many other students as you can. Report the answers.

Who's the	best singer funniest comedian most beautiful actress best-looking actor most interesting writer most intelligent politician	in the world? in this/your country?
What's the	most beautiful nicest most interesting most boring	place (that) you know?

Learn: world; place; better; best; worse; worst; easy; difficult; funny; beautiful; slow; boring; more; most.

Choose two or more to learn: politician; singer; comedian; actress; actor; writer.

Unit 13: Lesson C

Students learn to compare people, places and things.
Structures: comparative and superlative of adjectives; *a bit / much* before comparative adjectives.

Language notes and possible problems

1. Pronunciation You will want to point out the pronunciation of *longer/longest* (/ˈlɒŋɡə(r)/ /ˈlɒŋɡɪst/); of *younger/youngest* (/ˈjʌŋɡə(r)/ /ˈjʌŋɡɪst/); and of *comfortable* (/ˈkʌmftəbl/); and to remind students that *the* is pronounced /ðiː/ before vowels (e.g. *the oldest*).

2. *than I / than me* Tell the students that *I* and *me* are both correct after *than*; *I* is preferred in a more formal style, and is common in written English. (The same is true of *she/her*, etc.) Americans are more likely than British people to consider *me*, etc., as sounding uneducated.

3. Topics In Exercise 4, you may very well want to choose different topics to fit in better with your students' experience and knowledge.

---

1 Rules for comparing adjectives

• Ask students to look at the table of adjectives and try to see what is special about each group. Do not get them to offer suggestions aloud yet.
• Ask them to do Exercise 1 individually, to check their guesses.
• Get them to compare their answers in small groups before checking them with you.
• Ask them to tell you a rule for each group of words.
  Group 1: normal one-syllable adjectives add *-er*, *-est*.
  Group 2: one-syllable adjectives that end in one vowel + one consonant: these double the consonant and add *-er*, *-est*.
  Group 3: two-syllable adjectives ending in *y* change the *y* to *i* and add *-er*, *-est*.
  Group 4: one-syllable adjectives ending in *e* add *-r*, *-st*.
  Group 5: irregular.
  Group 6: longer adjectives prefix *more*, *most*.
• As a working rule, you can tell students to use *more* and *most* with adjectives of more than one syllable, except for two-syllable words ending in *-y*.
• Explain any words the students don't know.

2 Comparing people (age and appearance)

• In a class where this will not cause discomfort, you can get the students to compare people in the class. Teach the use of a *much / a bit* and make sure students use them in their sentences.
• One way of making this exercise more interesting is to get each student to make one comparison and then get everyone to try to write as many as they can remember.
• Point out the use of *in* after superlatives and make sure students say *in my family* or *in the class*.

3 Comparing countries and cars

• You will want to introduce the new adjectives before you begin the exercise, or as you go along.
• According to your students' interests, you may wish to talk about countries or cars or both.
• Point out that the *w* in *slow* is considered a vowel, not a consonant, so isn't doubled for comparative and superlative.

4 Class survey (superlatives)

• Go over the new vocabulary with the students.
• Practise the pronunciation of the first question in each group (*Who's the best singer in the world?* and *What's the most beautiful place you know?*).
• Ask students to suggest other questions, or add other questions yourself that correspond to the students' interests and knowledge (e.g. *best football team*, *best rock group*).
• Each student should choose one question and practise it with a partner a few times until they are both satisfied with each other's pronunciation. Problems can be referred to you.
• Students should then get up and walk round, if possible, and try to get answers for their questions from everyone else in the class.
• When they have finished, ask for reports, e.g. *'Everybody thinks Rome is the most interesting place they know.'* *'Half the class thinks Mishima is the most interesting writer in the world.'*

Practice Book exercises: choose two or more
1. Writing comparatives and superlatives.
2. Writing the simple forms of comparative and superlative adjectives.
3. Writing sentences with comparatives.
4. Writing true sentences with superlatives.
5. Recreational reading: *Believe it or not*.

Unit 13: Lesson D

Students learn to talk about similarities and differences.
Structures: *the same as; different from; (not) as . . . as.*
Phonology: weak forms of *as* and *from*; stress and rhythm recognition.

Language note
Stress Because English is a 'stress-timed' language, some words are pronounced more quickly and lightly than others. Students whose own languages are not stress-timed find this difficult to get used to, and they often have trouble actually hearing some of the words in a sentence, particularly words such as *from, can, and, but, than,* and *as*, which have a 'weak form' with the vowel /ə/. Exercise 3 will help them to become more sensitive to unstressed words.

Optional extra materials
Sets of brochures on countries, cars, or other things to compare (Exercise 4).

1 The same or different?
• Get students to read through the list of pairs, using their dictionaries where necessary, to decide whether the things in each pair are the same or different.
• They should put numbers down the page, and *the same* or *different* by each number.
• Walk round while they work; make sure they are not omitting *the* in *the same*.
• Then each student should write three sentences with *the same as* and three with *different from*, like the ones in the examples.
• Get them to read out their sentences; emphasise correct stress, teaching the unstressed pronunciation of *as* (/əz/), and reminding them of the unstressed pronunciation of *from* (/frəm/). These pronunciations will be easier to realise if they say their sentences with a good rhythm.

Answers to Exercise 1

1. the same	9. different
2. different	10. different
3. the same	11. different
4. different	12. different
5. the same	13. different
6. the same	14. the same
7. different	15. different
8. different	

2 *(not) as . . . as . . .*
• Practise the pronunciation of the example sentences (using the recording if you wish), paying careful attention to the pronunciation of *as* (/əz/) and to the rhythm.
• Get students to write their sentences; go round helping as necessary.
• When they are ready, ask them to read their sentences to each other or to the class.
• At this stage, it is probably better not to introduce the alternative structure *not so . . . as . . .* ; *not as* is equally correct and less confusing.

3 How many words?
• Play the sentences through twice or more, pausing afterwards each time so students can note their answers.
• When you have played the ten sentences, let the students compare notes in small groups and then play the sentences again so they can listen more carefully to those where they differ.
• Then check their answers.

Tapescript and answers to Exercise 3
1. He can swim as well as a fish. (8)
2. These oranges are much better than the others. (8)
3. Is this different from Ann's? (5)
4. There are some much better ones in the fridge. (9)
5. Do you think the new book's better than the old one? (12)
6. They said it was an interesting film. (7)
7. Mary and Tom are both taller than me. (8)
8. It will be easier to talk at seven o'clock. (9)
9. What's the most expensive car in the world? (9)
10. I'd like a cup of tea better than a glass of beer. (13)

Optional activity after Exercise 3
• Ask students to say each sentence in Exercise 3 after the recording or after you.
• Get them to decide how many stressed syllables there are in each case. For example, the first sentence has eight words, but only three stressed syllables.
• If they pronounce the stressed syllables slowly and clearly, they will find it easier to say the other syllables quickly and lightly.
• In problem cases you can help them by 'backchaining': start by saying from the last stressed syllable to the end of the sentence; then the next-to-last stressed syllable to the end of the sentence, and so on.

4 Detailed comparisons
• For this exercise, it will help students if you can collect brochures on countries, cars, or anything else you think they might like to compare. It is not important in a monolingual class if the brochures are in their native language rather than in English, as they are only a starting point for their work.
• If you do have brochures, pass them around after dividing the class into groups of about four.
• If you do not have brochures, tell the groups they must choose two countries or two cars or two famous people. Be prepared to suggest specific ones if they are stuck.
• Tell each group they must decide which two things they are going to compare, and write down at least eight points of comparison.
• Enthusiastic groups will always go on if they have reached the target.
• Walk round to give any help that is needed.
• You may need to help with suggestions of points.
• Make sure each group has a secretary noting the sentences down as they produce them.
• The final products can be read out or posted up for the other groups to read.

Practice Book exercises: choose two or more
1. Writing sentences with *(not) as . . . as.*
2. Writing sentences with *the same as* and *different from.*
3. Check on revision vocabulary.
4. Revision of stress patterns in some longer adjectives.
5. Translation of sentences from the unit.
6. Extended writing: comparison of two people.
7. Reading: Part 12 of *It's a Long Story.*

13D The same or different?

More comparisons; *the same as* and *different from*;
as . . . as.

1 The same or different? Use your dictionary;
write three sentences with *the same as* and three
sentences with *different from*. Examples:

Three o'clock in the afternoon is the same
as 15.00.

A café is different from a pub.

1. 7 × 12 and 3 × 28
2. Britain and England
3. The Netherlands and Holland
4. The USSR and Russia
5. Peking and Beijing
6. three o'clock and 15.00
7. a café and a pub
8. handsome and pretty
9. a woman and a wife
10. a pen and a pencil
11. 4,718 and 4.718
12. a cooker and a cook
13. a typewriter and a typist
14. a telephone number and a phone number
15. a restaurant and a hotel

2 Compare some of these people and things. Use
(*not*) *as . . . as . . .* Examples:

I'm as good-looking as a film star.

A Volkswagen is not as quiet as a
Rolls-Royce.

| I/me   a film star   a Volkswagen |
| a Rolls-Royce   the President   Bach |
| an elephant   a cat   Canada |
| rock music   Kenya   a piano |

| tall   heavy   good-looking |
| strong   old   fast   economical |
| cold   warm   cheap   expensive |
| big   noisy   quiet   comfortable |
| intelligent   nice |

3 Listen to the recording. How many words are
there in each sentence? What are they? (Contractions
like *I'm* count as two words.)

4 Work in groups. In each group, make a detailed
comparison between two people, or two countries, or
two cars, or two other things. Write at least eight
sentences.

"How do you mean I'm as fit as
a man of thirty – I am thirty!"

As and *than*
I can run faster *than* my brother.
My brother can't run *as* fast *as* me.
My brother can run *as* fast *as* my father.
Peking is the same *as* Beijing.

Learn: pencil; restaurant; hotel; economical;
comfortable; noisy; quiet; warm; heavy; fast;
handsome; typewriter.

Learn if you want: typist; film star; president;
piano; rock (music); cooker; pub.

Unit 14 Personal information

14A How old are you?

dinosaur

Le Mans Sports Bentley

statue by Degas

early telephone

Great Pyramid of Giza

1 Look at the pictures. How old do you think the different things are? How heavy? How big? Examples:

'I think the dinosaur is 75 million years old.'
'I think the car is 3 metres long.'
'I think the pyramid is 120 metres high.'
'I think the statue weighs 50 kilos.'
'I think the dinosaur weighed 30 tonnes.'

2 Listen to the descriptions. What is the person describing – the dinosaur, the car, the pyramid, the statue or the telephone?

3 Say the numbers.

75 57 48 21 99
151 278 984 602
1,000 1,500 75,000 1,000,000 6,000,000

4 Make sentences about yourself and other people. Examples:

'I'm 1m 65.'
'My husband is 1m 85, and he weighs 70 kilos.'
'I weigh about 55 kilos.'
'My baby's six months old.'
'My mother's 66, but she looks older.'
'I'm 34, and I look my age.'
'I'm over 21.'

5 Ask some other students.

'How old/tall are you?'
'How much do you weigh?'

6 Describe somebody. The class must try to say who it is.

'She's a bit taller than me – about 1m 75. She weighs about 60 kilos. She's as old as me – over 20 and under 30. She's got dark hair.'

---

1 inch = 2½cm
12 inches = 1 foot (30cm)
1 pound = about 450gm
2.2 pounds = 1 kilogram

Learn: height; weight; metre; month; pound; think (thought); weigh; high; over (= 'more than'); under (= 'less than').

68

Unit 14: Lesson A

Students learn to talk about weights and measures.
Structures: *be* with ages and measures; comparatives and superlatives.

Language notes and possible problems

1. Metric and imperial measures Metric measures are used in the lesson. Students who are in an English-speaking country or planning to go to one will need to learn about the basic imperial units (inch, foot, pound) and to have a feeling for how much they represent; you may want to spend a little time on this. The table at the bottom of the Student's Book page gives rough equivalents.

Note that British people calculate their weight in *stones* (1 stone = 14 pounds); Americans calculate their weight in pounds.

A British *ton* (2,240 pounds) is very slightly heavier than a metric tonne; an American ton (2,000 pounds) is rather lighter.

2. Ages In talking about people (but not things) we tend to drop the expression *years old*.

3. Tall This word is used mostly for people; sometimes for objects, especially buildings and trees. You may wish to tell students that *high* is the usual word for mountains and hills.

4. Pronunciations *Height* (/haɪt/) and *weight* (/weɪt/) are confusing.

5. People's weights (Exercises 4–6) You may want to avoid or adapt these exercises in classes where somebody has a weight problem.

6. Saying numbers (Exercise 3) Note that *1,000* and *1,000,000* can be said as either *a thousand/million* or *one thousand/million*. But *1,500* can only be said as *one thousand five hundred*.

Students may add *-s* wrongly to larger numbers: look out for mistakes like **seventy-five thousands*.

Note also: British English *two hundred and seventy-eight, nine hundred and eighty-four*; American English *two hundred seventy-eight, nine hundred eighty-four*.

Optional extra materials
Pictures of people of various ages (Exercise 1).

1 Guessing ages, sizes etc.
• Look over the examples and practise the pronunciation of the new words.
• Get students to say how old, heavy and big they think the various things might be. They should use the structures illustrated in the examples.

Answers to Exercise 1
– The dinosaur lived about 150 million years ago. Dinosaurs of this species (diplodocus) were up to 26 metres long, and may have weighed up to 80 tonnes.
– The Great Pyramid of Giza was built about 4,500 years ago. It is about 135 metres high; the sides measure about 270 metres at the base.
– The telephone was designed by the German engineer Philipp Reis in about 1861. The box which holds the microphone is 11.5cm square at the base and 11cm high; the other part (the receiver) measures 24cm × 9cm at the base and is 9cm high. The microphone and its box weigh about 225gm; the receiver weighs about 110gm.
– The statue was made by Edgar Degas in 1880. It is 98cm high, and weighs about 40kg.
– The Bentley was built in 1930. It is 4.4 metres long and 1.75 metres wide. It weighs about 1.7 tonnes (1,727kg).

2 Listening to descriptions
• Play the recording (or read out the descriptions), pausing after each sentence so that students can say or write which object they think is being described.

Tapescript and answers to Exercise 2
1. It's about 150 million years old. (*the dinosaur*)
2. It's about 4,500 years old. (*the pyramid*)
3. It's about four and a half metres long. (*the car*)
4. It's about one metre high, and weighs about 40 kilograms. (*the statue*)
5. It's about 135 metres high. (*the pyramid*)
6. It's older than the telephone, but it's not as old as the dinosaur. (*the pyramid*)
7. It's bigger than the telephone, but it's not as long as the dinosaur. (*the car*)
8. It weighs more than the car, but not as much as the pyramid. (*the dinosaur*)
9. It's not as old as the telephone or the statue, but it's heavier than both of them. (*the car*)
10. It's not as heavy as the car, and it's older than the statue. (*the telephone*)
11. It's the highest of the five things. (*the pyramid*)
12. It's the oldest of the five things. (*the dinosaur*)
13. It's the fastest of the five things. (*the car*)

3 Saying numbers
• This gives students some quick revision practice in saying larger numbers aloud. See *Language notes* for some possible problems.

4 People's heights and weights
• Go over the examples and get students to make similar sentences.
• Follow up by asking students to guess your height and weight (if these are not sensitive areas!) and those of two volunteers.
• Then ask them to guess the heights and weights of things in the room (use *high*, not *tall*).

5 Asking other students
• Students can ask their neighbours or do it as a walk-round exercise. Avoid the activity if it is likely to embarrass anybody.

6 Identifying people from descriptions
• Go over the example.
• Ask students to prepare a description of another student, or somebody that everybody knows, using the structures illustrated in the example.
• Get students to give their descriptions; the others try to guess who is being described.
• In a large class, do the exercise in groups.

Optional activity
• Think of a person; don't say who it is. Students ask questions about the person (age, height, weight, appearance) until they can work out who it is.
• Follow up by getting students to do it in groups.

Practice Book exercises: choose two or more
1. Dialogue completion: questions about height, weight and age.
2. Information transfer: sentences about height, weight and age.
3. Writing numbers in words.
4. Writing descriptions.
5. Writing times from clocks.
6. Crossword (vocabulary from Unit 13).

Unit 14: Lesson B

Students learn to say more about people's appearances, relating them to professional and personality types.
Structures: *What does X look like?*; *look like* + noun phrase; *look* + adjective; *What is X like?*

Language notes and possible problems
Look like The structures *What does X look like?* and *What is X like?* are complex and not easy for students to master. They may tend to use *How . . . ?* instead of *What . . . like?* to elicit descriptions, or to confuse *What is X like?* and *What does X like?*

1 What do they do?
● Give students a minute or two to look at the photographs.
● Explain the words and practise their pronunciation.
● Spend a few minutes in general discussion, getting students to use the expressions illustrated in the examples (*I don't agree*; *looks like*; *looks more like*).
● Put students in groups of three or four. Each group *must* draw up an agreed group list, saying what profession each person has.
● When they are ready, see whether all the groups have reached similar conclusions.

Answers to Exercise 1
A is a footballer.
B is a poet.
C is an actor playing a criminal.
D is a scientist.
E is a politician.
F is a secretary.

2 Personality types
● Exercise 2 can be done in the same way.
● Explain and practise the vocabulary and the example sentences.
● Start with a general discussion, and then ask for groups to produce lists.
● There are no 'right answers'.

3 Personalisation
● Start by getting students to write at least one sentence each (preferably about themselves).
● In a friendly class, they can read their sentences out to everybody; less confident students might prefer just to show you what they have written.
● Then get students to ask and answer questions as in the example.

4 Information transfer: personality chart
● Look over the chart and the examples with the students. Explain the new words and practise the pronunciation. Make sure students all understand how to 'read' the chart. Point out if necessary that *self-c.*, *opt.* and *pess.* stand for *self-confident*, *optimistic* and *pessimistic* respectively.
● Get students to write two or three sentences each about Harry and Claire. They can read them out to the class or compare notes in groups.
● Here and in the next exercise, note that *a bit* is used mainly with more negative characteristics – one is more likely to say *a bit shy* than *a bit calm*.

5 Personalisation: comparing impressions of personality
● If possible, students in each pair should know each other quite well.
● Tell students to copy the chart (without the letters *H* and *C*).
● They should first enter their own initial in an appropriate place on each line, according to how calm/nervy, patient/impatient etc. they feel they are. Tell them not to show their partners what they have written.
● Next, they should enter their partner's initial, according to their impression of his/her personality.
● Then tell them to compare charts and see what differences there are between their own assessments and their partner's.
● Finally, look over the example and tell students to report some of their findings to the class in the same way.

Practice Book exercises: choose two or more
1. Further work on *look*, *look like* and *be like*.
2. Revision of articles.
3. Word stress.
4. Distinguishing *as* and *than*.
5. Students read a short text about their personality and write a few sentences about themselves.
6. Reading: students read a description and choose the illustration that corresponds to the text.

14B You look shy

People's appearance and personality.

A

B

C

D

E

F

1 What do they do? Look at the pictures.
The six people are: a *criminal*, a *poet*, a *footballer*, a
secretary, a *scientist* and a *politician*. Discuss who
does what. Examples:

*'I think C is a poet.'   'I don't agree. I think C's a
  criminal.'*
*'D looks like a scientist.'   'No, E looks more like a
  scientist.'*

2 What are they like? Look at the pictures and
discuss the people's personalities. Useful words:

> kind   shy   sensitive   self-confident
> intelligent   stupid   bad-tempered   calm
> friendly   nervy   optimistic   pessimistic

Examples:

'What is B like, do you think?'   'Very shy.'
*'I think A looks quite friendly.'   'I don't agree.
  A looks very bad-tempered to me.'*

3 Say some things about yourself and other people.
Ask about other people. Examples:

'I look shy, but I'm not.'
'What's your sister like?'   'She's quite bad-tempered.'

4 Look at the personality chart. What can you say
about Harry and Claire? Use *not at all, not very, a
bit, quite, very* and *extremely*. Examples:

'Harry's a bit pessimistic.'   H = Harry
'Claire's extremely self-confident.'   C = Claire

CALM	......H............................C.....	NERVY
PATIENT	H...............................C.............	IMPATIENT
SHY	.................H....................C.....	SELF-C.
QUIET	.................H.............C.............	TALKATIVE
OPT.	..........C..................H..............	PESS.

5 Copy the chart. Work with a partner. Fill in the
chart for yourself and your partner. Then compare
charts with your partner and see what he/she has
written. Report to the class. Example:

*'Celia thinks I'm a bit nervy, but I think I'm
extremely calm. I think Celia's quite talkative, but
she doesn't agree. We both agree that I'm more
optimistic than her.'*

> 'What **is** she **like**?'   'She's very shy.'
> 'What **does** he **look like**?'   'He looks like
>   a scientist.'

> **Learn:** agree; look; extremely; that (*conjunction*).
>
> **Learn four or more of these:** calm; nervy; patient;
> impatient; optimistic; pessimistic; shy; self-confident;
> sensitive; stupid; bad-tempered; friendly; talkative.

14C When is your birthday?

Dates.

1 🔊 Pronounce the names of the months.

January February **March** April **May**
June July **August** September October
November December

And can you pronounce these?

week month year

2 Can you say the numbers?

1st first	10th	30th
2nd	11th	31st
3rd	12th twelfth	40th
4th	13th	52nd
5th	14th	63rd
6th	18th	70th
7th	20th twentieth	99th
8th	21st twenty-first	100th
9th	22nd twenty-second	

3 Ask and answer.

'*What's the eighth month?*' '*August.*'

4 When is your birthday? Examples:

'*My birthday is on March the twenty-first.*'
  (OR: '*. . . the twenty-first of March.*')
'*My birthday is on November the third.*'
  (OR: '*. . . the third of November.*')
'*My birthday is today.*' '*Happy Birthday!*'

5 How to say and write dates.

WRITE	SAY
14 Jan(uary) 1990 14.1.90 (GB) 1.14.90 (US)	January the fourteenth, nineteen ninety (GB) January fourteenth . . . (US)
5 Apr(il) 1892	April the fifth, eighteen ninety-two
9 Dec(ember) 1600	December the ninth, sixteen hundred

5 Nov(ember) 1804	November the fifth,
	  eighteen hundred and
	  four
	OR: . . . eighteen oh four

Say these dates:

14 Jan 1978	17 May 1936	30 Dec 1983
3 Aug 1066	10 Oct 1906	3 Mar 1860
21 Sept 1980	20 July 1840	1 April 1900

**What is today's date? What about tomorrow, the day
after tomorrow, yesterday, and the day before
yesterday?**

6 Listen to the recording and write the dates.

7 Can you match the dates and the pictures?
(There are too many dates.)

12 Oct 1492	6 May 1525	4 July 1776
8 June 1876	17 Dec 1903	17 Jan 1910
29 May 1953	22 Nov 1963	20 July 1969
6 Oct 1980		

*Columbus reached America
on . . .*

*J. F. Kennedy was assassinated
on . . .*

*Mount Everest was climbed for
the first time on . . .*

*The United States declared its
independence from Britain on . . .*

*The first person walked on the
moon on . . .*

*The first heavier-than-air flight
took place on . . .*

Learn: *the names of the months; ordinal numbers
from* tenth *to* hundredth; *week; birthday; date; new;
today; tomorrow; the day before yesterday;
the day after tomorrow; after; Happy Birthday.*

Unit 14: Lesson C

Students learn to talk about dates.
Structures: article in *January the fourteenth* etc.; *on* before dates.
Phonology: more practice of /θ/.

Language notes and possible problems

1. Written dates   There are various conventions for writing dates. Not all of them are taught here.

2. Stress (Exercise 5)   *Thirteen, fourteen, fifteen*, etc. are stressed at the end when alone. However, the stress can move to the beginning, especially if a stressed syllable follows immediately – for example in *'fourteen ninety-two, 'thirteen seventy-eight*. Some other words behave like this – e.g. *afternoon* (compare *this 'after'noon* and *'afternoon 'tea*).

3. Vocabulary   This lesson may have too much new vocabulary for students to manage in one go. If so, come back to the ordinals and the months again later.

Optional extra materials

Specially prepared parcel for 'pass the parcel'. (See Optional activity.)

1   The names of the months

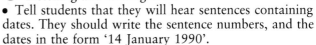

- Practise these, paying attention to stress. The recording can be used as a model.
- Practise *week, month* (/mʌnθ/) and *year* (/jɪə(r)/). Ask students if they can think of any other words like *month* in which *o* is pronounced like *u*. (Examples: *son, mother, some, one, money*.)
- Close books and go round the class seeing if students can remember the months.

2   Ordinal numbers

- Students have already learnt the first nine of these. The rest should present little difficulty except for pronunciation.
- Explain that there are three syllables in *twentieth* (/'twentiəθ/), *thirtieth* (/'θɜːtiəθ/) etc.
- You may like to add *thousandth* to the list, but it is very difficult to pronounce.
- The recording can be used as a model if you wish.

3   'What's the eighth month?'

- Students can test each other in a 'chain': A makes up a question for B, who answers and makes a question for C, and so on.
- The question is something of a tongue-twister, but gives good practice in pronouncing /θ/.

4   'When is your birthday?'

- Look over the examples and explain any difficulties.
- Then ask everybody. If it is somebody's birthday, teach the class *Happy Birthday To You*. (Use the recording as a guide if necessary.)
- If you want more practice, do a walk-round exercise.

5   Saying and writing dates

- Look over the examples and deal with any problems.
- Get the students to say the dates. Note that *1906* can be said as either *nineteen hundred and six* or *nineteen O six* (like 'nineteen oh six').

6   Listening and writing dates

- Tell students that they will hear sentences containing dates. They should write the sentence numbers, and the dates in the form '14 January 1990'.
- Play the recording, stopping after each section for students to write.
- Play the recording again if necessary.
- Let students compare notes before checking answers.

Tapescript and answers to Exercise 6

1. I was born on July the first, nineteen sixty-five.
2. 'What date's the meeting?' 'September the seventeenth.'
3. She was married on April the seventh, nineteen twenty.
4. 'I'll never forget the day I first met you.' 'When was it, then?' 'August the first, nineteen eighty-nine. It was raining.'
5. 'When are you leaving?' 'On a Tuesday.' 'Which Tuesday?' 'The sixth, I think.' 'The sixth of what?' 'November, of course.'
6. She died on May the twentieth, 1886, in the early afternoon, at the age of ninety-seven.

7   Matching dates and pictures

- Students can do the exercise by group discussion.

Answers to Exercise 7

– Columbus reached America on 12 October 1492.
– J. F. Kennedy was killed on 22 November 1963.
– Mount Everest was first climbed on 29 May 1953.
– The United States declared its independence from Britain on 4 July 1776.
– The first moon-walk was on 20 July 1969.
– The first heavier-than-air flight took place on 17 December 1903.

Optional activity: 'Pass the parcel'

- Before the lesson, prepare a parcel. It must have a number of wrappings, one outside the other; inside *each* wrapping there is a picture of a 'present' (or a card with the name of a present on). Students must know the words for the 'presents'.
- Students and teacher sit in a circle and pass the parcel, saying the names of the months in turn.
- The teacher positions himself or herself so as to get the parcel on the month of his/her birthday, and says *It's my birthday!*
- Students say (or sing) *Happy Birthday!*
- The teacher opens the parcel, takes out the first picture or word, looks at it and says *'Oh! A car!'* (or whatever) *'How lovely!'*
- The teacher passes the parcel on. Whenever a student says the name of his or her birth month, he or she opens a wrapping.
- If there are twelve (or twenty-four) students, the teacher must continue to play to make a thirteenth, so that the months change for each person. Otherwise he/she can drop out.
- In larger classes, the game can be played in groups.

Practice Book exercises: choose two or more

1. Saying dates.
2. Answering questions about dates and times.
3. Word stress.
4. Student's Cassette exercise (Student's Book Exercise 1). Saying the names of the months.
5. Controlled writing: description of a room.
6. Free writing: description of a room.
7. Recreational reading: *Believe it or not*.

Unit 14: Lesson D

Students learn to make phone calls in English.
Structures: difficult question structures.
Phonology: stress and rhythm.

Language notes and possible problems
1. *Can* and *could* both occur in the dialogues. Point out that *could* makes a request less direct.
2. Demonstratives Note that British people use *this* to identify themselves on the phone, and *that* to ask who the other person is. Americans use *this* in both cases.
3. *What sort of . . . ?, How many . . . ? etc*. Questions which begin with *interrogative expression + noun* are difficult to construct when the noun is the object. Exercise 1 includes some practice on this point.

1 Constructing questions
• The students' task here is to make the questions that they will have to answer in Exercise 2.
• Some of the questions are difficult to construct, and students may need to think a bit.
• If you mix written and oral work, you can make sure that everybody solves at least some of the problems.
• Students should finish by writing a complete list of the questions; they will need this for Exercise 2.

Answers to Exercise 1
1. What is Dan's phone number?
2. What is Sue's phone number?
3. When is Sue's birthday?
4. How old is Sue?
5. Is Sue as old as Dan?
6. What time is the party?
7. What sort of food does Sue want?
8. What sort of CDs does she want?
9. How many brothers has Sue got?
10. What sort of job does Sue do?
11. What is Sue's boss's name?
12. Is Dan as old as Sue's boss?
13. Is Dan's hair the same colour as John's?

2 Listening for specific information
• Tell students to close their books. Play the first conversation, more than once if necessary, while students write the answer to the first question.
• Play the second conversation right through.
• Tell students, individually or in groups, to write as many of the other answers as they can manage.
• Play the conversation again and see if they can get some more answers.
• Go through the conversations with books open. Play the recording again and deal with any problems.
• Point out the expressions that are typical of telephone calls (*Could I speak to . . . ?*; *This is . . .*; *Is that . . . ?*; *Can I take a message?*, etc.).

Tapescript for Exercise 2
BEN: Brighton *936022*.
SUE: Hello. Could I speak to Dan, please?
BEN: Just a moment. Dan! . . . Dan! . . . I'm sorry. He's not in. Can I take a message?
SUE: Yes. Could you ask him to phone me? It's Sue.
BEN: OK.
SUE: Thanks very much. Bye.
BEN: You're welcome. Bye.

* * *

SUE: Brighton *914406*.
DAN: Hello. This is Dan. Is that Sue?
SUE: Yes. Hi, Dan. Listen. It's my birthday on *Saturday*.
DAN: Yes? How old are you?
SUE: Never mind. Well, *22*.
DAN: Yes? You're *nearly* as old as me. You don't look it.
SUE: Yes, well, I'm having a party. Would you like to come?
DAN: Yes. Great. What time?
SUE: Oh, *nine* o'clock.
DAN: Can I bring something?
SUE: Something to eat, if you like. *Cheese, bread*. Or a bottle of wine. And some CDs.
DAN: OK. What sort?
SUE: It doesn't matter. Something good for *dancing*.
DAN: Who's coming?
SUE: Oh, about twenty people. Jim and Bob. *Both* my brothers. My boss and the girls from the *shop*.
DAN: Your boss?
SUE: Yes, *John*. He's really nice. He's very young. Only *28*. Tall and *dark*. I like him.
DAN: Do you? Yes. Great. OK. Thanks. See you on Saturday, then.
SUE: Right. See you. Bye, Dan.
DAN: Bye.

Answers to Exercise 2 (= Answers to the questions in Exercise 1)
1. Brighton 936022.
2. Brighton 914406.
3. On Saturday.
4. 21; 22 on Saturday.
5. No. (He says she's nearly as old as him.)
6. Nine o'clock.
7. Bread, cheese.
8. Something good for dancing.
9. Two. (She says 'Both my brothers'.)
10. She probably works in a shop. (She says 'My boss and the girls from the shop'.)
11. John.
12. No. (Sue, at 22, is nearly as old as Dan; John is 28.)
13. No. John is dark; Dan is fair (see illustration).

3 Stress and rhythm
• Get students to try saying the sentences.
• Then demonstrate the rhythm (using the recording as a guide if you wish), and get them to try again until they find it easy to get a natural rhythm.

4 Asking for and giving telephone numbers
• Check that students know how to say phone numbers.
• Get them to spend a minute asking for their neighbours' phone numbers or going round the class.

5 Students' conversations
• Don't let this exercise take too long. Students should use some expressions from Exercise 2, but should keep the conversations reasonably short.
• When groups are ready, listen to them, making essential corrections only.

Practice Book exercises: choose two or more
1. Writing questions with *What sort of . . . ?* and *How many . . . ?*
2. Telephone language.
3. Countable and uncountable nouns.
4. Check on revision vocabulary.
5. Translation of material from the unit.
6. Student's Cassette exercise (Student's Book Exercise 2, first conversation). Students listen and practise saying the sentences.
7. Students write about a person's life.
8. Reading: Part 13 of *It's a Long Story*.

14D Could I speak to Dan?

Telephoning.

Hello.

1 Make questions.

1. Dan's | phone number?
2. Sue's | phone number?
3. When | Sue's birthday?
4. How old | Sue?
5. Sue | as old | Dan?
6. time | party?
7. What sort | food | Sue | want?
8. What sort | CDs | she | want?
9. How many brothers | Sue | ?
10. What sort | job | Sue | do?
11. Sue's | boss's | name?
12. Dan | as old | Sue's boss?
13. Dan's hair | same colour | John's?

2 🔊 Listen to the conversations and answer the questions in Exercise 1.

BEN: Brighton ....
SUE: Hello. Could I speak to Dan, please?
BEN: Just a moment. Dan! . . . Dan! . . . I'm sorry. He's not in. Can I take a message?
SUE: Yes. Could you ask him to phone me? It's Sue.
BEN: OK.
SUE: Thanks very much. Bye.
BEN: You're welcome. Bye.

*   *   *

SUE: Brighton ....
DAN: Hello. This is Dan. Is that Sue?
SUE: Yes. Hi, Dan. Listen. It's my birthday on ....
DAN: Yes? How old are you?
SUE: Never mind. Well, ...
DAN: Yes? You're .... as old as me. You don't look it.
SUE: Yes, well, I'm having a party. Would you like to come?
DAN: Yes. Great. What time?
SUE: Oh, ... o'clock.
DAN: Can I bring something?
SUE: Something to eat, if you like. ...., ... Or a bottle of wine. And some CDs.
DAN: OK. What sort?
SUE: It doesn't matter. Something good for ....
DAN: Who's coming?
SUE: Oh, about twenty people. Jim and Bob. .... my brothers. My boss and the girls from the ....
DAN: Your boss?
SUE: Yes, ... He's really nice. He's very young. Only .... Tall and .... I like him.
DAN: Do you? Yes. Great. OK. Thanks. See you on Saturday, then.
SUE: Right. See you. Bye, Dan.
DAN: Bye.

4 Ask other people's phone numbers and give yours.

'What's your phone number?'
'Milan three oh seven double two eight six.'

5 Work in groups of three. Prepare and practise two short telephone conversations. (A telephones B and asks to speak to C; A invites C to a party.)

> **Learn:** party; boss; eat (ate); (tele)phone (*verb*); bring (brought); This is . . . ; Is that . . .?; Could I speak to . . . ?; He's not in; Can I take a message?; You're welcome; It doesn't matter.

This is Dan. Is that Sue?

3 Practise these sentences.

Could I **speak** to **Dan**, please?
Just a moment.
Can I take a **message**?

Could you **ask** him to **phone** me?
I'm **having** a **party**.
Would you like to **come**?

Unit 15 Present and future

15A What's happening?

Present Progressive tense.

1 Who is the man talking to? What does she think is happening in the room? What is really happening? What is she doing? Examples:

'Some people are dancing.'
'Somebody is lying on the floor.'

Hello, darling . . . Yes . . . Are you having a good time? . . . How's your mother? . . . What? . . . What do you mean, 'What's happening?' . . . Oh, the noise . . . Yes, it's the TV – I'm watching something good on the TV . . . What? . . .

2 What is your wife/husband/father/mother/boyfriend/girlfriend/boss, etc. doing just now? Useful expressions: *I think, I know, probably.*

'I think my boyfriend's working. My mother's shopping. John's probably getting up.'

3 Pronouncing the letter *e*. Say these words.

1. red   dress   get
2. he   eat   sleep

1 or 2? Decide how to pronounce these words, and then check with your teacher.

went   meat   men   bed
be   left   reading   mean
me   speak

1 or 2?

many   friend   head   any

4 Prepare questions about the picture. Examples:

'What is the woman in the red dress doing?'
'What is the man with fair hair doing?'
'Is anybody smoking?'

Can you answer all the questions?

5 Memory test. Work in groups. One group asks its questions from Exercise 4; another group tries to answer with books closed.

Present Progressive tense		
I am (I'm) talking	am I talking?	I am (I'm) not talking
you are (you're) talking	are you talking?	you are not (aren't) talking
he/she is (he's/she's) talking	is he/she talking?	he/she is not (isn't) talking
we are (we're) talking	are we talking?	we are not (aren't) talking
you are (you're) talking	are you talking?	you are not (aren't) talking
they are (they're) talking	are they talking?	they are not (aren't) talking

Learn: head; noise; happen; lie (lying, lay); stand (stood); sit (sat); drink (drank); smoke; shave; shop (*verb*); answer (*verb*); somebody; anybody; probably; have a good time.

Unit 15: Lesson A

Students learn to talk about temporary present actions and states.
Structures: Present Progressive (Continuous) tense; *the girl in jeans*; *the man with a beard*.
Phonology: pronunciations of the letter *e*.

Language notes and possible problems

1. Present Progressive: forms The tense is easy for students to construct. The only formal problem is likely to be the word order in questions with noun-phrase subjects like *What is the girl in red doing?* Students may tend to put the subject in the wrong place (*What is doing the girl in red?* or *The girl in red, what is doing?*), because they are reluctant to separate the two parts of the verb.

2. Present Progressive: meaning This is a more difficult problem. Most languages do not have a special verb form for *temporary* present states or actions, so it is difficult for students to get used to the fact that one has to make this distinction when speaking English.

Note that it is important (and not very easy) to practise the tense realistically as far as possible. People generally ask or say what *is happening* in a situation where somebody can't see or understand what is going on – when talking on the telephone, for instance.

3. *Stand, sit* etc. State-verbs like *stand, sit, lie, kneel, lean* may present problems for some students. The equivalent in some languages of, for instance, *he's standing*, might not be constructed with an active verb form at all, but with a passive, a reflexive or even an adjective.

4. Prepositions Note that *in* is used when we talk about clothing and colours (*in jeans, in red*); *with* is used when we refer to hair, beards, moustaches and (usually) glasses.

1 Presentation

- Give students time to look at the picture and see what is happening.
- Read through the man's side of the phone conversation with them and make sure they understand everything.
- Ask them who they think the man is talking to, and what they think she says.
- Ask what *she* thinks is happening in the room.
- Get students to say as much as they can about what is happening in the picture. Supply vocabulary as needed.
- To finish the exercise, ask students what they think the man's wife is doing.
- Talk about the grammar of the Present Progressive. Make sure students realise that we say, for example, *he is talking* or *she is dancing* (and not *he talks* or *she dances*) when we want to say what is happening just now.

2 Personalisation

- Look at the examples and explain *probably*.
- Ask for as many sentences as possible – you may have to supply vocabulary.
- If somebody uses the verb *sleeping*, you may want to point out that in informal British English it is more common to say *asleep*.

3 Pronouncing the letter *e*

- This is an easy exercise, and is perhaps not worth doing in a class which does not contain a number of bad spellers.
- It is, however, useful for students to realise that the three words in the second section all contain the same vowel.
- After getting students to say the words in the two sections, ask them to work in groups putting the next ten words in the right places.
- Note that the last four words have irregular spellings: they are all in group 2.

Optional activities: mime

1. Miming actions

- Mime creates a natural context for the use of the Present Progressive (because it is not completely clear what is happening, so students need to talk about it to find out).
- Ask individuals (or small groups) to take it in turns to mime an action. The others have to say what it is.
- If students are short of ideas, suggest that they mime playing an instrument or a game (the others say what they are playing); or cooking or eating a particular food (the others say what they are doing).
- Make sure the mime continues while the class are making their guesses, so that students associate the idea of *present* activity with the tense.

2. Phone calls

- Put students in groups of three (it's better if the people in each group are some distance away from each other).
- Student A 'telephones' student B, who pretends to answer the phone.
- A says '*Can I speak to C, please?*' (naming the third student in the group).
- As soon as C is named, he or she starts miming an activity which makes it impossible for him or her to come to the phone.
- B decides what C is doing, and says to A:
  '*I'm sorry, he/she's having a bath / cooking / washing his/her hair / working, etc. Can you ring back later?*'

4 Preparing questions

- Look over the examples with the students and make sure they understand how the questions are constructed. Write on the board: *What is/are + subject + doing?*
- Give students a few minutes, working in groups, to prepare lists of ten or so questions. (Try to make sure that there is an even number of groups.)
- When each group has got its questions ready, tell them to see if they know how to answer them in English. Supply any vocabulary needed.

5 Memory test

- This can be done group against group. Students in one group close their books; students in another group ask their questions. Then the groups change over.
- Finish by letting the class test *your* memory of the picture.

Practice Book exercises: choose two or more
1. Students write about what they are wearing.
2. Students write about what people are doing.
3. Stress and rhythm.
4. Describing a picture: what is happening?

Students practise writing about temporary present actions and states; they learn to talk about the weather.
Structures: Present Progressive; spelling of *-ing* forms.

Practice Book exercises: choose two or more
1. Writing *-ing* forms.
2. Completing conversations.
3. Students write sentences about what is happening around them.
4. Further practice on vocabulary relating to weather.
5. Students write about what they did yesterday or last weekend.

Optional extra materials
Pairs of similar pictures (see Optional activity).

1 *-ing* forms
• Let students try the exercise themselves, to see how far they can get without help.
• They should be able to get the first and second sections right, but they may need help to see the rule that applies in the third section.
• Only one-syllable words have been put in, so as to avoid the complication introduced by the fact that we don't double letters at the end of unstressed syllables (compare *be'ginning* and *'happening*). Don't mention this unless students ask about it.

2 Holiday postcards
• Look over the exercise with the students, and help them to understand the system.
• Explain unknown vocabulary in the 'dictionary', or let students look words up.
• In order to write the postcard, they must fill in each blank with a word from one of the columns of the 'dictionary'.
• The letter in the blank shows which column to look in.
• Start off by filling in one or two blanks on the board, and then let students continue on their own.
• They should write out the complete text.
• If you like, they can send their 'postcards' to other students.

Optional activity: similar pictures
• Before the lesson, collect pairs of pictures (e.g. advertisements) which look fairly similar.
• Advertisements for cars and clothes in glossy magazines are a good source of material. You can often get two similar pictures by cutting a full-page advertisement in half.
• Hand out pictures to two volunteers. They should sit face to face (so that they can't see each other's pictures) and describe them in turn (e.g. *'There's a woman. She's wearing a red dress. She's standing by a car.'*)
• The students' task is to find some differences (decide in advance how many).
• When the volunteers have finished, hand out pairs of pictures to other students.
• It's worth building up a library of pairs of pictures of this kind. Each pair can be kept in a separate envelope, with the subject and the number of differences to be found written on the outside.

Optional activity: imagining
• Ask students to close their eyes and spend five minutes imagining themselves (as vividly as possible) in another place – a very beautiful place, where they are having a very good time.
• When they are ready, ask them to tell you about the place, and what they are doing, in as much detail as possible, without opening their eyes.

15B The Universal Holiday Postcard Machine

Present Progressive tense; weather; places.

1 Spelling. Make the -ing form.

1. sing singing
   play playing
   stand ....
   read ....

   work ....
   start ....
   eat ....
   go ....

3. stop stopping
   sit sitting
   get ....

   shop ....
   run ....
   begin ....

4. lie lying

   die ....

2. make making
   smoke smoking
   write ....

   dance ....
   drive ....
   like ....

2 It's easy to write holiday postcards! Write one now and send it to a friend.

Dear ..N..
   Well, here we are in
..T.... ..W.., and we are
having a/an ..A.. time.
   I am sitting/lying ..Pr..
..Pl.., writing postcards,
drinking ..D... and looking
at ..L.... ..N.. is ..V..., and
..PN. are ..V... ..Pr. ..Pl...
   Tomorrow we are going to
..T.... I'm sure it will be ..A...
Wish you were here,
Love, ..N..

POSTCARD DICTIONARY

N (*name*)
John
Mary
Alexandra
Mother
etc.

T (*town, city, village*)
Rome
Manchester
Honolulu
etc.

W (*weather*)
The sun is shining
It is raining
It is snowing
There is a hurricane
etc.

A (*adjective*)
wonderful   terrible
beautiful   awful
lovely   horrible
exciting   catastrophic
interesting   boring
magnificent   *etc.*

Pr (*preposition*)
in
on
at
under
by
near
opposite
etc.

Pl (*place*)
my room
their room
the bar
the beach
a café
a tree
a mountain
etc.

D (*drink*)
coffee
beer
wine
etc.

L (*things to look at*)
the sea
the mountains
the tourists
the rain
the sheep
etc.

V (*verb*)
shopping
sightseeing
sleeping
drinking beer
dancing
playing cards
having a bath
etc.

PN (*plural noun*)
the children
Mummy and Daddy
George and Sue
etc.

Learn: postcard; town; city; sun; sea; mountain; weather; Love; send (sent); sure.

Learn some more words from the lesson if you want to.

15C Who's doing what when?

Present Progressive tense with future meaning; plans and invitations.

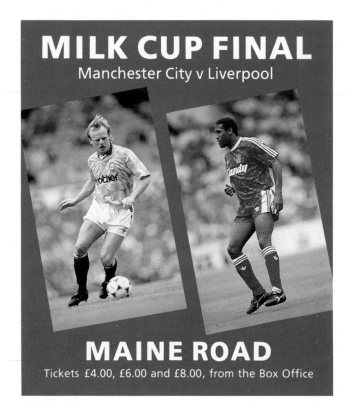

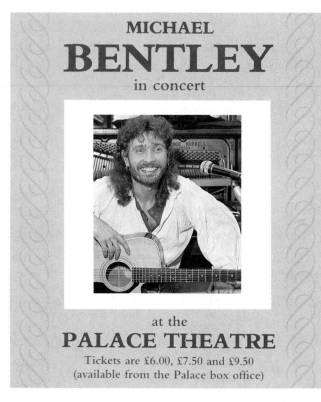

1 🔊 **Listen to the conversation and fill in the missing information.**

WHO?	WHAT?	WHEN?
Michael Bentley	is ....ing at the Palace	on .... evening.
City	are playing at home	....
Jane	is working	....
Bill	is ....ing	on Wednesday evening.
Jane's granny	is probably coming	....
Jane	is	on Tuesday evening.

2 **Can you think of some things that are happening during the next week or so (concerts, football matches, . . .)? What are you doing this evening, next weekend, for your next holiday?**

3 **Listen to the recording. How many words do you hear in each sentence? (Contractions like *I'm* count as two words.)**

4 **Complete this conversation and practise it in pairs. You can make some changes if you want to.**

A: Are you doing anything this evening?
B: I'm not sure. Why?
A: Well, would you like to .... with me?
B: I'd love to, but I'm probably ....ing.
A: Well, what about tomorrow? Are you free?
B: Perhaps. ....
A: ....

Learn: (football) match; concert; free; perhaps; I'd love to; What about . . . ?

74

Unit 15: Lesson C

Students learn to talk about plans and arrangements for the future, to invite, and to reply to invitations.
Structure: Present Progressive with future reference.
Phonology: perceiving unstressed syllables and decoding rapid speech.

Language notes and possible problems
The future   This is one of the most complex areas of English grammar. Here students work on one way of talking about the future in English – using the Present Progressive to talk about future events which are planned for a particular time or date.

Note that the Simple Present is not often used like this. Typical mistakes: *I see her tomorrow* or *Do you come on Friday evening?* In main clauses, the Simple Present is only used to talk about the future in certain special contexts – for example, in talking about timetables.

Other ways of talking about the future will be studied later.

1 Listening for information

● Look through the table and answer any queries. You may need to explain that 'City' are a football team. See if students can guess what *playing at home* means. (And note the plural verb with a collective noun – *City are playing . . .*)
● Play the recording through once without stopping. Then ask students to work in groups and see how many of the sentences they can complete.
● Play the recording again, and see if students can fill in any missing answers.
● Discuss the answers.
● Students may ask you to write up the whole of the conversation on the board, explaining every word. This is unnecessary, and would take up time which could probably be used better in other ways.

Tapescript for Exercise 1
BILL: Hello, Jane. Are you doing anything this evening?
JANE: Oh, hello, Bill. I'm not sure. Perhaps. What's today? Monday. I don't know. Why?
BILL: Well, Michael Bentley's singing at the Palace. Would you like to come?
JANE: I don't know, I'm a bit tired. I don't really want to go out tonight.
BILL: What about tomorrow, then? Would you like to see a film, have something to eat?
JANE: Oh, dear. I'd love to, but I'm going to a concert in London. What about Wednesday? Can we do something on Wednesday?
BILL: No, I'm working on Wednesday evening. What about Thursday?
JANE: No, I'm working on Thursday, and my granny's probably coming on Friday.
BILL: Well, let's do something at the weekend. City are playing at home on Saturday. Would you like to go?
JANE: Perhaps. Yes, why not?
BILL: OK. See you outside the ground about two o'clock, OK?
JANE: Right. See you then. Bye.
BILL: Bye.

Answers to Exercise 1
Michael Bentley is *sing*ing at the Palace on *Monday* evening.
City are playing at home *on Saturday.*
Jane is working *on Thursday (evening).*
Bill is *work*ing on Wednesday evening.
Jane's granny is probably coming *on Friday (evening).*
Jane is *going to a concert (in London)* on Tuesday evening.

2 Personalisation
● Give students a few moments to think, and then ask for their sentences.
● Try to get at least one sentence from every student.

3 Unstressed syllables: decoding fast speech
● Play each sentence and ask students to write down the number of words they think they hear.
● Play the sentence again and give students a chance to change their answers if they want to.
● Let them compare notes. Tell them how many words there are in each sentence, and see if they can tell you what the words are.
● Finish the exercise by getting students to say the sentences after the recording.

Tapescript and answers to Exercise 3
1. Are you doing anything this evening? (6)
2. I don't know. (4)
3. I'm working on Wednesday evening. (6)
4. I don't really want to go out tonight. (9)
5. My granny's coming on Friday. (6)
6. I don't know what she's doing. (8)
7. What's the girl in the red dress doing? (9)
8. I'm looking for a sweater. (6)
9. Have you got anything in blue? (6)

4 Students' conversations
● Give students ten minutes or so to prepare and practise their conversations. Don't let them make them too long.
● If they come up with amusing dialogues, you may want to let them perform for the class.

Practice Book exercises: choose two or more
1. Follow-up to lesson: completing a conversation.
2. Students write sentences to say what they are doing in the near future.
3. Choosing between comparatives and superlatives.
4. Student's Cassette exercise (Student's Book Exercise 1). Students try to say and write sentences from the dialogue.
5. Reading: two logic problems.

Listening and reading for specific information
Not all spoken and written texts are meant to be studied in detail. Some texts are used just to present certain language points; the students' task is to extract particular pieces of information from the text, but not to study and understand every word.

Students may have followed other courses in which nothing is presented without being immediately explained. So they may be uncomfortable if they leave a text without having studied every word in every line. It is important for them to realise that there are different ways of reading and listening for different purposes, and that it is not always necessary to understand everything in order to 'get the message'. Indeed, they must get used to coping with writing and speech in which not everything is clear – they will have to do this all the time in real-life use of English.

So if students ask you to spend an extra half hour or so 'going through' a text which is not meant to be studied in this way, it is probably best to refuse (telling the students why), unless you are very sure that the time could not be used more profitably for other purposes.

Unit 15: Lesson D

Students learn ways of referring to future time; they practise reading quickly for specific information.
Structures: Present Progressive with future reference; *going to* (preview); prepositions of time.

Language notes and possible problems
Prepositions of time   Students should revise or learn the following facts:
1. *On* is used with names of days of the week (e.g. *on Tuesday, on Monday morning*), and with dates (*on the 22nd*).
2. *At* is used in *at the weekend*, and also in *at Christmas, at Easter* etc.
3. *At* is also used (as students should already know) in *at . . . o'clock*.
4. *In* is used to say how close a future event is to the present – how soon it is going to happen (e.g. *in ten minutes; in six weeks*).
5. *In* is also used in the expressions *in the morning/afternoon/evening* (not exemplified in the dialogue).
6. *For* is used to say how long something lasts (e.g. *for three weeks*).
7. No preposition is used before *today, tomorrow,* (and *yesterday*); *this* and *next* (and *last*) *week/Monday/weekend* etc.
Note that American usage is slightly different in some cases (*on* is often dropped before the names of days of the week: Americans say *on the weekend*).

1 Scanning
• This exercise gives practice in the skill of reading quickly for specific information.
• It can be done as a competition if you wish.
• The correct answer is: I, C, K, L, A, H, G, D, E, B, J, F.
• After the scanning exercise, the dialogue can be used for language study if you wish.
• The most important thing to do is to see how prepositions of time are used – get students to look through, noting all expressions like *on Wednesday morning, at the weekend*.
• You may like to say a brief word about the use of *going to*, which is previewed here. Its use will be studied systematically in Unit 21. *Must* also occurs; it will be studied in Level 2.

2 Adverbials of time
• This can be done either orally or in writing.
• If you do it orally, you may like to make up a few more examples so that everybody has a turn.

3 Personalisation
• Again, you can make up more examples, depending on the time of year and what public events, public holidays etc. are close.

4 Test on prepositions
• This will show you whether any individuals are having difficulty in learning the correct use of the prepositions.

5 Journeys
• Get students to talk about their journeys in the Present Progressive tense (as far as possible).
• An amusing variant is to ask two students to tell the class about complicated journeys they are planning, one after the other, and then to ask the class to try to recall the details without mixing up the two separate journeys.

Practice Book exercises: choose two or more
1. Vocabulary: units of time.
2. *In* as a preposition of time.
3. Prepositions of time.
4. Writing: students describe an imaginary travel schedule.
5. Check on revision vocabulary.
6. Translation of material from the unit.
7. Reading: Part 14 of *It's a Long Story*.

15D We're leaving on Monday

Talking about the future; prepositions of time.

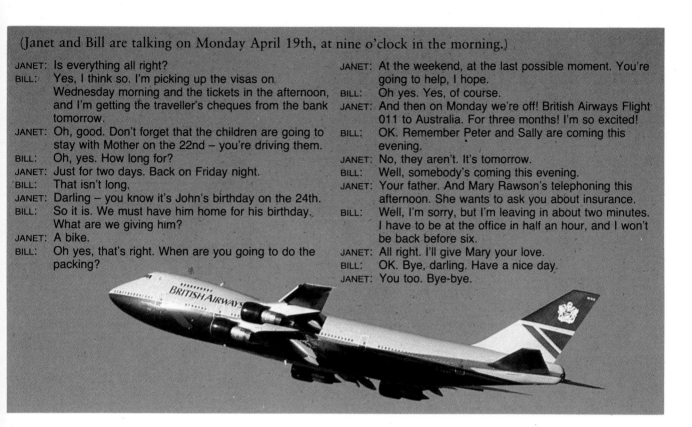

(Janet and Bill are talking on Monday April 19th, at nine o'clock in the morning.)

JANET: Is everything all right?
BILL: Yes, I think so. I'm picking up the visas on Wednesday morning and the tickets in the afternoon, and I'm getting the traveller's cheques from the bank tomorrow.
JANET: Oh, good. Don't forget that the children are going to stay with Mother on the 22nd – you're driving them.
BILL: Oh, yes. How long for?
JANET: Just for two days. Back on Friday night.
BILL: That isn't long.
JANET: Darling – you know it's John's birthday on the 24th.
BILL: So it is. We must have him home for his birthday. What are we giving him?
JANET: A bike.
BILL: Oh yes, that's right. When are you going to do the packing?

JANET: At the weekend, at the last possible moment. You're going to help, I hope.
BILL: Oh yes. Yes, of course.
JANET: And then on Monday we're off! British Airways Flight 011 to Australia. For three months! I'm so excited!
BILL: OK. Remember Peter and Sally are coming this evening.
JANET: No, they aren't. It's tomorrow.
BILL: Well, somebody's coming this evening.
JANET: Your father. And Mary Rawson's telephoning this afternoon. She wants to ask you about insurance.
BILL: Well, I'm sorry, but I'm leaving in about two minutes. I have to be at the office in half an hour, and I won't be back before six.
JANET: All right. I'll give Mary your love.
BILL: OK. Bye, darling. Have a nice day.
JANET: You too. Bye-bye.

1 Put these events in the right order as fast as you can.

A Bill's visit to the bank
B John's birthday
C Mary Rawson's phone call
D Bill picking up the tickets
E children leaving to stay with their grandmother
F family leaving for Australia
G Bill picking up the visas
H Peter and Sally's visit
I Bill leaving for the office
J Janet packing (with Bill's help)
K Bill coming back from the office
L Bill's father's visit

2 Janet and Bill are talking at nine o'clock on Monday April 19th. They can talk about the future in two or three different ways. Examples:

on the 22nd = on Thursday = in three days
at ten o'clock = in an hour
at ten past nine = in ten minutes

How could Bill and Janet say these differently?

on Wednesday   on the 24th   in a week
at eleven o'clock   in three hours
in twenty minutes   in four days   at 9.05

3 How soon are the following: your birthday; Christmas; the end of your English course; the end of this lesson? (Use *in*.)

4 Put *at, on, in, for* or no preposition.

1. What are you doing .... the weekend?
2. I'm seeing Carlo .... Tuesday.
3. My mother's telephoning .... three o'clock.
4. 'Can I talk to you?' 'Sorry, I'm leaving .... five minutes.'
5. I think it's going to rain .... this afternoon.
6. We're going to Dakar in June .... three weeks.
7. Would you like to go out with me .... Monday evening?
8. Telephone me .... tomorrow if you have time.
9. 'I'm going to Norway .... August.' 'That's nice. How long ....?'

5 Are you going on a journey soon? If so, tell the class about it. If not, imagine that you are going on a journey (a really interesting one) next week, and tell the class about it.

Learn: minute; hour; half an hour; ticket; forget (forgot); get (got) (= obtain); give (gave); leave (left); stay; long (= a long time); back.

Unit 16 Consolidation

16A Things to remember: Units 13, 14 and 15

Present Progressive tense

I am (I'm) eating you are (you're) eating he/she/it is (he's/she's/it's) eating we are (we're) eating you are (you're) eating they are (they're) eating	am I eating? are you eating? is he *etc*. eating? are we eating? are you eating? are they eating?

I am (I'm) not eating you are not (aren't) eating she *etc*. is not (isn't) eating we are not (aren't) eating you are not (aren't) eating they are not (aren't) eating

Examples:
Some people **are dancing**.
What **is** the woman in the red dress **doing**?
  (~~What is doing the woman . . . ?~~)
John **is** probably **getting** up now.

Spelling of *-ing* forms

ORDINARY VERBS:	sing ⟶ singing eat ⟶ eating
ENDING IN *-e*:	make ⟶ making (~~makeing~~) write ⟶ writing
ENDING IN ONE VOWEL + ONE CONSONANT:	stop ⟶ stopping sit ⟶ sitting run ⟶ running
ENDING IN *-ie*:	lie ⟶ lying

Talking about the future

Are you **doing** anything this evening?
I'm **working** next Thursday.
  (~~I work next Thursday.~~)
We're **leaving** on Monday.
We're **going** to Australia for three months.
Jane's granny is probably **coming** on Thursday.

Can

I can go (~~I can to go~~) you can go he/she/it can go (~~he/she/it cans go~~) we can go you can go they can go
can I go? (~~do I can go?~~)
I cannot (can't) go

Examples:
I **can** sing, but I **can't** dance.
Diego **can** dance, but Alice **can't**.
'**Can** you swim?' 'Yes, I **can**.'
'**Can** you cook?' 'No, I **can't**.'

Pronunciation and stress

I can (/kən/) **swim**, but I **can't** (/kɑ:nt/) **dance**.
Yes, I **can** (/kæn/).

Comparative and superlative adjectives

	ADJECTIVE	COMPARATIVE	SUPERLATIVE
SHORT ADJECTIVES:	short cheap young	shorter cheaper younger (/ˈjʌŋgə(r)/)	shortest cheapest youngest (/ˈjʌŋgɪst/)
ENDING IN ONE VOWEL + ONE CONSONANT:	fat slim big	fatter slimmer bigger	fattest slimmest biggest
ENDING IN *-e*:	late	later	latest
ENDING IN *-y*:	happy	happier	happiest
IRREGULAR:	good bad far	better worse farther	best worst farthest
LONG ADJECTIVES:	interesting beautiful	**more** interesting **more** beautiful	**most** interesting **most** beautiful

This lesson summarises and displays the language that students should have learnt in the last three units. Spend a short time going over the lesson pages with the students. Make especially sure that the forms of the Present Progressive are thoroughly mastered: in Lesson 16B students will study the contrast between this tense and the Simple Present.

Note that expressions which occur in the grammatical and functional sections of the summary are not necessarily listed again in the vocabulary section.

Practice Book exercises: choose two or more
1. Writing comparatives and superlatives.
2. Comparative structures in sentences.
3. Writing dates in words.
4. Dialogue completion: replying to an unwelcome invitation.
5. Text completion: Present Progressive and vocabulary.
6. Revision crossword.

Video

Sequence 4 in *The New Cambridge English Course 1 Video*, **The trip**, can be used around this point in the book, as it relates to Units 13–15 of the coursebook. The topics are travel; describing places; making comparisons. Language focus is on making plans and arrangements; comparative and superlative forms; descriptive adjectives.

Ways of comparing

I'm **taller than** my mother.
I'm **much** taller than my brother.
He's fatter **than me.**
Mario's **a bit** older than his
  brother.

I can speak English **better than** my
  father.
My father can speak Spanish
  better now **than** he could when I
  was younger.

I'm **the tallest** in my family.
What's **the most beautiful** place
  (that) you know?

I'm **as good-looking as** a film star.
A Volkswagen is not **as quiet as** a
  Rolls-Royce.
He can't run as fast as **me.**

Peking is **the same as** Beijing.
England is **not the same as** Britain.
A pen is **different from** a pencil.

As and *than*

faster **than**
more beautiful **than**
as fast **as**
the same **as**

Be like, *look* (*like*)

What is she **like?** (How is she?)
She's a bit shy, but very nice.

He **looks like** a footballer.
I think he **looks more like** a
  businessman.
She **looks like** her mother.

She **looks** bad-tempered.
You **look** tired.

Ages, heights and weights

The Great Pyramid **is** 4,500
  years **old.**
It **is** 135 metres **high.**
The car **is** 4 metres **long.**
The statue **weighs** three kilos.

Lucy **is** four months **old.**
Her mother **is** 40 (years old).
I **am** 1 metre 91.
I **weigh** 85 kilos.

She's **over** 21 and **under** 30.

How old/tall are you?
How much do you weigh?

British and US measures

1 inch = 2½cm
12 inches = 1 foot (30cm)
1 pound = about 450gm
2.2 pounds = 1 kilogram

Large numbers

100: a hundred OR one hundred
125: a/one hundred and
  twenty-five
  (US a/one hundred twenty-five)
300: three hundred
  (three hundreds)
1,000: a/one thousand
1,467: one thousand, four
  hundred and sixty-seven
4,000: four thousand
  (four thousands)
1,000,000: a/one million
1,400,000: one million, four
  hundred thousand

Ordinal numbers

10th: tenth
11th: eleventh
12th: twelfth
13th: thirteenth
20th: twentieth (/'twentɪəθ/)
21st: twenty-first
22nd: twenty-second
30th: thirtieth
100th: hundredth

Dates

WRITE	SAY
14 Jan(uary) 1990	January the fourteenth, nineteen ninety (GB)
14.1.90 (GB)	
1.14.90 (US)	January fourteenth . . . (US)
5 Apr(il) 1892	April the fifth, eighteen ninety-two
9 Dec(ember) 1600	December the ninth, sixteen hundred
14 May 1906	May the fourteenth, nineteen hundred and six
	OR: . . . nineteen oh six

Question expression + object

What sort of food do your
  children like?
How many children have you got?

Prepositions

on June 22nd
on Thursday
in three days
at ten o'clock
in an hour
the girl **in** jeans
the man **with** a beard
good **at** maths/running *etc.*
the highest mountain **in** the world

Agree

I agree. (I am agree.)
He doesn't agree.
We both agree.

Telephoning

Can/Could I speak to . . . ?
This is . . .
Is that . . . ?
He/She's not in.
Can I take a message?

Inviting; answering invitations

Are you doing anything this evening?
Would you like to see a film?
I don't know, I'm a bit tired.
I don't really want to go out tonight.
Well, what about tomorrow?
I'd love to, but I'm probably going to a
  concert in London.

Let's do something at the weekend.
Are you free?
Perhaps.
Yes, why not?
See you about two o'clock.
Right, see you then.

Words and expressions

Nouns

sleep	boss
glasses	head
world	noise
place	postcard
pencil	town
restaurant	city
hotel	sun
typewriter	sea
height	mountain
weight	weather
metre	(football) match
month	concert
pound (*weight*)	minute
week	hour
birthday	half an hour
date	ticket
party	

Verbs

can (could)	eat (ate)
cook	(tele)phone
dance	bring (brought)
drive (drove)	happen
make (made)	lie (lying, lay)
run (ran)	stand (stood)
see (saw)	sit (sat)
sleep (slept)	drink (drank)
swim (swam)	smoke
write (wrote)	shave
count	shop
draw (drew)	answer
sing (sang)	send (sent)
ski	forget (forgot)
think (thought)	get (got)
weigh	give (gave)
agree	leave (left)
look	stay

Adjectives

foreign	comfortable
better	noisy
best	quiet
worse	warm
worst	heavy
easy	fast
difficult	handsome
funny	high
beautiful	new
slow	sure
boring	free
economical	

Adverbs

better	probably
fast	perhaps
faster	long
extremely	back

Prepositions

without
than
over (= more than)
under (= less than)
after

Months

January	July
February	August
March	September
April	October
May	November
June	December

Other words and expressions

somebody	that (*conjunction*)
anybody	Happy Birthday
today	You're welcome
tomorrow	It doesn't matter
the day before yesterday	have a good time
the day after tomorrow	Love (*end of a letter*)
good at . . .ing	

Optional words and expressions to learn

cake; chess; piano; tennis; violin; politician; singer; comedian; actress;
actor; writer; typist; film star; president; rock (music); cooker; pub; type;
calm; nervy; patient; impatient; optimistic; pessimistic; shy; self-confident;
sensitive; stupid; bad-tempered; talkative; in the daytime; go without sleep.

Unit 16: Lesson B

Students look at and contrast the 'central' meanings of the two present tenses.
Structures: Present Progressive tense; Simple Present tense.

Language notes and possible problems
1. Meanings of the tenses Both of the 'present' tenses have several uses. Students are only concerned here with the more 'central' meanings.
2. Grammatical explanations Students (and teachers) vary widely in their reactions to explicit grammatical information. The tense usage dealt with here is difficult, and knowledge of the rules will serve as a valuable support to many students. It will not, however, stop them making mistakes – they are likely to confuse the two tenses for some time to come, and frequent revision will be necessary.

1 Presentation
• Give students plenty of time to look at the table and study the examples.
• Go through the four rules with them and ask them to decide which two rules are for the Present Progressive and which are for the Simple Present.
• Let them discuss this in groups before you give them the answers (Present Progressive: A and D; Simple Present: B and C).

2 Discrimination test
• This will help to fix students' grasp of the rules.
• It is probably better to ask for written answers (at least to some of the questions) so that you can check up on everybody's understanding of the point.
• Discuss the reasons for the choice of tense in each case.

Answers to Exercise 2
1. 'm working
2. Do you work
3. I don't smoke
4. do you speak
5. are you wearing
6. always spends
7. plays
8. 's shopping
9. are you eating
10. Do you speak
11. are staying
12. 's cleaning.

3 Answering questions
• Play the recording (or ask the questions), pausing for students to answer.
• Either pick out individuals to answer the questions, or tell students to write the answers.

The questions
1. What are you wearing?
2. What colours do you usually wear?
3. Are you wearing them now?
4. Who smokes in the class?
5. Who is smoking?
6. Who is sitting next to you now?
7. Does he or she usually sit there?
8. What's the weather like just now?
9. Is it raining?
10. Does it often rain?
11. What language are you speaking?
12. What languages do you speak?

4 Listening for information – introduction
• Go over the list of verbs with the students. They should know most of them.
• Tell them to copy the list if you don't want them to write in their books.
• Play the conversation through once without stopping; then again with a few pauses so that students can circle the verbs.
• Let them compare notes and tell them the answers (*spending, staying, having, washing, doing, eating, cleaning, cooking*).

5 Listening for information
• Students can probably start Exercise 5 without hearing the conversation again.
• Get them to copy the table and fill in as much of it as they can manage, and then play the recording once more.
• They will not understand everything; this does not matter.
• Let them compare notes, and discuss the answers with them.

Answers to Exercise 5
Jane is talking to Polly.
Polly is talking to Jane.
Jane's mother is staying with Jane's sister.
Bill: we don't know what he's doing. Possibly cleaning the car or having a drink.
The baby is eating the newspaper.
Sue is having breakfast.
Frank is washing his hair.

Tapescript for Exercises 4 and 5
Hello. 656 790. Jane Parker speaking . . . Oh, Polly! Hello! How are you? . . . Me? Oh, I'm OK. . . . Yes . . . No. . . . No, we're spending Christmas at home . . . No, we usually go to my mother's, but she's staying with my sister this year, so we didn't go.
 . . . No. No, it's terrible when the kids are at home. It's murder, Polly. I mean it. They're everywhere. Sue's just got up: she's having lunch.
(SUE: No, I'm not! I'm having breakfast.)
Frank's washing his feet in the kitchen.
(FRANK: No, I'm not, Mum. I'm washing my hair!)
And the baby. God knows what the baby's doing.
(SUE: He's eating the newspaper!)
 . . . Bill? He's out somewhere. Probably cleaning the car, or having a drink at the pub. I don't know. . . . Yes. Look, I'm sorry, Poll, I must go. I'm just cooking lunch. I'll call you back, OK? Bye.

Practice Book exercises: choose two or more
1. Choosing between Present Progressive and Simple Present.
2. Rhythm and stress in interrogative sentences.
3. Vocabulary revision: things in a room.
4. Putting a jumbled story in order.
5. Writing past narrative.
6. Reading: a choice of short factual passages.

16B Present tenses

The difference between the two present tenses.

1 Look at the table and examples, and choose the best rules for each tense.

PRESENT PROGRESSIVE TENSE	SIMPLE PRESENT TENSE
I am working, you are working *etc.* am I working? *etc.* I am not working *etc.*	I work, you work, he/she works *etc.* do I/you work? does he/she work? *etc.* I/you do not work, he/she does not work *etc.*

'Are you free now?' 'Sorry, **I'm studying**.'
'Look. Helen**'s wearing** a lovely dress.'
The cat**'s eating** your steak.
What **are** you **doing** tomorrow?
He**'s** not **working** on Saturday.
We**'re spending** Christmas with Ann and
  Peter again this year.
	I always **study** from five to seven o'clock.
	Helen often **wears** red.
	Cats **eat** meat.
	What **do** you **do** at weekends?
	He never **works** on Saturdays.
	We always **stay** with Ann and Peter at
	  Christmas.

Rules
We use the Present Progressive to talk about:
1. ....
2. ....

Rules
We use the Simple Present to talk about:
1. ....
2. ....

A things that are happening now, these days
B things that are always true
C things that happen often, usually, always, never, *etc.*
D plans for the future

2 Put in the correct tense.

1. 'Can you help me for a minute?' 'I'm sorry, I
   ....' (*'m working / work*)
2. .... on Saturdays? (*Are you working / Do
   you work*)
3. 'Have you got a light?' 'Sorry, ...' (*I'm
   not smoking / I don't smoke*)
4. How many languages ....? (*are you
   speaking / do you speak*)
5. Why .... a sweater? It isn't cold. (*are you
   wearing / do you wear*)
6. My father .... August in Ireland. (*is always
   spending / always spends*)
7. Robert .... football most weekends. (*is
   playing / plays*)
8. 'Where's Lucy?' 'She ....' (*'s shopping /
   shops*)
9. 'What ....?' 'Chocolate.' (*are you eating /
   do you eat*)
10. '................. English?' 'Yes, a bit.' (*Are you
    speaking / Do you speak*)
11. The children .... with Granny this week.
    (*are staying / stay*)
12. 'Is John in the bathroom?' 'No, he's outside.
    He .... the car.' (*'s cleaning / cleans*)

3 🔘 Listen to the recording and answer the
questions.

4 What are they doing? Listen to the conversation
and circle any of these verbs that you hear.

sending   spending   standing   staying
playing   having   working   watching
washing   doing   reading   eating   writing
raining   cleaning   drinking   thinking
looking   cooking   going

5 Who is doing what? First copy the table, then
listen again and fill it in.

JANE	
POLLY	
JANE'S MOTHER	
BILL	
THE BABY	
SUE	
FRANK	

16C   Choose

A choice of vocabulary, pronunciation, listening and speaking exercises.

Look at the exercises, decide which ones are useful to you, and do two or more.

VOCABULARY

1 **Which one is different?**

1. Monday, Wednesday, Friday, Sunday
2. Britain, Brazil, Australia, Japan
3. station, hotel, restaurant, phone box
4. beer, cheese, bread, banana

5. aunt, sister, father, girlfriend
6. bus, train, horse, car
7. short, big, large, tall
8. dark, long, grey, big
9. blue, brown, black, green
10. sun, rain, snow, weather

2 **Choose a word from Units 1–15 and draw it. Other students will try to say what it is.**

LISTENING

1 🔊 **Listen to the song (*Anything You Can Do, I Can Do Better*). You will hear most of these comparatives. Which two do you *not* hear?**

better   older   greater   higher   cheaper   shorter   softer
longer   faster

2 🔊 **Look at the picture and listen to the recording. How many differences can you find?**

Unit 16: Lesson C

Students and teacher choose vocabulary, pronunciation, listening and speaking exercises.

Note
There is 3–4 hours' work in this lesson. You might get students to vote for the most useful exercises.

VOCABULARY

1 'Odd word out'
• Look at each group of words and get students to discuss which one doesn't belong.
• There may be more than one possible answer.

Possible answers to Exercise 1
1. Sunday (not a weekday); Wednesday (9 letters)
2. Brazil (not surrounded by water); Australia (continent).
3. phone box (you can't sit down in it)
4. beer (drink); cheese (doesn't begin with *b*); banana (not made by people)
5. girlfriend (not a relative); father (male)
6. horse
7. short
8. big (the others can all be used for hair)
9. black (eyes aren't black); green (doesn't begin with *b*)
10. weather (not a particular kind of weather)

2 Drawing words
• Volunteers draw things they have already learnt the names of (they can look back through the book).
• The class should try to say what the things are.
• Encourage use of *I think*, *perhaps* and *I'm not sure*.

LISTENING

1 Song: *Anything You Can Do, I Can Do Better*
• This song is from the musical *Annie Get Your Gun*.
• Explain the title (*anything* may cause difficulty).
• Play the song, and help students to get a general idea of what it is about.
• Play it again, while students decide which of the listed comparatives come in the song, and which two don't (*older*; *shorter*).
• Play it once more and help students to understand the words. In successive verses, one person tells another that he or she can:
  do anything better; be anything greater; sing anything higher; buy anything cheaper; say anything softer; hold any note longer; wear anything better; say anything faster.
(For copyright reasons we are not able to reproduce the exact words.)

2 Detecting differences
• There are a large number of differences between the picture in the Student's Book and the description on the recording.
• Tell students to look at the picture for a minute or two.
• Get them to talk about it, as far as their limited vocabulary permits. Make sure everybody understands what is going on.
• Play the recording once through without stopping. Ask students if they noticed any differences.
• Play it again; ask students to write down the differences they noticed.
• Play it a third time, stopping at intervals to compare the recording and the picture. Make sure everybody speaks.

Tapescript for Exercise 2
This is a picture of a bank – Barclay's Bank. There are four people in the bank: the cashier, another man, a woman and a small child. The cashier is dark. The other man, who is tall and fair, is taking money from the cashier. The woman is neither tall nor short; she's dark and very pretty. She is on the man's right. She has got two dogs with her. The child is sitting in a chair by the window. There are three doors in the picture. The time is twenty to three in the afternoon; it is Tuesday March 18th.

Answers to Exercise 2
– It's Lloyds Bank.
– There are at least five people (two children).
– The cashier is fair.
– The other man is short.
– He is not taking money from the cashier (yet).
– The woman is fair, and not very pretty.
– She has got one dog.
– There is one door; there are no windows.
– The children are sitting by the door.
– It is March 8th.

PRONUNCIATION

1 Spelling and pronunciation: the letter *i*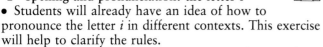

- Students will already have an idea of how to pronounce the letter *i* in different contexts. This exercise will help to clarify the rules.
- Practise the words in each group (using the recording if you wish), and get students to discuss when *i* is pronounced /ɪ/, when /aɪ/ and when /ɜ:/.
- Now look at the other words. Students should now be able to pronounce correctly not only the words they know but also the ones they don't know.

Answers to Exercise 1
Group 1: with; fin; skip
Group 2: like; arrive; tights; white; light; slight; bright; excite; ride
Group 3: girl; skirt; bird; stir

2 Word stress and resultant /ə/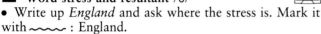

- Write up *England* and ask where the stress is. Mark it with ⁓: England.
- Ask students to do the same with the other words.
- Demonstrate the words while they check the answers.
- Point out the neutral, weak pronunciation of *a* in England (/ˈɪŋglənd/). Explain that it is weak because it isn't stressed.
- Get students to listen again, circling the vowels that are pronounced /ə/. Check their answers.
- Let them practise pronouncing the words themselves.

Answers to Exercise 2
England /ˈɪŋglənd/
Brazil /brəˈzɪl/
Italy /ˈɪtəli/
Russia /ˈrʌʃə/
Japan /dʒəˈpæn/
America /əˈmerɪkə/
Lebanon /ˈlebənən/
Canada /ˈkænədə/
Africa /ˈæfrɪkə/
London /ˈlʌndən/

SPEAKING

1 Interviewing English-speaking people

ARRANGING INTERVIEWS
If you do this exercise, you will need to arrange for one or more English-speaking people to visit your class in the near future. If you can't find anybody else, you can use other English teachers from the school – preferably teachers that the students don't know well. Ideally, you should have several groups of students, each with a set of questions prepared; and as many visitors as groups, so that they can rotate.

Alternatively, you may be able to arrange for students to interview English-speaking people outside the school. (If they are studying in an English-speaking country, they will be able to organise this for themselves.)

PREPARING QUESTIONS
Get students to work in groups of four or so.

Encourage them to prepare interesting questions to which they will really want to know the answers. They shouldn't be afraid to ask personal questions – you will obviously choose visitors who won't mind talking about themselves.

Get students to use plenty of the structures illustrated in the exercise instructions.

Explain the point about 'follow-up' questions, and see how many they can prepare for each of their basic questions.

2 Sketch: shops

INTRODUCTORY NOTE
Students have already done one or two sketches. But they will still need support and encouragement. Be generous with praise, and try not to let anyone feel a failure – a sketch which doesn't come off may still teach a lot of English.

You may want to tape- or video-record the sketches. This gives students feedback, and motivates them to aim at a high standard.

PRESENTATION
Make up mixed-ability groups of three or four.

Go over the instructions, and let students decide what to do. Warn them if you are going to record.

You might work briefly with one group in front of the class, demonstrating how to start:

All right. Who wants to buy something?
What do you want to buy?
Who's a shop assistant?
Who's going to start? What are you going to say?

PLANNING AND WRITING SKETCHES
Walk around and help while groups are working.

If any group is really stuck, suggest roles and things to buy.

They will want to look at Unit 10 as they work.

Discourage people from writing complicated material which only they will understand. Their task is to *reuse creatively what has been learnt.*

Set a time limit (20–30 minutes) for this phase.

Each student should end up with a clear copy of the sketch, with his/her part underlined.

PRACTICE
Get groups to practise their sketches when ready, with appropriate actions and movements.

Correct grammar and pronunciation where necessary.

PERFORMANCE
If there is time for students to learn their parts, it will give brighter, more natural performances. Otherwise, let them read from their scripts.

Don't start with the best or the worst group.

Make sure other students are attentive; encourage them to applaud after each sketch.

IMPROVISATION
The exercise can continue with an improvisation.

Shop assistants position themselves round the room, with signs saying what they are selling.

Customers visit all the shops trying to buy things.

Practice Book exercises: choose two or more
1. Word order in Present Progressive and Simple questions with noun-phrase subjects.
2. Vocabulary revision and comparisons.
3. Word stress.
4. *Look(s)*, *look(s) like* and *like*.
5. Students choose words to write sentences about themselves with.
6. Translation of material recently learnt.
7. Student's Cassette exercise (Student's Book Listening Exercise 2). Students try to write three or more sentences from the recording.
8. Reading: Part 15 of *It's a Long Story*.

PRONUNCIATION

1 Pronunciation of the letter *i*. Say these words.

1. sit   in   big
2. wine   five   night   right
3. first   shirt

Now decide how to pronounce these words. Are they in group 1, 2 or 3? Check with your teacher or the recording.

girl   like   arrive   tights   white
skirt   light   with   fin   bird   stir
slight   bright   excite   ride   skip

2 Word stress.
1. Copy the names from the box. Under each word draw a ∼∼∼ for stress. Example: England.
2. Listen and check your answers.
3. Listen again. Circle the vowel where you hear /ə/. Example: Engl(a)nd.

   Pronounce the words.

England	Brazil	Italy	Russia	Japan
America	Lebanon	Canada	Africa	
London				

SPEAKING

1 Prepare questions for an interview with an English-speaking stranger. Some ideas for questions:

How old . . . ?   What did you . . . ?   . . . favourite . . . ?
Are you . . . ?   What was . . . ?   What sort of . . . ?
Where do . . . ?   What do you . . . ?   Can you . . . ?
Where were you . . . ?   Have you got a/any . . . ?   Do you like . . . ?
Where did you . . . ?   How many . . . ?   Do you know . . . ?

Prepare 'follow-up' questions for some of your questions. Examples:

'Have you got a car?'
'Yes, I have.'
'What sort of car? What colour is it? Do you drive to
   work? . . . '

'Did you study languages at school?'
'Yes, I did.'
'What languages?'

2 Work in groups of three or four.
Some of you are shop assistants;

and some of you want to buy things.

Prepare and practise a sketch. Use all the English you can.

81

16D Test yourself

LISTENING

1 Listen to the conversation and answer the questions.

1. How many bedrooms are there?
2. Is the kitchen big or small?
3. Is there a toilet downstairs?
4. Is there a garage?
5. How much is the rent?

2 Listen and answer these questions about the speaker.

1. How old is she?
2. Where was she born?
3. What is her best friend's name?
4. What happened when she was seven?
5. When did she begin to like school?
6. How old are her sister and brothers?
7. Where is her sister working now?
8. Does she see her little brother very often?

GRAMMAR

1 Write five things that are happening in your school or home now. Example:

Some students are playing table-tennis.

2 Give the *-ing* forms. Example:

play playing

work; write; stop; sit; eat; run; lie; make.

3 Choose the correct forms.

1. .... John tomorrow? (*Are you seeing / Do you see*)
2. .... on Saturdays? (*Are you working / Do you work*)
3. What .... with my bicycle? (*are you doing / do you do*)
4. 'Have you got a cigarette?' 'Sorry, I ....' (*'m not smoking / don't smoke*)

4 Give the comparative and superlative. Example:

old older oldest

young; big; important; interesting; fat; happy; late; good.

5 Complete the sentences using the words in brackets (and any other words that you need).

1. She can run .... I can. (*faster*)
2. These oranges cost .... the others. (*the same*)
3. 'I think it's a really good film.' 'No, I ....' (*not agree*)
4. Do you think she .... her mother? (*look like*)
5. 'What ....?' 'She's a bit shy, but very nice.' (*like*)

6 Write the object pronouns. Example:

I me

you; he; she; it; we; they.

7 Write sentences beginning:

1. What sort of . . .
2. How much . . .
3. How many . . .
4. I can . . .
5. I can't . . .
6. He weighs . . .
7. How tall . . .

82

Unit 16: Lesson D

Students do a simple revision test.

The purpose of the test

This test, like the others in the book, is provided for teachers who feel that it will be useful. It covers several different areas: it is not of course necessary to do all of the sections, and teachers should select according to their students' needs. Teachers who do not feel the test will be useful should simply drop it altogether.

The test has three main functions:

1. To show you and the students whether there are any points that have not been properly learnt for any reason.
2. To identify any students who are having serious difficulty with the course, if this is not already evident.
3. To motivate the students to look back over the work they have done and do some serious revision before they move on.

If possible, try to make the students feel that they are 'testing themselves', rather than 'being tested'. It is not intended that students should 'pass' or 'fail' the test, and it is not particularly useful to give marks. (If the school or education system requires that this be done, you will need to work out a simple marking scheme.) But students should of course be told whether you feel their performance is satisfactory. In principle, most students ought to get most answers right. If this does not happen, efficient learning is not taking place (because of poor motivation, too rapid a pace, absenteeism, failure to do Practice Book work or follow-up study outside class, or for some other reason).

Administration

The test can be administered in various ways, depending on how strictly you want to control students' performance; whether you want to collect the answers and mark them, or allow the students to correct them in class; and so on.

The 'speaking' test will need to be done individually, with students interrupting their work on the other tests to come and talk to you one at a time.

If you are not collecting students' scripts, correction can be done by class discussion when everybody has finished.

Notes, tapescripts and answers are given below.

LISTENING

- Tapescripts and answers are as follows. Before starting, go over the instructions and questions and clear up any problems.
- A possible approach is to play each recording two or three times, pausing for a few moments after each playing so that students can write their answers.

1 Tapescript

'Well, this is the flat. There are two bedrooms, both with double beds, and a spare room upstairs. Then downstairs there's a living room, a study and a kitchen. I'm afraid the kitchen's rather small, but it's fully equipped. Two toilets: one in the bathroom and a separate one downstairs. And there's a double garage. I expect you'd like to know the rent. It's £750 a month.'
'My God!'

Answers
1. two
2. small
3. yes
4. yes
5. £750 (a month)

2 Tapescript

'I'm 18 years old. I was born in Oxford. Erm, I had quite a nice early childhood, I think, erm, I grew up with a guy called Dan, who I'm still friends with, he's my best friend. Erm, my parents divorced when I was seven. Erm, I didn't like school much until about three years ago. I've got, erm, an older sister, twenty, and a younger brother of fourteen, another brother of three and a half.'
'How well do you get on with them?'
'I don't get on *too* well with my sister, but I get on pretty well with my younger brother. Erm, my sister, she's working in a pub at the moment, so I don't see *that* much of her, so I suppose we get on better. Erm, my brother I get on pretty well with, and my little brother I don't see that often.'

Answers
1. 18
2. Oxford
3. Dan
4. Her parents divorced.
5. about three years ago
6. 20, 14 and three and a half
7. in a pub
8. no

GRAMMAR

1 (Various possible answers.)

2 working; writing; stopping; sitting; eating; running; lying; making.

3 1. Are you seeing
  2. Do you work
  3. are you doing
  4. don't smoke

4 younger, youngest; bigger, biggest; more important, most important; more interesting, most interesting; fatter, fattest; happier, happiest; later, latest; better, best.

5 1. faster than
  2. the same as
  3. don't agree
  4. looks like
  5. is she like

6 you, him, her, it, us, them

7 (Various possible answers.)

VOCABULARY

1 fourteen; forty; a/one hundred; two hundred and thirty-four; six thousand, seven hundred and ninety-eight; a/one million; twelfth; twentieth; hundredth.

2 1. birthday (*not a period of time*)
   2. noisy (*not a verb*)
   3. goodbye (*not a verb*)
   4. ticket (*not an adjective*)
   5. answer (*not a movement*)
   6. station (*not a place where people live*)

3 1. on; for
   2. in; at
   3. in
   4. under
   5. in
   6. at
   7. in

LANGUAGE IN USE

1 1. understand
   2. know/remember
   3. mean
   4. What do you
   5. How do you
   6. How are you
   7. Can/could I speak to (*name*); message
   8. (Various possible answers.)
   9. what about / how about / are you free / are you doing anything
   10. (Various possible answers.)
   11. All right. / OK. / See you then.

PRONUNCIATION

1 1. weigh
   2. pound
   3. easy
   4. best
   5. place
   6. town
   7. month
   8. got

2 **type**writer; **birth**day; **post**card; **moun**tain; **con**cert; **tele**phone; for**get**; **for**eign; **com**fortable; eco**nom**ical; **hand**some; ex**treme**ly; to**mor**row; to**day**; per**haps**; with**out**.

WRITING

When correcting this, it is best to judge students on their ability to communicate successfully, using appropriate vocabulary and structures. Don't give too much importance to minor errors of grammar and spelling – this can damage students' confidence.

SPEAKING

Go over the instructions with the whole class and make sure they understand what they have to do. Then test the students one by one. The conversation could run more or less as follows, but all sorts of variations are possible.

YOU: (*give phone number*)
STUDENT: Can/Could I speak to (*name*)?
YOU: Speaking. Who's that?
STUDENT: Oh, hello, (*name*), this is (*name*).
YOU: Oh, hi. How are you?
STUDENT: Fine, thanks. Listen, are you free this evening?
YOU: I'm not sure. Why?
STUDENT: Would you like to see a film?
YOU: I don't know. I'm a bit tired. I don't really want to go out tonight.
STUDENT: Well, what about tomorrow?
YOU: Perhaps. What film?
STUDENT: (*name of film*)
YOU: OK. What time?
STUDENT: It's at 7.45. See you outside the cinema at half past seven.
YOU: OK. See you then. Bye.
STUDENT: Bye.

Test Book recordings
A recording for Test 4 in the Test Book follows this lesson on the Class Cassette.

VOCABULARY

1 Write these numbers in words.

14; 40; 100; 234; 6,798; 1,000,000;
12th; 20th; 100th.

2 Which word is different?

1. hour   birthday   week   month
2. eat   drink   draw   noisy
3. goodbye   think   remember   forget
4. noisy   comfortable   quiet   ticket
5. ski   swim   run   answer
6. city   town   station   village

3 Put in the right preposition.

1. We're leaving .... Monday: we're going to Australia .... three months.
2. I'm not free now, but I can see you .... an hour, ... ten o'clock.
3. I'm the tallest .... my family.
4. She's over 21 and .... 30.
5. Who's the girl .... jeans and a red sweater?
6. I was very bad .... maths at school.
7. Which is the hottest country .... the world?

LANGUAGE IN USE

1 Complete these conversational exchanges.

1. 'Agresti, kunsti sifnit?'   'I'm sorry, I don't ....'
2. 'What's that girl's name?'   'I'm sorry, I don't ....'
3. 'What does *shut* ....?'   'The same as *closed*.'
4. '................ do?'   'I'm a photographer.'
5. '................ do?'   'How do you do?'
6. '................?'   'Fine, thanks.'
7. '................?'   'I'm afraid she's not in. Can I take a ....?'
8. 'Are you doing anything this evening?'   '................ .'
9. 'I don't really want to go out tonight.'   'Well, ... tomorrow?'
10. 'Would you like to see a film tomorrow?'   '................ .'
11. 'See you about two o'clock.'   '................ .'

PRONUNCIATION

1 Which word is different?

1. high   height   weigh   lie
2. cook   look   pound   could
3. easy   head   heavy   weather
4. metre   best   ski   leave
5. any   many   send   place
6. town   slow   smoke   post
7. month   boss   shop   got
8. warm   thought   got   saw

2 Which syllable is stressed?

typewriter; birthday; postcard; mountain; concert; telephone; forget; foreign; comfortable; economical; handsome; extremely; tomorrow; today; perhaps; without.

WRITING

1 Write about the differences between you and another person in your family (100–200 words).

SPEAKING

1 Act out this conversation. The teacher will take the other part.

TELEPHONE CALL
Telephone a friend. You want to ask him/her to go and see a film with you. Try to find an evening when you are both free.

Unit 17 Ordering and asking

17A I'll have roast beef

Eating in a restaurant; *no = not any*; *some* and *something* in offers and requests.

1 Try to put the sentences in order. Then listen and check your answers.

'Yes, sir. Over here, by the window.'
'Have you got a table for two?'

'How would you like your steak?'
'Oh, all right then. I'll have a rump steak.'
'I'll start with soup, please, and then I'll have roast beef.'
'I'm sorry, madam, there's no more roast beef.'
'Rare, please.'

'Vegetables, sir?'
'Chicken for me, please.'
'Mushrooms and a green salad, please.'
'And for you, sir?'

2 The conversations continue. Try to guess what goes in the blanks. Then listen and check.

'............... you .... something to ....?'
'Just .... water, please.'
'Certainly, madam.'
'I'll .... a lager, ... And .... you .... me some water, too?'
'............... course, sir.'

      *   *   *

'How's the chicken?'
'Not too bad. .... about .... steak?'
'A bit tough. The vegetables are ...., though.'

      *   *   *

'Is .... all right?'
'Oh, yes, excellent, ... you.'
'............... good.'

      *   *   *

'............... I .... you a little more coffee?'
'No, thank you.' 'Yes, ...'

      *   *   *

'............... you .... us the bill, please?'
'..............., madam.'
'Is service included?'
'No, ...'

3 🔊 Listen to the questions on the tape, and try to remember the answers. Example:

'Have you got a table for two?'
'Yes, sir. Over here, by the window.'

4 Make up your own restaurant conversations and practise them.

Learn: (the) bill; everything; all right; for (you, *etc*.); though; just; then; certainly; how; I'll have; a little more; no more; Is service included?

Learn some of these if you want: soup; (roast) beef; (rump) steak; chicken; vegetable; mushroom; salad; lager; coffee; tough; rare; excellent; over here; not too bad.

Unit 17: Lesson A

Students learn how to order meals in English.
Structures: *no = not any*; *some* (and *something*) used in offers and requests; *I'll* to announce decisions (preview of future tense).

Language notes and possible problems

1. Preview Some of the expressions taught in this lesson contain structures which will be learnt in detail later. For the moment, it is enough for students to use and understand the expressions as if they were new vocabulary items. These include: *I'll* used to announce decisions; and *a little* (in *a little more*).

2. *Bring* and *give* are followed by two objects, and the same pronouns are used for direct and indirect objects.

3. *Everything* Make sure that students note that *everything* is singular.

Optional extra materials

If you are going to finish the lesson with an improvisation, you may like to prepare menus (one for each group).

1 Unscrambling dialogues

- Divide the class into groups, and ask them to try to put the dialogues into the right order.
- They can use their dictionaries or consult you for new words.
- When they are ready, play the recording for them to check their answers.
- Then play the recording again and point out the following items:
- *for* is used to indicate eventual possession. Get the students to pronounce these expressions with 'weak' /fə/: *Have you got a table for two?*; *And for you, sir?*; *Chicken for me, please.*
- *I'll* is used to announce decisions. Students have already come across this in Lesson 7A; they will study *will* more fully later in the course. Get them to practise these sentences, paying special attention to the pronunciation of *I'll*: *I'll start with soup*; *I'll have roast beef*; *I'll have a rump steak*.
- *no more* is an emphatic way of saying *not any more*.
- *sir* and *madam* are used by people in service professions: waiters, shop assistants, etc. In other situations British people tend to use title plus surname (e.g. *Mrs Abbott*) or first names.

Tapescript and answers to Exercise 1: see page 141

2 Predicting conversations

- Ask students to work individually at first, trying to find a word for each blank. Once again, they can use their dictionaries or consult you about new words.
- They should compare answers in small groups.
- When they are ready, play the recording so they can check their answers.
- Play the recording again; note these points:
- *Some* and *something* are used in questions when they are requests or offers. Get the students to practise *Would you like something to drink?* and *Could you bring me some water?*
- *Just* means 'only'.
- To refuse an offer, we say *No, thank you* (not just *Thank you*).
- You may have to explain *Is service included?*

Tapescript and answers to Exercise 2: see page 141

Optional activity: pronunciation practice

- Tell students to say any sentence from the text that they want to (one sentence at a time).
- Don't comment in any way, but just say the same sentence with a correct pronunciation.
- If a student is not satisfied with his/her pronunciation, he/she can say the same sentence several times, checking against your version each time.

3 Answering questions from the recording

- Ask students to close their books. Play the recording, pausing after each question.
- In a small class, students can take turns answering the questions aloud; in a large class, you may prefer to get the students to write down the answers, and ask one person to give his or her answer aloud.
- (The answers are given after the questions.)

Tapescript for Exercise 3: see page 141

4 Students' conversations

- Divide the class into groups of three (one or two groups of four is all right).
- Each group should prepare and practise a short sketch in a restaurant. One student is a waiter; the others are customers.
- They should try to use language from the dialogue.
- Tell them the waiter or the customers have to have at least one problem in the sketch.
- Don't let them spend too long in preparation; tell them to practise acting out the sketch after they have prepared it.
- Walk round to give any help that is needed.
- Ask selected groups to perform their sketches for other groups or for the class.

Optional activity: improvisation

- First of all, get three or four volunteers to improvise a restaurant scene.
- Don't correct mistakes unless they really impede communication.
- Then turn the whole classroom into a restaurant (with one waiter for every two tables, more or less), and let students act out the situation as they wish.
- You may like to prepare menus in advance.
- Alternatively, you can put the menu on the board.

Practice Book exercises: choose two or more

1. Changing *not any* to *no* and vice versa.
2. Completing restaurant conversations.
3. Looking for meal-related words in the dictionary.
4. Student's Cassette exercise (Student's Book Exercise 3). Students try to answer the questions and then write down three or more of the questions and answers.
5. Recreational reading: diaries of adolescent London boys.

Unit 17: Lesson B

Students learn to borrow things, and to reply to requests (formally and informally).
Structures: *Could you* + infinitive without *to*; verbs with two objects (*lend, give, show*).
Phonology: polite intonation for requests.

Language notes and possible problems

1. Lend and borrow Students may confuse these. If so, concentrate on practising *lend* and leave *borrow* for another time.

2. Requests Make sure students understand the differences of formality (very polite, polite and casual) illustrated here. The degree of politeness depends on social equality or inequality; how well the people know one another; and the importance of the request.

Note that we normally use *yes/no* questions to ask for things (*Could you . . . ?*; *Have you got . . . ?*). It is the question form (with appropriate intonation) that makes a request polite; an imperative request (even with *please*) generally sounds like a command.

3. Pronunciation Remind students of the pronunciations of *minute* /ˈmɪnɪt/ and *hour* /ˈaʊə(r)/ (Exercise 2).

4. Cultural differences Students from some cultures may be taken aback by the situation here: calling casually on a neighbour one doesn't know in order to borrow something. You may need to explain that this is normal behaviour in most of the English-speaking world.

1 Completing the conversation

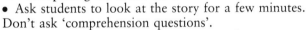

- Ask students to look at the story for a few minutes. Don't ask 'comprehension questions'.
- Explain any difficulties. Make sure students understand the exact meaning of *lend*.
- Ask for ideas about how the conversation might continue. (There are innumerable possibilities.)
- Get students to write the end of the conversation in pairs. You will need to supply some words and expressions.
- Go over the text in the picture story, practising rhythm, intonation and linking. Use the recording as a model if you wish.
- Then get students to practise their completed conversations. If there is time, they can perform their conversations for other groups.

2 Requests and replies; formality

- First of all, look at the requests with the students.
- Explain any difficulties and practise the pronunciation; if you get the students to repeat after you, rather than after the recording, make sure that you use a polite intonation.
- Ask students to suggest possible answers to the first request – there are five possible answers. They should understand clearly why answers with *them* or *one* are not possible.
- Ask students to continue the exercise alone or in groups. Get them to compare notes; go over the answers with them.
- Get them to practise the exchanges in pairs. Pay special attention to intonation.

Possible answers to first part of Exercise 2

1. a, b, c, e, g
2. a, b, c, d, g
3. a, b, e, g
4. a, b, d, f
5. a, b, c, d, g
6. a, b, c, e
7. a, b, c, d
8. a, b, d, e, f

- Then get them to look at the requests again individually, trying to decide which two are very polite and why. (1 is marked as very polite by *Sorry to trouble you, but . . .* ; 5 is very polite because of *possibly*).
- Then get them to try and decide which two requests are casual (2 and 8, because of the absence of *please* or any other 'softener' like *for a moment*).
- Tell them that the other requests can be more or less polite depending on how they are said; and that this is why intonation is important.
- If you speak their language(s), you can ask them for examples of when they need to speak politely or very politely.

3 Vocabulary extension

- Before doing Exercise 4, students need to learn the names of some common possessions.
- Get them to look in their bags and pockets for things to ask you about.
- Before giving the answers, you might ask '*Does anybody know?*'

4 Borrowing and lending

- Get half the class to become borrowers and the other half lenders.
- The borrowers walk round trying to borrow as many things as they can (using the expressions from Exercise 2). Lenders should answer appropriately.
- If your class will cooperate easily, you might want to make sure levels of formality are practised by putting a label on one or two lenders saying '*Stranger*' (explain what it means); and on another one or two with the name of a monarch or head of state. Make sure appropriate polite forms are used with these people.
- Before switching roles, the lenders should go and ask for their possessions back, as in the example.

Optional activity: sketch

- Get students to prepare and perform sketches based on the situation in the picture story.
- They can start with the idea of borrowing something from the person/people in the next flat, and develop it as they wish.
- (For suggestions about organising this kind of work, see Teacher's Book Lesson 16C.)

Practice Book exercises: choose two or more

1. Completing sentences with formulae from the lesson.
2. Appropriate polite or casual ways of requesting and refusing requests.
3. *Lend* or *borrow*; correct verb tenses.
4. Vocabulary revision: rooms of a house. Writing sentences with appropriate verbs.
5. Student's Cassette exercise (Student's Book Exercise 2, sentences 1 to 5). Stress and intonation practice.
6. Quick crossword.

Lending and borrowing.

1 Read the story and complete the conversation. Practise the complete conversation with a partner.

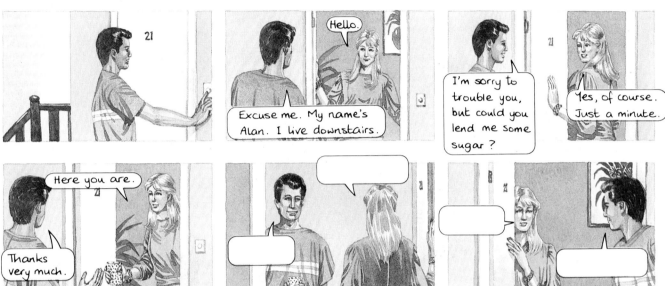

2 ☺ Match the questions and answers. You can find more than one answer to each question.

QUESTIONS
1. Sorry to trouble you, but could you lend me some bread?
2. Could you lend me a dictionary?
3. Could you show me some black sweaters, please?
4. Excuse me. Have you got a light, please?
5. Could you possibly lend me your car for half an hour?
6. Could I borrow your keys for a moment?
7. Could I borrow your umbrella, please?
8. Have you got a cigarette?

ANSWERS
a. I think so . . . Yes, here you are.
b. Yes, of course. Just a minute.
c. I'm sorry. I need it/them.
d. I'm afraid I haven't got one.
e. I'm afraid I haven't got any.
f. Sorry, I don't smoke.
g. I'm sorry, I'm afraid I can't.

Look at the questions again; find two very polite questions and two very casual questions.

3 Ask the teacher the names of some of your possessions. Examples:

'What's this?'
'What's this called in English, please?'
'Is this a pen or a pencil?'
'Is this a lighter?'

4 Ask other students to lend, give or show you things. Examples:

'Could you lend me your Practice Book for a moment?'
'Yes, here you are.' / 'I'm sorry. I haven't got one.'

'Could you possibly lend me your watch?'
'Yes, of course. Here you are.' / 'I'm sorry, I need it.'

Now ask for your possessions back. Example:

'Could I have my watch back, please?'
'Yes, of course. Here you are. Thanks.'

Learn: cigarette; lend (lent); borrow; show; need; (I'm) sorry to trouble you; Could you possibly lend me . . . ?; Here you are; Just a moment/minute; Have you got a light?

Learn if you want to: sugar; bread (*uncountable*); dictionary; key; umbrella; *some of the possessions you lent or borrowed in Exercise 4.*

17C Somewhere different

Making suggestions; agreeing, disagreeing and negotiating.

1 📻 **What are they talking about? Look at the pictures; then listen to the recording.**

2 Can you remember? Try and put words and expressions in each blank from the dialogue. Then listen again to check.

1. .... go to Turkey for our holiday
2. Yeah, OK, ...?
3. Hey, ..., ... think about this.
4. .... we can get package holidays
5. ...., darling?
6. I think ....
7. ...., ..., Sarah, find out about it.
8. .... I'll phone tomorrow morning.

3 Can you fill in the blanks and put this conversation in order?

BOB: ...., ... ask her to come with us – can you phone her?

BOB: .... I'll get the paper and see what's on.

BOB: .... go to the cinema tonight?

SUSAN: Yes, ...? The last film we saw was months ago. I'll phone.

SUSAN: I'd love to, but Anne is coming for supper.

4 Listen to the recording. How many words are there? What are they? (Contractions like *don't* count as two words.)

5 Work in groups of four to try and solve the problem.

You are a group of eighteen-year-olds. Your parents have agreed to give you holiday money for six weeks if:
– you all travel together
– you spend two weeks learning something: for example, a new sport; a new skill (typing, bricklaying, . . .); a foreign language; . . .
– you camp in the mountains or at the seaside for two weeks.

Agree on how and where you will spend your six weeks.

> **Learn:** idea; paper; find out (found); spend (spent); wait (a minute); let's; Why don't we . . . ?; Why not?; Well, . . . ; all right; fine; about; somewhere; with.

Unit 17: Lesson C

Students learn to make and reply to suggestions and to negotiate in disagreements.
Structures: *Why don't we* + infinitive without *to*; *Let's* + infinitive without *to*.
Phonology: decoding rapid colloquial pronunciation.

Language notes and possible problems
1. *Let's*   The structure with *Let's* corresponds to a first-person plural imperative verb form in many European languages.
2. **Infinitives without *to*** are used after *Let's*. You may have to watch that students do not use *to*-forms.

1 Sensitisation

- Give students a few minutes to look over the pictures and take in the situation.
- Ask them how old they think the people are and who they think they are (i.e., their relationship to one another).
- Get them to look at the speech bubbles and tell you what the conversation is about. Explain that *package holiday* means a holiday where you pay a single price and transport, hotel, and meals are all included.
- Ask them if you think the people all agree about their holiday in the first two pictures.
- Then play the recording without comment as they follow the pictures in their books.

Tapescript and answers to Exercises 1 and 2: see page 141

2 Presentation: remembering
- Get the students to work individually trying to remember the words from the dialogue that complete the fragments in the book.
- Then let them compare answers in small groups. Make sure that each student ends up with a written list of the answers.
- Play the recording again so that they can check their answers. You may have to play the recording more than once.
- Help them with the meanings of new words and expressions.
- Point out the following:
  – *Let's* is followed by infinitives without *to*.
  – *Let's* is a contraction for *Let us*, but the full form is very rarely used.
  – *idea* is stressed on the second syllable (/aɪˈdɪə/).

3 Focus on requests and negotiation
- Ask students to work in pairs to order the conversation and fill in the blanks.
- Make sure they understand that each blank can contain one word or more.
- Answer any questions they have about meanings of words and expressions.
- When they are ready, get them to help you write the conversation on the board. Write up all the plausible answers that they suggest.

Possible answers to Exercise 3
BOB: *Why don't we / Would you like to* go to the cinema tonight?
SUSAN: I'd love to, but Anne is coming for supper.
BOB: *Well, let's / why don't we/you* ask her to come with us – can you phone her?
SUSAN: Yes, *why not / why don't we*? The last film we saw was months ago. I'll phone.
BOB: *Fine / All right / OK*. I'll get the paper and see about the film.

4 How many words?

- Play the first sentence and ask students how many words they think it contains.
- Then ask them to try to write it down.
- Play the recording again two or three times if necessary.
- Deal with the other sentences in the same way.
- This exercise should be done individually, not in groups. Good students should keep their answers to themselves until weak students have had time to try to work out the sentences.
- It may be necessary to remind students that the pronunciations they hear in this exercise are not 'careless' or 'incorrect' – they are normal ways of saying the phrases in fast colloquial speech. This kind of practice is essential if students are to understand natural spoken English.

Tapescript and answers to Exercise 4
1. Wait a minute. (3)
2. Why don't we go to the seaside? (8)
3. It's a bad idea. (5)
4. There's a phone here somewhere. (6)
5. There are some beautiful places in Turkey. (7)
6. How high are those mountains, do you know? (8)
7. Let's talk about that later. (6)
8. All right. (2)
9. Can you find out about it? (6)
10. She's spending her holiday with her father. (8)

5 Role play task: planning a holiday
- Divide the class into groups of four (one or two groups of three will be all right).
- Read over the instructions with them and make sure they understand them.
- Give them a time limit, and tell them they will have to report their decisions to the class at the end of that time.
- Depending on your students, you may want to require each group to choose a leader, who will make sure that everybody's opinions get expressed and that decisions are made in time.
- Alert them a few minutes before the time limit is up; then when time is up get each group to say briefly what they have decided (they should use the Present Progressive for this as far as possible, e.g. '*We are spending our first two weeks . . .* ').

Practice Book exercises: choose two or more
1. Completing conversations: asking directions, telephoning, suggesting and negotiating.
2. Revision of prepositions.
3. Student's Cassette exercise (Student's Book Exercise 1). Students listen to the first part of the conversation and try to write it down.
4. Reading and reacting: students read a text about a dream and answer a few questions about their reactions to it. You may want to have a short discussion about students' answers in class.

Unit 17: Lesson D

Students practise writing and replying to informal invitations.
Structures: *Shall we*; revision of various structures used for suggesting and requesting; preview of imperatives.

1 and 2 Inviting and replying

• Let the students spend a few minutes looking at the notes and asking questions. Point out:
– the use of *Shall we* + infinitive without *to* for suggestions.
– the use of imperatives (including negative imperatives with *don't*).
• The students should try to match up the invitations and replies (there is no reply to Judy's note).
• Tell them to make up a diary page (like the one in the book) for the next seven days, with space for two or three appointments each day. The names of the days should be in English.
• Now they start writing each other invitations, using words and expressions from the notes in the book.
• Their purpose is to make appointments with as many people as possible, so that they really fill up their diary pages.
• They should reply to each invitation they receive.
• If you notice a student who isn't getting invitations, send him/her one yourself.
• You will probably need to deliver the students' letters to everyone.

Practice Book exercises: choose two or more
1. Pronunciation: sentence stress.
2. Check on revision vocabulary.
3. Translation of material from the unit.
4. Filling blanks in a story.
5. Writing the story of a dream.
6. Reading: Part 16 of *It's a Long Story*.

Writing: inviting and replying; *Shall we . . . ?*

1 Read the notes. Ask your teacher for help with any difficult words or expressions.

2 Write similar notes to other students. Reply to the notes that you get. Fill up your diary for the next week with a list of appointments.

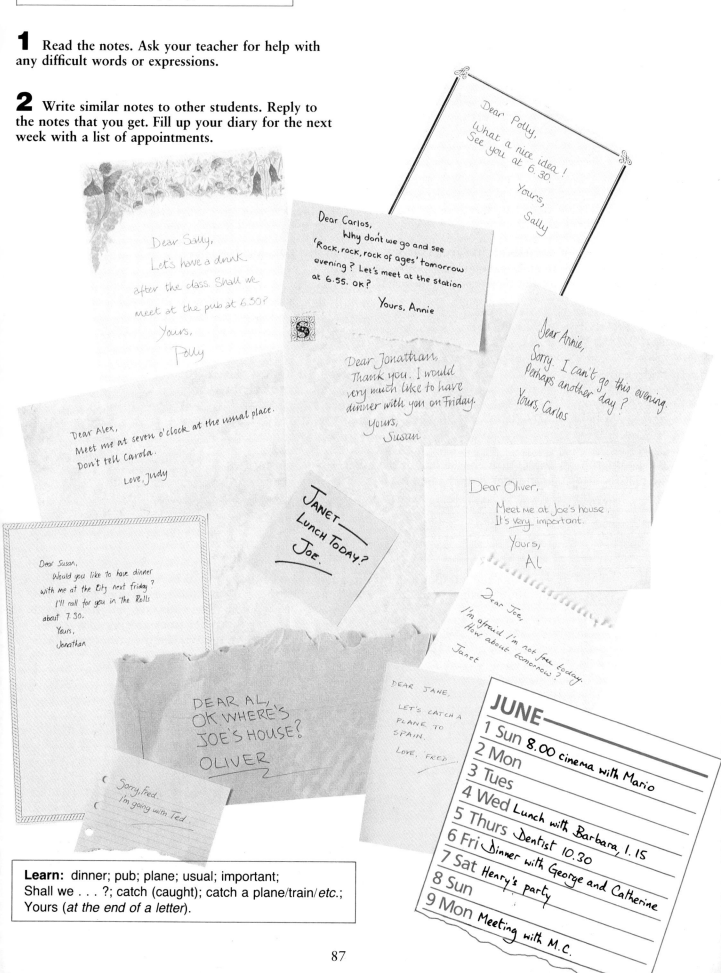

Dear Polly,
What a nice idea! See you at 6.30.
Yours,
Sally

Dear Sally,
Let's have a drink after the class. Shall we meet at the pub at 6.30?
Yours,
Polly

Dear Carlos,
Why don't we go and see 'Rock, rock, rock of ages' tomorrow evening? Let's meet at the station at 6.55. OK?
Yours, Annie

Dear Annie,
Sorry. I can't go this evening. Perhaps another day?
Yours, Carlos

Dear Jonathan,
Thank you. I would very much like to have dinner with you on Friday.
Yours,
Susan

Dear Alex,
Meet me at seven o'clock at the usual place. Don't tell Carola.
Love, Judy

JANET —
LUNCH TODAY?
JOE.

Dear Oliver,
Meet me at Joe's house. It's very important.
Yours,
Al

Dear Susan,
Would you like to have dinner with me at the Ritz next Friday? I'll call for you in the Rolls about 7.30.
Yours,
Jonathan

Dear Joe,
I'm afraid I'm not free today. How about tomorrow?
Janet

DEAR AL,
OK. WHERE'S JOE'S HOUSE?
OLIVER

DEAR JANE,
LET'S CATCH A PLANE TO SPAIN.
LOVE, FRED

Sorry, Fred.
I'm going with Ted.

JUNE
1 Sun 8.00 cinema with Mario
2 Mon
3 Tues
4 Wed Lunch with Barbara, 1.15
5 Thurs Dentist 10.30
6 Fri Dinner with George and Catherine
7 Sat Henry's party
8 Sun
9 Mon Meeting with M.C.

Learn: dinner; pub; plane; usual; important; *Shall we . . . ?*; catch (caught); catch a plane/train/*etc.*; Yours (*at the end of a letter*).

Unit 18 More about the past

18A Where was Galileo born?

> More about people's pasts.

Galileo

Amelia Earhart

Marie and Pierre Curie

Ho Chi Minh

1 Match four of the phrases with each picture. You can use a dictionary.

A
born in Paris, France and Warsaw, Poland
born in Annam, Vietnam
born in Atchison, Kansas, USA
born in Pisa, Italy

B
student in Saigon
student at the University of Pisa, Italy
student at Columbia University, New York
students at the Sorbonne, Paris

C
mathematician, astronomer and physicist
politician and poet
professors of physics
pilot and writer

D
first woman to fly a plane across the Atlantic
people who discovered radium
founder of the People's Republic of Vietnam
man who discovered sunspots

2 Look at the example; then choose one of the other people and turn the phrases into complete sentences. Example:

Ho Chi Minh was born in Annam, Vietnam. He was a student in Saigon. He was a politician and poet, and the founder of the People's Republic of Vietnam.

3 🔊 First, read through the questions and try to guess some of the answers. Next, listen to the recording, and then see how many of the questions you can answer.

1. Galileo was born in the (a) *15th* (b) *16th* (c) *17th* century.
2. Was he a professor at Pisa? (a) *Yes.* (b) *No.* (c) *We don't know.*
3. Students came to Galileo (a) *to hear his lectures* (b) *to work with him* (c) *to study sunspots.*
4. Amelia Earhart stopped studying at (a) *18* (b) *22* (c) *33.*
5. She stopped studying because she (a) *didn't have enough money* (b) *wanted to fly* (c) *wanted to work.*
6. She paid for her flying lessons (a) *with her father's help* (b) *with a lorry driver's help* (c) *by doing several jobs.*
7. She worked as a lorry driver because (a) *the money was good* (b) *there was plenty of free time* (c) *she liked driving.*
8. Her Atlantic flight finished in (a) *Newfoundland* (b) *Iceland* (c) *Ireland.*
9. Which places did Ho Chi Minh visit? (a) *South Africa* (b) *the USSR* (c) *England* (d) *France.*
10. He worked as a photographer in (a) *North Africa* (b) *the USA* (c) *Paris.*
11. The Curies met in (a) *Poland* (b) *Paris* (c) *Germany.*
12. In 1903, (a) *Marie Curie* (b) *Pierre Curie* (c) *both of them* got the Nobel Prize.

4 Prepare a short talk (2–3 minutes) about somebody's life. Give your talk, and then ask the other students questions to see how much they can remember.

Learn: century; learn (learnt); fly (flew); pay (paid); pay for something; because; plenty of; round; round the world; across; together; (at a) university; the first man/woman/person to . . .; who; the woman/man/person who . . .

Learn these if you want to:
republic; Atlantic; free time; finish.

88

Unit 18: Lesson A

Students practise the Simple Past tense by talking about historical personalities.
Structures: Simple Past tense; article and prepositional usage; preview of relatives and infinitive of purpose.
Phonology: weak forms of *was* and *were*.

Language notes and possible problems

1. Articles   Students may need to pay attention to the use of articles in Exercise 2. The indefinite article *a* is used here to classify people (*He was a student in Saigon*); the definite article *the* is used to give a unique identification (*She was the first woman to fly . . .*; *They were the people who discovered . . .*).
2. Prepositions (Exercise 1)   Note the difference between *student in Saigon* (name of city) and *students at the Sorbonne* (name of university).
3. Centuries (Exercise 3)   Students may need to learn that the 1400s are called *the 15th century*, the 1500s *the 16th century*, etc.
4. Relatives   Relative clauses with *who* occur in Exercise 1. These will be studied in detail later.
5. Infinitive of purpose (Exercise 3)   Note the use of the infinitive in *Students came from all over Europe to hear his lectures*. This, too, will be studied in detail later.

1 Presentation

• Get the students to do the matching exercise, using their dictionaries where necessary. (If students speak the same language they can work in groups, dividing up the dictionary work between them.)
• Make sure they understand that for each person there is one item in list A, one item in list B and so forth.
• No special historical knowledge is needed for this exercise – it can be done by observation and common sense.
• When students are ready, let them compare notes to check that they have all got the same solution.

2 Building up text

• Ask students to choose one of the people and combine the notes into a complete short text, putting in articles, auxiliary verbs etc. where necessary.
• Make sure students get the articles correct in *a student, the first woman to . . .*, etc.
• Look out for mistakes with *born* (* *Galileo born in Pisa* or * *Galileo is born in Pisa*).
• Get some or all of the students to read out their texts. They should be careful about stress and rhythm, and aim for correct pronunciation of the weak forms *was* (/wəz/) and *were* (/wə(r)/).

3 Listening for specific information

• As an introduction to the listening exercise, look through the questions, explain any difficulties and ask students to try to guess some of the answers.
• Play the recording, and then get students to work individually or in groups to see how many of the answers they can remember.
• Play the recording again once or twice until students have got as many answers as they can.

Answers to Exercise 3

1b; 2c; 3a; 4b; 5b; 6c; 7a; 8c;
9c,d; 10c; 11b; 12c.

Tapescript for Exercise 3

Galileo Galilei was born in Pisa, Italy, in 1564. He was a mathematician, astronomer and physicist and made valuable discoveries in all these fields. For example, he discovered sunspots for the first time. Galileo was a student at the University of Pisa when he was young, and later a professor at different universities in Italy. He was famous for his lectures, and students came from all over Europe to hear them.

Amelia Earhart was a famous aeroplane pilot. She was born in Atchison, Kansas in 1898. When she was 22, she stopped her studies at Columbia University, New York, to learn to pilot a plane. Flying lessons were expensive and she took several jobs to pay for them: once she worked as a lorry driver because the pay was good. In 1932 she was the first woman to fly her own plane across the Atlantic, from Newfoundland to Ireland.

Ho Chi Minh was a Vietnamese politician and poet. He was born in Annam in 1892 and studied in Hué and Saigon. Later he visited North Africa, the USA, England and France, working on ships, sweeping snow, and, in Paris, working as a photographer. He was the founder of the People's Republic of Vietnam and worked all his life to liberate and unify his country. It was only after his death that this dream came true.

Marie Sklodowska was born in Warsaw, Poland in 1867. She later went to Paris, where she met and married Pierre Curie. The Curies were both physicists, and became famous for their work. One of their first discoveries was the element radium. They were both professors of physics at the Sorbonne, and they shared the Nobel Prize for physics in 1903.

4 Students' talks

• If students are all from different countries or educational backgrounds, it should be easy for them to find subjects that will be new and interesting for other people in the class.
• If they all share the same culture, the exercise may not work well in this form. In this case, you can do the exercise with volunteers who do have special knowledge about a particular person (e.g. a singer, a sports personality, a historical figure).
• An entertaining alternative is for students to imagine that they are future historians, looking back on their own (or other students') enormously successful and colourful careers.
• Students should prepare brief notes for the talks, but *not* write them out in detail. They should also prepare a few comprehension questions for the audience. (It's best if these are 'open-ended' questions; 'multiple-choice' questions like those in Exercise 3 would take too long to prepare.)

Practice Book exercises: choose two or more

1. Writing past questions.
2. Writing past negative sentences.
3. Student's Cassette exercise (Student's Book Exercise 3, second section). Students try to write down some of the sentences and practise saying them.
4. Reading and making notes.
5. Writing a paragraph about somebody's life.

Unit 18: Lesson B

Students learn to structure narrative.
Structures: Simple Past tense; sequencing and linking words.
Phonology: linking initial vowel to previous word.

Language notes and possible problems

1. Reading for meaning   There are a fair number of new words and expressions in the reading text in this lesson, and students may be a little daunted at first sight. During their first reading, tell them to try to guess some of the new vocabulary: they should look up (or ask you about) only those words they really need to put the pictures in order.

2. Sequencing and linking   In this lesson students learn some of the words and expressions used in English to signal time sequence and link ideas. Since these items are more common in written than in spoken language, the work is mostly writing-based. But this need not mean a dull and silent lesson if students work in groups to carry out the tasks.

3. Linking words in speech (Exercise 3)   In some languages, a word that begins with a vowel is clearly separated from the word before by a glottal stop. In English, the tendency is to link the vowel to the preceding word (so that, for example, *pack it* sounds exactly the same as *packet*). Check whether your students need practice in this.

---

1 Reading for meaning

- Before the students begin to read, look at the pictures with them, eliciting or teaching a few words as you do so (*ship, gun, fight, . . .*).
- Then tell them that the pictures are not in order, and that they must read the story to put them in order.
- Explain that they can ask you for words or look them up, but that you would like them to do this as little as possible during their first reading, and to try to guess some of the new words. (Encourage them to try to do the exercise without looking up any words at all, if they feel this is possible.)
- When students are ready, get them to compare notes and discuss their answers.

Answer to Exercise 1
The correct sequence is: A, D, C, B.

2 Sequencing and linking words

- Tell students to write the numbers 1–11 on a piece of paper.
- Look over the expressions in the box, and make sure they are all understood.
- Then ask students to work in pairs or groups to decide which of the expressions belongs in each gap in the text.
- Let them look up more words (or ask you for explanations) if necessary.

Answers to Exercise 2
1. who   2. that   3. So (*or* And)   4. as   5. and
6. Then (*or* Next)   7. First of all   8. Next (*or* Then)
9. but   10. Finally   11. where

3 Linking in speech

- This need not take very long unless students have a lot of difficulty.
- Get them to practise the sentences once or twice after you or the recording; then give them a minute or two to work on their own.
- The links are marked. Some students may find vowel-vowel links difficult. Tell them to pronounce a very light *y* after /iː/ and a very light *w* after /uː/: '*freeyof*', '*heyarrived*', '*theyinn*' and '*intowit*'.

4 Reading aloud

- Let students choose for themselves how much they want to try reading.
- Don't try to correct everything – concentrate on rhythm, weak forms and linking, and leave vowel and consonant mistakes unless they are really serious.

5 Writing narrative

- Unless you have a lot of spare time, you will probably want students to keep this short – just one or two paragraphs.
- Go round helping and correcting where necessary (but don't over-correct – the aim at this stage is successful communication, not perfection).
- Make sure students use plenty of the sequencing and linking words from Exercise 2.
- When students have finished, get them to put their work up on the walls or notice board for everybody to read.

Practice Book exercises: choose two or more
1. Writing infinitives of irregular pasts.
2. Using irregular pasts in sentences.
3. Using sequencing and linking words in sentences.
4. Word stress.
5. Vocabulary revision: words used for describing personality.
6. Reading and writing: putting a jumbled text in order.

18B America invades Britain!

Connecting sentences into stories.

1 Read the text and put the pictures in the correct order. Use your
dictionary where necessary, but try not to use it too much.

Here is a piece of history that British people don't
learn at school.

In 1778 the British had the strongest navy in the
world. They laughed at the small navy of their
American colonies, ...1....... were fighting to be free
of Britain.

One American captain thought he would like to
show the British ......2...... size was not everything.
......3....... this is what he did.

On the night of April 24, 1778, Captain John Paul
Jones quietly brought his ship *Ranger* to Whitehaven,
in the north-west of England. As soon ......4....... he
arrived, he took a group of his men to one of the
inns in the town, broke into it, ...5....... had a drink
with them.

......6...... they started work. ......7......, they went to
the fort and destroyed the guns. ......8......, they began
burning British ships. The British sailors woke up and
started fighting against the Americans, ...9...... they
could not stop Jones and his men.

......10......, the Americans left Whitehaven and sailed
to the south of Scotland, ...11....... they carried out
more attacks.

After Jones' visit, the British stopped laughing at
the small American navy.

2 Complete the text with the words and
expressions from the box. (There are two words
too many.)

and	as	because	but	finally
first of all	next	so	that	then
where	who	why		

3 Pronunciation: linking. Read these phrases and
sentences aloud. Be careful to join the words as
shown.

1. Here is a piece of history
2. They laughed at the small navy
3. to be free of Britain
4. as soon as he arrived
5. he took a group of his men
6. to one of the inns in the town
7. broke into it
8. first of all

4 Choose a section of the story (one sentence or
more) and read it aloud.

5 Write a short story using some of the words in
the box from Exercise 2 (as many as you can). You
can write about a journey, a holiday, a party, a
strange thing that happened to you, a historical
event, or anything else you like.

Learn: piece; north; south; west; east; so;
first of all; next; finally; where.

89

18C Who? What? Which? How? Where? When?

Question-word questions.

1 Put one of these words into each question: *Who, What, Which, How, Where, When.* Can you answer any of the questions? The picture will help.

HISTORY QUIZ

1. .... did Louis Blériot travel from France to England in 1909?
2. .... animals did Hannibal take across the Alps when he invaded Italy?
3. .... in Israel was Jesus Christ born?
4. .... was the name of the man who built the Eiffel Tower?
5. Copernicus disagreed with Ptolemy. .... about?
6. .... was 'New Amsterdam'?
7. .... did the Second World War start (month and year)?
8. .... led the 'Long March' in China?
9. .... starred in the film *The Sound of Music*?
10. .... of these was not a member of the Beatles: John Lennon, Mick Jagger, George Harrison, Ringo Starr, Paul McCartney?
11. .... wrote the James Bond novels?
12. .... of these sports was Pele famous for: baseball, running, football, tennis?

GUSTAVE BETHLEHEM

JULIE FLEMING

MICK EIFFEL

MAO DZE JAGGER

1939

SEPTEMBER ANDREWS

IAN DONG

2 Can you make a better quiz than the one in Exercise 1? Work in groups. Make at least ten questions, and use all of the question words.

Learn: when; animal; film; build (built); disagree; lead (led); famous.

Unit 18: Lesson C

Students revise past interrogative structures with question words.

Language notes and possible problems

1. Question word as subject   Students may have problems with questions in which *who, what* or *which* is (or accompanies) the subject of the sentence (e.g. *Who wrote Hamlet?; Which train goes to Edinburgh?*), since the auxiliary *do* is not used in these questions. The point will be studied in detail later, but look out for mistakes like **Who did write . . . ?*

2. *Which* and *what*   The differences between interrogative *which* and *what* are quite complicated, involving questions of both meaning and grammar. For the moment, students simply need to learn that *which* (not *who* or *what*) is used before *of.*

3. Cultural problems   The quiz in Exercise 1 will obviously be suitable for some students and totally unsuitable for others, depending on their cultural background and level of education. Those who don't know any of the answers should be able to guess a lot of them by using the clues in the picture; but if you think your class will react negatively to the exercise, you may like to prepare your own substitute quiz using items that are likely to be more familiar to the students. In any case, you should not spend too much time on Exercise 1 – the most important part of the lesson is Exercise 2, where students get a chance to design their own quizzes.

1 History quiz: interrogatives

• This can be done by class discussion or as an individual or group exercise. Don't take too long over it; the main purpose is to make sure that students can handle the various interrogative words correctly.

• The answers to the questions can be found, if necessary, in a mixed-up form in the picture.

Answers to Exercise 1
1. (*How*) By air (first Channel crossing by aeroplane).
2. (*What* or *Which*) Elephants.
3. (*Where*) In Bethlehem.
4. (*What*) Gustave Eiffel.
5. (*What*) The structure of the solar system: Ptolemy said the sun went round the earth, and Copernicus said the opposite.
6. (*Where* or *What*) It was the old name for New York City.
7. (*When*) In September 1939.
8. (*Who*) Mao Dze Dong (Mao Tse Tung).
9. (*Who*) Julie Andrews.
10. (*Which*) Mick Jagger.
11. (*Who*) Ian Fleming.
12. (*Which*) Football.

2 Students' quizzes

• Students must often feel that they could write a better textbook themselves. This exercise gives them an opportunity to make a start.

• Put them in groups and give them fifteen minutes or so to prepare a set of questions.

• The questions should be neither too difficult nor too easy. Each set of questions will have to be answered by other students, so there shouldn't be too much difficult vocabulary. All of the question words *who, which* etc. should be used. And the questions should be about the past.

• Go round helping if necessary.

• When students are ready, they should try out their quizzes on each other (group asking group, or each group asking the whole class, as you like).

Practice Book exercises: choose two or more
1. Students work on past tense forms.
2. Punctuation and capitalisation.
3. Articles.
4. Word stress.
5. Formation of past questions.
6. Crossword.

Unit 18: Lesson D

Students practise talking about daily routines and the recent past, and reporting what people have said.
Stuctures: Simple Past tense; *say* and *tell*; *both . . . and*; *neither . . . nor*, elementary reported speech.
Phonology: contrastive stress.

Language notes and possible problems
1. Reported speech is introduced in contexts without tense-shift or special word order.
2. Neither Contrast US /ˈniːðər/ (and non-standard British /ˈniːðə(r)/) and standard British /ˈnaɪðə(r)/.
3. Tell and say Remind students that *tell* has a direct object before a clause (*tell somebody that . . .*), while *say* does not (*say that . . .*). Look out for mistakes like **He told that . . .* ; **He said met that . . .*
4. Contrastive stress In Exercises 2 and 3, students indicate a contrast or contradiction by saying the key word or expression louder and on a higher pitch than normal. Some students may find this difficult.

1 Presentation: *both . . . and*; *neither . . . nor*
• After looking at the pictures, go through the list of actions and help with the new vocabulary.
• Ask all students to write at least one sentence with *both . . . and*, and one with *neither . . . nor*. Invite them to add more orally.

2 Finding differences; contrastive stress 🔲
• Practise the example, making sure students say *eight* and *ten* louder and on a high pitch.
• Play the recording, and elicit differences between Al's statement and the picture strip. Students should begin 'Al told the policeman . . . ' and use contrastive stress.
• Play the recording again, pausing to let students take notes, and see if they find more differences.

Answers to Exercise 2

AL TOLD THE POLICEMAN THAT	BUT ACTUALLY
he got up at eight	he got up at ten
he shaved	he didn't
he wrote to his mother	he didn't
he met Jake outside the Super Cinema at about twelve	they met outside a bank at 11.15
they went for a walk, talked about music etc.	they robbed the bank
they had lunch in a pub	they went to the Ritz
they bought flowers and went to an art gallery.	Al went to buy a Rolls
that evening he listened to the radio and read	he watched TV
his aunt gave him the Rolls	he bought it

Tapescript for Exercise 2
Yeah, well, I got up about eight o'clock, didn't I? Washed and shaved, had breakfast. Wrote a letter to my old mother. Went out of the house about, say, 11.30. Met my friend Jake outside the Super Cinema at about twelve. We went for a drink, then we went for a walk in the park. Talked about music and books, things like that. Then we had lunch in a pub somewhere – sandwiches and a glass of orange juice. Then we went to a flower shop to buy some flowers to give to the hospital. After that we went to the art gallery for an hour or two – 'cos old Jake's very interested in pictures. Then I went home, and spent the evening listening to the radio and reading philosophy.
   Rolls-Royce? Yes, my Aunt Lucy gave it to me. That's right. Kind of her, wasn't it? Yes, she really loves me, Aunt Lucy does.

3 Listening: finding differences, contrastive stress (continued) 🔲
• Practise the examples; work on the contrastive stress on *art gallery* and *football match*.
• Carry on as in Exercise 2; this time the students should report the differences using 'Al said that . . . '

Answers to Exercise 3
– Al said that they met outside the Super Cinema at about twelve, but Jake said that they met outside the ABC at 12.30.
– Al said that they went for a walk in the park, but Jake said that they walked in the town centre.
– Al said they talked about music and books, but Jake said that they talked about sport and girls.
– Al said that they had sandwiches and orange juice in a pub, but Jake said that they had a hamburger.
– Al said that they bought flowers and went to an art gallery, but Jake said that they went to a football match.

Tapescript for Exercise 3
Yeah, well, I got up about seven o'clock. Washed and shaved, had breakfast. Listened to some music on the radio. Wrote letters. Went out of the house about, I dunno, twelve. Met my friend Al outside the ABC Cinema at half past twelve. We went for a walk in the town centre. Talked about sport, girls, things like that. Went and had a hamburger. Then we went to watch the football. It was a good match. Then I came home. Watched TV, took the dog for a walk, . . .
   All that money under my bed? Yeah, well, I found it in the street, didn't I? While I was out walking with the dog. Yes, I was going to bring it to the police station tomorrow. See, it was late. I didn't want to wake you up, did I?

4 Students' stories
• Give students a minute or two to prepare, and then ask a volunteer to say as much as possible about what he/she did yesterday, including at least one lie.
• Get the class to decide which statement is not true.
• Continue the exercise in groups.

Optional activity: 'Alibi'
• Two students go out. They are murder suspects, and must prepare an untrue story about their activities yesterday (they were together all day).
• The rest of the class are policemen investigating the crime. They prepare questions for the suspects.
• After five minutes, one suspect is brought in, and questioned about what they did yesterday.
• Then the second is brought in and questioned. The class must 'break the alibi' by finding three contradictions between the two accounts.

Practice Book exercises: choose two or more
1. Contrastive stress.
2. *Both . . . and*; *neither . . . nor*; *but*.
3. *Tell* and *say*.
4. Check on revision vocabulary.
5. Translation of material from the unit.
6. Student's Cassette exercise (Student's Book Exercise 2). Students listen to Al's statement and try to write some of it down.
7. Reading: Part 17 of *It's a Long Story*.

Talking about the past; understanding spoken
English; building sentences.

AL'S DAY

JAKE'S DAY

1 Look at the pictures. Which of these things
did both Al and Jake do? Which did neither Al nor
Jake do? Examples:

'Both Al and Jake robbed a bank.'
'Neither Al nor Jake went to bed early.'

got up late washed shaved had breakfast	

robbed a bank   wore masks   carried guns
had lunch at the Ritz   went to a football match
bought flowers   went to an art gallery
listened to the radio   took the dog for a walk
went to bed early

2 Listen to Al's statement to the police. Can
you find anything that is not true? Example (practise
the pronunciation):

*'He told the policeman that he got up at **eight**
o'clock, but actually he got up at **ten** o'clock.'*

3 Listen to Jake. Can you find any differences
between his statement and Al's? Example (practise
the pronunciation):

*'Al said that they went to an **art gallery** together, but
Jake said that they went to a **football match**.'*

4 Tell the other students what you did yesterday.
Include two or more things that are not true.
Example:

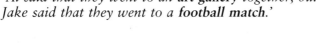

... then I went to have lunch with the President.

Not true!

No, you didn't!

You had lunch with Pedro.

Learn: policeman; gun; flower; radio; dog;
walk (*noun and verb*); wash; carry; early; true;
listen to the radio; watch TV.

Unit 19 Getting to know you

19A Is this seat free?

Permission (asking, giving, refusing); starting conversations; *Do you mind if . . . ?*

1 Look at the pictures. What do you think the people are saying in each picture?

2 Pronunciation. Say these words and expressions.

a. Is this seat free?
b. seat   sit   eat   it   sheep   ship
c. heat   need   cheap   steam   steel   leak
   seek   peach   keep
d. win   spit   hit   pick   lip

3 Work with another student. You are on a train, and you want to sit down, open the window, etc. Ask and answer.

ASK FOR PERMISSION	REFUSE PERMISSION
Do you mind if I sit here?	I'm sorry. It's not free.
Do you mind if I open the window?	Well, it's a bit cold.
Do you mind if I smoke?	Well, I'd rather you didn't.
Do you mind if I look at your paper?	Well, I'm reading it myself, actually.
	GIVE PERMISSION
	Not at all.
	No, please do.
	Go ahead.

4 📼 Close your books, listen to the recording and answer.
a. Refuse permission.
b. Give permission.

5 Improvisation. Work in groups of between four and six. You are sitting together on a train. Begin a conversation.
OR: Work in pairs. You are both in a coffee-bar, a pub or a park. Begin a conversation.

Learn: seat; myself; open; mind; Do you mind if . . . ?; for a moment; please do; go ahead; I'd rather you didn't.

Unit 19: Lesson A

Students learn how to ask for, give and refuse permission; how to initiate a polite conversation with a stranger.
Structure: *Do you mind if . . . ?*
Phonology: /iː/ and /ɪ/.

Language notes and possible problems

1. Subject-matter The basic situation here (getting into conversation with strangers) will be familiar to most students. Some of them, indeed, are likely to be experts at it, and there will probably be a lot of questions about how to formulate this or that expression in English. (Encourage *How do you say . . . ?* or *How can I say . . . ?*) Note, however, that students from certain cultural backgrounds may find the situation unfamiliar; they may have more difficulty with this lesson, especially with Exercise 5.

2. *Do you mind if . . . ?* is likely to cause difficulty (because the answer *No* means 'Yes, you can' and *Yes* means 'No, you can't'). You can explain *mind* as 'not want' or 'not like'. *If* is previewed here, but is not studied in detail at this stage.

3. *Can* and *could* reappear here. Remind students that *could* is used when we want to be more polite.

1 Predicting a conversation

- Ask students to look at the pictures for a minute or two.
- Get them to suggest sentences for the six speech-balloons.
- Ask how they think the conversation continues.
- Build up the complete conversation (with alternatives) on the board.
- Play the recording, and answer any questions.
- Get students to note down the sentence *Do you mind if I sit here?*
- Ask volunteers to try to act out the recorded conversation from memory.

Tapescript for Exercise 1
'Excuse me. Is this seat free?'
'Yes, it is.'
'Do you mind if I sit here?'
'Not at all.'
'Could I borrow your newspaper?'
'Yes, of course.'

2 Pronunciation

- The sentence *Is this seat free?* makes a good jumping-off point for further work on the contrast between /iː/ and /ɪ/.
- The second part of the exercise (b) can be extended and done as an ear training activity:
  – Write on the board: *seat   sit*
                     eat   it
  – Say one of the words and ask students which side it is on, left or right.
  – Do this a few times, then add some more pairs such as *sheep/ship, Jean/gin, feet/fit*.
  – Ask students to choose words and say them; you and the rest of the class will say which side of the board they are from.
  – Finish by dictating some of the words, chosen at random.
- The third part of the exercise (c) reminds students that they can generally pronounce words written with *ea* and *ee* even if they don't know them. (They may be able to think of a few cases where these letters are pronounced differently; for example, *bread, steak*.)
- The fourth part (d) does the same for words written with *i*.
- The recording can be used as a model if you wish.

3 *Do you mind if . . . ?*

- Look over the examples with the students.
- Practise the intonation with the recording, and pay special attention to the sound /ɪ/ in *if* and *sit*.
- It is important for them to realise the meaning of *mind*, and to understand that a negative answer to *Do you mind if . . . ?* means 'It's all right'.
- They must also realise that it is common to refuse a 'Do you mind if . . . ?' request by giving some sort of reason.
- When students are ready, ask them to close their books and practise asking and answering with a partner.
- If they have difficulty, let them look back at their books and then try again.

4 Listening and answering

- Tell students to look again at the answers used for refusing permission in Exercises 2 and 3.
- Get them to close their books.
- Play the recording straight through, while students answer the requests by refusing permission.
- *Do you mind . . . ?* and *Can/Could I . . . ?* are mixed here, so students will have to pay attention to the form of the question.
- Students can answer all together or in turn, as you wish.
- If they are slow, stop the recording so as to give more time.
- When you have gone through all the requests, get students to open their books and look again at ways of giving permission.
- Then tell them to close their books; play the requests again from the beginning while students give permission.

Tapescript for Exercise 4
Do you mind if I sit here?
Do you mind if I smoke?
Do you mind if I use your dictionary?
Do you mind if I ask you a question?
Can I look at your newspaper?
Could I open the window?
Do you mind if I make a telephone call?
Could I possibly borrow your pen?
Do you mind if I play some records?
Could I borrow your keys for a moment?

5 Improvisation

- The second alternative will work best in mixed classes; in a single-sex class the railway-carriage situation may go better.
- The conversations will probably not go on for very long; the important thing is to get them started.

Practice Book exercises: choose two or more
1. Completing conversations about permission.
2. /iː/ and /ɪ/.
3. Writing sentences with quantifiers.
4. Student's Cassette exercise (Student's Book Exercise 4). Students listen to requests, and first refuse, then give permission.
5. Recreational reading, with limited use of dictionaries.

Unit 19: Lesson B

Students learn more about how to express the idea of frequency, and practise reply questions and *So . . . I* in the context of polite conversational exchanges.
Structures: position of adverbs and adverbials of frequency; *once a week, twice a month* etc.; *every three days* etc.; reply questions; *So . . . I.*
Phonology: rising intonation in reply questions.

Language notes and possible problems

1. Word order Students have already learnt that frequency adverbs tend to go before the main verb. This is not true of most adverbials (longer expressions which function as adverbs): these often go at the end of a clause. Exercise 2 practises the point.
2. Reply questions There may be some resistance to reply questions, which often seem silly to speakers of languages which do not have a similar device. Point out that *Is it?*, *Do you?* and so on are not real questions but simply show interest on the part of the listener.
 Students who find it too difficult to produce all the different combinations of subject + auxiliary can just say *Oh, yes?* or *Really?* instead.
3. So . . . I This structure uses auxiliary verbs in the same way as reply questions. If manipulating all the different auxiliaries is too difficult for some students, you may want to teach them to say *Me too*.
4. Articles Note the 'generalising' use of the article in *the cinema/opera/hairdresser*.
5. Come and go both occur in the conversation; you may wish to explain the difference.
6. Actually is a 'false friend' – speakers of European languages may think it means 'now'.
7. A drink Note the common use of *a drink* to mean 'an alcoholic drink'. Compare *something to drink* (which might also be coffee, fruit juice etc.).
8. Every is used here with plural numerical expressions; point out that it is normally followed by a singular noun.

Presentation: the illustration

• Before doing Exercise 1, let students have a good look at the illustration and dialogue.
• Answer questions on the text and explain difficulties.
• Draw students' attention to the position of frequency adverbs and adverbials.
• Then tell them to close their books and see how much they can remember of the exchanges.

1 *How often?*

• Look at the possible questions and answers.
• Explain vocabulary; practise pronunciation.
• Get students to ask you as many questions as they can; try to give true answers.
• Then set up a 'chain-drill': ask one of the students a question; he/she answers it and asks another student.

2 Word order

• Ask students to write three or more sentences of each kind, so that they can get a fair amount of practice in putting the adverbs in the right place.

Optional activity: class survey

• Get each student to go round the class finding out how often everybody does one of the things mentioned in Exercise 1 (or anything else).
• Students note the answers and report.
• Example: '*Six people go to the cinema once a week. Three people go twice a week. One never goes.*'

3 Reply questions

• First of all, tell students to decide which is the right answer to each sentence. Help them to see why.
• Play the recording of the eight sentences with the replies, and practise the intonation.
• Play the recording of the rest of the exercise: students have to produce reply questions spontaneously.
• If they find it difficult, play the recording twice: the first time, students answer '*Oh, yes?*' or '*Really?*', and the second time they try the forms with auxiliary verbs.

Tapescript for Exercise 3
'My sister's a doctor.' 'Is she?'
'My brother's got five children.' 'Has he?'
'Maria likes fast cars.' 'Does she?'
'It's raining again.' 'Is it?'
'I slept badly last night.' 'Did you?'
'I love skiing.' 'Do you?'
'My father can speak five languages.' 'Can he?'
'I'm tired.' 'Are you?'

It's three o'clock.
I'm hungry.
We live in a very small house.
I like dancing.
Mary telephoned yesterday.
Mr and Mrs Harris are coming tomorrow.
I forgot to buy bread.
We're going on holiday next week.
It's snowing.
You're late.
John's here.
My sister works in a cinema.

4 *So . . . I / I . . . not*: presentation

• Explain that *So can I* means 'I can too', *So do I* means 'I do too', and so on.
• The exercise will help students to grasp the details of the structure, if they find this difficult.
• It is probably best to ask them to write the answers, so that you can make sure everybody has understood the point.

5 Personalisation

• This can either be done as a 'real' or a 'role' activity.
• Ask each student to write five true sentences, or five untrue sentences, about him- or herself. If students are inventing untrue facts, make sure they understand that these can be perfectly outlandish.
• Go over the examples with the students and then ask them to work in pairs, using the sentences they have written as jumping-off points for dialogues.
• Walk round while they are working to give any help that is needed.
• For extra practice, students can change partners after a few minutes.

Practice Book exercises: choose two or more
1. Completing sentences with frequency adverbs.
2. Answering questions about frequency.
3. Writing reply questions.
4. Completing sentences with *So . . . I.*
5. Student's Cassette exercise: (Student's Book Exercise 3, second set of sentences). Students listen and make reply questions.

19B How often do you come here?

Frequency; showing interest; comparing interests and habits; reply questions; *So . . . I.*

● *I always come here on Sunday mornings.*
♥ Oh, do you? So do I.

♥ *I'm Pisces.*
● Are you? So am I.

● Do you like 'Top of the Pops'?
♥ *I never watch it.*

♥ My brother . . .
● *Does he?*

♥ I go to the cinema at least once a week.

● *How often do you . . . ?*
♥ Every two or three days . . .

♥ I've got a . . .
● *Oh, have you? . . .*

● Do you ever go to the opera?
♥ Oh, yes, I love opera.
● *So do I. Actually, I've got two tickets for 'Carmen' tonight.*
♥ Oh, have you?
● *Would you like to go with me?*
♥ I'd love to.
● *Let's have a drink before it starts.*
♥ Why not?

1 Ask and answer.

How often do you:
go to the hairdresser / watch TV /
travel by train / go on holiday / go for a walk /
go to the cinema / listen to music at home /
go skiing / write letters / drink coffee?

Very often.   Sometimes.   Hardly ever.
Quite often.   Occasionally.   Never.

Once	a day.
Twice	a week.
Three times	a month.
	a year.

Every day/week/month/Tuesday.
Every three days / six weeks.

2 Word order. Write sentences like the examples.

I never go to the cinema.
I often listen to records.
I go skiing twice a year.
I travel by train every Tuesday.

3 [cassette icon] Reply questions. Match sentences and answers. Practise the intonation. Then close your books and answer the recorded sentences.

My sister's a doctor.
My brother's got five children.
Maria likes fast cars.
It's raining again.
I slept badly last night.
I love skiing.
My father can speak five languages.
I'm tired.

Oh yes?	Has he?
Really?	Are you?
Do you?	Can he?
Is it?	Does she?
Is she?	Did you?

4 Match the sentences and the answers. (Two answers for each sentence.)

I like fish.
I'm tired.
I've got too much work.
I can speak German.

So can I.	I haven't.
I don't.	So am I.
So have I.	I can't.
I'm not.	So do I.

5 Compare real or imaginary interests and habits. Tell your partner things about yourself. Your partner will answer beginning '. . . you? So . . . I.' or '. . . you? I . . .n't/not.' Examples:

'I've got a pink Rolls-Royce.'
'Have you? So have I. I've got a yellow one, too.'
'Really? I don't like yellow, but . . .'

'I go skiing twice a year.'
'Do you? I don't; I can't ski. But I've got a brother who skis very well.'
'Oh, yes? . . .'

Learn: cinema; go to the cinema; go for a walk; tonight; occasionally; hardly ever; once; twice; three times *etc.*; once a week/month *etc.*; every day/week *etc.*; every three days *etc.*; badly; How often . . . ?; So (do/am/have I *etc.*).

19C What do you think of . . . ?

1 Look at the questions in the picture. Choose possible answers from these.

Yes, I do.   Terrible!   Cheesecake.
Yes, I went to Senegal last year.
No, I don't.   Yes, lots of times.   Not bad.
We played it at my school.   No, never.
No, I haven't.   Great!   Not much.
I saw it in Paris three years ago.

What do you think of the government?
Have you ever been to Africa?
Do you like modern jazz?

How do you like this place?
Have you seen 'Carmen' before?
What's your favourite food?
Have you ever played baseball?

2 Look at the table of verb forms and choose words to complete the sentences.

1. 'Have you .... *Carmen* before?' 'Yes, I .... it three years ago.'
2. 'Have you ever .... to America?' 'Yes, I .... to California last summer.'
3. 'Have you ever .... fish curry?' 'No, I haven't.'
4. 'Do you like modern jazz?' 'I don't know. I haven't .... much.'
5. 'Do you like driving?' 'Actually, I've never .... to drive.'
6. 'Have another drink.' 'No, thanks. I've .... enough.'
7. 'I .... my job last week.' 'I've .... my job three times this year.'
8. 'Have you ever .... in a shop?' 'Yes, I .... in my uncle's shop every summer when I was younger.'
9. 'Have you ever .... in a car crash?' 'Yes, I .... in a bad crash when I was eighteen.'
10. 'I've .... in three different countries.' 'I've always .... here – I've never wanted to live anywhere else.'

3 Class survey. Write three questions:
a. One question beginning 'What do you think of . . . ?'
b. One question beginning 'What's/Who's your favourite . . . ?'
c. One question beginning 'Have you ever . . . ?'

4 Ask other students your questions. Example:

'What do you think of classical music?' 'Not much.'
'Who's your favourite musician?' 'Tracy Chapman.'
'Have you ever heard her in person?' 'Yes, I have.' / 'No, I haven't.'

Then report to the class. Example:

'Seven people like classical music, three think it isn't bad, and two think it's terrible. Favourite musicians are: Tracy Chapman, . . . One person has heard her favourite musician in person.'

Present Perfect tense	
I have ('ve) been	we have ('ve) been
you have ('ve) been	you have ('ve) been
he/she/it has ('s) been	they have ('ve) been
have I been?	have we been?
have you been?	have you been?
has he/she/it been?	have they been?
I have not (haven't) been	
you have not (haven't) been	
he/she/it has not (hasn't) been	
we have not (haven't) been	
you have not (haven't) been	
they have not (haven't) been	

Verb forms		
INFINITIVE	PAST TENSE	PAST PARTICIPLE
be	was/were	been
have	had	had
see	saw	seen
hear	heard	heard
eat	ate	eaten
learn	learnt	learnt
go	went	gone/been
change	changed	changed
work	worked	worked
live	lived	lived

Learn: great; ever; anywhere; anywhere else; *past participles of the irregular verbs in the table.*

Unit 19: Lesson C

Students learn how to ask and talk about opinions and experiences.
Structures: *What do you think of . . . ?*; Present Perfect tense.

Language notes and possible problems

1. Present Perfect tense – formation In this lesson, students are introduced to 'past participles' (a misleading name – the meaning of this participle has nothing to do with past time). Speakers of most European languages will find the structure **have** + **past participle** familiar. Speakers of other languages may not have a mother-tongue equivalent of the past participle or of the verb forms that are constructed with it; they may consequently take some time to get used to the formation of the Present Perfect.

2. Present Perfect tense – use In this lesson, students concentrate on one use of the Present Perfect – to talk about things that have happened at some indefinite or unknown time in the past, or that have not happened at any time in the past. The key concept here is 'at any time up to now'. Adverbs like *ever*, *never* and *before* are common in this context.

When explaining the use of the tense, you might want to make a time line like this:

THEN ——?——?——?——?——?——?—— NOW

The contrast between the Present Perfect and Simple Past is illustrated in Exercise 2, but is studied more systematically in Unit 20.

For further notes on the Present Perfect, see the panel at the end of this page.

1 Matching questions and answers
• Look over the questions; make sure students understand the meaning of *Have you ever . . . ?* and *Have you . . . before?*
• The exercise can be done by group discussion. There are of course several possible ways to match up some of the questions and answers.
• Ask students if they can suggest other answers that are not on the page.

2 Past participles and past tenses
• Look over the table of verb forms with the students. The main thing for them to realise is that some (irregular) verbs have a special third form besides the infinitive and past tense, and that this form (the so-called 'past participle') is used after *have* to make the Present Perfect tense. Note that *been* can be used as a past participle of *go* (you may prefer to leave more detailed explanations until later).
• Go through the exercise, getting students to write some of the answers so as to make sure that everybody has understood.

Answers to Exercise 2
1. seen, saw
2. been, went
3. eaten
4. heard
5. learnt
6. had
7. changed, changed
8. worked, worked
9. been, was
10. lived, lived

Use of the Present Perfect – explanation
• This is a suitable moment to tell students something about how the Present Perfect is used in English. It's probably best to keep to the use mainly illustrated here (things that have or have not happened 'at any time up to the present'). See *Language notes* for details and suggestions.

3 Class survey: writing questions
• Ask each student to write three questions as shown in the examples.
• Point out the table of irregular verbs at the back of the book – this will give them past participles of verbs not listed in this lesson.
• Walk round and give help where needed.

4 Class survey: asking questions and reporting
• Go over the examples with the students.
• Then each student should ask his or her questions of as many others as possible, preferably by getting up and walking round the room.
• They should note the answers they get.
• When they have finished, get each student to report the results of his or her survey.

Practice Book exercises: choose two or more
1. Writing sentences about favourite things and people.
2. Answering questions about opinions and experiences.
3. Making Present Perfect questions.
4. Sentence stress and rhythm.

The Present Perfect tense
The Present Perfect is not an easy tense for students. It has several meanings (continuation up to the present; current relevance; completion); these ideas may not be expressed by choice of tense in the students' languages, and the use of the Present Perfect may therefore seem abstract and difficult to grasp.

Many European languages have a form which looks like the Present Perfect, but which is not used in the same way – it may correspond to the English Simple Past, leading to mistakes like *I have seen the lawyer yesterday*.

Conversely, students' languages may use a present tense to talk about duration up to the present, causing mistakes like *I am here since last Tuesday*.

Unit 19: Lesson D

Students learn to refer to periods of time extending up to the present, and to say how long they have known people, lived in places, etc.
Structures: Present Perfect tense referring to states (*know, have, live, be*); *since* and *for*.

Language notes and possible problems
1. The Present Perfect is used here in its meaning of continuation up to the present. In some students' languages, this meaning may be expressed by a present tense. Watch out for mistakes like **I am here since Tuesday*.

The focus here is on the simple tense. The Present Perfect Progressive is studied in Level 2 of the course.
2. *Since* and *for* may present problems for students whose language has only one word for the two meanings. Look out for mistakes like **I have known her since three years*.

---

1 Restoring a text
• Look over the two 'letter fragments' and vocabulary with the students, and answer any questions.
• The exercise can be done in groups.
• Only the language for the 'torn-off' right-hand part of each page is provided; the letters remain incomplete at the top and the bottom.
• When the students have finished and checked their answers with you, point out the use of the Present Perfect in *I've only known him since yesterday* and *I've only known her for 24 hours*. Explain that the Present Perfect is used for states starting in the past and continuing in the present.
• You may want to put a time line on the board:

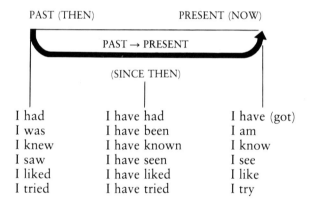

PAST (THEN)   PRESENT (NOW)

PAST → PRESENT

(SINCE THEN)

I had	I have had	I have (got)
I was	I have been	I am
I knew	I have known	I know
I saw	I have seen	I see
I liked	I have liked	I like
I tried	I have tried	I try

• Remind students that regular past participles have got the same form as past tense forms, but that irregular past participles are often different and must be learnt.

Answers to Exercise 1

. . . the nicest *man*
I've met for years. I've only *known him*
since yesterday, but I'm already *sure*
it's going to be very important. *He's*
tall and slim, with a beautiful *smile*
and – believe it or not, Sally – *he's*
interested in the same things as *I am:*
films, music, travel and so on. *He's*
Pisces, and so *am I.*

. . . met this wonderful *woman.*
John, I really think *I'm in love.*
It's funny. I've only *known her*
for 24 hours, but I feel *we've always*
known each other. And *we've got*
so many interests in common; *music,*
films, travel . . . We're both *Pisces.*

2 *Since* and *for*
• Look at the examples with the students.
• They should see that *since* is used with a reference to the beginning of a period, while *for* introduces an expression naming the whole period.
• Get students to fill in the gaps.

3 Questions with *How long*
• Ask students to work in pairs. After looking at the examples, explain that each student should ask his or her partner as many questions as possible beginning with *How long have you . . .*
• They should write down the answers to at least four questions, in the form *This person has lived here for twelve years*, etc.
• Walk round while they are working to give any help that is needed.

4 Reading and guessing
• Collect the papers from Exercise 3 and shuffle them.
• Pass them out again at random. Each student should read the paper you give them and write on the back who they think it is about.
• Then they should pass it along, until all the students have read all the papers (or, in a large class, until ten or so people have written on the back of each paper).
• Quickly read out the papers and let the students claim them.

Practice Book exercises: choose two or more
1. Past tenses and participles.
2. Completing sentences with past participles.
3. Choosing the correct verb form (Simple Present or Present Perfect).
4. Translation of material from the unit.
5. Check on revision vocabulary.
6. Reading: Part 18 of *It's a Long Story*.

19D I've only known her for twenty-four hours, but . . .

Present Perfect tense; *How long*, *for* and *since*.

1 Can you complete the sentences in the two torn letters? These words and expressions will help.

LETTER 1		
sure	he's	He's
I am:	man	
known him		am I.
smile	He's	

LETTER 2	
we've got	music
Pisces.	known her
woman.	we've always
in love	

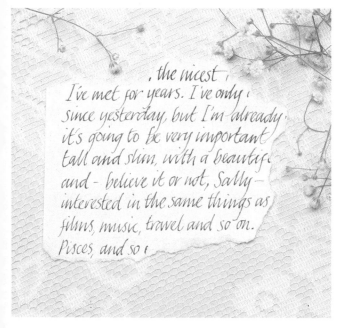

, the nicest
I've met for years. I've only
since yesterday, but I'm already
it's going to be very important
tall and slim, with a beautif
and - believe it or not, Sally -
interested in the same things as
films, music, travel and so on.
Pisces, and so

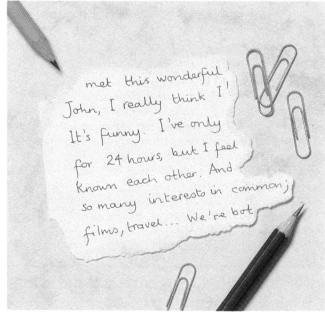

met this wonderful
John, I really think I
It's funny. I've only
for 24 hours, but I feel
known each other. And
so many interests in common;
films, travel... We're bot

2 *Since* and *for*.

since yesterday = for 24 hours
for 400 years = since the 16th century
since last Tuesday = for ....
since last .... = for five days
since 1977 = for ....
.... I was born = all my life
.... = since my birthday
since nine o'clock = ...
since last July = ...
for ten years = ...

3 Make questions with *How long* and ask a partner. Write down four of the answers. Examples:

How long have you | *lived in this town/city?*
| *been in this class?*
| *been married?*
| *been learning English?*
| *been studying karate / the*
| *violin etc.?*
| *had that watch/sweater/ring etc.?*
| *had long/short hair?*
| *known your friend Maria etc.?*

4 Give your partner's answers to the teacher, who will shuffle the papers and pass them round. Try to guess who answered the questions.

Learn: smile (*noun*); believe; feel (felt, felt); funny; wonderful; already; since; for (*with time*); all my life; in love; and so on; each other.

95

Unit 20 Consolidation

20A Things to remember: Units 17, 18 and 19

Present Perfect tense

I have ('ve) been	have I been?	I have not (haven't) been
you have ('ve) been	have you been?	you have not (haven't) been
he/she/it has ('s) been	has he *etc.* been?	she *etc.* has not (hasn't) been
we have ('ve) been	have we been?	we have not (haven't) been
you have ('ve) been	have you been?	you have not (haven't) been
they have ('ve) been	have they been?	they have not (haven't) been

Examples:
'**Have** you ever **been** to Africa?' 'Yes, I **have**.'
'**Have** you **seen** *Carmen* before?' 'No, I **haven't**.'
I've never **learnt** to drive.
I've **changed** my job three times this year.
How long **have** you **lived** in this town?
(How long do you live in this town?)
How long **have** you **known** Maria?
(How long do you know Maria?)
How long **have** you **been** learning English?
I've **been** in this class for three weeks.
(I am in this class for three weeks.)
(I've been in this class since three weeks.)
I've **known** her since 1986.
(I know her since 1986.)

Since and *for*
since yesterday = **for** 24 hours
since the 16th century = **for** 400 years

Present Perfect and Simple Past
– I've **changed** my job three times **this year**.
  I **changed** my job three times **last year**.
– **Have** you **seen** *Carmen* before?
  I **saw** it **three years ago**.
– **Have** you **ever worked** in a shop?
  I **worked** in my uncle's shop **when I was younger**.

Infinitive, past tense and past participle

INFINITIVE	PAST TENSE	PAST PARTICIPLE
Regular verbs		
work	worked	worked
live	lived	lived
stop	stopped	stopped
try	tried	tried
play	played	played
Irregular verbs		
be	was/were	been
bring	brought	brought
buy	bought	bought
catch	caught	caught
come	came	come
cost	cost	cost
draw	drew	drawn
drink	drank	drunk
eat	ate	eaten

(For a complete list of irregular verbs from Units 1–24, see page 136.)

Verbs with two objects
Could you bring **me some water**?
Can I give **you a little more coffee**?
Could you lend **me some sugar**?
Could you show **me some black sweaters**, please?

Imperatives
Meet me at seven o'clock.
Don't tell Carola.

Reported speech; *say* and *tell*
He **told the policeman that** he got up at eight o'clock.
(He told that he got up . . . .)
He **said that** they went to an art gallery.
(He said the policeman that . . . .)

Question words
How did Louis Blériot travel from France to England? (How travelled . . . ?)
When did the Second World War start? (When started . . . ?)
What animals did Hannibal take across the Alps?
Where was Jesus Christ born? (Where was born Jesus Christ?)

Question word as subject
Who wrote the James Bond novels? (Who did write . . . ?)

Which of . . . ?
Which of these was not a member of the Beatles? (Who of these . . . ?)
Which of these sports was Pele famous for?

This lesson summarises and displays the language that students should have learnt in the last three units. Spend a short time going over the lesson pages with the students, making sure that everything is clearly understood.

Note that expressions which occur in the grammatical and functional sections of the summary are not necessarily listed again in the vocabulary section. On the other hand, words which have occurred before in the course may appear again in the vocabulary lists if they are used in a new way in Units 17–19 (e.g. *with* meaning 'accompanying', *who* and *where* as relatives).

Ask the students to look over the lesson again at home.

Practice Book exercises: choose two or more
1. Students construct sentences with *neither . . . nor*.
2. Students write sentences about themselves with *neither . . . nor*.
3. Reply questions and short answers; *So am I* etc.
4. Place names: nouns and adjectives.
5. Conversational responses.
6. Students write about what they did yesterday evening.
7. Recreational reading.

Video

Sequences 5A and 5B in *The New Cambridge English Course 1 Video* can be used around this point in the book, as they relate to Units 17–19 of the coursebook.

In Sequence 5A, **Getting to know you**, the topics are meeting people and keeping conversation going; food. Language focus is on Present Perfect tense; ordering and asking; frequency adverbs.

In Sequence 5B, **One man's life**, the topics are a person's life; historical information. Language focus is on Simple Past tense; dates.

Determiners and pronouns

I'm sorry, there's **no more** roast beef.
Would you like **something** to drink?
Could you bring me **some** water?
Is everything all right?
 (Are everything . . . ?)

Articles

He was **a** student in Saigon.
 (He was student . . .)
She was **a** pilot and writer.
She was **the** first woman to fly a plane across the Atlantic.
He was **the** man who discovered sunspots.

Frequency adverbs and adverbials

How often do you go to the cinema?
Do you ever go to the opera?

| I | always
very often
quite often
sometimes
occasionally
hardly ever
never | come here on Sunday mornings. |

| I come here | every day.
every three days.
once a day.
twice a week.
three times a year. |

Joining subjects

Both Al **and** Jake robbed a bank.
Neither Al **nor** Jake went to bed early.

Joining sentences

Then they started work. **First of all** they went to the fort and destroyed the guns. **Next,** they began burning British ships . . . **Finally,** the Americans left Whitehaven . . .

Joining clauses into sentences

The British sailors woke up **and** started fighting, **but** they could not stop Jones and his men.
One American captain wanted to show the British **that** size was not everything.
They laughed at the small navy of the Americans, **who** were fighting to be free of Britain.
The Americans left Whitehaven and sailed to Scotland, **where** they carried out more attacks.
As soon as he arrived, he took a group of his men to an inn.
Amelia Earhart stopped studying **because** she wanted to learn to fly.

Showing interest: reply questions

'I'm Pisces.' '**Are** you?'
'I've got a . . . ' 'Oh, **have** you?'
'My father **can** speak five languages.' '**Can** he?'
'I love skiing.' '**Do** you?'
'I **slept** badly last night.' 'Oh, **did** you?'

So am I etc.

'I've got a pink Rolls-Royce.' '**So have I.**'
 '**I haven't.**'
'I'm tired.' '**So am I.**' '**I'm not.**'
'Mary **can** swim.' '**So can** Alice.' 'Louise **can't.**'
'I go skiing twice a year.' '**So do I.**' 'I **don't.**'
'John **phoned** last night.' '**So did** your mother.'

Lending and borrowing

I'm sorry to trouble you, but could you lend me some sugar?
Could you possibly lend me your car?
Could I borrow your keys **for a moment**?
Yes, **here you are.**
Yes, **of course.**
I'm sorry, I need it/them.
I'm afraid I haven't got one/any.
I'm sorry, I'm afraid I can't.

Lend and *borrow*

Could you **lend** me some sugar?
Could I **borrow** some sugar?
 (Could I borrow you some sugar?)

Suggestions; inviting; replying to invitations

Let's have a drink.
Shall we meet at 6.30?
Why don't we go and see a film?
Would you like to have dinner with me?
What a nice idea!
Why not?
I'm afraid I'm not free today. **How about** tomorrow?

Ordering and asking

I'll start with soup, please, and then **I'll have** roast beef.
Chicken **for me**, please.
Could you bring me some water?
Just some water, please.
a little more coffee
Could you bring us the bill, please?
Is service included?

Asking for and giving permission: *Do you mind if . . . ?*

Do you mind if I	sit here?
	open the window?
	smoke?
	look at your paper?

Not at all.	I'm sorry, it's not free.
No, please do.	Well, it's a bit cold.
Go ahead.	Well, I'd rather you didn't.
	Well, I'm reading it myself, actually.

Opinions

'How do you like this place?' 'Great / Not bad / Not much / Terrible.'
Do you like modern jazz?
What do you think of the government?
What's your favourite food?

Asking about English

What's this?
What's this called in English, please?
Is this a pen or a pencil?
Is this a lighter?

Pronunciation: linking

Here is a piece of history.

as soon as he arrived

first of all

Pronunciation: contrastive stress

He said he got up at **eight** o'clock, but actually he got up at **ten** o'clock.
Al said they went to an **art gallery**, but **Jake** said they went to a **football match**.

Words and expressions

Nouns

bill	film
cigarette	policeman
idea	gun
paper (= newspaper)	flower
dinner	radio
pub	dog
plane	walk
century	seat
university	cinema
piece	smile
animal	

Verbs

lend (lent, lent)	build (built, built)
borrow	disagree
show (showed, shown)	lead (led, led)
need	walk
find out (found, found)	wash
spend (spent, spent)	carry
wait	open
catch (caught, caught)	mind
learn (learnt, learnt)	believe
fly (flew, flown)	feel (felt, felt)
pay (paid, paid)	

Adjectives

fine	true
usual	great
important	funny
famous	wonderful

Prepositions

round	for (*time*)
across	about
since	with
for (*person*)	

Adverbs

though	hardly ever
just	once
then	twice
certainly	three times *etc.*
so	once a week *etc.*
first of all	every day *etc.*
next	every three days *etc.*
finally	badly
early	ever
tonight	already
occasionally	all my life

Other words and expressions

north	Have you got a light?
south	wait a minute
east	Well, . . .
west	all right
something	catch a plane *etc.*
everything	listen to the radio
somewhere	watch TV
anywhere	go to the cinema
anywhere else	go for a walk
how	pay for (*something*)
How often . . . ?	Yours (*end of a letter*)
because	round the world
who	at a university
where	in love
all right	the first woman *etc.* to . . .
no more	the man *etc.* who . . .
plenty of	and so on
Just a moment/minute	each other
for a moment	

Optional words and expressions to learn

soup; (roast) beef; (rump) steak; chicken; vegetable; mushroom; salad; lager; coffee; sugar; bread; excellent; over here; not too bad; tough; rare; dictionary; key; umbrella; republic; Atlantic; free time; finish.

Unit 20: Lesson B

Students look at and contrast some uses of the Simple Past, Present Perfect and Simple Present tenses.

Language notes and possible problems
Past, Perfect and Present tenses   Usage in this area is notoriously complex and difficult to pin down. The purpose of the lesson is to give students some simple rules of thumb which will help them to avoid the commonest mistakes (e.g. *I have seen him yesterday, *I am here since Tuesday). Obviously these rules are not intended as complete and watertight descriptions of the use of the tenses in question, and teachers will have little difficulty in finding counter-examples. It is probably best, however, not to confuse students by trying to give them more comprehensive rules at this stage.

Some language learners find explicit rules useful; others do not. In any case, although knowledge of the rules mentioned here will act as a valuable support to some students, it will not stop them making mistakes overnight. If a high level of accuracy is important to your students, you will need to revise the use of tenses quite frequently. On the other hand, confusions between the Present Perfect and the Simple Past do not usually result in serious misunderstanding, and you may prefer not to spend too much time on a difficult area of grammar which does not have great communicative importance.

---

1 Present Perfect and Simple Past: presentation
• Give students plenty of time to look at the table and study the examples.
• Go through the five rules with them and ask them to decide which rules are for the Present Perfect and which are for the Simple Past.
• Let them discuss this in groups before you give them the answers (Present Perfect B, C and D; Simple Past A and E).

2 Discrimination test
• This will help to fix students' grasp of the rules studied in Exercise 1.
• It is probably better to ask for written answers (at least to some of the questions) so that you can check up on everybody's understanding of the point.
• Discuss the reasons for the choice of tense in each case.

Answers to Exercise 2
1. Have you read
2. read
3. saw
4. Have you ever been
5. went
6. have never seen
7. has been
8. has crashed
9. was
10. has been

3 Perfect, Past and Present
• This exercise focuses on the 'How long . . . ?' use of the Present Perfect, studied in Lesson 19D. For many students, it will seem natural to use a present tense in these contexts.
• The exercise can be done in writing or by class discussion, as you prefer.

Answers to Exercise 3
1. have you lived
2. have known
3. know
4. have you had
5. bought
6. have been

4 *Since, for* and *ago*
• Some students may still confuse these adverbs. If not, you may prefer to drop the exercise.

Answers to Exercise 4
1. for
2. since
3. ago
4. since
5. for
6. for
7. ago
8. ago
9. for

Practice Book exercises: choose two or more
1. Collocations: matching verbs and nouns.
2. Word stress.
3. Tense revision: students choose the correct verb forms to complete a letter.
4. Guided composition: students write a letter using material from Exercise 3.
5. Crossword.

20B   Past, Perfect and Present

> The differences between the Simple Past, the
> Present Perfect and the Simple Present.

1 Look at the table and examples, and choose the best rules for each tense.

PRESENT PERFECT TENSE	SIMPLE PAST TENSE
I have seen, you have seen *etc.* have I seen? *etc.* I have not seen *etc.*	I saw, you saw *etc.* did I see? did you see? *etc.* I did not see, you did not see *etc.*
I've changed my job three times this year. **Have** you **seen** *Carmen* before? **Have** you ever **been** to America? She **has** never **learnt** to drive.	**I changed** my job last week. **I saw** *Carmen* three years ago. **Did** you **go** to California last summer? She **learnt** to fly when she was eighteen.

Rules
We use the Present Perfect:

Rules
We use the Simple Past:

    A when we are thinking of a period of time that is finished.
    B when we are thinking of a period of time that is not finished.
    C when we mean 'at any time up to now'.
    D with *ever, never, before, this week/month/year* etc., *since.*
    E with *ago, yesterday, last week/month/year* etc., *then, when.*

2 Present Perfect or Simple Past?

1. .... this book before? (*Have you read / Did you read*)
2. Yes, I .... it last year. (*have read / read*)
3. 'Do you know where Alice is?' 'She's at home. I .... her yesterday.' (*have seen / saw*)
4. .... to Alaska? (*Have you ever been / Did you ever go*)
5. I .... to eight different schools when I was a child. (*have been / went*)
6. 'Do you like Chaplin?' 'Actually, I .... any of his films.' (*have never seen / never saw*)
7. Ann .... to a lot of parties this year. (*has been / went*)
8. Joe .... his car three times since Christmas. (*has crashed / crashed*)
9. The weather .... terrible last summer. (*has been / was*)
10. This summer .... nice and warm. (*has been / was*)

3 Present Perfect, Simple Past or Simple Present?

1. How long .... here? (*do you live / have you lived / did you live*)
2. I .... Mary since 1980. (*know / have known / knew*)
3. I think I .... her very well. (*know / have known / knew*)
4. How long .... that watch? (*do you have / have you had / did you have*)
5. I .... it last year. (*buy / have bought / bought*)
6. I .... in this school since February. (*am / have been / was*)

4 *Since, for* or *ago*?

1. We've lived in London .... eight years.
2. I've only known her .... yesterday.
3. My grandmother died three years ....
4. I've been working .... four o'clock this morning.
5. She's been a teacher .... eighteen years.
6. It's been raining .... three days.
7. I first went to Africa about seven years ....
8. Mary phoned a few minutes ....
9. I haven't seen her .... weeks.

20C Choose

A choice of listening, writing, pronunciation and speaking exercises.

Look at the exercises, decide which ones are useful to you, and do two or more.

LISTENING

1 Listen to the sounds. What is happening?
Example:

1. 'Somebody is walking.'

2 Listen, and choose the correct one. Example:

1. 'It's smaller than a piano; it's got more strings than a violin.' **Answer:** *'Guitar.'*

1. piano   clarinet   organ   guitar   violin
2. cloud   snow   sun   ice   rain
3. dog   mouse   kangaroo   cat   elephant
4. fridge   car   cooker   typewriter   bus
5. horse   taxi   bicycle   car   bus
6. Everest   Mont Blanc   Eiffel Tower   tree
7. Japan   Kenya   France   Germany   Norway
8. champagne   whisky   Coca-Cola   milk
9. sofa   chair   table   wardrobe   TV

Now make your own questions about these.

10. shirt   raincoat   skirt   shoe   belt
11. India   Tibet   Bolivia   Switzerland   Canada
12. the USA   the USSR   China   Norway   Ghana
13. London   Paris   New York   Hong Kong   Cairo
14. doctor   teacher   dentist   shop assistant   footballer
15. cheese   carrot   potato   ice cream   apple

3 Read these questions about Thomas Morley, an English musician. Then listen to the recording and try to answer the questions.

1. When was Morley born?
2. Who was Queen at the time?
3. What was the name of Morley's writer friend?
4. What was the date of Morley's own book?
5. Was Morley's best music dramatic or light?

4 🔊 Listen to the song and try to write down the words.

WRITING

1 Copy the text, and put one of these words or expressions into each blank.

after   at midnight   began
finally   as soon as   about
dancing   and then   others
on the night of   some   so
sang   some of them   went

.... December 31st, we invited .... friends to a New Year's Eve party. .... the first guests arrived, we offered them drinks, ... we put on some music. .... half an hour there were .... thirty people in our small flat. .... to dance .... just went on talking, eating and drinking. .... we all joined hands and .... an old Scottish song called *Auld Lang Syne;* then we went on ....

At seven o'clock in the morning there were still eight people left, ... we had breakfast. .... the last guest went home, and we .... to bed.

2 Write about a party that you have been to, using at least five of the words and expressions from the box in Exercise 1.

Unit 20: Lesson C

Students and teacher choose listening, writing, speaking and pronunciation exercises.

Note

There is enough work in this lesson for 3–4 hours. Students could vote for the most useful exercises.

LISTENING

1 Sounds

• Play the recording straight through once. Then play it again, stopping for students to write the answers.
• They should answer as in the example.

Answers to Exercise 1
1. Somebody is walking.
2. A man is having a bath.
3. A woman is singing.
4. Some people are drinking.
5. Some cats are fighting.
6. It is raining.
7. Children are playing.
8. Somebody is typing.
9. Somebody is eating.

2 Comparisons

• Go through the lists and clear up any difficulties.
• Play or read the definitions; students should write the words they think the speaker is referring to.
• Finally, students make up definitions for words in the last six lists and try them out on each other.

Tapescript and answers to Exercise 2
1. It's smaller than a piano; it's got more strings than a violin. (*guitar*)
2. It's colder than rain; it's not as hard as ice. (*snow*)
3. It's bigger than a dog; it lives farther south than an elephant. (*kangaroo*)
4. It's bigger than a typewriter; it's colder than a cooker. (*fridge*)
5. It goes faster than a bicycle; it takes more people than a car. (*bus*)
6. It's not as high as Everest; it's higher than the Eiffel Tower. (*Mont Blanc*)
7. It's twice as big as Norway; it's hotter than Germany. (*Kenya*)
8. It's cheaper than champagne; it's darker than whisky. (*Coca-Cola*)
9. It's smaller than a sofa; it's more interesting than a wardrobe. (*TV*)

3 Listening for information: Thomas Morley

• Make sure the students understand the questions they are to answer.
• Tell them that they need not worry about understanding the rest of the recording, but only need listen for the answers to the questions.
• Then play the recording once through.
• Give the students a chance to compare answers with one another before playing the recording a second time.
• Some classes may want you to play the recording a third time before checking the answers with you.

Answers to Exercise 3
1. 1557   2. Queen Elizabeth I   3. Shakespeare
4. 1597   5. light music

Tapescript for Exercise 3: see page 141

4 Song: *Hello Goodbye*

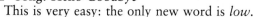

• This is very easy: the only new word is *low*.
• Play the song twice; ask students what they have understood. Then play it again with pauses and let them write down what they hear.
• Let them compare notes; then tell them the words.

Text of the song for Exercise 4

You say yes, I say no,
You say stop and I say go, go, go.
Oh no.
You say goodbye, and I say hello.
Hello, hello.
I don't know why you say goodbye,
I say hello.
Hello, hello.
I don't know why you say goodbye,
I say hello.

I say high, you say low,
You say why and I say I don't know,
Oh no.
You say goodbye, and I say hello.
Hello, hello.
I don't know why you say goodbye,
I say hello.
Hello, hello.
I don't know why you say goodbye,
I say hello.
Hello.

(Lennon and McCartney)

WRITING

1 Text completion

• Divide the class into small groups, and get them to put one of the words or expressions into each blank.
• Walk round to give any help they may need.
• To check the answers, get students to come to the board in turn to write up the sentences.

Answers to Exercise 1
On the night of December 31st, we invited *some* friends to a New Year's Eve party. *As soon as* the first guests arrived, we offered them drinks, *and then* we put on some music.
    After half an hour there were *about* thirty people in our small flat. *Some of them began* to dance; *others* just went on talking, eating and drinking. *At midnight* we all joined hands and *sang* an old Scottish song called 'Auld Lang Syne'; then we went on *dancing*.
    At seven o'clock in the morning there were still eight people left, *so* we had breakfast. *Finally* the last guest went home, and we *went* to bed.

2 Guided composition

• Get the students to write their own stories, using at least five items from the box in Exercise 1.

PRONUNCIATION

1 Pronunciation and spelling: the letter *u*

- The three common pronunciations of the letter *u* correspond in general to three different spellings:
  - *u* followed by *e* or *consonant + e* = /juː/ or /uː/ (e.g. *excuse, due, blue*). American English has /uː/ after /t/, /d/, /n/, /s/, /z/, /θ/, /r/ and /l/, and /juː/ in other positions. British English differs from American in having /juː/ everywhere except after /r/ and sometimes /l/ and /s/.
  - *ur* = /ɜː/ (e.g. *Thursday*).
  - In most other cases, *u* = /ʌ/ (e.g. *under*).
- When students have done the exercise and compared notes, go over the answers with them, and practise the pronunciation some more if necessary. Use the recording as a model if necessary.
- Common exceptions: *minute* (/ˈmɪnɪt/); *business* (/ˈbɪznɪs/).

Answers to Exercise 1
1. (/ʌ/) lunch   supper   number   uncle   summer   sun
2. (/uː/) supermarket   true   June
3. (/ɜː/) furniture   turn

2 Intonation: questions and statements

- Students should by now have some feeling for the difference between rising intonation (common in *yes/no* questions) and falling intonation (common in statements).
- Look over the instructions and examples.
- Demonstrate the two different intonations in the example sentences (using the recording if you wish).
- Tell students to write the ten words and expressions on a separate paper.
- Play the recording. Students should write *Q* or *S* after each expression.
- Play the recording again, so that students can change their answers if necessary.
- Let them compare notes.
- Discuss the answers with them.

Answers to Exercise 2

Michael *S*	a cigarette *S*
Tuesday *Q*	two pounds *S*
a girl *Q*	Washington *Q*
at the pub *Q*	trinitrotoluene *Q*

(The last example will help students to realise that they can understand that a word is a question even if they don't know what it means.)

SPEAKING

1 Problem: Who is who?

- Students can work in groups (pooling the information they obtain) or individually. Make sure everybody asks questions.
- To help them keep track of the answers, students may like to copy the grid from the book and fill it in square by square.
- Use the following table to answer their questions.

Alice	Joe	Pete	Jane
good-looking	blue-eyed	dark	tall
19	36	47	22
artist	dentist	doctor	shop assistant
London	Canberra	New York	Birmingham
Greek	Chinese	German	French

2 General revision sketch

- The purpose of this exercise is to give students practice in combining what they have learnt into longer communicative exchanges.
- The simplest approach is for a group to prepare a sketch that has four main sections, as follows:
  - getting to know somebody (as in Lesson 17B or Lesson 19A)
  - developing a conversation (as in Lesson 19B and Lesson 19C)
  - an invitation (as in Lesson 17D or Lesson 19B)
  - a meal at a restaurant (as in Lesson 17A)
- For this sketch, three characters are needed (the two main actors and a third person to play the waiter/barman etc.), but more can of course be added.
- Given enough time, students can work in rather larger groups and prepare sketches containing a wider variety of material, more episodes and more characters.
- If practicable, it is a good idea to spread the preparation over parts of several lessons, so that students' scripts can be worked out in groups, corrected, copied and learnt, and so that there is adequate time for practice before students perform their sketches. (For detailed suggestions about how to organise the work, see notes to Lesson 16C, Speaking Exercise 2.)
- If there is a lot of time available (and if students are well-motivated and reasonably confident), the activity can be done as a play involving the whole class, with several scenes and as many characters as students. The more gifted and enthusiastic students will do most of the writing and planning and take the bigger parts; less confident students can be given easier writing jobs and smaller parts. This takes a lot of time and work, but is an extremely rich and rewarding activity, which can give impressive results in terms of increased fluency, confidence and motivation.

Practice Book exercises: choose two or more
1. Irregular verbs.
2. Quantifiers with *more*.
3. Student's Cassette exercise (Student's Book Pronunciation Exercise 2). Students listen and practise the pronunciation.
4. Vocabulary revision: text completion.
5. Reading: Part 19 of *It's a Long Story*.

PRONUNCIATION

1 **Say these words after the recording or after your teacher.**

1. hungry   husband   under   much
2. blue   Tuesday   excuse   July
3. purple   burn   surname   Thursday

1, 2 or 3? Decide how to pronounce these words and check with your teacher or the recording.

furniture   lunch   supermarket   supper   true   number   uncle   turn   June   summer   sun

2 🔊 **Intonation. Look at these two conversations, and listen to the recording.**

1. 'Cambridge 31453.' 'Mary?' 'No, this is Sally.'
2. 'What's your name?' 'Mary.'

In the first conversation, *Mary* is a question. The voice goes up. Mary↗? In the second conversation, *Mary* is a statement. The voice goes down. Mary↘.

Now copy these words and expressions; then listen to the recording and decide whether they are questions or statements. Write *Q* or *S* after the words.

three o'clock ....Q....
London ....S....
Michael   Tuesday   a girl
at the pub   a cigarette
two pounds   Washington
trinitrotoluene

SPEAKING

1 **Who is who?**

Jane, Pete, Joe and Alice are from Birmingham, London, New York and Canberra (not in that order).
One is a doctor, one a dentist, one an artist and one a shop assistant.
Their ages are 19, 22, 36 and 47.
Apart from English, one of them speaks French, one German, one Greek and one Chinese.

Only one of them is tall, only one is good-looking, only one is blue-eyed, only one is dark. The tall one is 22.
One of them is a 36-year-old blue-eyed dentist from Canberra who speaks Chinese. What are the others?

Ask your teacher questions. He or she can only answer *Yes* or *No*. Examples:

'Is Jane a dentist?' *'No.'*
'Is the artist good-looking?' *'Yes.'*
'Does Joe speak Chinese?' *'Yes.'*

		ALICE	JOE	PETE	JANE
APPEARANCE	Tall				
	Good-looking				
	Blue-eyed				
	Dark				
AGE	19				
	22				
	36				
	47				
PROFESSION	Doctor				
	Dentist				
	Artist				
	Shop assistant				
HOME	Birmingham				
	London				
	New York				
	Canberra				
LANGUAGES	French				
	German				
	Greek				
	Chinese				

2 **Getting to know somebody. Work in groups. Prepare and practise a sketch with several characters. Include some of the following:**

getting to know somebody   asking for things   a letter
lending and borrowing   inviting   exchanging opinions
addresses   saying how often you do things   a meal in a restaurant
names   spelling   telephone numbers   telling the time
telephoning   asking the way

20D Test yourself

LISTENING

1 Look at the picture and listen to the description. Can you find five differences?

GRAMMAR

1 Which is correct – *a*, *b*, or both *a* and *b*?

1. .... this film before?
   a. *Have you seen*
   b. *Did you see*
2. .... to Australia?
   a. *Have you ever been*
   b. *Did you ever go*
3. I .... the doctor yesterday.
   a. *have seen*
   b. *saw*
4. I .... a lot of tennis this year.
   a. *have played*
   b. *played*
5. We've lived in this house .... 50 years.
   a. *since*
   b. *for*
6. Could you .... me where the station is?
   a. *tell*
   b. *say*

7. I always .... what I think.
   a. *tell*
   b. *say*
8. .... everything all right?
   a. *Is*
   b. *Are*
9. Could you .... me some sugar?
   a. *borrow*
   b. *lend*
10. Let's .... a drink.
    a. *to have*
    b. *have*
11. Would you like .... dinner with me?
    a. *to have*
    b. *have*
12. He was .... in Saigon.
    a. *a student*
    b. *student*

2 Write the past tense and past participle. Example:

go *went gone (or been)*

bring; buy; catch; come; cost; draw drink; eat.

3 Put the words in the right order

1. water me could bring some you ?
2. I little can you more give a coffee ?

4 Write questions to find out:

1. how Louis Blériot travelled from France to England.
2. when the Second World War started.
3. what animals Hannibal took across the Alps.
4. where Napoleon was born.
5. who wrote the James Bond novels.

Unit 20: Lesson D

Students do a simple revision test.

The purpose of the test

This test, like the others in the book, is provided for teachers who feel it will be useful. It covers several different areas: it is not of course necessary to do all of the sections, and teachers should select according to their students' needs. Teachers who do not feel the test will be useful should simply drop it altogether.

The test has three main functions:

1. To show you and the students whether there are any points that have not been properly learnt for any reason.
2. To identify any students who are having serious difficulty with the course, if this is not already evident.
3. To motivate the students to look back over the work they have done and do some serious revision before they move on.

If possible, try to make the students feel that they are 'testing themselves', rather than 'being tested'. It is not intended that students should 'pass' or 'fail' the test, and it is not particularly useful to give marks. (If the school or education system requires that this be done, you will need to work out a simple marking scheme.) But students should of course be told whether you feel their performance is satisfactory. In principle, most students ought to get most answers right. If this does not happen, efficient learning is not taking place (because of poor motivation, too rapid a pace, absenteeism, failure to do Practice Book work or follow-up study outside class, or for some other reason).

Administration

The test can be administered in various ways, depending on how strictly you want to control students' performance; whether you want to collect the answers and mark them, or allow the students to correct them in class; and so on.

The 'speaking' test will need to be done individually, with students interrupting their work on the other tests to come and talk to you one at a time.

If you are not collecting students' scripts, correction can be done by class discussion when everybody has finished.

Notes, tapescript and answers are given below.

LISTENING

- Before starting, go over the instructions and clear up any problems.
- Get the students to say what is in the picture, making sure they know the following words: *sofa, sweater, jeans, shoes, ear-rings, watch, ring, cat*.
- Play the recording once and give students a minute or two (working individually) to note any differences they have spotted.
- Play the recording again, one or more times, pausing after playing so that students can complete their lists of differences.
- Note that students will not understand every word in the recording. Make sure they realise that this does not matter.

1 Tapescript

(The items in italics are those where the recording differs from the picture.)

In the picture, you can see a woman called Catherine Stewart, sitting on a *chair* in her *kitchen*. She lives in a small town in the north of England, and works in a bank. She's *58*, divorced, with two *grown-up children*. Catherine has *grey* hair, and *looks like a grandmother*. In fact, she isn't one yet, but *she will be soon – one of her daughters is expecting a baby next month*.

She has a *friendly* face. In the picture, she's wearing a *white blouse* and blue jeans – she usually wears jeans when she's at home, but of course she wears a dress or a suit to work. She *isn't wearing shoes*. She's got a pair of *small* ear-rings, and a watch on her *right* arm, but no necklace *or rings*. She's wearing *glasses* in the picture, because she's reading a *newspaper* – she reads two newspapers every day. While she's reading, she's also *eating breakfast* and playing with her *dog*. Catherine's good at doing more than one thing at the same time.

GRAMMAR

1 1a; 2a; 3b; 4a; 5b; 6a; 7b; 8a; 9b; 10b; 11a; 12a.

2 brought, brought
bought, bought
caught, caught
came, come
cost, cost
drew, drawn
drank, drunk
ate, eaten

3 1. Could you bring me some water?
  2. Can I give you a little more coffee?

4 1. How did Louis Blériot travel from France to England?
  2. When did the Second World War start?
  3. What animals did Hannibal take across the Alps?
  4. Where was Napoleon born?
  5. Who wrote the James Bond novels?

VOCABULARY

1 (Other answers are possible in some cases.)

1. free
2. favourite
3. born
4. (Various possible answers.)
5. have
6. eat, drink, read, *etc.*
7. ago
8. (Various possibilities – answer should contain a comparative adjective.)
9. give me some; give me the; pass (me) the
10. afraid
11. included
12. I'm just
13. are you; do you take; shoes do you take; *etc.*
14. try them (on)

LANGUAGE IN USE

1 (Too many possible answers to list.)

PRONUNCIATION

1 1. fine
2. June
3. though
4. walk
5. great
6. who
7. dog
8. piece

2 **mo**ment; ciga**rette**; i**dea**; **cen**tury; **an**imal; po**lice**man; **ra**dio; disa**gree**; be**lieve**; **u**sual; im**por**tant; **fa**mous; **won**derful; **some**where; to**ge**ther; **fi**nally; al**rea**dy; to**night**; oc**ca**sionally; a**bout**; a**cross**; **eve**rything.

WRITING

When correcting this, it is best to judge students mainly on their ability to communicate successfully, using appropriate vocabulary and structures. Part of the test involves the correct use and positioning of frequency adverbs, but don't give this more importance than it is worth. Excessive emphasis on minor errors of grammar and spelling can damage students' confidence.

SPEAKING

Go over the instructions with the whole class and make sure they understand what they have to do. Then test the students one by one. Sit beside the student who is being tested, and pretend you are the stranger. Help the student to get a conversation going (making the first move yourself if necessary). The student should ask questions as well as answering them.

Test Book recordings
A recording for Test 5 in the Test Book follows this lesson on the Class Cassette.

VOCABULARY

1 Put in suitable words or expressions.

1. Is this seat ....?
2. 'What is your .... colour?' 'Red.'
3. Karl Marx was .... in 1818.
4. I'm very good at ...., but I'm bad at ....
5. 'What would you like?' 'I'll .... roast beef.'
6. Would you like something to ....?
7. I first met Annie seven years ....
8. I'm much .... than my mother.
9. Could you .... water?
10. 'Could you lend me £5?' 'I'm sorry, I'm .... I can't.'
11. Is service ....?
12. 'Can I help you?' '................ looking.'
13. What size ....?
14. Those shoes are nice. Can I ....?

LANGUAGE IN USE

1 Give suitable answers to these sentences.
Example:

I'm tired. *So am I.*

OR: *Are you?*

1. John's got a new car.
2. My sister works in New York.
3. My father can speak five languages.
4. Would you like to come to a party?
5. Let's go and have a drink.
6. Do you mind if I smoke?
7. Do you like mountains?
8. I love skiing.
9. I slept very badly last night.
10. Could I borrow your pen for a moment?

PRONUNCIATION

1 Which word is different?

1. dinner   since   fine   build
2. funny   just   once   June
3. south   though   round   out
4. walk   wash   on   not
5. lead   great   seat   east
6. so   show   who   though
7. caught   north   walk   dog
8. twice   piece   fly   mind

2 Which syllable is stressed?

moment; cigarette; idea; century; animal; policeman; radio; disagree; believe; usual; important; famous; wonderful; somewhere; together; finally; already; tonight; occasionally; about; across; everything.

WRITING

1 Write 100–200 words about what you do at weekends. Use some of the following words and expressions:

always; usually; often; quite often; sometimes; hardly ever; never.

SPEAKING

1 Act out this conversation. The teacher will act the other part.

You are sitting next to a stranger on a plane or a train. The two of you start talking. Answer the other person's questions, give some information about yourself, and find out something about him or her. Try to find at least three things that you have in common.

21A I'm going to learn Chinese

Plans for the future; *going to.*

1 What are your plans for this evening? Are you going to do any of these things?

write letters   see a film
play cards   see friends
watch TV   wash your hair
listen to music   study

Examples:

'I'm going to write letters.'
'I'm not going to watch TV.'

Have you got any plans for the next year or so? Are you going to make any changes in your life? Think of something that you are never going to do again in your life.

2 You are going to hear a man talking about what he is going to do next year. First, look at the pictures and see if you can guess some of the things he is going to do. Example:

'I think he's going to learn Chinese.'

3 📼 Now listen to the conversation. Which of these things is the man going to do during his year off work?

take a big rest; listen to the radio; watch videos; study biology; walk right across Ireland; write a novel; play some rugby; travel round the world; learn karate; get married.

Listen again. Can you make a complete list of the things he is going to do?

4 Pronunciation. Say these words and expressions.

1. first   first of all   third
   thirsty   thirty
2. certain   certainly
3. Thursday   on Thursday
   burn
4. world   round the world
   word   work
5. learn   early   heard

Can you think of any other words that are pronounced with the vowel /ɜː/?

5 Work in groups. Each group has £100,000; you must use it to do some good to three or more groups of people in your country or somewhere else in the world. What are you going to do with the money? You have fifteen minutes to decide. Useful structures:
Let's . . . ; Why don't we . . . ?
Example:

'Let's give most of the money to poor people in Africa.' *'No, why don't we use it to help people in this country?'*

Learn: rest (*noun*); video; use; decide; get married (got, got); right across; do good to somebody (did, done).

104

Unit 21: Lesson A

Students learn to talk about future plans using the *be going* + infinitive structure.
Structures: *be going* + infinitive.
Phonology: spellings of /ɜː/; pronunciation of *going to*.

Language notes and possible problems

Be going + infinitive Students have already learnt to use the Present Progressive to talk about the future (Unit 15). The *going-to* structure is used in similar ways, and there is a lot of overlap between the two. Because they are present tenses, it is most appropriate to use them when the future is seen as already fixed or determined by the present situation.

The Present Progressive is used particularly to talk about future actions or events which have been planned for a specific time or date, and the tense is often used with adverbs or adverbials of future time. *Going to* has a rather wider use than the Present Progressive. It is more often used, as here, to talk about plans and resolutions with no fixed date; and it can be used to talk about other kinds of future event besides those that are planned (see Lesson 21C).

It is probably best if students simply pick up the use of the structure through practice at this stage, leaving a study of the rules until later. Just tell them that *going to* is another way of talking about future plans.

Note the common casual pronunciation /gənə/ (often spelt *gonna* in American written dialogue).

1 Students' plans

• Write on the board:
I'm seeing some friends this evening.
I'm going to see some friends this evening.
• Explain that *going to* is another structure used when talking about plans for the future.
• Talk about what you are going to do this evening.
• Get students to tell you their plans, and also some of the things that they are not going to do (see list of actions in exercise instructions).
• Note that *going to go* is unusual; we are more likely to say, for example, *I'm going to the cinema* than *I'm going to go to the cinema*.
• Get students to tell you their plans and intentions for the more distant future.
• Work on the stress and pronunciation of students' sentences. The *to* of *going to* is usually pronounced as a weak form (/tə/) except before a vowel. In fast speech *going to* sounds more or less like *gonna* (/gənə/).

2 Preparation for listening: guessing

• Give students a minute or two to look at the pictures and try to guess what the person on the recording is going to do.

3 Listening for specific information

• Explain that students will hear somebody who is going to take a year off work to do things that he has always wanted to do.
• Look at the list of activities. Students have to listen for these; they will not hear all of them.
• Play the recording once, and see if students can tell you which of the items on the list they heard.
• Play the recording again and get students to work in groups trying to draw up a complete list.

Answers to Exercise 3

The speaker is going to:
– take a big rest
– read his books
– listen to music
– watch videos
– learn Chinese
– study astronomy
– play the violin
– walk across Scotland
– take up skiing
– write a novel
– play football
– travel round the world
– learn karate

The speaker does not say he is going to:
– listen to the radio
– study biology
– walk across Ireland
– play rugby
– get married

Tapescript for Exercise 3

MAN: I'm taking a year off next year.
WOMAN: Yes? Lucky you. Can you afford it?
MAN: Well, one of my uncles died last year and left me some money. So I'm going to buy some free time.
WOMAN: Oh, great. What are you going to do?
MAN: Oh, lots of things. First of all I'm going to take a big rest. Read my books, listen to music, watch some of my videos, that sort of thing. Then I'm going to do all the things I've always wanted to do. I'm going to learn Chinese, study astronomy, start playing the violin again, walk right across Scotland, take up skiing, write a novel, play some football.
WOMAN: Yes, well, I hope you have a good time. One year, you said?
MAN: No, that's just the spring. Then in summer I'm going to travel round the world, learn karate, . . .

4 Spellings of /ɜː/

• Students already know some words containing /ɜː/, and probably realise that it is usually spelt *er*, *ir* or *ur*.
• First of all, ask whether students think the words in the five groups have the same or different vowels.
• Get them to try pronouncing the words.
• If they have difficulty, demonstrate the words or play the recording while students imitate.
• If they want a standard British accent, they should not pronounce *r* after the vowel.
• The last two groups are exceptions: *or* is not normally pronounced /ɜː/; this only happens after *w*. And *ear* is more often /ɪə/ (as in *beard*). Ask if students can add any words to the lists. Note that *year* can be /jɪə(r)/ or /jɜː(r)/.

5 Discussion

• Make groups of 4–6, and explain the task. Students will need *should* for the discussion.
• Don't let them go on too long; they should reach an agreed group decision within a quarter of an hour.
• Each group should appoint a spokesperson to tell the class what the group are going to do with the money.

Practice Book exercises: choose two or more
1. Sentences with *going to*.
2. Stress and rhythm with *going to*.
3. Choice of tenses (Present Perfect, Present Progressive and Simple Present).
4. Student's Cassette exercise (Student's Book Exercise 3). Students listen and try to write down the conversation.
5. Guided writing: plans for the future.

Unit 21: Lesson B

Students practise *be going* + infinitive; they revise and extend their knowledge of language relating to houses.
Structures: *going to be.*

Language notes and possible problems
Going to be   Although students have used the present and past tenses of *be* a good deal, they may not be familiar with the infinitive, and may find the sequence *going to be* complicated at first.

1 Information gap exercise: what are the rooms going to be?
● Revise the names of the main rooms in a house, and the expressions *ground floor* and *first floor.*
● Get students to look at the plan and say which room they think is going to be the bathroom. They will probably say room 7: tell them this is correct.
● Then put them in pairs. In each pair, one student should turn to page 133, and the other to page 134. They will find information and questions.
● Tell them to read the information and ask each other the questions. By combining what they know, they should be able to decide where each room is going to be.

Answers to Exercise 1
1. study
2. living room
3. kitchen
4. dining room
5. Alice's bedroom
6. parents' bedroom
7. bathroom
8. Mary's bedroom
9. playroom

2 Vocabulary revision and expansion
● This can be done in groups, with students pooling their knowledge and sharing the task of looking up new words.
● Students may wish to ask for more words in this area. Don't let this go on too long, or students will simply fill their notebooks with unlearnt vocabulary.

3 Redesigning the school
● Tell students to imagine that they can redesign the school as they wish – they can turn it into something quite different if they want to.
● Give them ten minutes or so, working alone or in groups as you prefer, to make their decisions. Help with vocabulary when required; and encourage them to use some of the words from Exercise 2.
● Then get students to tell the others what the various rooms are going to be.

Practice Book exercises: choose two or more
1. Questions with *is/are going to.*
2. Logic problem.
3. Word stress.
4. Irregular verbs.
5. Vocabulary revision; names of vehicles.

Correctness and correction
Fluency practice activities (like Exercise 3 above) work best if the students are allowed to talk without being corrected. Mistakes which seriously impede communication are worth dealing with on the spot, but anything else should be noted for attention later or ignored. Teachers sometimes feel (and students may encourage them to feel) that they are not doing their jobs unless they correct every mistake. This is quite unrealistic: casual correction has very little effect on students' accuracy, and it is much more constructive to pick out a limited number of high-priority errors and deal with them by systematic work at another time.

Planning a house; *going to*; vocabulary study.

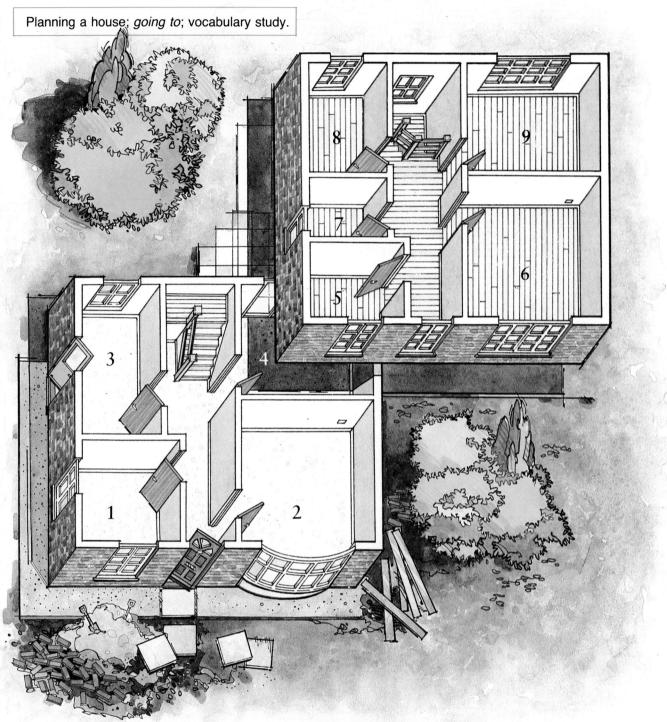

1 Look at the plan. The house isn't finished yet. Which room do you think is going to be the bathroom? Work in pairs. Turn to page 133 OR page 134: you will find some more information about the house. Exchange information with your partner until you know what all the rooms are going to be.

2 Vocabulary revision and extension. How many of these words do you know already? Find out what the rest mean. How many of them can you see?

carpet   ceiling   door   floor   garden
lift   light   paint   roof   stairs
steps   switch   wall   wallpaper   window

3 Redesign your school. Decide what the different rooms are going to be. Tell the class. Example:

'Classroom 6 is going to be a games room. This is going to be my bathroom.'
'I'm going to put purple wallpaper in all the rooms.'
'I'm going to move all the furniture out of this room and put cushions on the floor.'

Learn: bedroom; bathroom; kitchen; living room; dining room; information (*uncountable*); find (found, found); put (put, put); move; finished; over; out of.

Learn three or more other words from the lesson.

21C It's going to rain

Predictions with *going to*.

1 Look at the pictures. What is going to happen? (If you don't know the words, use your dictionary or ask your teacher.)

1

2

3

4

5

6

7

8

2 Pronunciation: 'long *o*' (/əʊ/). Can you say these words and expressions?

go   so   no   home   don't   know   coat
Don't go.   I don't know.   I don't think so.
I'm going home.   It's going to rain.

Can you think of any more words that are pronounced with /əʊ/?

3 Other pronunciations of *o*. Can you say these words?

1. holiday   Scotland   not   job   stop   cost
2. north   more   born   short   or   organise
3. work   world   worse
4. some   one   mother   cover   tough
   young   country

Which groups do these words go in?

on   sport   brother   got   bored   come
forty   word   dog   morning   clock
love   worst

Can you add more words to any of the groups?

4 Read the advertisement. Then make up advertisements yourself (working in groups and using the phrases in the box) to get people to join your holiday trip. Useful words: *spring, summer, autumn, winter.*

> ...to October.
> tact box 1391 for brochure.
>
> **HOLIDAY IN SCOTLAND**
> We are organising a holiday
> walking tour in the north of
> Scotland this summer.
> We are going to cover 150
> miles of mountainous coun-
> try in ten days.
> It's going to be hard work.
> It's going to be tough.
> You're going to be wet, cold
> and tired a lot of the time.
> But it's going to be fun!
> If you're young and fit, and if
> you like beautiful places –
> why not join us?
> Cost £95 inclusive.
> For more details, write Box
> 1346, *Edinburgh Times.*

We are organising a trip to . . .
We are going to . . .
It's going to be . . .
It's going to be . . .
And/But it's going to be . . .
If you're . . . , and if . . . , why not join us?
Cost: £ . . . inclusive.

Learn: advertisement; fun; spring; summer; autumn; winter; baby; have a baby (had, had); win (won, won); crash; fall (fell, fallen); break (broke, broken).

Unit 21: Lesson C

Students learn to make predictions in English.
Structures: *be going* + infinitive.
Phonology: pronunciations of the letter *o*.

Language notes and possible problems
Be going + **infinitive** is not only used to talk about people's plans and resolutions. It can also be used to make predictions about what is going to happen. This is especially the case where there is 'present evidence' for the future event – when it is obviously on the way, or starting to happen. In cases where we are predicting without obvious present evidence, *going to* and *will* are both possible; the differences are subtle and not important for students at this level.

Optional extra materials
Pictures to illustrate things that are going to happen (Exercise 1).

1 Pictures
• Each picture shows a situation in which it would be natural to talk about the future with *going to*.
• Let students look at the pictures and decide (individually or in groups) what is going to happen.
• Tell them to write their answers – they will need to ask you for vocabulary.
• When they have compared notes, go over the answers with them.
• Additional pictures taken from magazines, showing things that are going to happen, would be a great help.

2 The vowel /əʊ/
• British /əʊ/ is a difficult sound, and it is not very important for students to get it correct unless they are aiming at a high standard of pronunciation. However, it will do them no harm to improve their production of it a bit.
• The best approach is to break the sound down into its two parts: the first is like the *er* of *mother* or the *a* of *about*; the second part is like the *oo* of *too*. Get students to make the sounds separately and then put them together.
• Use the recording or your own pronunciation to help them practise the words and expressions in the book: then see if they can think of some more words with /əʊ/.

3 Other pronunciations of *o*

• Get students to say the words in each group; demonstrate or play the recording if necessary.
• See if students can see the pattern in the different pronunciations:
  – *o* is pronounced /əʊ/ especially at the ends of words, in *oa* and before consonant + *e*
  – *o* is pronounced /ɒ/ in most other cases
  – *or* is usually pronounced /ɔ:/
  – *wor* is usually pronounced /wɜ:/
  – *o* and *ou* are pronounced /ʌ/ in a limited number of very common words
• Get students to try to put the other words into the various groups. When they are ready, say the words or play the recording and let them check.
• See if they can add some words to the groups.

Answers to Exercise 3
1. on, got, dog, clock
2. sport, bored, forty, morning
3. word, worst
4. brother, come, love

4 Guided composition
• Go over the advertisement with the students, explaining difficulties.
• Then give them 15–20 minutes to compose one or more similar advertisements in groups, using the framework provided but choosing a different situation.
• When they are ready, get a student from each group to read out what they have written.
• The class could vote for the holiday they would most like to go on.

Practice Book exercises: choose two or more
1. Pictures: what is going to happen?
2. Students say what is going to happen in the next hour.
3. Rhythm and stress in sentences with *going to*.
4. Revision vocabulary: parts of the body.

Unit 21: Lesson D

Students learn to talk about purposes; they practise building up paragraphs with sequencing expressions.
Structures: infinitive of purpose; paragraph-structuring adverbials.

Language notes and possible problems

1. Infinitive of purpose   English can express purpose with a simple infinitive; this may not be possible in your students' languages. Look out for mistakes like *for go, *for going or *for to go instead of *to go.

2. Building up paragraphs   Prose is not organised in the same way in all languages. Your students may not be familiar with the paragraph as a unit of organisation; and the use of structuring words (to join sentences into paragraphs and show the structure of discourse) may need practice. Exercise 2 gives training in using sequencing adverbials.

3. Library (Exercise 1)   When students learn this, make sure they don't confuse *library* and *bookshop* – *library* is a 'false friend' for some European learners.

4. Butcher's, baker's (Exercise 1)   You will need to explain the reason for the possessive *'s*; mention other common examples like *the doctor's* (also possible in Exercise 1).

1 Places and purposes

• Look at the exercise instruction. Explain that we can use the *to*-infinitive to answer the question *Why?*
• Get students to say or write answers to as many questions as they can manage. Tell them the words they don't know.
• You may like to take the opportunity to mention the names of other kinds of shop.

Possible answers to Exercise 1

(Answers may vary a good deal from one culture to another.)
study: school, university, polytechnic, college
buy books: bookshop
borrow books: library
post letters: post office, letter box
catch a train: station
catch a plane: airport
get a visa: embassy, consulate
have a drink: pub, bar, café
have a meal: restaurant, pub
meet people: club, party
buy meat: butcher's, supermarket
buy bread: baker's, supermarket
borrow money: bank
get an injection: doctor('s), hospital
see animals: zoo

2 Paragraph writing

• First of all, get the students to match the 'where' pictures and the 'why' pictures.
• Supply words where they are needed; practise pronunciation.
• Then tell students to try to make sentences about where Mr Andrews is going. (The Present Progressive – *is going* – is more natural than *is going to go*.)
• Put the sentences on the board.
• Get students to link the sentences into a paragraph (they can decide themselves what order the actions will be done in).
• Obviously this exercise is not going to produce an elegant piece of writing, but it will help to sensitise students to the way in which written language can be structured by adverbials expressing time and sequence.
• This is particularly important for students speaking non-European languages, in which writing may be structured in very different ways.

Possible answer to Exercise 2

A possible paragraph is as follows:
First of all, Mr Andrews is going to the embassy to get a visa. Then he is going to the bank, to pick up his traveller's cheques, and to the travel agent to buy an air ticket. Next, he is going to the doctor('s) to get an injection. After that he is going to Harrods to buy a suitcase, and then he is going home to pack. Tomorrow he is going to the airport to catch his plane.

3 Reasons for learning English

• If some of your students have definite reasons for learning English, ask what they are. Supply vocabulary where necessary, and write the reasons on the board.
• Look through the list of possible reasons and clear up any difficulties.
• Put students into groups and ask them to list the reasons in order of priority, with the reason why they think most people learn English at the top, and the reason what they think fewest people learn at the bottom. Tell them they must reach a group decision.
• When groups are ready, ask them to read their lists to the class.

Practice Book exercises: choose two or more
1. Infinitive of purpose (reasons for travelling).
2. Infinitive of purpose (negative sentences).
3. Infinitive of purpose (students' reasons for travelling).
4. Check on revision vocabulary.
5. Translation of material from the unit.
6. Reading: Part 20 of *It's a Long Story*.

21D Why? To . . .

Why we do things: *to . . .* ; joining sentences into paragraphs.

1 Vocabulary study. You go to a supermarket to
buy food. Do you know where you go:

to study; to buy books; to borrow books; to post letters; to catch a train;
to catch a plane; to get a visa; to have a drink; to have a meal; to meet people;
to buy meat; to buy bread; to borrow money; to get an injection;
to see interesting animals?

WHERE?

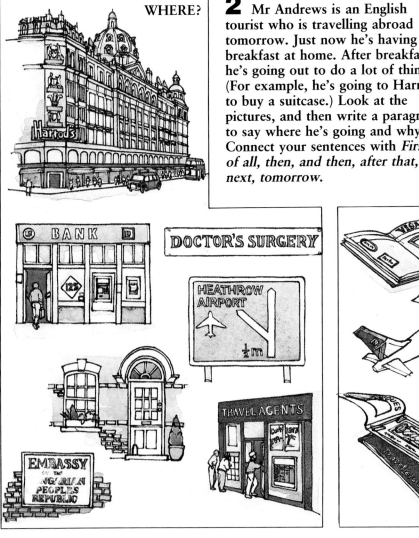

2 Mr Andrews is an English
tourist who is travelling abroad
tomorrow. Just now he's having
breakfast at home. After breakfast,
he's going out to do a lot of things.
(For example, he's going to Harrods
to buy a suitcase.) Look at the
pictures, and then write a paragraph
to say where he's going and why.
Connect your sentences with *First
of all, then, and then, after that,
next, tomorrow.*

WHY?

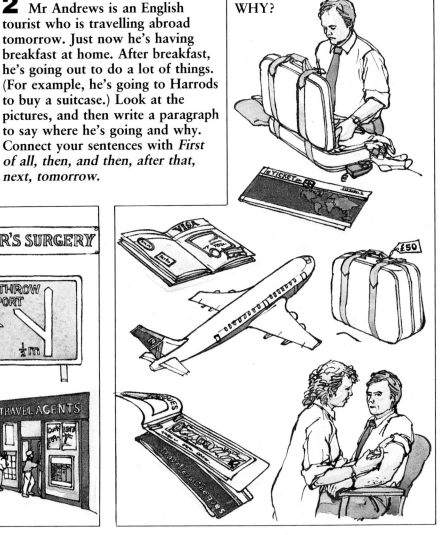

3 Why are you learning English? People learn English all over the world. Why do you
think most of them do it? Put these reasons in order of importance.

– to read English literature
– to travel to English-speaking countries
– to do business in English
– to understand songs and films in English

– to use English for international communication
– just because they like the language
– because they have to learn it at school
– for other reasons (what?)

> **Learn:** meal; meat; bread (*uncountable*); reason; country; song;
> airport; business; do business (did, done); international.
>
> **Learn these if you want to:** injection; suitcase; embassy; visa;
> travel agent; literature; communication; pack.

Unit 22 Telling people to do things

22A I feel ill

1 Use your dictionary to match the pictures and the words. Then match the problems and the suggestions.

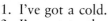

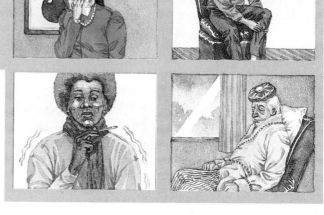

1. I've got a cold.
2. I've got toothache.
3. I've got a temperature.
4. I've got flu.
5. I've got a headache.
6. My leg hurts.

a. Why don't you go home and lie down?
b. Why don't you take an aspirin?
c. Why don't you see the doctor?
d. Why don't you see the dentist?

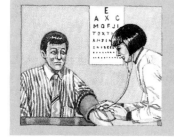  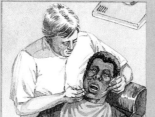 

2 🔊 What do you think they will say next? Listen to check.

3 Use your dictionary to look up three other words or expressions you can use at the doctor's.

4 At the doctor's. Work in groups to write the other half of this dialogue.

DOCTOR: Good morning. What's the problem?
YOU: Well, ...
DOCTOR: I see. Does it / Do they hurt very badly?
YOU: ....
DOCTOR: How long have you had this?
YOU: ....
DOCTOR: Yes, right. I'd like to examine you, then. Mmm . . . Mmm . . .

YOU: ....?
DOCTOR: No, it doesn't look too bad. Here's a prescription for some medicine. Phone me if you're not better by the day after tomorrow.
YOU: ....
DOCTOR: Goodbye.
YOU: ....

> **Learn:** headache; aspirin; problem; temperature; (a) cold; flu (*uncountable*); toothache (*uncountable*); medicine (*uncountable*); catch (caught, caught) (flu, *etc.*); hurt (hurt, hurt); hope; What's the matter?; take medicine (took, taken).

Unit 22: Lesson A

Students learn how to ask and talk about common physical problems and to express sympathy, as well as practising making suggestions.
Structures: no new structures.

Language notes and possible problems

1. Countable and uncountable nouns   Note that *headache* and *temperature* are countable, while *toothache* and *flu* are both uncountable in British English (and therefore not used with the article *a*). (In American English, only *flu* is uncountable.)

2. Pronunciation   Make sure students note the pronunciation of *aspirin* (/ˈæsprɪn/) and *medicine* (/ˈmedsən/) – each word has two syllables, not three; and of *temperature* (/ˈtemprɪtʃə/), which has only three syllables.

1 Presentation: matching

- Divide the class into groups, so students can pool the English they have learnt outside your class.
- Let the students look at the illustrations for a moment, and ask them to match the words and the pictures.
- Tell them they can use their dictionaries.
- Then ask them to match the numbered physical problems with the lettered solutions.
- Of course, the students can differ on what solution to propose for each problem; there are at least two 'correct' answers in each case.
- Go over the pronunciation of the sentences with the students and answer any questions they may have. Point out the absence of an article in *I've got toothache* and *I've got flu*.

2 Dialogue construction

- Write on the board:
  Good ...., Mr Culham. How ....?
- Get students to suggest what might go in the blanks. Accept *morning*, *afternoon*, or *evening* for the first blank; write them up, along with any plausible suggestions for the second blank.
- Then play or read out the first line of the dialogue; erase the suggestions and put the words from the dialogue in the blanks.
- Then write *Man:* on the second line and get students to suggest things for the man to say.
- Accept (and write up) any suggestions that would be logical answers to the woman's questions (*Fine, thanks, and you?*; *I'm not very well today*, etc.).
- Play or read the second line of the dialogue, and get the students to repeat what the man actually says, paying attention to the intonation pattern and to the pronunciation of /ɪ/ and /iː/.
- Erase the suggestions and write *I feel ill* on the second line.
- Continue in the same way for the succeeding sentences in the dialogue.
- Make sure the students give you several sentences with *hurt/hurts*, so that they become aware of the coverage of this verb.
- When the entire dialogue has been put on the board, play it through without stopping.
- Divide the class into pairs and ask them to make new dialogues by changing some of the words. When a pair has finished they should change partners and make another dialogue.
- You may like to tape/video-record their dialogues.

Tapescript for Exercise 2

WOMAN: Good morning, Mr Culham. How are you?
MAN: I feel ill.
WOMAN: I am sorry. What's the matter?
MAN: My eyes hurt, and I've got a bad headache.
WOMAN: Oh, I hope you aren't catching flu. Why don't you take an aspirin?
MAN: That's a good idea.

3 Vocabulary extension

- Students will need to use their bilingual dictionaries for this exercise, unless you speak their language(s).
- Ask each student to make a list of three or more words or expressions to use at the doctor's.
- If you think it is appropriate for your class, get them to walk round the classroom seeing if they can find out what they want to know from another student.
- Then they should look the words up in their dictionaries; walk round while they are working to give any help that is needed.
- If you speak their language(s), you can ask them to write you notes instead, asking, '*How do you say . . . in English?*', '*Can you say . . . in English?*' and so on.

4 Extension

- Divide the class into groups of three or four and let them try to invent the other half of the dialogue.
- Make sure they understand that there is no one 'correct' answer.
- Move around helping with problems and checking that sentences are correct.
- You may wish one or more groups to perform their dialogues for the class.

Optional activity

- When students have produced a corrected version of the 'half dialogue' in Exercise 4, they can practise it with the recording. This contains the doctor's part, with pauses left for the patient's part.
- The object of the exercise is for the students to say their sentences, to their own satisfaction, in the allotted time.

Practice Book exercises: choose two or more

1. Completing conversations with material from the lesson.
2. Writing two or three true sentences about how one feels.
3. Revision of pronouns and possessives.
4. Student's Cassette exercise (Student's Book Exercise 2). Students listen and repeat, trying for good stress and intonation.
5. Reading: putting a text in order to match with pictures.

Unit 22: Lesson B

Students practise giving instructions and advice.
Structures: imperative and negative imperative; position of *always* and *never* imperatives; simple *if*-clauses.
Phonology: letter *o* pronounced /ɒ/ and /ʌ/ (revision).

Language notes and possible problems
1. Word order *Always* and *never* come before imperatives.
2. Advice Students may tend to use *advice* as a countable noun; look out for *an advice* and *advices*.

---

1 Advice about running

• Make sure students understand the task: they are supposed to decide which pieces of advice are good and which are not.
• Go through the text, explaining any difficulties and teaching the pronunciation of the new words. Point out that the numbered words in the text are illustrated by the pictures on the right. Note *comfortable* (three syllables: /ˈkʌmftəbl/).
• Students will probably start classifying the advice into good and bad as you go through the text.
• Don't give your own opinion at this stage.
• Ask students to discuss the question in groups, and to produce a group decision (if possible).
• After they have got into their stride, you may like to tell them that four of the DOs and four of the DON'Ts are good advice.

Answers to Exercise 1
Good advice: Wear good running shoes.
　　　　　　　Wear comfortable clothing.
　　　　　　　Always warm up before you run.
　　　　　　　Walk for a few minutes after you finish.
　　　　　　　Don't run if you feel tired.
　　　　　　　Don't run until two hours after eating.
　　　　　　　Don't run if you have got a cold.
　　　　　　　Don't run on roads in fog.
Misleading: Never drink water while you are running.
The other pieces of advice are of no value.

2 Listening

• The list in the Student's Book contains words and expressions that the native speakers in the recording use to indicate whether they think the advice is good or bad.
• Get your students to look over the list using their dictionaries; or go over the list with them. Explain that *should* will be dealt with later in the course.
• Ask the students to copy down the list of advice, if they have not already done so for Exercise 1.
• Tell them that they will hear two speakers giving their answers to Exercise 1. (If your students have particular difficulty with listening, you may want to use only the first speaker, who goes through the advice in the same order as the text.)
• All the students must do is put a tick, a cross or a question mark according to whether the speaker says that the bit of advice is good, bad, or s/he doesn't know.
• Play the recording, more than once if necessary, until students are happy that they have understood what they can.
• Let them compare answers in groups of four or five, and play the recording again if necessary.
• Ask the students to work in groups again, deciding how many times each speaker was wrong.
• Finally check the answers with them.

Answers to Exercise 2

Speaker 1 was wrong 3 times (he says it is bad advice not to run if you feel tired; that it doesn't matter if you run when you've got a cold; that it's good advice not to run fast downhill).

Speaker 2 was wrong once (she said you shouldn't drink while you're actually running) and unsure twice (she didn't know about running when you have a cold or feel tired).

Tapescript for Exercise 2: see page 142

3 Revision of pronunciation

• This gives students another chance to practise the normal pronunciation of 'short' *o* (/ɒ/), and to note the words where *o* is pronounced /ʌ/.
• Other words in group 2 (/ʌ/): *mother, one, once, some, love, money, come, colour, son.*

4 Listening to instructions

• Go over the words in the box with the students, explaining any that are new to them.
• Make sure they have a blank piece of paper and a pen or pencil ready, and remind them what *draw* means.
• Play the recording once through without stopping.
• Play it again, stopping at the pauses to give students time to draw.
• Draw the table and chairs yourself, very simply, so that students can see it is unnecessary to be good at drawing to do the exercise.
• Play the recording a third time, giving students a chance to make any changes they wish.

Tapescript for Exercise 4
Draw a table and two chairs in a room.
Don't draw a window. Draw a cat under one of the chairs.
Draw a knife and a fork on the table, and draw a spoon to their right.
Draw some men or women in the room; don't draw any children.
Draw one other thing in the room, but don't put it on the table.

5 Giving advice

• Students can either take this seriously (giving good advice), or choose a more entertaining treatment by deliberately thinking up misleading advice.
• Help with vocabulary, but discourage students from using too many words that have not already been learnt.
• If there is time, you may want the groups to make posters of their advice, to post up in the room for the other students to see.
• Otherwise, when groups are ready, let each one read out its advice.

Practice Book exercises: choose two or more
1. Putting *always*, *never* and *don't* in negative imperative sentences about driving a car.
2. Revision of irregular verbs.
3. Student's Cassette exercise (Student's Book Exercise 2, part of Speaker 1's answer). Students listen and write down as much as they can.
4. Reading for gist: students read a text and put pictures in order.
5. Reading quickly for detailed understanding: students follow written instructions.

22B   Always warm up

Instructions and advice; imperatives.

1 Here is some advice about running. Some of it is good, and some is not. Which sentences give you good advice?

RUNNING[1] – DOs and DON'Ts

Wear good running shoes.
Run early in the morning – it's better.
Wear comfortable clothing[2].
Always warm up[3] before you run.
Always run with somebody – never run alone.
Rest every ten minutes or so.
Walk for a few minutes after you finish.

Don't run if you feel tired.
Never drink water while you are running.
Don't run until two hours after eating.
Don't run if you have got a cold[4].
Don't run fast downhill[5].
Don't run if you are over 50.
Don't run on roads in fog[6].

2 Listen to two English people doing Exercise 1. Are all their answers right? Words to listen for:

a good/bad idea   not true
a good piece of advice
you should/shouldn't
I don't think it matters
it's up to you   your own choice

3 Say these words after the recording or your teacher.

1. fog   hot   long   doctor
   dollar   office
2. comfortable   front
   another   brother

Find some more words that go in group 1.
Can you find any more that go in group 2?

4 Make sure you know what the words in the box mean. Then listen, and try to draw the picture.

cat   chair   fork   knife
spoon   table   window
child/children   man/men
woman/women   in   on
under   to the right of

5 Work in groups. Think of some advice (good or bad) for somebody who:

– is a tourist in your country
– is learning to drive
– is learning your language
– is learning English
– wants to get rich
– wants more friends

Make a list of three (or more) DOs and three (or more) DON'Ts.

Learn: advice (*uncountable*); shoe; picture; fork; knife; spoon; rest (*verb*); right; wrong; alone; before (*conjunction*); after (*conjunction*); while; mistake; make a mistake (made, made).

22C Look out!

1 Put the following expressions into the pictures.

Please hurry, darling.
Take your time, darling.   Don't worry.
Look.   Please come in.   Wait here, please.
Be careful, dear.   Follow me, please.   Look out!

1

2

3

4

5

6

7

8

9

2 Listen to the recording. Write ✓ every time you hear an imperative (like *Walk, Come in, Be careful*), and ✗ every time you hear a negative imperative (like *Don't run, Don't worry*). Listen again, and then try to remember some of the imperatives and negative imperatives.

3 Work in groups. Prepare and practise a very short sketch using one or more of the expressions from Exercise 1.

Learn: be; darling; dear; hurry; Look out!; (Don't) worry; follow; Follow me; (Be) careful; Take your time.

Students learn a number of common phrases used for advising and directing people.
Structures: imperative and negative imperative.

1 Matching expressions and pictures

- Let students try this by themselves, using dictionaries or consulting each other to find out the meanings of the expressions.
- Help them out if they get stuck.
- When they are ready and have compared notes, go over the answers with them. Practise saying the expressions. *Look out!* and *Be careful* are similar. However, *Look out!* (which draws somebody's attention to a danger he/she is unaware of) is more appropriate to picture 1, and *Be careful* (which simply advises caution) is more appropriate to picture 6.

Answers to Exercise 1
1. Look out!   2. Wait here, please.   3. Please come in.
4. Follow me, please.   5. Look.   6. Be careful, dear.
7. Don't worry.   8. Please hurry, darling.
9. Take your time, darling.

2 Listening for specific points

- You will probably need to play the conversation at least twice for students to pick out some of the imperatives and negative imperatives.
- After the second time, ask them how many they have noticed, and see whether they can remember some of them. (The answer is six imperatives and four negative imperatives.)

Tapescript for Exercise 2
Sit down, children. Time for your story. Are you all sitting comfortably? Good. Then I'll begin. Once upon a time, long long ago, there was a beautiful girl who lived with her mother and father in a small village. She – don't do that, George – she worked very hard on her father's farm looking after the cows – George, stop that! Mary, sit down at once – looking after the cows and the horses and the sheep. No, Sally, you are not a sweet little baby baa-lamb. You are a nice sensible little girl who is listening to a story. Every day – Bill, take that out of your mouth – she got up very early and milked the cows – don't make that stupid noise, Alice, please. Then she cleaned the house, and fed the animals, and made breakfast – Don't do that, George – breakfast for her mother and father.

One day, while she was cleaning the kitchen, she looked out of the window, and she saw – what do you think she saw, children? No, George, not Superman. No, Sylvia, not Mickey Mouse. Now don't be stupid, children. Think. What do you think she saw? James Bond, Louisa? Really! Sit down, please, Mary. And you, Celia. George . . .

(Inspired by a sketch by Joyce Grenfell.)

3 Mini-sketches

- The instruction asks students to illustrate one or more of the expressions in a brief sketch.
- However, confident and ambitious students ought to be able to get several of the expressions in.
- Don't let the exercise go on too long; elaborate sketches which take a long time to write are not required.
- If video is available, you might record the sketches.
- As a follow-up, you can ask groups to mime a situation involving one of the expressions. The class has to guess which it is.

Practice Book exercises: choose two or more
1. Common written instructions and prohibitions: matching words and pictures.
2. Writing notices for the students' school.
3. Vocabulary: choosing appropriate expressions from the lesson.
4. Revision of irregular verbs.
5. Check on revision vocabulary.
6. Student's Cassette exercise (Student's Book Exercise 2). Students listen to the first part of the monologue and try to write it down.
7. Crossword.

Unit 22: Lesson D

Students learn to say more about the ways in which things are done.
Structures: formation, use and position of adverbs of manner; distinction between adjectives and adverbs.

Language notes and possible problems

Adverbs   Not all languages distinguish 'adverbs' and 'adjectives' as separate grammatical categories. And in some European languages, adverbs of manner often have the same form as the corresponding adjectives. So many students have difficulty in using adverbs correctly in English, or in distinguishing them from adjectives.

In this lesson, students concentrate on adverbs of manner. Most of the ones practised end in -ly. Note, however, that *fast* is both adjective and adverb, and one or two words ending in -ly (e.g. *lovely, friendly*) are adjectives. *Loud* can often be used as an adverb, but *loudly* is used in this lesson to avoid confusion.

Position and spelling of adverbs can cause problems. For rules, see below in the notes on the exercises.

Optional extra materials

Verb and adverb cue-cards (Optional activity before Exercise 6).

1   Listening and matching

• Run over the list of adverbs with the students and make sure of meaning and pronunciation. (The ending -ily is usually pronounced /əli/.)
• Tell the students to write the numbers 1–6.
• Play the first sentence. Each student writes down an adverb that describes how the sentence is spoken.
• Note that they are not asked to *understand* the sentence, only to interpret the tone of the voice.
• Let students compare notes, and then play the sentences a second time so that they can check their answers before you go over the answers with them.

Tapescript and answers to Exercise 1
1. If you take my records again there's going to be trouble. (*angrily*)
2. Good morning. Are there any letters for me? (*sleepily*)
3. I'm sorry. I can't help you. (*coldly*)
4. Don't play with those! (*loudly*)
5. What a lovely surprise! Flowers – that *is* nice. (*happily*)
6. All right, Mary, just wait there for a minute and I'll see what I can do for you. (*kindly*)

2   Extension

• This exercise is similar to Exercise 1, except that students have to supply the adverbs themselves.
• The words required are already known, or correspond to known adjectives.
• Again, students do not need to understand everything.

Tapescript and answers to Exercise 2
1. The trouble with this government is that they think they know what's happening. (*fast*)
2. 'Can you understand what I'm saying?' 'Please speak more slowly.' (*slowly*)
3. Erm, excuse me, erm, do you mind if I sit here? (*shyly*)
4. There's no need to shout. I'm not deaf. (*quietly*)
5. Oh dear, it's terrible. He doesn't love me any more. (*unhappily*)

3   Spelling of adverbs

• Help students to work out the rules for the formation of adverbs ending in -ly. They are:
1. Add -ly to the adjective.
2. Don't drop -e (*extremely*, not *extremly*).
3. Change y to i (*happily*). Exception: *shyly*.
4. If the adjective ends in -ble the adverb ends in -bly (*comfortably*).

4   Adjective or adverb?

• It should be clear to students that adverbs are used after most verbs, to say how things are done. They already know how adjectives are used.
• Note that sentence 6 contains an example of a different structure: an adverb emphasizes an adjective.
• The last two sentences illustrate the relationship between the adjective *good* and the adverb *well*, and show adjective and adverb positions.

5   Position of adverbs

• This exercise discourages the common mistake of putting an adverb between the verb and the direct object (e.g. *I like very much skiing*).
• More than one answer is sometimes possible, but it is best just to teach students to put the adverb after the object at this stage.
• Ask students how well they speak English (and other languages if appropriate) to get personal examples.

Optional activity: miming
• Prepare two sets of cue-cards as follows: (verbs) write, eat, drink, walk, sing, speak, run, drive, fly, sleep, cook, dance, swim, smoke, type, wash, play (the guitar/piano/etc.); (adverbs) fast, slowly, loudly, quietly, happily, unhappily, angrily, sleepily, coldly, kindly, shyly, noisily, badly.
• Each student takes a verb-card and an adverb-card.
• They must demonstrate or mime the action (for example: *walk happily*; *drink slowly*); other students say what they are doing and how they are doing it.
• They should be told to reject absurd combinations (e.g. *sleep kindly*) and take new cards.

6   Practice

• Write the list of adverbs from Exercises 1 and 2 on the board; *angrily, coldly, happily, kindly, loudly, sleepily, fast, slowly, shyly, quietly, unhappily*.
• Practise the pronunciation.
• Ask students to try saying *Hello* in all ten ways.
• Give them a minute or two to work in pairs preparing a short conversation (two sentences each is enough).
• Each conversation should contain an instruction (like those in Lesson 22C, Exercise 1); and each student should speak in one of the ways listed on the board.
• Get the class (or a group of students) to listen to each conversation and try to identify the adverbs.

Practice Book exercises: choose two or more
1. Making adverbs from adjectives.
2. Putting adverbs in the right position.
3. Revision of past tenses of some irregular verbs.
4. Translation of material from the unit.
5. Student's Cassette exercise (Student's Book Exercise 1). Students listen and try to write the sentences.
6. Reading and writing: students read a letter and write one of their own.
7. Reading: Part 21 of *It's a Long Story*.

111

22D Please speak more slowly

1 📼 How are the people speaking? Listen to the recording, and choose one adverb for each sentence.

angrily	coldly	happily	kindly
loudly	sleepily		

2 Now listen to the next five sentences, and find more adverbs to say how the people are speaking.

3 Spelling. Look carefully at these adverbs.

badly	quietly	nicely	completely
carefully	angrily	happily	comfortably

Now make adverbs from these adjectives.

warm	great	extreme	sincere
hungry	lazy	real	terrible

4 Adjective or adverb?

1. I'm very .... with you. (*angry/angrily*)
2. She spoke to me .... (*angry/angrily*)
3. I don't think your mother drives very .... (*good/well*)
4. You've got a .... face. (*nice/nicely*)
5. I play the guitar very .... (*bad/badly*)
6. It's .... cold. (*terrible/terribly*)
7. Your father's got a very .... voice. (*loud/loudly*)
8. Why are you looking at me ....? (*cold/coldly*)
9. You speak very .... English. (*good/well*)
10. You speak English very .... (*good/well*)

5 Put the adverb in the right place.

1. He read the letter without speaking. (*slowly*)
   He read the letter slowly without speaking.
2. She speaks French. (*badly*)
3. I like dancing. (*very much*)
4. Please write your name. (*clearly*)
5. You should eat your food. (*slowly*)
6. She read his letter. (*carefully*)
7. I said 'Hello' and walked away. (*coldly*)

6 Now work with a partner and make up a short conversation. One partner tells the other to be careful, or to look out, or to wait, etc. Each partner speaks coldly, or angrily, or fast, etc.; the other students must say how you are speaking.

Learn: lazy; angry; clear; complete; loud; sleepy.

Unit 23 Predictions

23A Are you sure you'll be all right?

> Talking about the future with *will*.

1 Read the dialogue and then practise it in pairs.

A: I'm going to hitchhike round the world.
B: Oh, that's very dangerous.
A: No, it isn't. I'll be all right.
B: Where will you sleep?
A: Oh, I don't know. In youth hostels. Cheap hotels.
B: You'll get lost.
A: No, I won't.
B: You won't get lifts.
A: Yes, I will.
B: What will you do for money?
A: I'll take money with me.
B: You haven't got enough.
A: If I need money I'll find jobs.
B: Well . . . are you sure you'll be all right?
A: Of course I'll be all right.

2 Write and practise the contractions.

I will _I'll_   we will   I will not _I won't_
you will   they will   you will not
he will   it will not
she will
it will

3 Listen. Which sentence do you hear?

1. I stop work at six.
   I'll stop work at six.
2. You know the answer.
   You'll know the answer.
3. I have coffee for breakfast.
   I'll have coffee for breakfast.
4. You have to change at Coventry.
   You'll have to change at Coventry.
5. I drive carefully.
   I'll drive carefully.
6. I know you like my brother.
   I know you'll like my brother.

4 Work in pairs. Complete one of these dialogues and practise it.

A: I'm going to be a racing driver.
B: dangerous
A: isn't | all right
B: crash | get killed
A: won't
B: find a job
A: will | good driver
B: sure | all right
A: course

A: I'm going to be a doctor.
B: have to study | seven years
A: know | I don't mind
B: finish your studies
A: will
B: have | really hard life
A: interesting
B: have to work very long hours
A: know | don't mind
B: OK – if that's what you want.
A: is

5 Make up and practise a short conversation beginning:

    A: *'I'm going to get married.'*
or A: *'I'm going to work in a circus.'*
or A: *'I'm going to be a teacher.'*
or A: *'I'm going to ski down Everest.'*
or A: *'I'm going to be a pilot.'*

Will

I will go (~~I will to go~~) (I'll go)
you will go (you'll go)
he/she/it will go (~~he wills go~~) (he'll/she'll/it'll go)
we will go (we'll go)
you will go (you'll go)
they will go (they'll go)

will I go? (~~do I will go?~~)

I will not (won't) go

Learn: finish; get lost (got, got); get killed; have to do something (had, had); dangerous; all right; if; I don't mind.

Learn some other words and expressions from the lesson if you want to.

112

Unit 23: Lesson A

Students practise predicting, warning, and raising and countering objections.
Structures: the *will*-future; *get lost/killed/married*; preview of *have to*.
Phonology: /w/; 'dark *l*'; *won't*.

Language notes and possible problems

1. *Will* and *shall* *Will* is taught here as a future auxiliary for all persons. (*Shall* is also common in the first person, but *will* is usually equally correct as a first-person future auxiliary.) Students should work on the contractions; full affirmative and negative forms are rare in speech.

2. *Will*, *going to* and Present Progressive The differences between these three ways of talking about the future are complicated and difficult to analyse. It is enough if students practise each one in context for the moment, without paying too much attention to the rules. Some basic guidelines for reference:

a. The Present Progressive and *going to* are both used to talk about plans.
For the differences, see notes to Lesson 21A.

b. *Going to* and *will* are both used to predict the future. *Going to* is preferred when we talk about an event that is already starting to happen, or on the way, so that we can see it coming. (See notes to Lesson 21C.) Sentences with *going to* can often be re-expressed with a present tense (for instance, *She's going to have a baby* means *She's pregnant*). *Will* is used for more subjective predictions, when something is not already determined but we still feel that it is likely or certain to happen.
Compare: – *Look out! We're going to crash!*
– *Don't drive so fast, or you'll crash.*

3. *Get* Students meet *get* used as a kind of passive auxiliary (*get lost, get killed, get married*).

4. *Have to* Students also meet examples of *have to*. The contrast with *must* will be studied later.

5. Pronunciation 'Dark *l*' is the variety of *l* which occurs after a vowel (as in *I'll, feel, tell*). It is almost a separate syllable. Many students will find the dark *l* in *'ll* difficult to pronounce correctly (which does not matter very much), and difficult to hear (which does). To pronounce a good dark *l*, students should begin by saying /ʊ/ (the vowel in *good*), and then make an *l* while continuing the vowel.

You may also want to pay special attention in this unit to the pronunciation of *w* (for students who find it difficult) and /əʊ/ (as in *won't*). Students should make a clear distinction between *won't* and *want*.

---

1 Dialogue 📼

- Present this first with books closed. Play the recording once; then ask how much students have understood, and see if they can remember some words and expressions (not necessarily in order).
- Ask what is the relationship between the speakers.
- Open books. Study the text and answer questions.
- Practise the pronunciation.
- Get students to practise the dialogue in pairs.

2 Contractions 📼

- Get students to write out the affirmative and negative contractions, and then practise the pronunciation. (See *Language notes*.)
- Use the recording as a model if necessary.

3 Ear-training 📼

- Play each sentence and ask students to write the key words (e.g. *I stop* or *I'll stop*).
- Repeat the exercise if they are having difficulty.

Tapescript and answers to Exercise 3

1. I stop work at six.
2. You'll know the answer.
3. I'll have coffee for breakfast.
4. You'll have to change at Coventry.
5. I drive carefully.
6. I know you'll like my brother.

4 Completing dialogues

- Tell students to work in pairs.
- They should choose one of the dialogues (weaker students will find the first easier), and expand the notes into sentences, using Exercise 1 as a guide.
- Go round helping where necessary.
- When they are ready, they should practise their dialogues a few times.

Answers to Exercise 4

Some of the sentences can be completed in more than one way. Possible answers are as follows:

A: I'm going to be a racing driver.
B: Oh, that's very dangerous.
A: No, it isn't. I'll be all right.
B: You'll crash. You'll get killed.
A: No, I won't.
B: You won't find a job.
A: Yes, I will. I'm a good driver.
B: Well, are you sure you'll be all right?
A: Of course I'll be all right.

A: I'm going to be a doctor.
B: You'll have to study for seven years.
A: Yes, I know. I don't mind.
B: You won't finish your studies.
A: Yes, I will.
B: You'll have a really hard life.
A: Yes, but it'll be interesting.
B: You'll have to work very long hours.
A: Yes, I know. I don't mind.
B: OK – if that's what you want.
A: Yes, it is.

5 Students' dialogues

- Students should build up their conversations by taking elements from the dialogues they have just studied. The conversations should be short.
- They may need help with vocabulary.
- When ready, students should practise their conversations until they can say them from memory. Pay attention to pronunciation.
- If time allows, get students to perform their conversations for the class.
- You may like to tape- or video-record the conversations. If so, warn the students in advance – this will motivate them to aim for a high standard.

Practice Book exercises: choose two or more

1. Students predict what presents people will give them at Christmas etc.
2. Rhythm and stress.
3. Students write sentences about themselves, using a choice of words.
4. Irregular verbs.
5. Student's Cassette exercise (Student's Book Exercise 1). Students listen and practise the pronunciation.

Unit 23: Lesson B

Students learn to use simple conditional structures; they study the different meanings of *get*.
Structures: conditional structures with *will* in the main clause; *get* + direct object; *get* + adverb particle/preposition; *get* + adjective.
Phonology: /iː/ and /ɪ/.

Language notes and possible problems

1. If Like many conjunctions, *if* is used with 'simplified' tenses: present instead of future, and past instead of conditional. In this lesson, students practise sentences with *will* in the main clause and a present tense in the *if*-clause. Some students may find it natural to use a future tense with *if* in these sentences: look out for mistakes like **I'll phone you if I will have time.*

Conditional structures are often divided, rather misleadingly, into three types; the type studied here is the so-called 'first conditional'.

2. Get Students have met three main uses of *get*:

a. *Get* + direct object (e.g. *Where can I get stamps?*). The meaning here is *obtain, receive, fetch, buy* or something similar, depending on the context.

b. *Get* + adverb particle or preposition (e.g. *I get up at six; He got to the station twenty minutes late.*) In this case, the meaning generally involves some kind of movement – the exact meaning depends on the particular expression.

c. *Get* + adjective (e.g. *I'm getting old; my English is getting better*). Here *get* means *become*, and is used to refer to changes. With a past participle, *get* functions as a kind of passive auxiliary (e.g. *get lost*).

Note also the use of *get* (with no separate meaning) as part of the verb *have* in certain of its uses, especially in an informal style (e.g. *I've got two children*).

3. Get and go Students may confuse these two verbs from time to time. This is partly because of the second meaning of *get* referred to above, which is quite close to that of *go* (compare *I go to work by bus; I get to work at eight o'clock*). It is also unfortunate that *got* looks more like the past of *go* than *went* does.

---

1 The machine: *if*; *get* + direct object
• Look at the 'clouds' and explain the new vocabulary (or see if students can tell you what the words mean).
• Ask students to try to guess what you get from the different buttons, levers and handles, and to write one or more sentences with their guesses. Help with vocabulary if necessary.
• Get them to compare notes in groups.
• Then tell them to ask you for the right answers, making questions as in the example.

Answers to Exercise 1
– If you press button A, you'll get a surprise.
– If you push lever B, you'll get an electric shock.
– If you pull lever C, you'll get a hamburger.
– If you turn handle D, you'll get a flower.
– If you turn handle E, you'll hear music.
– If you push button F, you'll get a hot drink.

2 Tenses in sentences with *if*
• Ask students to look again at the sentences in Exercise 1. Point out that the Simple Present is used with *if* to refer to the future.
• Go through the exercise orally with the class, but get everybody to write one or two of the sentences to make sure that all the students have understood.

Answers to Exercise 2
(Full and contracted forms of *will* are of course both possible.)
1. press; will get
2. have; will come
3. rains; will have
4. will tell; need
5. will come; are
6. open; will see
7. will be; arrives
8. eat; will have
9. get; will take
10. will sell; go

3 Pronunciation: /iː/ and /ɪ/
• This is for students who confuse /iː/ and /ɪ/ (as in *eat* and *it*). If your students don't have trouble, drop the exercise.
• Say or play the words and expressions in each section, getting students to imitate.
• Note that the difference is mainly one of vowel quality, though length is also a factor.
• In Exercises 4 and 5, encourage students to pronounce these two vowels correctly as they occur.

4 *Get* + adjective
• This is a straightforward vocabulary exercise which also gives practice in *if*-structures.

Possible answers to Exercise 4
1. hungry 2. fat 3. thirsty 4. drunk
5. tired 6. wet 7. cold 8. dark 9. older

5 *Get*: deducing the rules
• Explain what you want students to do (starting the exercise on the board if necessary).
• Give them five or ten minutes to do the exercise and compare notes.
• They will probably not manage to sort out the sentences into exactly the right categories, but they will go some way towards understanding the point.
• Go over the answers. Note that students' answers may be valid even if they are different from those given below (for instance, they may put *get some stamps* and *get a letter* into different groups because *get* means *buy* in one case and *receive* in the other).
• Show how the meaning depends on the structure.

Answers to Exercise 5
1. *Get* + *direct object* (= 'receive', 'obtain')
   Where can I get some stamps?
   I get a letter from my mother every week.
   If you go to the shops, can you get me some bread, please?
2. *Get* + *adverb particle/preposition* (= 'move')
   What time to you usually get up?
   John got into his car and drove away.
   It takes me an hour to get to work.
   Get on the bus outside the station, and get off at Park Street.
   Get out! I don't want to see you any more. Get out of my life!
3. *Get* + *adjective* (= 'become')
   It's getting late.
   My English is getting better.
   The housing problem is getting worse.
4. *Have got* (= 'possess')
   You've got beautiful eyes.

Practice Book exercises: choose two or more
1. Vocabulary revision: sentence completion.
2. Students say where they got some of their possessions.
3. Rhythm and stress.
4. Reading quickly for specific information.

113

23B   If you push lever B, . . .

If and will; meanings of get.

1 How does the machine work? Write sentences.

| If you | press
pull
push
turn | button
lever
handle | A,
B,
C,
D,
E,
F, | I think you'll
get . . . |

Check with the teacher. Example:

'If you push lever B, what will you get?'

2 Put in the correct verb forms.

1. If you .... that button, you .... a cup of coffee. (*press; get*)
2. If I .... time, I .... and see you. (*have; come*)
3. If it ...., we .... the party inside. (*rain; have*)
4. I .... you if I .... help. (*tell; need*)
5. I hope you .... and see us if you .... in Chicago again. (*come; be*)
6. If you .... that door, you .... something strange. (*open; see*)
7. I .... surprised if she .... before 7 o'clock. (*be; arrive*)
8. If you .... fast, we .... time to play a game of tennis. (*eat; have*)
9. If you .... up early tomorrow, I .... you swimming. (*get; take*)
10. I .... my car if I .... to live in London. (*sell; go*)

3 Pronunciation. Say these words and expressions.

1. if   it   is   will   drink   him   his swimming   without   English   women minute
2. eat   east   feel   see   need   tea   meat free   week   please
3. evening   seeing   feeling   eating   needing extremely
4. I think it is.   I think I agree. if you eat too much   if you see him if you meet him   if you feel ill

4 Do you know the right adjectives to complete these sentences?

1. If you don't eat, you'll get ....
2. If you eat too much, you'll get ....
3. If you don't drink, you'll get ....
4. If you drink too much alcohol, you'll get ....
5. If you run a long way, you'll get ....
6. If you go out in the rain without an umbrella, you'll get ....
7. If you go out in the snow without a coat, you'll get ....
8. In the evening, when the sun goes down, it gets ....
9. We are all getting ....

5 *Get* has several different meanings. Put these sentences in four groups, according to the meaning of *get*.

What time do you usually get up?
It's getting late.
My English is getting better.
Where can I get some stamps?
John got into his car and drove away.
It takes me an hour to get to work.
I get a letter from my mother every week.
Get on the bus outside the station, and get off at Park Street.
The housing problem is getting worse.
If you go to the shops, can you get me some bread, please?
Get out! I don't want to see you any more. Get out of my life!
You've got beautiful eyes.

Learn: press; push; pull; turn; get on (got, got); get off; get in(to); get out (of); sell (sold, sold).

Learn four or more other words from the lesson.

113

23C   What do the stars say?

Predictions: people's futures.

AQUARIUS (Jan 21 – Feb 18)
An old friend will come back into your life, bringing new problems. Don't make any quick decisions.

PISCES (Feb 19 – Mar 20)
In three days you will receive an exciting offer. But your family will make difficulties.

ARIES (Mar 21 – Apr 20)
Money will come to you at the end of the week. If you're not careful it will go away again very fast.

TAURUS (Apr 21 – May 21)
You will have trouble with a child. Try to be patient. You will have a small accident on Sunday – nothing serious.

GEMINI (May 22 – June 21)
This will be a good time for love, but there will be a serious misunderstanding with somebody close to you. Try to tell the truth if you can.

CANCER (June 22 – July 22)
You will meet somebody who could change your life. Don't be too cautious – if you lose the opportunity, it won't come again.

LEO (July 23 – Aug 23)
Something very strange will happen next Thursday. Try to laugh about it.

VIRGO (Aug 24 – Sept 23)
This will be a terrible week. The weekend will be the worst time. Stay in bed on Sunday. Don't open the door. Don't answer the phone.

LIBRA (Sept 24 – Oct 23)
There will be bad news the day after tomorrow; but the bad news will turn to good.

SCORPIO (Oct 24 – Nov 22)
You will make an unexpected journey, and you will find something very good at the end of it.

SAGITTARIUS (Nov 23 – Dec 21)
You will have trouble from a person who loves you; and you will have help from a person who doesn't.

CAPRICORN (Dec 22 – Jan 20)
A letter will bring a very great surprise. If there are problems, a good friend will make things better.

1   Read your horoscope with a dictionary. Memorise it – and see if it comes true! Read some of the others too.

2   *There* or *it?*

1. There..... will be bad news the day after tomorrow.
2. It.......... will be cold and wet tomorrow.
3. .... will be rain at the weekend.
4. .... will be warm and sunny next week.
5. .... will be problems with somebody you love.
6. .... will probably be difficult to finish the work in time.
7. .... will be a meeting at 8.00 this evening.
8. .... will be a public holiday next Tuesday.
9. Do you think .... will be enough food for everybody?
10. 'We're going to Japan for our holiday.'   'That's nice, but .... will be expensive.'
11. We're late – .... will be after ten o'clock when we arrive.
12. .... won't be many cars on the road this evening.

3   If possible, work with somebody else who has the same sign as you. Write a new horoscope for your sign, and a new one for a different sign.

> **Learn:** decision; make a decision (made, made); trouble; truth; tell the truth (told, told); surprise; strange; bad news.
>
> **Learn some more words from the lesson if you want to.**

Unit 23: Lesson C

Students continue to practise predicting.
Structures: *will, if; there will be.*

1 Reading horoscopes

- Give students a few minutes to read their own horoscopes. Get them to read some or all of the others too.
- Tell them to memorise their predictions.
- In the next lesson, ask if any of the predicted things happened.

2 *There will be*: distinguishing *there* and *it*

- Students may find it difficult to use *there* as a subject with compound forms of *be*, and this may lead to confusion, for example, between *it will be* and *there will be*. This exercise should help them to sort things out.
- As you go through the exercise, help students to see that *there will be* is used to introduce nouns and noun phrases (e.g. *rain, bad news*), while *it will be* comes before adjectives (e.g. *wet*).

Answers to Exercise 2
3. There   4. It   5. There   6. It   7. There   8. There
9. there   10. it   11. it   12. There

3 Writing horoscopes

- If this can be done in groups of people who share the same sign it gives a nice focus to the exercise.
- For example, each group can write a splendid horoscope for its own sign and a terrible one for one of the other groups.
- Lone students can join one of the groups or work individually, as they wish.
- Encourage students to use *will, if,* and other words and expressions from the texts in the book.
- When the horoscopes are ready, get students to read them out.

Optional activity: telling fortunes

- There is usually somebody in the class who enjoys fortune-telling of one kind or another (for example, by reading people's palms or turning up cards).
- If so, ask them if they would prepare something for one of the next lessons with your help (unless they feel able to improvise in English).

Optional activity: predicting results

- Get students to make some predictions about sports results, the pop music charts, current events, the weather, or anything else that they are interested in.
- They should of course use *will* (e.g. *Manchester will beat Liverpool 3–1 next Saturday*; *'Baby come here' will go up to number one*).
- Get one of the students to act as class secretary and write down what everyone has said.
- Check in a week's time (or whenever) to see who was right.

Optional activity: ten years from now

- Ask students to say what they think they and other students will be like in ten years' time.

Practice Book exercises: choose two or more

1. Sentence completion: revision of *will*-future and Simple Past.
2. Vocabulary revision: lexical fields.
3. Learning irregular verbs.
4. Translation of material from the lesson.
5. Writing: imagining a dream holiday.
6. Reading: the *Which?* report on horoscopes.

Unit 23: Lesson D

Students predict how a story will end.
Structures: *will* or narrative present.

Language notes and possible problems
1. Tenses   Students are asked (Exercise 3) to predict what will happen in the third act. If one were actually in a theatre between the acts, it would be natural to use *will*. However, if students work in groups to continue the synopsis, as suggested, they are more likely to use present tenses.
2. Vocabulary   The text contains a good deal of new vocabulary. In order not to slow students' reading down to the point where they lose interest, essential words and expressions are taken out and taught in advance (Exercise 1).

1 Pre-teaching vocabulary
• Either go through the list (asking students if anybody knows the meanings of the words), or let students work through them with dictionaries.

2 Reading and remembering
• Give students ten minutes or so to read through the text and ask questions.
• Then tell them to close their books and see how much they can remember.
• You may like to prompt their memories by asking a few questions. For example:

Act 1   How old is Anna?
Where does she work?
What's her lover's name?
Why is he in prison?
Does she like her job?
Why not?
What happens when the Grand Duke sees her?
What does he tell her when she goes to the palace?
Does she agree?
What does she say to Boris?
What does Boris do?

Act 2   Who does Anna meet in Paris?
What is he doing now?
Who does he love?
Do you think Anna loves him?
Who is Yvette?
What does Boris say he will do?
Who does he say Anna is?
What does Yvette think?

3 Completing the synopsis
• Start by asking students to suggest what they think will happen.
• Then get them to form groups of three or four.
• Ask groups to plan and write out a synopsis of the third act. This will probably take some time: allow 20–30 minutes.
• Help with vocabulary as required.
• When everybody is ready, get a spokesperson from each group to read out the group's synopsis.

Practice Book exercises: choose two or more
1. Predicting fashions 50 years from now.
2. Pronunciation: words with the vowel /ɜː/.
3. Revision of prepositions.
4. Check on revision vocabulary.
5. Translation of material from the unit.
6. Reading: Part 22 of *It's a Long Story*.

115

Predicting the end of a story.

1 Find out what these words mean.
Ask your teacher or use a dictionary.

dead   prison   revolution   employer
royal   procession   duke   palace
mistress   famous   successful   heart
refuse   cousin

2 Read the opera synopsis. Then close your book
and see how much you can remember.

3 What do you think will happen in the third act?
Work in groups and finish the synopsis.

> **Learn:** heart; cousin; dream (dreamt, dreamt);
> pass; become (became, become); dead; away.
>
> **Learn three or more of these:** lover; prison;
> revolution; employer; mistress; refuse; join;
> unkind.

DEATH IN PARIS

An Opera in Three Acts
by Zoltan Grmljavina

SYNOPSIS

ACT ONE

Anna, a beautiful 18-year-old girl, works in a shop in
the old town of Goroda, in Central Moldenia. Her
parents are dead; her lover, Boris, is in prison for
revolutionary activities; her employer is very unkind
to her. She dreams of a happier life. One day a royal
procession passes in the street. The Grand Duke sees
Anna and falls in love with her. He sends for her; when
she goes to the palace he tells her that she must become
his mistress. If not, Boris will die. Anna agrees. Boris
is released from prison; in a letter Anna tells him that
she can never see him again. Boris leaves Moldenia.

ACT TWO

Three years have passed. Anna and the Duke are in
Paris. The Duke is dying – he has only six months to
live – but the doctors have not told him. Only Anna
knows the truth.
One day, Anna is walking in the Tuileries when a
man stops her. It is Boris. He tells her that he is now
a famous artist, rich and successful; but in his heart he still loves
Anna. 'Come away with me', he says. Anna refuses,
and Boris says that he will do something terrible. At
this moment, Yvette joins them. Boris tells Yvette that
Anna is his cousin from Moldenia, but Yvette does not
believe him.

ACT THREE

Anna and ...

Unit 24 Consolidation

24A Things to remember: Units 21, 22 and 23

Going to

I'm going to learn Chinese.
What are you going to do next year?
It's going to rain.
She's going to have a baby.

Will

I will go (~~I will to go~~) (I'll go)
you will go (you'll go)
he/she/it will go (~~he wills go~~) (he'll/she'll/it'll go)
we will go (we'll go)
you will go (you'll go)
they will go (they'll go)
will I go? (~~do I will go?~~)
I will not (won't) go

Examples:
Are you sure **you'll be** all right?
Manchester **will beat** Liverpool 2–0.
If you press button F, **you'll get** a cup of coffee.
This **will be** a terrible week.
There **will be** bad news the day after tomorrow.

If . . . will . . .

If you **press** button F, you'll get a cup of coffee.
  (~~If you will press . . .~~)
If I **have** time, I'll **come** and see you.
  (~~If I will have time . . .~~)
I'll be surprised **if** she **writes** to you.

There will be + noun; it will be + adjective

There will be rain at the weekend.
It will be warm next week.

Infinitive of purpose

You go to a supermarket **to buy** food.
He's going to Harrods **to buy** a suitcase.

Adjectives and adverbs

– Adjectives with nouns
  You've got a **nice** face.
  She speaks **good** English.

– Adjectives after *be*
  I am **angry** with you.

– Adverbs after other verbs
  She **spoke angrily**.
  She **speaks** English **well**.

– Adverbs with adjectives
  It's **terribly** cold.

Adverbs after objects

She speaks **English well**. (~~She speaks well English.~~)
I like **skiing very much**. (~~I like very much skiing.~~)

Adverbs of manner: spelling

slow ——————→ slowly
quiet ——————→ quietly
kind ——————→ kindly
bad ——————→ badly
careful ——————→ carefully (~~carefuly~~)
extreme ——————→ extremely (~~extremly~~)

happy ——————→ happily
angry ——————→ angrily

comfortable ——→ comfortably

Articles with words for illnesses

I've got **a cold.**
     a headache.   }   COUNTABLE
     a temperature.

I've got **toothache.** }   UNCOUNTABLE
     flu.

The meanings of *get*

– *Get* + direct object (= 'receive', 'obtain')
  Where can I **get some stamps**?
  I **get a letter** from my mother every week.
  Can you **get** me **some bread**, please?

– *Get* + adverb particle / preposition (= 'move')
  What time do you usually **get up**?
  It takes me an hour to **get to** work.
  Get on the bus outside the station, and **get off** at
    Park Street.
  Get out!!

– *Get* + adjective / past participle (= 'become')
  It's **getting late**.
  If you work too hard you'll **get tired**.
  get married/lost/killed

– *Have got* (= 'possess')
  You've **got** beautiful eyes.

Sentences with *before* and *after*

Always warm up **before** you run.
Walk for a few minutes **after** you finish.

Joining sentences into paragraphs

First of all he's going to buy a suitcase. **Then** he's going to go to the embassy, **and then** he's going to get his traveller's cheques from the bank. **After that** he's going to the doctor for a vaccination. **Next**, he's going to the travel agent's to get his tickets.

This lesson summarises and displays the language that students should have learnt in the last three units. There is less new material here than in previous sections: in this final section of the book, the main emphasis has been on consolidation and skills practice. Spend a short time going over the points with the students, clearing up any problems.

Note that expressions which occur in the grammatical and functional sections of the summary are not necessarily listed again in the vocabulary section.

Practice Book exercises: choose two or more
1. Adverb formation.
2. Adverb position.
3. Tenses in *if*-clauses.
4. Reading and guessing vocabulary.
5. Crossword.

Video

Sequence 6 in *The New Cambridge English Course 1 Video*, **The triathlon**, can be used around this point in the book, as it relates to Units 21–23 of the coursebook. The topics are sport; fitness and health. Language focus is on making predictions; future forms; imperatives; advice and warnings.

Telling stories with present tenses

One day, Anna **is walking** in the Tuileries when a man **stops** her. It **is** Boris. He **tells** her . . .

Feelings

I feel ill.
What's the matter?
My eyes hurt. My arm hurts.
Do they / Does it hurt very badly?
I've got a (bad) cold / a (bad) headache /
   (bad) toothache / flu / a temperature.
Why don't you see the doctor/dentist?

Giving advice and instructions

Run early in the morning – it's better.
Always wear comfortable clothing.
Never run in fog.
Don't run if you have got a cold.

Please hurry!	Wait here, please.
Take your time.	Be careful.
Don't worry.	Follow me, please.
Look.	Look out!
Come in.	

Words and expressions

Nouns

rest	summer	business	picture
video	autumn	headache	fork
bedroom	winter	aspirin	knife (knives)
bathroom	baby	problem	spoon
kitchen	meal	temperature	mistake
living room	meat	flu (*uncountable*)	decision
dining room	bread (*uncountable*)	toothache (*uncountable*)	trouble
information (*uncountable*)	reason	medicine (*uncountable*)	truth
advertisement	country	advice (*uncountable*)	surprise
fun	song	shoe	heart
spring	airport	cold	cousin

Verbs

use	fall (fell, fallen)	worry	turn
decide	break (broke, broken)	follow	sell (sold, sold)
find (found, found)	catch (caught, caught)	hurry	dream (dreamt, dreamt)
put (put, put)	hurt (hurt, hurt)	finish	pass
move	hope	press	become (became, become)
win (won, won)	rest	push	
crash	be (was/were, been)	pull	

Adjectives

international
right
wrong
alone
lazy
angry
clear
complete
loud
sleepy
dangerous
strange
dead

Prepositions

right across
over
out of
into

Other words and expressions to learn

get married (got, got)
do good to somebody (did, done)
have a baby (had, had)
do business
take medicine (took, taken)
make a mistake (made, made)
make a decision
get lost
get killed
get on
get off
get in(to)
get out (of)
tell the truth (told, told)

have to do something
darling
dear
before (*conjunction*)
after (*conjunction*)
while
if
finished
all right
away
bad news
What's the matter?
I don't mind

Optional words and expressions to learn

injection; suitcase; embassy; visa; travel agent; literature;
communication; pack; lover; prison; revolution; employer;
mistress; refuse; join; unkind.

24B Choose

A choice of listening, pronunciation and speaking exercises.

Look at the exercises, decide which ones are useful to you, and
do two or more.

LISTENING

1 Listen to the recording. When each sentence stops,
say what you think the next word will be. Example:

1. 'What's the time?' 'Three . . .'
'I think the next word will be "o'clock".'

2 Listen to the recording of a man dictating a
telegram over the telephone, and correct the following text.

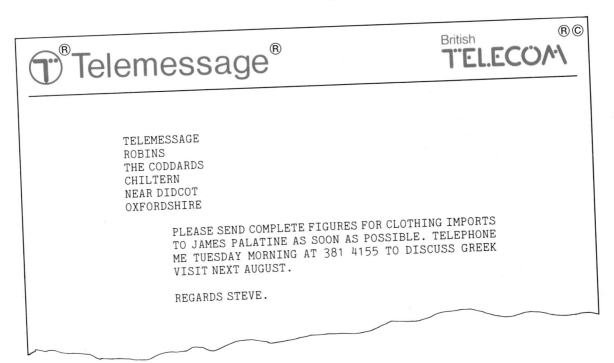

```
T®ⁱ Telemessage®                    British
                                    TELECOM  ®©


        TELEMESSAGE
        ROBINS
        THE CODDARDS
        CHILTERN
        NEAR DIDCOT
        OXFORDSHIRE
            PLEASE SEND COMPLETE FIGURES FOR CLOTHING IMPORTS
            TO JAMES PALATINE AS SOON AS POSSIBLE. TELEPHONE
            ME TUESDAY MORNING AT 381 4155 TO DISCUSS GREEK
            VISIT NEXT AUGUST.

            REGARDS STEVE.
```

3 ⊡ Listen to the song. Can you sing along?

Hush, little baby, don't say a word.
Mama's gonna buy you a mocking bird.

If that mocking bird don't sing,
Mama's gonna buy you a diamond ring.

If that diamond ring is brass,
Mama's gonna buy you a looking glass.

If that looking glass gets broke,
Mama's gonna buy you a billy goat.

If that billy goat don't pull,
Mama's gonna buy you a cart and bull.

If that cart and bull turn over,
Mama's gonna buy you a dog named Rover.

If that dog named Rover won't bark,
Mama's gonna buy you a horse and cart.

If that horse and cart fall down,
You'll still be the sweetest little baby in town.

Students and teacher choose from a selection of listening, pronunciation and speaking exercises.

Note
There is enough work in this lesson for 2–3 hours. You may like to get the students to vote for the exercises they consider most useful.

Optional extra materials
Flashcards for mime in Exercise 5.

LISTENING

1 What will the next word be?
• Play each sentence, and stop the recording at the break.
• Ask students to say or write what they think will come next. If you want to get examples of *will*, tell them to begin *I think the next word will be . . .*
• When they have decided, restart the recording so that they can check their answers.

Tapescript for Exercise 1
1. 'What's the time?' 'Three // o'clock.'
2. Europe, Asia, Africa, America, // Australia.
3. 'Can I speak to Alan?' 'Speaking. Who's // that?'
4. 'Excuse me, can you lend me £5?' 'I'm sorry, I'm afraid I // can't.'
5. One, four, seven, ten, thirteen, sixteen, // nineteen.
6. Darling, I love // you.
7. 'How long are you going to be away on holiday?' 'Oh, about three // weeks.'
8. To be or not to be, that is the // question.
9. 'Excuse me, have you got a light?' 'I'm sorry, I don't // smoke.'
10. 'Are you hungry?' 'Yes, I // am.'

2 Listening and correcting
• Ask students to read through the telemessage. Clear up any problems.
• Then tell them that there are some things wrong with the text in the book. They must listen to the recording and note the differences.

Answer to Exercise 2
The correct version is as follows:

Robbins
The *Goddards*
Chilton
Near Didcot
Oxfordshire.

Please *give* complete figures for *furniture* imports to James *Polixenes* as soon as possible. Telephone me *Thursday afternoon* at 3_7_1 41_99_ to discuss *German* visit next *April*.

Regards *Peter*.

3 Song: *Hush, Little Baby*
• This is a Southern United States version of a traditional folksong which originally came from Britain.
• Play the song once without comment.
• Go through the text explaining key vocabulary and clearing up any problems. (Note that there are various non-standard grammatical features.)
• Play the song again one or more times, and see if the students can sing along with it.

PRONUNCIATION

1 -e and pronunciation

• Get students to look at the first list, and see if they can work out for themselves, without your help, how *a* is pronounced in the first and second rows.
• When they are able to see the rule, ask them in turn to try to say the words in the list entitled NOW PRONOUNCE.
• Then ask them if they can think of any other words that fit into these patterns.
• Go on to do the same with the other three sections.
• Help them to see the overall rule: that *a, i, o* and *u* represent diphthongs or long vowels before *consonant + e,* and short vowels when there is no following *e.*
• (Note that the 'long' pronunciation of *u* is generally /juː/ in British English; but it is pronounced /uː/ after *r,* and in some words after *l* and *s.*)
• Finally, draw students' attention to the exceptions. Tell them that there are more exceptions, but that enough words follow the rule for it to be useful.
• Some students will probably ask what the new words mean. You can explain that they are not important words (except for pronunciation practice); students can look them up in their dictionaries if they really want to know their meanings.
• The recording can be used as a model if you wish.

SPEAKING

1 Mime: *going to*
• Get one or two volunteers to mime first (take part yourself if you like).
• Give students a couple of minutes to think, and then go round the class getting them to do their mimes.
• Encourage everybody to participate, but don't force a student who is really shy.
• It may help things along if you give students cards with the names of actions to mime.
• Possibilities: being about to eat, drink, shave, wash, go to bed, play chess, play the guitar/violin, write, read, cook something, drive, sneeze, faint, be sick, wake up, go to sleep.

2 Story

• Put the students in groups of three or four.
• Make sure they understand what they have to do. Their task is to work out a story which includes all the elements (pictures and sounds) which they are given.
• Play the recording twice, and then give them 15–20 minutes to work out their stories.
• They should make notes, but not write out complete versions of the stories.
• When they are ready, get one person from each group to tell the group's story to the class.
• The sounds are: breaking glass; heavy footsteps; a loud splash; a woman screaming; a violin playing.

Practice Book exercises: choose two or more
1. Students apply pronunciation rules to work out the pronunciation of words they don't know.
2. Stress.
3. Irregular pasts.
4. Check on revision vocabulary.
5. Putting linking and sequencing expressions into a text.
6. Writing: past narrative.

PRONUNCIATION

1 How does -e change the pronunciation?

WITHOUT -e: fat	cat	am	plan	hat	NOW PRONOUNCE: man same take that
WITH -e: gate	late	name	plane	hate	lemonade bale safe tap tape
WITHOUT -e: sit	in	begin	if	swim	NOW PRONOUNCE: fit inside still mile
WITH -e: invite	fine	wine	wife	time	hid ride tide like pipe strip
WITHOUT -e: stop	top	not	hot	clock	NOW PRONOUNCE: job stone rose God
WITH -e: hope	home	note	nose	smoke	joke dome bone on spot coke
WITHOUT -e: bus	run	pub	sun	just	NOW PRONOUNCE: much fuse cube cub
WITH -e: excuse	June	tube	rude	use	fuss tune gun fun duke luck
EXCEPTIONS: some come one have give live love							

SPEAKING

1 Mime a person who is going to do something. The other students will say what you are going to do.

You're going to swim.

2 Look at the pictures and listen to the recording. Prepare a story about the pictures and the sounds. When you are ready, tell the other students.

119

24C   When you grow up

Revision of tenses.

1 Listen to the recording. Which of these do you hear?

I'm not going to do anything at all.
I really am going to stop smoking now.
I'm never going to see you again.

I'm going to have the steak.
I'm going to have a bath.
I'm going to write a letter to the Prime Minister.

2 Choose the correct verb forms to complete the sentences.

1. 'Can you help me?' 'Sorry, not just now. I ....' (*work*)
2. 'What does she do?' 'I'm not sure. I think she .... in a bank.' (*work*)
3. We .... to Canada on holiday nearly every summer. (*go*)
4. But next summer we .... to Scotland. (*go*)
5. I .... Matthew yesterday. He sends you his love. (*see*)
6. I .... three good films this week. (*see*)
7. Alice .... her boyfriend for three weeks, and they're already talking about getting married. (*know*)
8. .... you ever .... to change your job? (*want*)
9. If you .... help I .... what I can. (*need*; *do*)
10. Look at those black clouds. I'm sure it .... (*rain*)
11. Your horoscope says that this .... a difficult week for you. You .... a tall dark stranger; he .... all your money. (*be*; *meet*; *take*)

3 🔲 Read the poems. Do you like them or not? Can you say why?

WHEN YOU GROW UP

If you are beautiful
when you grow up
we will be pleased.
And if you look like your father
we will still be quite pleased.

If you are angry at the world
we will understand.

If you fight us
we will try
not to fight back.

If you grow up
to be an artist
an airline pilot
or an import-export-expert
that will be fine.
Shop assistant
sheep farmer
professor of palaeontology
will be great.
Anything you want to be
will be fine
(except advertising
religion
or the military).

If you become rich and famous
don't worry.
We will not be too proud
to live on your money.

If you marry
marry anybody you want to
we will not mind
it will be your decision
you will be absolutely free.
Nobody will be good enough for you anyway.
(Only
don't marry somebody we don't like.)

If you realise
one day
that your parents are idiots
we hope you will tell us
in the nicest possible way.

Have a good life.

WEATHER FORECAST

Tomorrow
if it rains
I will dance in the rain with you.

If it snows
we will make snow pancakes
and eat them together.

If it is cold
I will warm myself
with your smile.

If it is hot
I will cool myself
with your slow clear voice.

If there is fog
I will be happy
to lose myself for a time.
(But please
come and find me
won't you?)

Unit 24: Lesson C

Students revise the use of tenses; they read and discuss two poems.
Structures: present, past and future verb forms.

1 Listening: *going to*

• Look through the list of sentences with the students and deal with any problems.
• Tell students to copy the sentences.
• Play the recording twice without stopping, while students check off the ones they hear.
• Let them compare notes before discussing the answers.

Answers to Exercise 1

I'm not going to do anything at all.
I'm going to have the steak.
I'm going to have a bath.

Tapescript for Exercise 1

'What are you going to do when you stop work, Steve? Must be difficult to decide.' 'Oh, no. It's easy. I'm not going to do anything at all. For the rest of my life. Nothing whatsoever.'

(*Cough, cough, cough*) I really am going to stop smoking. Next Monday morning. I'm going to stop – just like that. No more cigarettes. Never again. (*Cough, cough, cough*)

You dirty stinking liar! You toad! You disgusting creep! You awful little man! I'm never going to speak to you again! Never, as long as I live! Do you hear? Never!!!

'Have you decided, madam?' 'Yes, I'm going to have the steak with a green salad and French fried potatoes, thanks.' 'Very good, madam.'

'I'm going to have a bath. See you in half an hour.' 'Can I come and wash your back?' 'No.'

'That's it. That's enough. I'm not taking any more of it. I'm going to write to the Prime Minister. Today. I've had enough. I told them they couldn't do it. I told them and told them and told them. Didn't I, Tony? I told them.' 'You certainly did, Margaret. You told them.'

2 Revision of tenses

• This exercise gives a quick check on the main tense distinctions studied so far.
• If you want to make sure that everybody has grasped the basic rules, you may like to get the class to do the exercise in writing.

Answers to Exercise 2

1. 'm (am) working
2. works
3. go
4. 're (are) going
5. saw
6. 've (have) seen
7. has known
8. Have . . . wanted
9. need; 'll (will) do
10. 's (is) going to rain OR 'll (will) rain
11. 'll (will) be; 'll (will) meet; 'll (will) take

3 Poems

• Students will probably get more out of the poems if they hear them read. Read them yourself or play the recording while students follow in their books.
• Get students to say how they feel about the poems. They should feel free to express positive or negative reactions – if they don't like one or both poems, or aren't interested, get them to say so and, if possible, to explain why.
• You may need to suggest ways for the students to say what they have in mind. Useful expressions:

I like it.
I find it moving.
It's funny.
I think it's true.
I feel the same as the writer.
It's boring.
It doesn't say anything to me.
I think it's sentimental.
I find it silly.
It's empty.
I think it's badly written.

4 Sentences with *will* and *if*

• Get students to choose at least five of the sentences and complete them, using *will* in the main clause of each.

• If the sentences are carefully chosen, when they are put together they are likely to form a simple poem.

• If students are willing, get them to show their poems to each other or share them with the class.

5 Cartoons

• This is an easy exercise, suitable for group discussion. Students should have no difficulty in matching the captions to the cartoons; the choice of verb forms may need a little more thought.

Answers to Exercise 5
1. . . . Who shall I say *is calling*? (Cartoon C)
2. . . . You *always think* of something. (Cartoon B)
3. The milk*'s boiling* over. (Cartoon A)
4. Nobody *knows* what Ann*'ll do* next. (No cartoon)
5. . . . It*'s come* back without him. (Cartoon E)
6. We*'ve been* married for twenty-five years . . . (Cartoon D)

Practice Book exercises: choose two or more
1. Students write sentences comparing past and present.
2. Punctuation.
3. Vocabulary expansion.
4. Student's Cassette exercise (Student's Book Exercise 3, second poem). Students listen and practise saying the poem.
5. Reading: Part 23 of *It's a Long Story*.

4 Complete some of these sentences; make some more of your own if you want to. And if you like, put them together to make a poem.

Tomorrow, if I am happy, . . .
If I am unhappy, . . .
If life is difficult, . . .
If I see you, . . .
If I have no money, . . .
If I am tired, . . .

If I want to sing, . . .
If I break a cup, . . .
If the weather is bad, . . .
If I get bills in the post, . . .
If I am bored, . . .

5 Match the captions with the cartoons (there is one caption too many), and choose the right verb forms.

1. Yes, Ron's in. Who shall I say (*calls / is calling*)?
2. I'm not worried. You (*always think / 're always thinking*) of something.
3. The milk (*boils / 's boiling*) over.
4. Nobody (*knows / is knowing*) what Ann (*does / 'll do*) next.
5. Hello, police! It's my husband's hang-glider. It (*came / 's come*) back without him.
6. We (*are / were / 've been*) married for twenty-five years, Helen. You could at least give me a chance to run.

A

B

C

D

E

121

24D Test yourself

LISTENING

1 Copy the table. Then listen to the recording and fill in the information.

	DEPARTURE TIME	GOING TO	ARRIVAL TIME	CHANGE?
1				*no*
2		?		
3				
4				
5				

GRAMMAR

1 Write the adverbs. Example:

slow *slowly*

certain; cheap; complete; dangerous; easy; economical; expensive; free; happy; lazy; nice; possible; probable; terrible; usual; wonderful.

2 Put the adverb in the right place. Example:

I agree with you. (*certainly*)

I certainly agree with you.

1. She speaks English. (*well*)
2. I like skiing. (*very much*)
3. We go on holiday together. (*often*)
4. She is late for work. (*usually*)

3 Put in *a, an, the* or – (= no article). Examples:

What's *the* time?

She comes from *–* London.

I live in *a* small flat.

1. My brother's .... doctor.
2. Do you like .... music?
3. 'What are you eating?' '............... orange.'
4. Where's .... nearest toilet?
5. It's over there by .... stairs, on .... right.
6. Do you know, ... tomatoes are £3.50 a kilo?

4 Write the past tense and past participle. Example:

go *went gone*

become; fall; find; have; hear; hurt; know; make; put; read; see; sell; write.

5 Write out the letter with the correct forms of the words in brackets.

Agios Demetrios
Monday

Dear Jan and Phil,

Just a note to let you know that we (*have*) a wonderful holiday. This really is a great place – I (*never be*) anywhere like it before. The people are friendly, the food's great, and the weather's a lot better (*as/than*) at home. We (*be*) here (*for/since*) ten days now, and we (*have*) sun every day. Can you (*believe*) it?

Most days are pretty (*lazy/lazily*). I (*swim*) two or three times a day, but Bill just (*spend*) all his time lying on the beach with his eyes closed. Sometimes he (*write*) a postcard, but then he (*forget*) to post it.

Last Saturday I (*get*) on the bus and (*go*) to the north end of the island. It's much (*quiet*) there than here – very beautiful, but no tourists. Tomorrow we (*go*) across to the east coast (*see*) some of the old villages, if Bill (*wake*) up in time. And next week, if the weather (*be*) still nice, I (*think*) I (*do*) some walking in the mountains.

I (*learn*) Greek – I still can't (*say*) much, but it's fun to try. Bill actually (*speak*) it quite well, but he's afraid to open his mouth, so I'm the one who talks to people.

Love to Joe and the family. See you soon, I (*hope*).

Alex

122

Unit 24: Lesson D

Students do a simple revision test.

The purpose of the test

This final test, like the others in the book, is provided for teachers who feel that it will be useful. It covers several different areas, and includes points from earlier in the course as well as material from Units 21–23. It is not of course necessary to do all the sections, and teachers should select according to their students' needs. Teachers who do not feel the test will be useful should simply drop it altogether.

If possible, try to make the students feel that they are 'testing themselves', rather than 'being tested'. It is not intended that students should 'pass' or 'fail' the test, and it is not particularly useful to give marks. (If the school or education system requires that this be done, you will need to work out a simple marking scheme.) But students should of course be told whether you feel their performance is satisfactory. In principle, students who have worked systematically through the course ought to get most answers right.

Administration

The test can be administered in various ways, depending on how strictly you want to control students' performance; whether you want to collect the answers and mark them, or allow the students to correct them in class; and so on.

The 'speaking' test will need to be done individually, with students interrupting their work on the other tests to come and talk to you one at a time.

If you are not collecting students' scripts, correction can be done by class discussion when everybody has finished.

Notes, tapescript and answers are given below.

LISTENING

- Explain to students that they will hear five pieces of English.
- They will not understand everything, but this is not important.
- Their task is to note (in each case) the time of departure of the person or train referred to, the destination (if known), the time of arrival (if known) and whether it is necessary to change (if known).
- Stop after each extract for students to note their answers.
- Play the recording a second time, to give students a chance to catch any information they missed the first time round.

1 Tapescript and answers

1. The next train from platform one will be the four twenty for Hereford, calling at . . .

2. 'Oh God. It's going to take all day.'
   'What time do you leave?'
   'I'm catching the ten twenty from Victoria. I don't get there until half past nine in the evening.'
   'Half past nine?'
   'Yes. I have to change at Ashton, then I have to change at Stoke, Adderbury and Caldon. Change everywhere . . .'

3. 'What time's the next train for London?'
   'Three fifteen. Platform six. Change at Reading.'
   'What time does it get in?'
   'Four thirty-five.'

4. A: Excuse me.
   B: Yes?
   A: Is this the Birmingham train?
   B: Birmingham? Oh, no, dear. This is the 6.16 for Manchester.
   A: Manchester? But I don't want to go to Manchester.
   C: What's wrong with Manchester?
   A: Nothing. But I want to go to Birmingham. What time do we arrive?
   B: Ten to ten.
   C: No, ten past ten.
   CHORUS OF VOICES: Ten to ten.
   A: Oh, no!

5. 'I always take the 10.27, myself.'
   'Do you, dear?'
   'Yes. You get a nice cup of tea on the 10.27.'
   'D'you have to change?'
   'Oh, no. It's direct. I don't like changing.'
   'No, neither do I.'
   'I remember once, I was with Aunty Mary. It was during the war. We were living in Ashford . . .'

	DEPARTURE TIME	GOING TO	ARRIVAL TIME	CHANGE?
1	4.20	Hereford	?	no
2	10.20	?	9.30 (p.m.)	yes
3	3.15	London	4.35	yes
4	6.16	Manchester	9.50	?
5	10.27	?	?	no

GRAMMAR

1 certainly; cheaply; completely; dangerously; easily; economically; expensively; freely; happily; lazily; nicely; possibly; probably; terribly; usually; wonderfully

2 1. She speaks English well.
   2. I like skiing very much. / I very much like skiing.
   3. We often go on holiday together.
   4. She is usually late for work.

3 1. a
   2. –
   3. An
   4. the
   5. the; the
   6. –

4 became, become
   fell, fallen
   found, found
   had, had
   heard, heard
   hurt, hurt
   knew, known
   made, made
   put, put
   read, read
   saw, seen
   sold, sold
   wrote, written

5 (Contracted forms are not given in the answers, but are also correct.)

Agios Demetrios
Monday

Dear Jan and Phil,

Just a note to let you know that we *are having* a wonderful holiday. This really is a great place – I *have never been* anywhere like it before. The people are friendly, the food's great, and the weather's a lot better *than* at home. We *have been* here *for* ten days now, and we *have had* sun every day. Can you *believe* it?

Most days are pretty *lazy*. I *swim* two or three times a day, but Bill just *spends* all his time lying on the beach with his eyes closed. Sometimes he *writes* a postcard, but then he *forgets* to post it.

Last Saturday I *got* on the bus and *went* to the north end of the island. It's much *quieter* there than here – very beautiful, but no tourists. Tomorrow we *are going* (*are going to go* / *will go*) across to the east coast *to see* some of the old villages, if Bill *wakes* up in time. And next week, if the weather *is* still nice, I *think* I *will do* some walking in the mountains.

I *am learning* Greek – I still can't *say* much, but it's fun to try. Bill actually *speaks* it quite well, but he's afraid to open his mouth, so I'm the one who talks to people.

Love to Joe and and the family. See you soon, I *hope*.

Alex

VOCABULARY

1 small/little; expensive; fair/light; difficult/hard; slim/thin; unhappy; cold; short; quiet; fast; short/small; badly/ill; old.

2 1–3. (Various possible answers.)
   4. summer, autumn, winter
   5. south, east, west
   6. lunch/dinner, tea, dinner/supper
   7. knife, fork, cup, plate

3 1. (to a) bookshop
   2. (to a) library
   3. (to an) airport
   4. cousin
   5. glasses
   6. glass
   7. (Various possible answers.)

LANGUAGE IN USE

(Various possible answers.)

PRONUNCIATION

1 1. bread
   2. truth
   3. trouble
   4. heart
   5. one
   6. wrong
   7. but
   8. sorry

2 advertisement; advice; airport; alone; autumn; bathroom; become; business; complete; dangerous; decision; headache; information; international; medicine; mistake; picture; problem; surprise; temperature; video.

WRITING

When correcting this, it is best to judge students mainly on their ability to communicate successfully, using appropriate vocabulary and structures. Part of the test involves the correct use of verb forms to refer to the future, but don't give this more importance than it is worth. Excessive emphasis on minor errors of grammar and spelling can damage students' confidence.

SPEAKING

Go over the instructions with the whole class and make sure they understand what they have to do. Then test the students one by one. In the picture story, leave students free to use present or past tenses as they prefer. In the conversation, don't give students too much information at a time – make them ask plenty of questions.

Test Book recordings
A recording for Test 6 in the Test Book follows this lesson on the Class Cassette.

VOCABULARY

1 **Give the opposites of these words. Example:**

white ~black~

big; cheap; dark; easy; fat; happy; hot; long; noisy; slow; tall; well; young.

2 **Add some more words to these lists.**

1. uncle, sister, . . .
2. arm, nose, . . .
3. bathroom, . . .
4. spring, . . .
5. north, . . .
6. breakfast, . . .
7. spoon, . . .

3 **Answer these questions.**

1. Where do you go to buy a book?
2. Where do you go to read or borrow a book?
3. Where do you go to catch a plane?
4. Your aunt's daughter is your . . . .
5. What do you wear if you have bad eyes?
6. What is a window made of?
7. Give examples of: a noun, a verb, an adjective.

LANGUAGE IN USE

1 **Write a typical sentence or expression for each of these situations:**

1. in a restaurant
2. in a shop
3. on the telephone
4. at the doctor's
5. giving advice or instructions
6. inviting

PRONUNCIATION

1 **Which word is different?**

1. meal   meat   bread   reason
2. country   fun   summer   truth
3. trouble   flu   tooth   shoe
4. heart   turn   early   third
5. song   one   long   gone
6. fork   fall   wrong   caught
7. pull   push   but   put
8. worry   hurry   sorry

2 **Which syllable is stressed?**

advertisement; advice; airport; alone; autumn; bathroom; become; business; complete; dangerous; decision; headache; information; international; medicine; mistake; picture; problem; surprise; temperature; video.

WRITING

1 Write 100–200 words about what you are going to do *either* next weekend, *or* for your next holidays, *or* next year, *or* when you leave school, *or* when you stop work.

SPEAKING

1 Look at the pictures and tell the teacher the story.

2 Find out as much as you can about *either* the teacher's family, *or* the teacher's childhood, *or* the teacher's last holiday, *or* the teacher's plans for the next few years.

Vocabulary index

Word	Ref
child /tʃaɪld/ (children /'tʃɪldrən/)	3C
China /'tʃaɪnə/	1D
Chinese /tʃaɪ'ni:z/	1D
chips /tʃɪps/	7D
church /tʃɜ:tʃ/	5D
cigarette /sɪgə'ret/	17B
cinema /'sɪnəmə/	19B
city /'sɪti/	15B
clear /klɪə(r)/	22D
clothes /kləʊðz/	10B
coat /kəʊt/	3A
coffee /'kɒfi/	7A
cold (a cold) /kəʊld/	22B
cold (adjective)	10A
colour /'kʌlə(r)/	9B
colour: What colour is/ are . . . ?	9C
come /kʌm/	11D
comfortable /'kʌmftəbl/	13D
communication /kəmju:nɪ'keɪʃn/	21D
complete /kəm'pli:t/	22D
concert /'kɒnsət/	15C
cook /kʊk/	13A
cooker /'kʊkə(r)/	5A
cost (verb) /kɒst/	7B
could /kəd, kʊd/	17B
Could I speak to . . . ? /kʊd aɪ 'spi:k tə/	14D
Could you possibly . . . ? /'pɒsəbli/	17B
Could you speak more slowly, please? /'sləʊli/	10D
count /kaʊnt/	13B
country /'kʌntri/	21D
cousin /'kʌzn/	23D
crash /kræʃ/	21C
cup /kʌp/	7C
cupboard /'kʌbəd/	5A
dance (verb) /dɑ:ns/	13A
dangerous /'deɪndʒərəs/	23A
dark (e.g. dark green) /dɑ:k/	9B
dark (= not fair)	3B
darling /'dɑ:lɪŋ/	22C
date /deɪt/	14C
daughter /'dɔ:tə(r)/	3C
day /deɪ/	11A
day: the day after tomorrow /tə'mɒrəʊ/	14C
day: the day before yesterday /'jestədi/	14C
dead /ded/	23D
dear /dɪə(r)/	22C
Dear (e.g. Dear John)	9D
December /dɪ'sembə(r)/	14C
decide /dɪ'saɪd/	21A
decision /dɪ'sɪʒn/	23C
dentist /'dentɪst/	2A
depends: It depends /ɪt dɪ'pendz/	6A
dictionary /'dɪkʃənri/	17B
did /dɪd/	11C
didn't /'dɪdnt/	11C
die /daɪ/	11B
different /'dɪfrənt/	11A

Word	Ref
difficult /'dɪfɪkʊlt/	13C
dining room /'daɪnɪŋ ru:m/	21B
dinner /'dɪnə(r)/	17D
dirty /'dɜ:ti/	10A
disagree /dɪsə'gri:/	18C
dislike /dɪs'laɪk/	6A
divorced /dɪ'vɔ:st/	2D
do /də, dʊ, du:/	2A
do business /'bɪznɪs/	21D
do good to somebody	21A
Do you know? /də jʊ 'nəʊ/	7B
Do you mind if . . . ? /maɪnd/	19A
doctor /'dɒktə(r)/	2A
does /dəz, dʌz/	6A
doesn't /'dʌznt/	6A
dog /dɒg/	18D
don't /dəʊnt/	1B
Don't worry /'dəʊnt 'wʌri/	22C
door /dɔ:(r)/	5A
double (letters) /'dʌbl/	1B
downstairs /'daʊn'steəz/	5C
Dr /'dɒktə(r)/	2B
draw /drɔ:/	13B
dream (verb) /dri:m/	23D
dress (noun) /dres/	9B
drink (verb) /drɪŋk/	15A
drive /draɪv/	13A
each other /'i:tʃ 'ʌðə(r)/	19D
ear /ɪə(r)/	9A
ear-rings /'ɪərɪŋz/	9B
early /'ɜ:li/	18D
earn /ɜ:n/	11A
east /i:st/	18B
easy /'i:zi/	13C
eat /i:t/	14D
economical /ekə'nɒmɪkl/	13D
egg /eg/	7A
Egypt /'i:dʒɪpt/	1D
Egyptian /i:'dʒɪptʃən/	1D
eight /eɪt/	2C
eighteen /'eɪ'ti:n/	2C
eighteenth /'eɪ'ti:nθ/	14C
eighth /eɪtθ/	5B
eightieth /'eɪtiəθ/	14C
eighty /'eɪti/	2D
electrician /ɪlek'trɪʃn/	2A
eleven /ɪ'levn/	2C
eleventh /ɪ'levənθ/	14C
else: anywhere else /'eniweər 'els/	19C
embassy /'embəsi/	21D
employer /ɪm'plɔɪə(r)/	23D
engineer /endʒə'nɪə(r)/	2A
England /'ɪŋglənd/	1D
English /'ɪŋglɪʃ/	1D
enough /ɪ'nʌf/	7D
Europe /'jʊərəp/	11C
evening /'i:vnɪŋ/	2B
evening: in the evening	6B
ever /'evə(r)/	19C
ever: hardly ever /'hɑ:dli/	19B
every /'evri/	11A
every day etc.	19B
every three days etc.	19B

Word	Ref
everybody /'evribɒdi/	6A
everything /'evriθɪŋ/	17A
excellent /'eksələnt/	17A
except /ɪk'sept/	9C
Excuse me /ɪks'kju:z mi:/	1C
expensive /ɪks'pensɪv/	7B
extremely /ɪks'tri:mli/	14B
eye /aɪ/	9A
face /feɪs/	9A
fair (not dark) /feə(r)/	3B
fall /fɔ:l/	21C
family /'fæmli/	3C
famous /'feɪməs/	18C
far /fɑ:(r)/	5D
fast (adjective) /fɑ:st/	13D
fast (adverb)	13B
faster (adverb) /'fɑ:stə(r)/	13B
fat /fæt/	3B
father /'fɑ:ðə(r)/	3C
favourite /'feɪvrɪt/	11C
February /'februəri/	14C
feel /fi:l/	19D
fifteen /fɪf'ti:n/	2C
fifteenth /'fɪf'ti:nθ/	14C
fifth /fɪfθ/	5B
fiftieth /'fɪftɪəθ/	14C
fifty /'fɪfti/	2D
film /fɪlm/	18C
film star /'fɪlm stɑ:(r)/	13D
finally /'faɪnəli/	18B
find /faɪnd/	21B
find out /'faɪnd 'aʊt/	17C
fine (= satisfactory) /faɪn/	17C
Fine, thanks	1C
finish /'fɪnɪʃ/	23A
finished /'fɪnɪʃt/	21B
first /fɜ:st/	5B
first name /neɪm/	1B
first of all /əv 'ɔ:l/	18B
first: the first person etc. to	18A
fish /fɪʃ/	6D
five /faɪv/	1B
flat (noun) /flæt/	5B
floor /flɔ:(r)/	5B
flower /flaʊə(r)/	18D
flu /flu:/	22A
fly /flaɪ/	18A
follow /'fɒləʊ/	22C
Follow me	22C
food /fu:d/	7D
foot /fʊt/ (feet /fi:t/)	9A
football /'fʊtbɔ:l/	6D
football match /'fʊtbɔ:l 'mætʃ/	15C
for (e.g. for you) /fə(r), fɔ:(r)/	17A
for (distance)	5D
for (time)	19D
for a moment /'məʊmənt/	19A
foreign /'fɒrən/	13B
forget /fə'get/	15D
fork /fɔ:k/	22B
fortieth /'fɔ:tɪəθ/	14C
forty /'fɔ:ti/	2D
four /fɔ:(r)/	1B
fourteen /'fɔ:'ti:n/	2C

125

Is that . . . ? (phone) 14D
isn't /ˈɪznt/ 1A
It depends /dɪˈpendz/ 6A
It doesn't matter /ˈmætə(r)/ 14D
it /ɪt/ 1A
it's /ɪts/ 1A
Italian /ɪˈtælɪən/ 1D
Italy /ˈɪtəli/ 1D
jacket /ˈdʒækɪt/ 9B
January /ˈdʒænjəri/ 14C
Japan /dʒəˈpæn/ 1D
Japanese /dʒæpəˈniːz/ 1D
jeans /dʒiːnz/ 9B
job /dʒɒb/ 3D
job: between jobs /bɪˈtwiːn/ 2A
join /dʒɔɪn/ 23D
journey /ˈdʒɜːni/ 9D
juice /dʒuːs/ 7A
July /dʒəˈlaɪ/ 14C
June /dʒuːn/ 14C
just (= only) /dʒəst, dʒʌst/ 17A
just a minute /ˈmɪnɪt/ 17B
just a moment /ˈməʊmənt/ 17B
key /kiː/ 17B
killed: get killed /kɪld/ 23A
kilo /ˈkiːləʊ/ 7B
kind /kaɪnd/ 11B
kind to /ˈkaɪnd tə/ 11B
kiss /kɪs/ 11D
kitchen /ˈkɪtʃɪn/ 5A
knife /naɪf/ (knives /naɪvz/) 22B
know about /ˈnəʊ əˈbaʊt/ 11C
know: Do you know? 7B
know: I know 7B
know: I don't know 1B
lager /ˈlɑːgə(r)/ 17A
lamp /læmp/ 7C
language /ˈlæŋgwɪdʒ/ 6D
large /lɑːdʒ/ 10B
last night /ˈlɑːst ˈnaɪt/ 11D
late /leɪt/ 11D
lazy /ˈleɪzi/ 22D
lead (verb) /liːd/ 18C
learn /lɜːn/ 18A
leave (= depart) /liːv/ 15D
left (= not right) /left/ 5C
leg /leg/ 9A
lend /lend/ 17B
Let's /lets/ 17C
Let's go 9D
letter (e.g. Dear Susan) /ˈletə(r)/ 9D
letter (ABCDE etc.) 2C
lie (verb) /laɪ/ 15A
life /laɪf/ (lives /laɪvz/) 11B
life: all my life 19D
light (e.g. light green) /laɪt/ 9B
light (noun) 7C
light: Have you got a light? 17B
like: (e.g. look like) /laɪk/ 9C
like (verb) 6A
like: I'd like 10C
like: I'd like to 10C
like: Would you like . . . ? 10B

listen to /ˈlɪsn tə/ 7A
listen to the radio /ˈreɪdɪəʊ/ 18D
literature /ˈlɪtrətʃə(r)/ 21D
litre /ˈliːtə(r)/ 7A
little: a little /ə ˈlɪtl/ 1D
little: a little more /mɔː(r)/ 17A
live /lɪv/ 5B
living room /ˈlɪvɪŋ ruːm/ 5A
long /lɒŋ/ 9A
long (= a long time) 15D
look /lʊk/ 9D
look (= appear) 14B
look at /ət/ 9D
look for /fə(r)/ 10B
look like /laɪk/ 9C
look out /aʊt/ 22C
look: Can I look round? /raʊnd/ 10C
lost: get lost /lɒst/ 23A
lot: a lot of /ə ˈlɒt əv/ 7D
lots of /ˈlɒts əv/ 9C
loud /laʊd/ 22D
love (verb) /lʌv/ 6A
love: I'd love to 15C
Love (ending letter) 15B
love: in love /ɪn ˈlʌv/ 19D
lover /ˈlʌvə(r)/ 23D
lunch /lʌntʃ/ 6C
make /meɪk/ 13A
make a decision /dɪˈsɪʒn/ 23C
make a mistake /mɪsˈteɪk/ 22B
man /mæn/ (men /men/) 2B
many /ˈmeni/ 7D
many: How many . . . ? 7D
many: too many 7D
March /mɑːtʃ/ 14C
married /ˈmærɪd/ 2C
married: get married 21A
match (e.g. football match) /mætʃ/ 15C
maths /mæθs/ 6D
matter: It doesn't matter /ˈmætə(r)/ 14D
matter: What's the matter? 22A
May /meɪ/ 14C
me /miː/ 1C
meal /miːl/ 21D
mean: What does . . . mean? /miːn/ 3D
meat /miːt/ 21D
medical student /ˈmedɪkl ˈstjuːdənt/ 2A
medicine /ˈmedsən/ 22A
medicine: take medicine 22A
meet /miːt/ 9D
metre /ˈmiːtə(r)/ 14A
milk /mɪlk/ 7A
million /ˈmɪljən/ 11A
mind (verb) /maɪnd/ 19A
mind: Do you mind if . . . ? 19A
mind: I don't mind 23A
minute /ˈmɪnɪt/ 15D
minute: just a minute 17B
minute: wait a minute 17C
Miss /mɪs/ 2D
mistake /mɪsˈteɪk/ 22B

mistress /ˈmɪstrɪs/ 23D
moment /ˈməʊmənt/ 3D
moment: for a moment 19A
moment: just a moment 17B
Monday /ˈmʌndi/ 6C
money /ˈmʌni/ 7A
month /mʌnθ/ 14A
more (e.g. more interesting than . . .) /mɔː(r)/ 13C
more (e.g. more like Mum) 9C
more: a little more 17A
more: no more 17A
morning /ˈmɔːnɪŋ/ 2B
morning: in the morning 6B
morning: this morning 11D
most /məʊst/ 11C
most (e.g. the most beautiful) 13C
mother /ˈmʌðə(r)/ 3C
mountain /ˈmaʊntɪn/ 15B
mouth /maʊθ/ 9A
move /muːv/ 21B
Mr /ˈmɪstə(r)/ 2B
Mrs /ˈmɪsɪz/ 2D
Ms /mɪz, məz/ 2D
much /mʌtʃ/ 7D
much: How much . . . ? 7D
much: How much is/are . . . ? 10C
much: not much 6A
much: too much 7D
much: very much 6A
mushroom /ˈmʌʃrʊm/ 17A
music /ˈmjuːzɪk/ 6D
my /maɪ/ 1A
myself /maɪˈself/ 19A
name /neɪm/ 1A
name: first name /fɜːst/ 1B
near /nɪə(r)/ 3A
nearest /ˈnɪərɪst/ 5D
nearly /ˈnɪəli/ 11B
need /niːd/ 17B
nervy /ˈnɜːvi/ 14B
never /ˈnevə(r)/ 6D
new /njuː/ 14C
news /njuːz/ 11A
news: bad news 23C
newspaper /ˈnjuːspeɪpə(r)/ 6D
next (adjective) /nekst/ 9D
next (adverb) 18B
next to /ˈnekst tə/ 5D
nice /naɪs/ 9C
night /naɪt/ 2B
night: last night /lɑːst/ 11D
nine /naɪn/ 2C
nineteen /naɪnˈtiːn/ 2C
nineteenth /ˈnaɪnˈtiːnθ/ 14C
ninetieth /ˈnaɪntɪəθ/ 14C
ninety /ˈnaɪnti/ 2D
ninth /naɪnθ/ 5B
no /nəʊ/ 1A
no more /mɔː(r)/ 17A
nobody /ˈnəʊbədi/ 6A
noise /nɔɪz/ 15A
noisy /ˈnɔɪzi/ 13D
north /nɔːθ/ 18B

nose /nəʊz/	9A	pants /pænts/	9B	purple /ˈpɜːpl/	9B
not /nɒt/	1A	paper /ˈpeɪpə(r)/	11C	push /pʊʃ/	23B
not at all (*answering* Thanks) /nɒt ət ˈɔːl/	5C	paper (= newspaper)	17C	put /pʊt/	21B
not at all (*e.g.* I don't like it at all)	6A	Pardon? /ˈpɑːdn/	3D	quarter: a quarter /ˈkwɔːtə(r)/	6B
		parent /ˈpeərənt/	3C	question /ˈkwestʃən/	3D
not at all (*with adjectives*)	10A	party /ˈpɑːti/	14D	quiet /kwaɪət/	13D
not bad /bæd/	2B	pass (*verb*) /pɑːs/	23D	quite /kwaɪt/	3B
not much /mʌtʃ/	6A	passport /ˈpɑːspɔːt/	11C	radio /ˈreɪdiəʊ/	18D
not too bad /nɒt tuː ˈbæd/	17A	past (*preposition*) /pɑːst/	6B	railway station /ˈreɪlweɪ/	5D
not very /ˈveri/	3B	patient /ˈpeɪʃənt/	14B	rain /reɪn/	7C
not well /wel/	2B	pay /peɪ/	18A	rare /reə(r)/	17A
nothing /ˈnʌθɪŋ/	10C	pay for /ˈpeɪ fə/	18A	rather: I'd rather you didn't /ˈrɑːðə/	19A
November /nəʊˈvembə(r)/	14C	pen /pen/	3A		
now /naʊ/	11C	pence /pens/	7B	read /riːd/	6D
number /ˈnʌmbə(r)/	2C	pencil /ˈpensl/	13D	really /ˈrɪəli/	10B
number: phone number /fəʊn/	5B	people /ˈpiːpl/	7C	reason /ˈriːzn/	21D
numbers one to three	1A	perfume /ˈpɜːfjuːm/	7D	red /red/	9B
numbers four to six	1B	perhaps /pəˈhæps/	15C	refuse /rɪˈfjuːz/	23D
numbers seven to twenty	2C	person /ˈpɜːsn/	7D	remember /rɪˈmembə(r)/	9B
numbers twenty-one to a hundred	2D	pessimistic /pesɪˈmɪstɪk/	14B	republic /rɪˈpʌblɪk/	18A
		phone (*verb*) /fəʊn/	14D	rest (*noun*) /rest/	21A
numbers first to ninth	5B	phone box /ˈfəʊn bɒks/	5C	rest (*verb*)	22B
numbers tenth to hundredth	14C	phone number /ˈnʌmbə(r)/	5B	restaurant /ˈrestərɒnt/	5D
o'clock /əˈklɒk/	6B	photographer /fəˈtɒɡrəfə(r)/	2A	revolution /revəˈluːʃn/	23D
occasionally /əˈkeɪʒənli/	19B	piano /piˈænəʊ/	13A	rich /rɪtʃ/	11B
October /ɒkˈtəʊbə(r)/	14C	picture /ˈpɪktʃə(r)/	22B	right (= not left) /raɪt/	5C
of /əv, ɒv/	7A	piece /piːs/	18B	right (= not wrong)	22B
of course /əv ˈkɔːs/	3D	pink /pɪŋk/	9B	right across /əˈkrɒs/	21A
often /ˈɒfn/	6D	place /pleɪs/	13C	right: all right 17A, 17C, 23A	
often: How often . . . ?	19B	plane /pleɪn/	17D	right: That's right	1B
Oh /əʊ/	1C	play (*verb*) /pleɪ/	6D	road /rəʊd/	5B
Oh dear /ˈəʊ ˈdɪə(r)/	7B	please /pliːz/	3D	rock (music) /rɒk/	6D
OK /ˈəʊ ˈkeɪ/	2D	Please do	19A	room /ruːm/	5A
old /əʊld/	3B	plenty of /ˈplenti əv/	18A	round (*preposition*) /raʊnd/	18A
old: How old . . . ?	2D	p.m. /ˈpiː ˈem/	9D	round the world /wɜːld/	18A
on /ɒn/	3A	pocket /ˈpɒkɪt/	11C	round: Can I look round?	10C
on holiday /ˈhɒlədi/	6D	police /pəˈliːs/	5C	run /rʌn/	13A
on the left /left/	5C	police station /ˈsteɪʃn/	5C	Russia(n) /ˈrʌʃə(n)/	1D
on the right /raɪt/	5C	policeman /pəˈliːsmən/	18D	salad /ˈsæləd/	17A
once /wʌns/	19B	politician /pɒləˈtɪʃn/	13C	same: the same /ðə ˈseɪm/	11A
once a week *etc.*	19B	politics /ˈpɒlətɪks/	6D	Saturday /ˈsætədi/	6C
one (*number*) /wʌn/	1A	pool: swimming pool /ˈswɪmɪŋ puːl/	5D	say /seɪ/	11D
one: a . . . one /ə . . . wʌn/	10B			say: How do you say . . . ?	9B
only /ˈəʊnli/	6A	poor /pɔː(r)/	11B	school /skuːl/	6B
open (*verb*) /ˈəʊpn/	19A	possibly: Could you possibly . . . ? /ˈpɒsəbli/	17B	science fiction /ˈsaɪəns ˈfɪkʃən/	6D
opposite /ˈɒpəzɪt/	5D			Scotland /ˈskɒtlənd/	1D
optimistic /ɒptɪˈmɪstɪk/	14B	postcard /ˈpəʊstkɑːd/	15B	Scottish /ˈskɒtɪʃ/	1D
or /ɔː(r)/	2B	potato /pəˈteɪtəʊ/	7A	sea /siː/	15B
orange (*colour*) /ˈɒrɪndʒ/	9B	pound (*money*) /paʊnd/	7B	seat /siːt/	19A
orange (*fruit*)	7A	pound (*weight*)	14A	second /ˈsekənd/	5B
other /ˈʌðə(r)/	10B	president /ˈprezɪdənt/	13D	see /siː/	13A
other: each other	19D	press (*verb*) /pres/	23B	See you	1C
our /aʊə(r)/	3C	pretty /ˈprɪti/	3B	self-confident /selfˈkɒnfɪdənt/	14B
out /aʊt/	6B	price /praɪs/	7B	sell /sel/	23B
out of	21B	prison /ˈprɪzn/	23D	send /send/	15B
outside /aʊtˈsaɪd/	7C	probably /ˈprɒbəbli/	15A	sensitive /ˈsensətɪv/	14B
over (= more than) /ˈəʊvə(r)/	14A	problem /ˈprɒbləm/	22A	separated /ˈsepəreɪtɪd/	2D
over (*place*)	21B	pronounce: How do you pronounce . . . ? /prəˈnaʊns/	9B	September /sepˈtembə(r)/	14C
over here /ˈəʊvə ˈhɪə/	17A			service: Is service included? /ɪz ˈsɜːvɪs ɪŋˈkluːdɪd/	17A
over there /ˈəʊvə ˈðeə(r)/	5C				
p (= pence) /piː/	7B	pub /pʌb/	13D	seven /ˈsevən/	2C
pack /pæk/	21D	public /ˈpʌblɪk/	5D	seventeen /ˈsevənˈtiːn/	2C
		pull /pʊl/	23B	seventeenth /ˈsevənˈtiːnθ/	14C

129

tomorrow: the day after
    tomorrow 14C
tonight /tə'naɪt/ 19B
too /tu:/ 3D
too many 7D
too much 7D
toothache /'tu:θeɪk/ 22A
toothpaste /'tu:θpeɪst/ 7D
tough /tʌf/ 17A
town /taʊn/ 15B
train /treɪn/ 9D
travel (verb) /'trævl/ 6D
travel agent /'trævl 'eɪdʒənt/ 21D
trouble (noun) /'trʌbl/ 23C
trouble: Sorry to trouble you
    /'sɒri/ 17B
trousers /'traʊzəz/ 9B
true /tru:/ 18D
truth /tru:θ/ 23C
try (= attempt) /traɪ/ 7A
try (= try on) 10B
try on /'traɪ 'ɒn/ 10B
Tuesday /'tju:zdi/ 6C
turn /tɜ:n/ 23B
TV /'ti:'vi:/ 5A
twelfth /twelfθ/ 14C
twelve /twelv/ 2C
twentieth /'twentɪəθ/ 14C
twenty /'twenti/ 2C
twice /twaɪs/ 19B
two /tu:/ 1A
type /taɪp/ 13A
typewriter /'taɪpraɪtə(r)/ 13D
typist /'taɪpɪst/ 13D
umbrella /ʌm'brelə/ 17B
uncle /'ʌŋkl/ 9C
under (= less than)
    /'ʌndə(r)/ 14A
under (position) 3A
understand: I don't understand
    /ʌndə'stænd/ 7C
unhappy /ʌn'hæpi/ 10A
United States, the
    /ðə ju'naɪtɪd 'steɪts/ 1D
university /ju:nə'vɜ:səti/ 18A
unkind /ʌn'kaɪnd/ 23D
until /ən'tɪl/ 6C
upstairs /'ʌp'steəz/ 5C
us /əs, ʌs/ 10C
use /ju:z/ 21A
USSR /ju: es es 'ɑ:(r)/ 1D
usual /'ju:ʒʊəl/ 17D
usually /'ju:ʒəli/ 6D
vegetable /'vedʒtəbl/ 17A
very /'veri/ 2B
very much 6A
very: not very 3B

video /'vɪdi:əʊ/ 21A
village /'vɪlɪdʒ/ 11B
violin /vaɪə'lɪn/ 13A
visa /'vi:zə/ 21D
wait /weɪt/ 17C
wait a minute /'mɪnɪt/ 17C
wake up /'weɪk 'ʌp/ 11D
walk (noun) /wɔ:k/ 18D
walk (verb) 18D
walk: go for a walk 19B
wall /wɔ:l/ 5A
want /wɒnt/ 11D
wardrobe /'wɔ:drəʊb/ 5A
warm /wɔ:m/ 13D
was /wəz, wɒz/ 7B
wasn't /'wɒznt/ 11B
was born /wəz 'bɔ:n/ 11B
wash /wɒʃ/ 18D
watch (noun) /wɒtʃ/ 10C
watch (verb) 6D
watch TV /'ti:'vi:/ 18D
water /'wɔ:tə(r)/ 7A
we /wi:/ 3B
we're /wɪə(r)/ 3B
we've /wi:v/ 3D
wear /weə(r)/ 9B
weather /'weðə(r)/ 15B
Wednesday /'wenzdi/ 6C
week /wi:k/ 14C
weekend /'wi:k'end/ 6C
weigh /weɪ/ 14A
weight /weɪt/ 14A
welcome: You're welcome
    /'welkəm/ 14D
well (adjective) /wel/ 2B
well (adverb) 10B
well (agreement) 17C
were /wə, wɜ:/ 7B
weren't /wɜ:nt/ 11B
west /west/ 18B
what /wɒt/ 1A
What a nice . . . ! /naɪs/ 10C
What about . . . ? /ə'baʊt/ 15C
What are these? 9A
What are these called? /kɔ:ld/ 9B
What colour is/are . . . ? /'kʌlər/ 9C
What do you do?
    /'wɒt də ju 'du:/ 2A
What does . . . mean? /mɪ:n/ 3D
What sort of . . . ? /sɔ:t/ 6D
What's the matter? /'mætə/ 22A
What's this? 9A
What's this called? /kɔ:ld/ 9B
What time is it? /taɪm/ 6B
when (conjunction) /wən/ 10A
when (question) 18C

where (question) /weə(r)/ 1D
where (relative) 18B
Where are you from? 1D
which /wɪtʃ/ 10D
while /waɪl/ 22B
white /waɪt/ 9B
who (question) /hu:/ 3C
who (relative) 18A
why /waɪ/ 11D
Why don't we . . . ? 17C
Why not? 17C
widow /'wɪdəʊ/ 2D
widower /'wɪdəʊə(r)/ 2D
wife /waɪf/ (wives /waɪvz/) 3C
will /wɪl/ 23A
win /wɪn/ 21C
window /'wɪndəʊ/ 5A
wine /waɪn/ 7D
winter /'wɪntə(r)/ 21C
with (= accompanying) /wɪð/ 17C
with (= having) 9D
without /wɪð'aʊt/ 13A
woman /'wʊmən/
    (women /'wɪmɪn/) 2B
wonderful /'wʌndəfl/ 19D
won't /wəʊnt/ 23A
word /wɜ:d/ 7D
work (noun) /wɜ:k/ 6B
work (verb) 5B
world /wɜ:ld/ 13C
world: round the world /raʊnd/ 18A
worry /'wʌri/ 22C
worse (adjective) /wɜ:s/ 13C
worst (adjective) /wɜ:st/ 13C
would /wəd, wʊd/ 10B
Would you like . . . ?
    /'wʊd ju 'laɪk/ 10B
write /raɪt/ 13A
writer /'raɪtə(r)/ 13C
wrong /rɒŋ/ 22B
yard /jɑ:d/ 5D
year /jɪə(r)/ 11C
yellow /'jeləʊ/ 9B
yes /jes/ 1A
yesterday /'jestədi/ 7B
yesterday: the day before
    yesterday 14C
you /ju:/ 1C
you're /jɔ:(r)/ 3D
You're welcome /'welkəm/ 14D
you've /ju:v/ 3D
young /jʌŋ/ 3B
your /jɔ:(r)/ 1A
Yours (ending letter) /jɔ:z/ 17D
Yours sincerely
    /'jɔ:z sɪn'sɪəli/ 9D

Additional material

Lesson 1C, Exercise 6

Mickey Mouse	Minnie Mouse
James Bond	Greta Garbo
William Shakespeare	Marlene Dietrich
Christopher Columbus	Marie Curie
Marco Polo	Maria Callas
Karl Marx	Rosa Luxembourg
Charles de Gaulle	Eleanor Roosevelt
Clark Kent	Lois Lane
Jesse James	Annie Oakley
Wolfgang Mozart	Marilyn Monroe

Lesson 3A, Exercise 3

Lesson 3A, Exercise 4, Student A

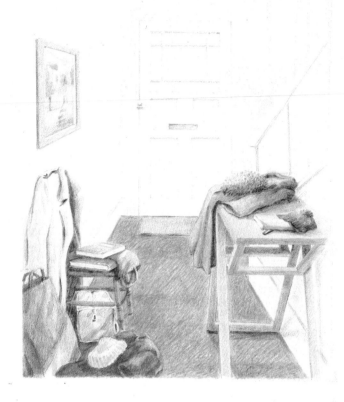

Lesson 4C, Exercise 1

A: Hello, Dan. How are you?
D: Oh, hi, Andrew. Not bad, not bad.
A: And how's your mother?
D: Oh, very well now, thanks. And you, Andrew? How are you?
A: Fine, thanks. Yes, very fine: I've got a new girlfriend.
D: Have you? I've got a new girlfriend, too.
A: Oh? Is she pretty?
D: Pretty, *and* intelligent.
A: What does she do?
D: She's a student, a business student.
A: Yeah? My girlfriend's a business student, too. She's very pretty: tall, and fair.
D: Er, is she English?
A: English? Oh, no, she's Swedish, in fact.
D: Swedish? From Stockholm?
A: No, from Malmö.
D: Oh. And her name is Kirsten, isn't it?
A: Well, yes, it is. Do you mean . . . ?
D: Yeah, I think Kirsten has got two new boyfriends.

Lesson 10C, Exercise 1

Lesson 11D, Exercise 4, Student A

A: ....

B: I'm really sorry. My car broke down and I couldn't get a taxi, and then I missed the train.

A: ....

B: I did, but your secretary didn't answer.

A: ....

B: The tennis? You know I couldn't get tickets.

A: ....

B: That's funny. People often tell me they know somebody who looks like me. You know, only yesterday . . .

Lesson 12B, Exercise 2

On Saturday I got up at seven and had a big breakfast. I read the newspaper until a quarter past eight, and then went shopping. In front of Anderson's, I met my sister Ruth, and she told me my mother was ill. I went to my mother's house, but she wasn't at home. When I arrived home, my sister phoned and said that my mother was in hospital. I went to the hospital to see her, and the doctor said that she was OK.

I had lunch with my friend Ann, and watched television until three. Then we played tennis and went to the swimming pool. In the evening we went to the cinema with friends.

Lesson 21B, Exercise 1, Student A

The study is going to be on the ground floor.
The living room is going to be next to the dining room.
The parents' bedroom is going to be over the living room.
The kitchen is going to be under the bathroom.

Ask your partner these questions:
'Where is Alice's bedroom going to be?'
'Where is Mary's bedroom going to be?'
'Where is the playroom going to be?'
'Where is the dining room going to be?'

Lesson 3A, Exercise 4, Student B

Lesson 11D, Exercise 4, Student B

A: Robin! It's two o'clock! Why didn't you come to work this morning?

B: ....

A: Well, why didn't you phone?

B: ....

A: You weren't watching the tennis, were you?

B: ....

A: Oh? Well, I saw the news on television at lunch, and there was a person there who looked a lot like you.

B: ....

Lesson 21B, Exercise 1, Student B

Alice's bedroom is going to be opposite the parents' bedroom.
Mary's bedroom is going to be over the kitchen.
The playroom is going to be on the first floor.
The dining room is going to be opposite the kitchen.

Ask your partner these questions:
'Where is the study going to be?'
'Where is the living room going to be?'
'Where is the parents' bedroom going to be?'
'Where is the kitchen going to be?'

Appendix: Teaching the articles

Introduction

If your students speak a Western European language such as German, Norwegian, Spanish or Greek, they will probably not have too much trouble with the English article system. These languages also contain definite and indefinite articles which (with a few exceptions) are used in similar ways to their English equivalents *a/an* and *the*.

In most other languages, however, there is nothing which corresponds at all closely to the English articles. Speakers of Russian, Japanese, Turkish or Chinese, for example, usually find it difficult to use articles correctly. They will tend to miss them out, to put them in where they are not required, or to confuse one article with another.

Unfortunately, it is not at all easy to teach correct article usage, especially to elementary students. This is for two reasons. First of all, the concepts which the articles express are relatively abstract: students will find them difficult to grasp and will not see why they have to be put into words. And secondly, a good deal of article usage is idiomatic – the rules have large numbers of exceptions, and these take a long time to get used to.

It is therefore important not to be perfectionist about articles. (Many foreigners communicate quite successfully in English without using them at all.) Although correctness is obviously desirable, students are certain to make mistakes, and these should be regarded with reasonable tolerance. The majority of article mistakes are unlikely to affect comprehensibility seriously.

However, you will probably want to do some additional work on this topic if your students are finding it difficult. The purpose of this appendix is to provide simple explanations, and a few basic supplementary exercises which can be copied and used in class. If possible, the explanations should be given to the students in their mother tongue. It will probably be necessary to make up additional exercises of your own to provide extra practice.

The explanations and exercises are arranged in order of difficulty, and follow roughly the order in which the points occur during the course. It is probably best to space them out over a long period.

A The use of *a/an*

Explanation

A noun such as *house, town, doctor, girl, name* symbolises a whole class of things. When we want to talk about just one member of this class, we generally put *a/an* in front of the noun. (The original meaning of *a/an* was 'one'.)

*She lives in **a** nice big house.*
***A** girl telephoned this morning.*
*There's **a** big fridge in our kitchen.*

A/an is common in definitions and descriptions (when we say what class somebody or something belongs to).

*He's **a** doctor.*
*She's **a** beautiful woman.*

1 Say whether each of these towns is on a river. Examples:

'Stoke is on a river.'
'Sheffield is not on a river.'

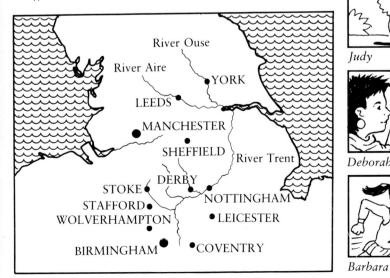

2 Make sentences about the people. Use the words in the box. Example:

*Hamida is **a** doctor.*

doctor	photographer	artist	pilot
driver	housewife	teacher	dancer
athlete	footballer	secretary	waiter

Hamida

Maurice

Paul

Judy

Desmond

Pat

Deborah

Ranjit

Mary

Barbara

Colin

Andrew

135

B When *a/an* is not used

Explanation
Students may need to learn that *a/an* is not used with plural nouns. (It means 'one'.)
   My parents are doctors. (Not * . . . *a doctors*.)
You may also have to point out that *a/an* cannot be used with adjectives when these are not followed by nouns. Compare:
   *She's **a** pretty girl.   She's pretty.*
      (Not *She's a pretty*.)

3 Put in *a/an* or nothing.

1. She's ......a...... pretty girl.
2. They are ......—...... pretty girls.
3. They are ......—...... pretty.
4. My father is .... doctor.
5. My parents are .... doctors.
6. There's .... post office near our house.
7. There are .... two cars in the garage.
8. You're .... very nice.
9. Wantage is .... small town near Oxford.
10. My house is .... very small.
11. 'My name is Schmidt.' 'That's .... German name, isn't it?'
12. Anna and Carola are .... housewives.
13. Their husbands work in .... offices.

C The use of *the*

Explanation
The meaning of *the* is something like 'that/those particular one(s) that you know about'. (*The* was originally the same word as *that*.) It is used with both singular and plural nouns.
Common uses of *the* are:
1. To refer to people and things that have already been mentioned.
   *She's got two children: a boy and a girl. **The** boy's fourteen and **the** girl's eight.*
2. To refer to people and things as we are identifying them.
   *Who's **the** girl in **the** car over there with John?*
3. To refer to people and things that are unique in the situation (so that the hearer can be in no doubt as to which one is meant).
   *Could you close **the** door?*
   *'Where's Ann?' 'In **the** kitchen.'*

4 Put in expressions from the box.

the bathroom	the first floor	the man
the newspaper	the potatoes	the red dress
the woman	the women	the window

1. 'Is that your wife?' 'No, my wife's .... in ....'
2. 'Where's ....?' 'On ....'
3. I work with a man and two women. .... is quite nice, but .... are not very friendly.
4. Could you shut ...., please?
5. What's in ....?
6. Could you pass ...., please?

D When *the* is not used (1)

Explanation
Students must learn that *the* is not used together with other 'determiners' (demonstratives and possessives; *some, any, which* and some other words).
   This is my uncle. (Not * . . . *the my uncle*.)
   That's John's car. (Not * . . . *the John's car*.)
   I like this house. (Not * . . . *the this house*.)
They must also realise that *the* is not generally used with proper names – the names of people and places. (There are some exceptions.)
   Mary lives in Birmingham. (Not *The Mary . . .*)
   England is a part of Britain.
      (Not *The England . . .*)

5 Put in *the* or nothing.

1. ......—...... Mary is ......—...... Peter's sister.
2. Could you shut ....the..... door?
3. 'Which is .... your car?' '............... blue one in front of .... house.'
4. Can you show me .... that book, please?
5. .... my aunt Susan lives in .... Canada.
6. 'Who is .... that woman?' 'It's .... Harry's mother.'
7. .... my husband is .... man in .... blue coat.

E The difference between *a/an* and *the*

Explanation
Some students confuse the two articles, and it may be useful to focus on the difference.
Very simply:
– *a/an* just means 'one of a class'.
– *the* refers to (a) particular identified ('labelled') member(s) of a class: it means 'that one / those ones that we know about'.
Compare *a* and *the* in this sentence:
   *I live in **a** small flat on **the** third floor of **an** old house.*
The speaker says *a small flat*, because this flat is not completely identified – there may be two or three on the third floor. *The* is used in *the third floor*, because the floor is completely identified – there is only one third floor in a house, and so we know exactly which floor is meant. The speaker says *an old house*, because he is not telling us (and we do not already know) exactly which house – it could be one of millions.

6 Put in *a/an* or *the*.

1. My brother is .... engineer.
2. I live in .... small flat.
3. Glasgow is .... industrial town in Scotland.
4. Could you open .... door, please?
5. What's .... name of .... woman in .... red dress?
6. I study English in .... language school.
7. .... school where I study is called 'The Universal Oxford and Cambridge Language Academy'.
8. I'd like .... drink of water, please.
9. There's some ice in .... fridge.

F When *the* is not used (2)

Explanation

In English, *the* is not normally used with nouns which have a 'general' sense. If we want to talk about books, life, people or anything else in general, we normally say *books*, *life* or *people*, not *the books* etc. (In this respect, English is different from most Western European languages, which tend to use the definite article in generalisations.) Compare:

Life is hard. (life in general)
The life of Beethoven . . . (a particular life)

Cheese is getting very expensive.
'*Where's* **the cheese**?' '*I ate it.*'

7 Put in *the* or nothing.

1. .... books are expensive.
2. Who are .... people you were talking to?
3. I forgot to buy .... eggs that you asked for.
4. I don't like .... whisky.
5. .... water turns into .... ice at 0°C.
6. Could you take .... books off the table, please?
7. .... light travels at 300,000km a second.
8. Could you put .... light on?

G Countable and uncountable nouns

Explanation

When students are familiar with the difference between countable and uncountable nouns, they are ready to learn two more rules about articles.
1. *A/an* cannot normally be used with an uncountable noun.
2. A singular countable noun must normally have an article (or other 'determiner') with it. (There are some common exceptions in prepositional phrases like *in bed*, *on holiday*.)

8 Can you put *a/an* with these nouns or not?

book **Yes**........ water **No**......... table ....
cheese .... wool .... work ....
address .... electricity ....

9 Can you use these nouns without an article?

book **No**........ men **Yes**......... child ....
children .... petrol .... car ....
soap .... pen .... hair ....

Answers to Appendix Exercises

1

York Leeds Derby Nottingham	is on a river.

Manchester Stafford Leicester Wolverhampton Birmingham Coventry	is not on a river.

2
Desmond is a photographer.	Ranjit is a driver.
Paul is a waiter.	Mary is a secretary.
Judy is a dancer.	Barbara is an athlete.
Maurice is a teacher.	Colin is a footballer.
Pat is a housewife.	Andrew is a pilot.
Deborah is an artist.	

3
4. My father is *a* doctor.
5. My parents are doctors.
6. There's *a* post office near our house.
7. There are two cars in the garage.
8. You're very nice.
9. Wantage is *a* small town near Oxford.
10. My house is very small.
11. 'My name is Schmidt.' 'That's *a* German name, isn't it?'
12. Anna and Carola are housewives.
13. Their husbands work in offices.

4
1. 'Is that your wife?' 'No, my wife's *the woman* in *the* red dress.'
2. 'Where's *the bathroom*?' 'On *the first floor*.'
3. I work with a man and two women. *The man* is quite nice, but *the women* are not very friendly.
4. Could you shut *the window*, please?
5. What's in *the newspaper*?
6. Could you pass *the potatoes*, please?

5
3. 'Which is your car?' '*The* blue one in front of *the* house.'
4. Can you show me that book, please?
5. My aunt Susan lives in Canada.
6. 'Who is that woman?' 'It's Harry's mother.'
7. My husband is *the* man in *the* blue coat.

6
1. My brother is *an* engineer.
2. I live in *a* small flat.
3. Glasgow is *an* industrial town in Scotland.
4. Could you open *the* door, please?
5. What's *the* name of *the* woman in *the* red dress?
6. I study English in *a* language school.
7. *The* school where I study is called 'The Universal Oxford and Cambridge Language Academy'.
8. I'd like *a* drink of water, please.
9. There's some ice in *the* fridge.

7
1. Books are expensive.
2. Who are *the* people you were talking to?
3. I forgot to buy *the* eggs that you asked for.
4. I don't like whisky.
5. Water turns into ice at 0°C.
6. Could you take *the* books off the table, please?
7. Light travels at 300,000km a second.
8. Could you put *the* light on?

8
table – *Yes*   cheese – *No*   wool – *No*   work – *No*
address – *Yes*   electricity – *No*

9
child – *No*   children – *Yes*   petrol – *Yes*   car – *No*
soap – *Yes*   pen – *No*   hair – *Yes*

Additional material for Lesson 4C, Exercise 4

WHO'S WHO?

Family tree (for teacher's reference)

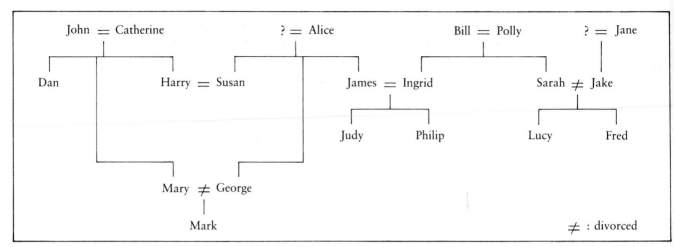

Role descriptions

1 NAME: James
  AGE: 34
  Tall, dark
  JOB: Doctor
  MOTHER: Alice (secretary; fair, not very tall)
  BROTHER: George (engineer)
  SISTER: Susan (doctor)
  You have got two children.
  Your wife's a housewife.
  Your wife's mother is a teacher.
  Find your wife.

2 NAME: Ingrid
  AGE: 33
  Quite tall, dark
  JOB: Housewife
  PARENTS: Bill (electrician)
           Polly (teacher)
  Your son is at school.
  Your husband is a doctor.
  Your daughter's age + 20 = your husband's age.
  Your daughter is fair, and quite tall. Find her.

3 NAME: Judy
  AGE: 14
  Fair, quite tall
  JOB: At school
  Your father's mother is a secretary.
  She is fair, and not very tall.
  Your mother is a housewife.
  Find your father.

4 NAME: Philip
  AGE: 15
  Tall, fair
  JOB: At school
  Your mother's father is an electrician.
  Your father's mother is a secretary.
  Find your sister.

5 NAME: Alice
  AGE: 64
  Fair, not very tall
  JOB: Secretary
  You've got three children.
  Two are doctors, and one is an engineer.
  The engineer is 38.
  One doctor is 34: what's his name?

6 NAME: George
  AGE: 38
  MARITAL STATUS: Divorced
  Quite tall, fair
  JOB: Engineer
  CHILD: Mark
  Your ex-wife is fair, and not very tall.
  Your brother's wife is 33.
  What's your mother's job?

7 NAME: Susan
  AGE: 39
  MARITAL STATUS: Married
  Not very tall, fair
  JOB: Doctor
  MOTHER: Alice
  You've got no children.
  One brother is divorced.
  One brother is married.
  What's your married brother's name?

8 NAME: Sarah
  AGE: 26
  MARITAL STATUS: Divorced
  Tall, dark
  JOB: Actress
  CHILDREN: Lucy (3), Fred (4)
  Your mother is a teacher.
  Your sister's son is fifteen.
  Find your sister.

9 NAME: Polly
AGE: 54
Quite tall, dark
JOB: Teacher
Your husband is a tall, dark electrician.
You've got two daughters; they're dark.
One daughter is 26; one daughter is 33.
How old are your daughters' children?

10 NAME: Bill
AGE: 55
Tall, dark
JOB: Electrician
Your wife is a teacher.
One daughter is an actress.
One daughter is a housewife.
How old is your wife?

11 NAME: Mark
AGE: 17
Fair, quite tall
JOB: At school
Your parents are divorced.
Your father is an engineer.
Your father's sister has got no children.
What is your father's sister's name?

12 NAME: Mary
AGE: 37
Fair, not very tall
JOB: Teacher
Your son is fair and quite tall.
Your ex-husband is an engineer.
How old is your son?

13 NAME: Harry
AGE: 35
Fair, not very tall
JOB: Between jobs
You've got no children.
Your wife is a doctor.
How old are your wife's brothers?

14 NAME: Dan
AGE: 32
MARITAL STATUS: Single
Fair, not very tall
JOB: Artist
Your sister is a teacher.
Your brother's wife is a doctor.
Find your brother.

15 NAME: Catherine
AGE: 57
Dark, not very tall
JOB: Housewife
You've got three children.
They're fair and not very tall.
One son is an artist.
One son is between jobs.
What's your daughter's job?

16 NAME: John
AGE: 59
Fair, not very tall
JOB: Electrician
You've got three children.
One son is an artist.
One son is between jobs.
Your daughter is a teacher.
Is your wife dark or fair?

17 NAME: Lucy
AGE: 3
Dark, not very tall
Your brother is 4.
He is dark and not very tall.
Your mother is an actress.
Find your mother's father.

18 NAME: Jake
AGE: 34
MARITAL STATUS: Divorced
Dark, tall
JOB: Artist
You've got a daughter; she's 3.
What is your ex-wife's name?

19 NAME: Fred
AGE: 4
Dark, not very tall
Your mother is an actress.
Your father is an artist.
Find your sister.

20 NAME: Jane
AGE: 59
Fair, quite tall
JOB: Secretary
Your son's children are 3 and 4.
Find your son's ex-wife.

Answers

1. (James) Ingrid is your wife.
2. (Ingrid) Judy is your daughter.
3. (Judy) James is your father.
4. (Philip) Judy is your sister.
5. (Alice) His name is James.
6. (George) Your mother is a secretary.
7. (Susan) Your married brother is James.
8. (Sarah) Ingrid is your sister.
9. (Polly) Your daughters are Ingrid and Sarah.
   Their children are 14 (Judy), 15 (Philip), 3
   (Lucy) and 4 (Fred).
10. (Bill) Your wife (Polly) is 54.
11. (Mark) Susan is your father's sister. (George is
    your father.)
12. (Mary) Your son (Mark) is 17.
13. (Harry) Your wife's brothers are 34 (James) and
    38 (George). (Susan is your wife.)
14. (Dan) Harry is your brother.
15. (Catherine) Your daughter (Mary) is a teacher.
16. (John) Your wife (Catherine) is dark.
17. (Lucy) Bill is your mother's father. (Sarah is your
    mother.)
18. (Jake) Sarah is your ex-wife.
19. (Fred) Lucy is your sister.
20. (Jane) Sarah is your son's ex-wife. (Jake is your
    son.)

Tapescripts

Lesson 4C, Exercise 1

A: Hello, Dan. How are you?
D: Oh, hi, Andrew. Not bad, not bad.
A: And how's your mother?
D: Oh, very well now, thanks. And you, Andrew? How are you?
A: Fine, thanks. Yes, very fine: I've got a new girlfriend.
D: Have you? I've got a new girlfriend, too.
A: Oh? Is she pretty?
D: Pretty, *and* intelligent.
A: What does she do?
D: She's a student, a business student.
A: Yeah? My girlfriend's a business student, too. She's very pretty: tall, and fair.
D: Er, is she English?
A: English? Oh, no, she's Swedish, in fact.
D: Swedish? From Stockholm?
A: No, from Malmö.
D: Oh. And her name is Kirsten, isn't it?
A: Well, yes, it is. Do you mean . . . ?
D: Yeah, I think Kirsten has got two new boyfriends.

Lesson 5B, Exercise 3

LESLIE: Excuse me, John. What's your address?
JOHN: A hundred and sixteen Market Street.
LESLIE: Thanks. And your phone number?
JOHN: What?
LESLIE: Your phone number.
JOHN: Oh, er, 314 6829.

OFFICER: Name, please.
ANN: ⎱ Ann Webber.
ROBERT: ⎰ Robert Webber.
OFFICER: And where do you live, Mr and Mrs Webber?
ANN: At number 60 Hamilton Road, Gloucester.
OFFICER: I see. And are you on the phone?
ROBERT: Yes, we are.
OFFICER: Could you tell me your number?
ANN: Our number? Yes, it's Gloucester 41785.

FLO: Hello, Alice. How are you?
ALICE: Not too bad, thanks. And you?
FLO: Oh, OK. Mustn't grumble. How's your mother?
ALICE: She's all right, considering. Yes, very well, really.
FLO: She lives in Oxford now, doesn't she?
ALICE: No, in Birmingham.

(*Doorbell. Door opens.*)
PETER: Excuse me.
SALLY: Yes?
PETER: My name's Peter Matthews. I live on the fourth floor. My telephone isn't working, and I was wondering if I could use yours.
SALLY: Yes, of course. Come in. The phone's over there, in the living room.
PETER: Thanks.

CHAIRMAN: Good morning, everybody. I'd like to introduce Mr Steven Billows, from New York. Mr Billows is going to talk to us about computer software delivery date problems . . .

MRS SIMON: Hello, Bedford 41632 . . . Yes . . . Yes, Mrs Simon speaking . . . Yes . . . No . . . No, my address is 16 Norris Road. N, O, double R, I, S, . . . Norris *Road*, not Norris *Street* . . . Yes, that's right. 16 Norris Road.

Lesson 7A, Exercise 3

1. Well, I did nought in a litre of water; 80 in 500 grams of ice cream; 50 in an orange; 115 in half a litre of milk; 320 in 100ml of coffee; 40 in a potato; . . .
2. A litre of water, nil; 500g of ice cream, eight hundred and fifty; an orange, 40; half a litre of milk, 90; 100ml of coffee with a teaspoon of sugar, 80; a potato, 175; . . .
3. A litre of water hasn't any; 500 grams of ice cream, 893, I think; 40 in an orange; 320 in half a litre of milk, I'm fairly sure of that one; 50 in 100mls of coffee with a teaspoonful of sugar; 175 in a potato – that's a guess, I suppose it depends how big the potato is; . . .
4. Well, er, I don't think there's anything in water at all; so there's zero calories in a litre of water; er, lots of fat in ice cream, so I think 893 calories in 500 grams; er, 50 in an orange; 320 in half a litre of milk, because of all the cream; erm, 80 er, in the coffee with the sugar; er, 40 in a potato . . .

Lesson 9C, Exercise 3

STEVE: 'She's about 5ft 8, about 9 stone, fair hair and a fairly thin face, slender figure, a slightly turned-up nose and a little double chin. And that's about it. And that's my wife. I don't know the colour of her eyes.'

LORNA: 'I'm going to describe my mum. She's 5ft 5, long wavy dark brown hair, dark brown eyes, fairly pretty – wearing well, I think – fairly slim, fairly pale complexion. That's about it.'

RUTH: 'I'm going to describe my best friend Dan, whom I grew up with. He's about 5ft 11, 5-10, 5-11, he's, um, dark brown hair, blue eyes I think, yeah, they are blue eyes. He's, um, quite slender build, nice legs (*laughter*), very nice face, lovely face, very nice face, in fact he's pretty good-looking, and I'm going to marry him. No –' 'Does he know?' 'No, he doesn't know.'

KATY: 'OK. My son is about 105cm tall. He's got fair hair, blue eyes, is fairly slim. I think he's very good-looking.'

SUE: 'My husband has fair hair going white, he's got lots of white hairs, greying rapidly; a beard and moustache – full beard and moustache – his eyes are blue, his height is around about 5-8, I think, 5-8, 5-9, and he's slightly overweight, and he's got a very round face. That's about it.'

Lesson 11A, Exercise 1

When I was younger, I hated school. I never studied, except just before exams; in fact, I stopped studying altogether when I was fourteen. I changed schools three times between the ages of eleven and sixteen. I hated school and the teachers, and I think they hated me. My parents were OK, though. At home, I listened to rock music, and watched science fiction and cartoons on TV. In the evenings and at weekends, I played my guitar, or I played snooker with friends. I started a rock group when I was sixteen, but that didn't last: I was in four different groups in the next four years.

I'm a successful rock star now, and I love my work; I get money for doing what I love. This year I earned £1,000,000. But I'm sorry I stopped studying at school.

Lesson 11B, Exercise 2

ADRIAN WEBBER
My name is Adrian Webber. My age is 42 years, and I was born in Delhi, India. This was due to the fact that my father had spent most of his adult life in India in the Indian police up to that time. I have a sister who's eight years older than myself. She was also born in India. And my childhood was very varied and quite happy as I remember.

LORNA HIGGS
My name's Lorna Higgs. I'm 19 years old, was born in Oxford and (have) lived here all my life. As far as childhood goes it's been quite mixed really. As far as family goes I've two brothers both younger than me. One's left school and has got a job, one of the lucky ones. The other one's still attending school.

SUE WARD
My name is Sue Ward. I was born in Tadcaster in Yorkshire. My father was in the Air Force and when I was seven months old we moved to Hong Kong and spent three years in the Far East, Hong Kong and Singapore. After that we moved every three years, back to England and around England, various places. When I was thirteen my parents went to Africa and I had to go to boarding school. My family consisted of three brothers and one sister, and I had a very happy childhood.

Lesson 17A, Exercise 1

'Have you got a table for two?'
'Yes, sir. Over here, by the window.'

* * *

'I'll start with soup, please, and then I'll have roast beef.'
'I'm sorry, madam, there's no more roast beef.'
'Oh, all right, then. I'll have a rump steak.'
'How would you like your steak?'
'Rare, please.'

* * *

'And for you, sir?'
'Chicken for me, please.'
'Vegetables, sir?'
'Mushrooms and a green salad, please.'

Lesson 17A, Exercise 2

'*Would* you *like* something to *drink?*'
'Just *some* water, please.'
'*Certainly*, madam.'
I'll *have* a lager, please. And *could* you *bring* me some water, too?'
'*Of* course, sir.'

* * *

'How's the chicken?'
'Not too bad. *What* about *the* steak?'
'A bit tough. The vegetables are *nice*, though.'

* * *

'Is *everything* all right?'
'Oh, yes, excellent, *thank* you.'
'*Very* good.'

* * *

'*Can* I *give* you a little more coffee?'
'No, thank you.'   'Yes, *please*.'

* * *

'*Could* you *bring* us the bill, please?'
'*Of course*, madam.'
'Is service included?'
'No, *sir*.'

Lesson 17A, Exercise 3

1. 'And for you, sir?' 'Chicken for me, please.'
2. 'Vegetables, sir?' 'Mushrooms and a green salad, please.'
3. 'Would you like something to drink?' 'Just some water, please.'
4. 'How's the chicken?' 'Not too bad.'
5. 'What about the steak?' 'A bit tough.'
6. 'Is everything all right?' 'Oh, yes, excellent, thank you.' 'Very good.'
7. 'Can I give you a little more coffee?' 'No, thank you.' 'Yes, please.'

Lesson 17C, Exercises 1 and 2

SARAH: Why don't we go to Turkey for our holiday this year?
FATHER: Yeah, OK, why not?
MOTHER: Hey, wait a minute, let's think about this. Turkey will be much more expensive than France. We can't really drive there – we haven't got the time.
SARAH: Yes, but we can get package holidays to Turkey. Ted went last year, and he said it was great, and really cheap. I can phone about it.
MOTHER: What do you think, darling?
FATHER: I think it's a good idea, if we can get a cheap package. Somewhere different.
MOTHER: Well, all right, Sarah, find out about it. I'd like to go somewhere different, too, if it doesn't cost too much.
SARAH: Fine. I'll phone tomorrow morning.

Lesson 20C, Listening Exercise 3

This is the third in a series of seven programmes devoted to the madrigal. Today's programme will explore the work of Thomas Morley, one of the greatest of English madrigal composers. Born in 1557, he became organist at St Paul's Cathedral, London, and, like so many of the great musicians of the time, a Gentleman of the Chapel Royal. This body of musicians performed for the Queen and composed church music for performance at her court. Queen Elizabeth I must have admired Morley's work, for in 1598 she granted him a monopoly which allowed him to control printing and importation of music and music-ruled paper for all of Britain. This must have represented a considerable financial advantage for the musician.

Morley was probably a friend of Shakespeare; he composed songs for some of the poet's plays. He was also a writer himself, and his *Plaine and Easie Introduction to Practicall Musicke*, published in 1597, was popular for 200 years. It is now one of our best sources of information about musical life in the sixteenth century.

Morley wrote church music, instrumental music, lute songs, and many of the finest madrigals of the period. Some of his best madrigals are in the light, rhythmic style called the ballet.

Our first selection for today is a madrigal from a collection called *The Triumphs of Oriana*, a collection of 29 madrigals by 26 different composers, generally thought to have been composed in praise of Queen Elizabeth.

By Thomas Morley, a madrigal from *The Triumphs of Oriana*.

Lesson 22B, Exercise 2

1. Erm, I think you should wear good running shoes. Erm, I don't think it matters if you run early in the morning or whatever time of day. I think you should wear comfortable clothing. You should warm up before you run. Erm, it's up to you whether you run with somebody or alone. Erm, definitely I don't think you should rest every ten minutes. I think you should walk for a bit after you've run, after you've finished. Erm, I think it's bad advice not to run if you feel tired; erm, bad advice not to drink water when you're running. Erm, I think don't run till two hours after eating is good advice. Erm, I don't think it matters if you run when you've got a cold or not. I think it's good advice not to run fast downhill. Erm, I think it's bad advice not to run if you're over fifty; and I think it's good advice not to run in fog.

2. I think it's a very good idea to wear good running shoes. I think running, the time of day you run would be, the, your own personal choice. If I go through the good advice, perhaps, I think wear comfortable clothing, warm up before you run, walk for a few minutes after you finish, erm, and certainly don't run on roads in fog. And I think the don't run until two hours after eating's a good piece of advice as well. I think the idea about drinking water is that you shouldn't drink while you're actually running, erm, because you get very hot, and it's better to wait until after you finish running to drink. As far as, I don't know exactly about some of the advice, like whether you have a cold or feel tired, erm, but certainly I think it's a bad idea to rest every ten minutes or so, and it's certainly not true to say that you can't run if you're over fifty.

Index of structures and functional/situational language

Acknowledgements

The authors and publishers are grateful to the following copyright owners for permission to reproduce photographs, illustrations, texts and music. Every endeavour has been made to contact copyright owners and apologies are expressed for any omissions.

page 28: *cl* Reprinted by permission of Royal Gallery of Paintings, Mauritshuis; *t* The Tate Gallery (The Tate Gallery, London); *cc* The British Museum (Copyright © Trustees of the British Museum); *cr* Ekdotike Athenon S.A. (Reprinted by permission of Ekdotike Athenon, S.A.)   page 54: The Bodleian Library (By permission of the Bodleian Library, Oxford.)   page 67: Reproduced by permission of *Punch*.   page 88: Hulton-Deutsch Collection (Hulton-Deutsch Collection).   page 118: ® British Telecom logo, and 'T' symbol are registered trade marks of British Telecommunications public limited company. ® TELEMESSAGE is a registered trade mark and service mark of British Telecommunications public limited company in the United Kingdom. © Copyright of British Telecommunications public limited company.
page 120: *r* Reprinted by permission of *The Daily Mirror*; *cl* and *cr* From *Weekend Book of Jokes 23* courtesy of Weekend; *bl* and *br* Reproduced by permission of *Punch*.

Happy Birthday To You by Mildred and Patti Hill (Lesson 14C, Exercise 4) is courtesy of International Music Publishers and the Mechanical Copyright Protection Society Ltd.   *Anything You Can Do, I Can Do Better* by Irving Berlin (Lesson 16C, Listening Exercise 3) is courtesy of Warner Chappell Music Ltd and the Mechanical Copyright Protection Society Ltd. *Hello, Goodbye* by Lennon and McCartney (Lesson 20C, Listening Exercise 4), lyrics by permission of SBK Songs, courtesy of SBK Songs and the Mechanical Copyright Protection Society Ltd.   *Hush, Little Baby* (Lesson 24B, Listening Exercise 3) is traditional.

The following songs were specially written by Steve Hall for *The New Cambridge English Course* Book 1: *If You Can Keep A Secret* (Lesson 8C, page 41); *Please Write* (Lesson 12C, page 60).

Artist Partners: Derek Brazell, pages 32 *b*, 55, 61, 81, 101, 110 *r*, 111; Biz Hull, pages 17, 86, 102; Tony Richards, pages 24, 72, 91, 105.   The Inkshed: Andrew Whiteley, pages 45, 66.   B. L. Kearley: Tony Kenyon, pages 15 *b*, 48 *b*, 50 *l*, 57, 65.   Maggie Mundy: Hemesh Alles, pages 8 *c*, 9 *t* and *c*, 15 *t*, 50 *r*, 51, 70, 73, 106, 108, 109, 112, 115; Nick Garner, page 113, 133; Sharon Pallent, pages 26, 107.   Young Artists: Amy Burch, pages 14 *c*, 16, 33, 132, 134; Pat Fogarty, pages 46, 47, 80; Sarah John, pages 8 *b*, 9 *bl*, 10 *b*, 22 *b*, 28 *bl*, 44, 45 *t* and *c*.

Nancy Anderson, pages 100, 104, 114.   John Blackman, pages 90, 123.   Caroline Church, page 89. Richard Deverell, pages 29, 39.   Joe McEwan, pages 11, 21 *t*, 34, 53, 60, 110 *l*.   Rodney Sutton, pages 14 *t*, 21 *b*, 25, 35, 40, 49.   Tony Watson, pages 64, 68.

Mark Edwards, pages 6, 9 *br*, 10 *tc*, *tr* and *cc*, 30, 31 *cl*.   Darren Marsh, pages 7, 8 *t*, 22 *t*, 48 *top row*, *second row cl* and *cr*, 52 *l*, 59, 69, 71, 84, 85, 92, 93, 94, 119 *l*, *cl*, *bl*, *cr* and *r*.   Ken Weedon, pages 20 and 21, 27, 32 *t*, 87, 95.   The Image Bank, pages 10 *tl*, *cl* and *cr*, 12, 13, 21 *bl*, *br* and *tl*, 31 *bl*, *c*, *t*, *cr* and *tr*, 48 *second row l*, *c* and *r*, 52 *r*, 74, 75, 119 *br*.

(*t* = top   *b* = bottom   *c* = centre   *r* = right   *l* = left)

Phonetic symbols

Vowels

symbol	example
/iː/	eat /iːt/
/i/	happy /ˈhæpi/
/ɪ/	it /ɪt/
/e/	when /wen/
/æ/	cat /kæt/
/ɑː/	hard /hɑːd/
/ɒ/	not /nɒt/
/ɔː/	sort /sɔːt/; all /ɔːl/
/ʊ/	look /lʊk/
/uː/	too /tuː/
/ʌ/	cup /kʌp/
/ɜː/	first /fɜːst/; turn /tɜːn/
/ə/	about /əˈbaʊt/; mother /ˈmʌðə(r)/
/eɪ/	day /deɪ/
/aɪ/	my /maɪ/
/ɔɪ/	boy /bɔɪ/
/aʊ/	now /naʊ/
/əʊ/	go /gəʊ/
/ɪə/	here /hɪə(r)/
/eə/	chair /tʃeə(r)/
/ʊə/	tourist /ˈtʊərɪst/

Consonants

symbol	example
/p/	pen /pen/
/b/	big /bɪg/
/t/	two /tuː/
/d/	do /duː/
/k/	look /lʊk/; cup /kʌp/
/g/	get /get/
/tʃ/	China /ˈtʃaɪnə/
/dʒ/	Japan /dʒəˈpæn/
/f/	fall /fɔːl/
/v/	very /ˈveri/
/θ/	think /θɪŋk/
/ð/	then /ðen/
/s/	see /siː/
/z/	zoo /zuː/; is /ɪz/
/ʃ/	shoe /ʃuː/
/ʒ/	measure /ˈmeʒə(r)/; decision /dɪˈsɪʒn/
/h/	who /huː/; how /haʊ/
/m/	meet /miːt/
/n/	no /nəʊ/
/ŋ/	sing /sɪŋ/
/l/	long /lɒŋ/
/r/	right /raɪt/
/j/	yes /jes/
/w/	will /wɪl/

Stress

Stress is shown by a mark (ˈ) in front of the stressed syllable.

mother /ˈmʌðə(r)/   China /ˈtʃaɪnə/
about /əˈbaʊt/   Japan /dʒəˈpæn/

Irregular verbs

Infinitive/Present	Simple Past	Participle
be /biː/	was /wəz, wɒz/ were /wə(r), wɜː(r)/	been /bɪn, biːn/
become /bɪˈkʌm/	became /bɪˈkeɪm/	become /bɪˈkʌm/
break /breɪk/	broke /brəʊk/	broken /ˈbrəʊkn/
bring /brɪŋ/	brought /brɔːt/	brought /brɔːt/
build /bɪld/	built /bɪlt/	built /bɪlt/
buy /baɪ/	bought /bɔːt/	bought /bɔːt/
can /k(ə)n, kæn/	could /kʊd/	been able /bɪn ˈeɪbl/
catch /kætʃ/	caught /kɔːt/	caught /kɔːt/
come /kʌm/	came /keɪm/	come /kʌm/
cost /kɒst/	cost /kɒst/	cost /kɒst/
do /dʊ, də, duː/	did /dɪd/	done /dʌn/
draw /drɔː/	drew /druː/	drawn /drɔːn/
dream /driːm/	dreamt /dremt/	dreamt /dremt/
drink /drɪŋk/	drank /dræŋk/	drunk /drʌŋk/
drive /draɪv/	drove /drəʊv/	driven /ˈdrɪvn/
eat /iːt/	ate /et/	eaten /ˈiːtn/
fall /fɔːl/	fell /fel/	fallen /ˈfɔːlən/
feel /fiːl/	felt /felt/	felt /felt/
find /faɪnd/	found /faʊnd/	found /faʊnd/
fly /flaɪ/	flew /fluː/	flown /fləʊn/
forget /fəˈget/	forgot /fəˈgɒt/	forgotten /fəˈgɒtn/
get /get/	got /gɒt/	got /gɒt/
give /gɪv/	gave /geɪv/	given /ˈgɪvn/
go /gəʊ/	went /went/	gone /gɒn/, been /bɪn, biːn/
have /(h)əv, hæv/	had /(h)əd, hæd/	had /hæd/
hear /hɪə(r)/	heard /hɜːd/	heard /hɜːd/
hurt /hɜːt/	hurt /hɜːt/	hurt /hɜːt/
know /nəʊ/	knew /njuː/	known /nəʊn/
lead /liːd/	led /led/	led /led/
learn /lɜːn/	learnt /lɜːnt/	learnt /lɜːnt/
leave /liːv/	left /left/	left /left/
lend /lend/	lent /lent/	lent /lent/
lie /laɪ/	lay /leɪ/	lain /leɪn/
make /meɪk/	made /meɪd/	made /meɪd/
meet /miːt/	met /met/	met /met/
pay /peɪ/	paid /peɪd/	paid /peɪd/
put /pʊt/	put /pʊt/	put /pʊt/
read /riːd/	read /red/	read /red/
run /rʌn/	ran /ræn/	run /rʌn/
say /seɪ/	said /sed/	said /sed/
see /siː/	saw /sɔː/	seen /siːn/
sell /sel/	sold /səʊld/	sold /səʊld/
send /send/	sent /sent/	sent /sent/
show /ʃəʊ/	showed /ʃəʊd/	shown /ʃəʊn/
sing /sɪŋ/	sang /sæŋ/	sung /sʌŋ/
sit /sɪt/	sat /sæt/	sat /sæt/
sleep /sliːp/	slept /slept/	slept /slept/
speak /spiːk/	spoke /spəʊk/	spoken /ˈspəʊkn/
spend /spend/	spent /spent/	spent /spent/
stand /stænd/	stood /stʊd/	stood /stʊd/
swim /swɪm/	swam /swæm/	swum /swʌm/
take /teɪk/	took /tʊk/	taken /ˈteɪkn/
tell /tel/	told /təʊld/	told /təʊld/
think /θɪŋk/	thought /θɔːt/	thought /θɔːt/
wake up /ˈweɪk ˈʌp/	woke up /ˈwəʊk ˈʌp/	woken up /ˈwəʊkn ˈʌp/
wear /weə(r)/	wore /wɔː(r)/	worn /wɔːn/
will /wɪl/	would /wʊd/	—
win /wɪn/	won /wʌn/	won /wʌn/
write /raɪt/	wrote /rəʊt/	written /ˈrɪtn/